Ready-to-Use

P.E. ACTIVITIES

for Grades 5-6

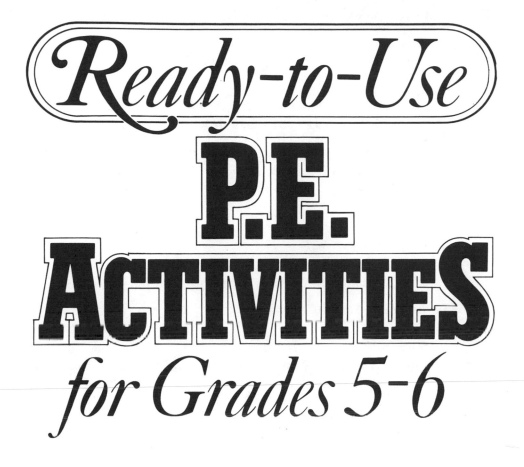

Joanne M. Landy · Maxwell J. Landy

PARKER PUBLISHING COMPANY
West Nyack, New York 10995

Library of Congress Cataloging-in-Publication Data

Landy, Maxwell J.
 Ready-to-use P.E. activities / Maxwell J. Landy, Joanne Landy.
  p. cm.
 Contents: bk. 1. For grades K–2—bk. 2. For grades 3–4—bk.
3. For grades 5–6—bk. 4. For grades 7–9.
 ISBN 0-13-673054-X (v.1)—ISBN 0-13-673070-1
 1. Physical education for children—Curricula. 2. Physical
education for children—Planning. I. Landy, Joanne. II. Title.
III. Title: Ready-to-use PE activities.
 GV443.L334 1992   92-21049
 372.86—dc20   CIP

Printed in the United States of America

10   9

*Dedicated in loving memory of my husband Max and to his children,
Matthew, Alan, and Jane. Thank you for your support and interest in
our project over the years.*

ISBN 0-13-673070-1

PARKER PUBLISHING COMPANY
West Nyack, New York 10994

On the World Wide Web at http://www.phdirect.com

About the Authors

Maxwell J. Landy, PED, New South Wales, B.S. and M.Ed., University of Oregon, Associate Professor Emeritus, University of Regina, Canada, was actively involved in the field of physical education for thirty-nine years. For eighteen of those years, Max served as a K–12 P.E. specialist and consultant in Canadian and Australian schools. For twenty years he taught at the university level, where he developed innovative programs in physical education and health, specializing in the P.E. internship program. Max passed away on May 7, 1991.

Joanne M. Landy, B.Ed., University of Regina, has fifteen years of experience as an elementary and high school P.E. specialist in the Saskatchewan school system. She also became involved as a demonstration P.E. teacher in liaison with the University of Regina, Faculty of Education pre-internship and internship programs, and presented at several workshops for elementary and secondary teachers. Joanne and her two children now reside in Perth, Western Australia.

Max and Joanne co-presented at several major P.E./Health conferences in Canada, the United States, and Australia. In 1988 they were involved in the USA National Fitness Foundation–Youth Fitness Camp in Los Angeles, spearheaded by John Cates of UCLA. Between them they combined over fifty years of Physical Education teaching knowledge and experience to produce the *Complete Physical Education Activities Program.*

Forewords

It is with extreme pleasure that I submit this foreword on behalf of Max and Joanne's wonderful contribution to improve the health and fitness of our youth.

I first met Joanne and Max in 1986 when they were selected as faculty members of a model youth fitness camp sponsored by George Allen's National Fitness Foundation.

During the camp, I had the opportunity to observe firsthand the wonderful physical education materials that Joanne and Max had created. Classroom teachers, with no formal physical education training, were able to involve their students in fun activities that emphasized all of the components of fitness. User-friendly lesson plans provided the teachers with games and activities for the progressive development of motor skills. Students, teachers, administrators, and parents soon became advocates of quality daily physical education.

I am delighted that the Landys have published their wonderful *Complete Physical Education Activities Program.*

In the United States, the level of youth fitness has continued to decline over the past twenty years. Physical education specialists and classroom teachers have been searching for physical education materials that will address the individual health and fitness needs of children while developing self-confidence and self-esteem. Joanne and Max have provided the materials that can put quality into daily physical education.

John Cates, Supervisor
Department of Physical Education
University of California, San Diego
Assistant to Arnold Schwarzenegger
Chairman, President's Council
  Physical Fitness and Sports

I am proud to say that Max Landy was, before his unfortunate death in 1991, one of my closest personal and professional friends. I had the pleasure of working with Max at the University of Regina from 1978 to 1980. He was my mentor, and out of this a lasting friendship developed with both him and his wife Joanne. I came to know and appreciate both Max and Joanne as two extraordinary physical educators. I was immediately impressed by their dedication to the profession and, in particular, to the development of a physical education program that they believed worth working and sacrificing for. Their goal was to develop a "user-friendly, activity-oriented" curriculum for teachers, designed to help promote a physically active lifestyle among children and youth. Their commitment to this work has been long term in nature, spanning more than twelve years. After Max's death, Joanne carried on to see their project come to fruition. Now it is available for all of us in their new series of books, the *Complete Physical Education Activities Program.*

To me, this series is first of all a jumping off place for the inexperienced teacher of physical education, whether a classroom teacher or a physical education specialist, who wants specific ideas about what to teach and how to go about teaching it. In this regard, an especially unique and attractive characteristic of these books are the many delightful cartoon-like illustrations designed to clarify the correct action, organization, and/or arrangement of students. In addition, teaching instructions are written in step-by-step form and can be read directly to students. My more than twenty years of in- and preservice work with teachers indicates that this is exactly the kind of direction they will most benefit from. Their initial teaching experiences will prove enjoyable for both themselves and their students, thus encouraging further involvement. Their students can only benefit!

Although the *Complete Physical Education Activities Program* is of most obvious help to the teacher who has not had an in-depth background in physical education, it is a time saver even for the experienced physical education teacher. It contains a myriad of practical, ready-to-use, and easy-to-follow activity ideas. These are organized sequentially to ensure proper progressions and allow for individualized teaching. The curriculum is divided into warm-up, fitness, core, and closing activity sections. This organization permits a flexibility and facility in lesson planning that would not be possible if detailed lesson plans were provided. The teacher is able to compile complete, well-balanced lesson plans merely by selecting activities from the various sections. Thus, teachers are encouraged to be creative in their implementation efforts.

Max and Joanne have skillfully blended together traditional activity ideas with more current ones in an effort to preserve the very best that both have to offer. However, they offer more than an academic approach. They provide many new and meaningful activity ideas, including many new, fun-packed fitness activities, which have evolved from their more than fifty years of teaching physical education in Australia and Canada. Notably, their curriculum has been field-tested in Regina schools, where it received high ratings from the many teachers and student-teachers who used it. Finally, it is divided into four books or teaching units, each tailored to the specific developmental needs of the students at that level. Thus, teachers need only purchase the book(s) appropriate for their grade level.

Through Max and Joanne's professional dedication and hard work, we have moved one step closer to providing quality daily physical education experiences in our schools. They have provided teaching units that will no doubt be used by a great many classroom teachers and physical education specialists who believe that physical activity is important for our children and youth. If the ultimate utility of information lies in its ability to enhance the quality of human experience, then their work represents a substantial contribution to the literature. I am honored that Joanne has asked me to write this foreword and wish her every success in this and all her future endeavors.

Dennis Caine, Ph.D.
Western Washington University

About Ready-to-Use P.E. Activities for Grades 5–6

This practical resource is one of four books presenting a unique curriculum for elementary and middle/junior high school educators entitled *Complete Physical Education Activities Program* (CPEP). The curriculum is designed to help classroom teachers and P.E. specialists successfully prepare and teach interesting, fun-packed physical education lessons in a sequential co-educational program. It includes the following specialized teaching units, each tailored to the specific developmental needs at the particular level:

Book 1 *Ready-to-Use P.E. Activities for Grades K–2*

Book 2 *Ready-to-Use P.E. Activities for Grades 3–4*

Book 3 *Ready-to-Use P.E. Activities for Grades 5–6*

Book 4 *Ready-to-Use P.E. Activities for Grades 7–9*

The CPEP curriculum provides a comprehensive continuity program from kindergarten through grade 9, with a strong emphasis on the *fitness* component. It is based on sound education principles, research in motor learning, exercise physiology, and teaching methodology and meets the requirements as a delivery system and resource for current P.E. curricula in the United States and Canada. Its primary objectives are as follows:

- to foster in children a love of physical activity and play
- to instill a need for physical fitness in each child
- to develop coordination, grace, and control
- to provide opportunities for increased responsibility in planning, organizing, and leadership
- to give children as wide a skill, games, and dance experience as possible
- to present opportunities for children to belong to a group in which each child is accepted
- to provide experiences that will develop initiative, self-reliance, self-worth, loyalty, honesty, kindness to others, and a love of learning
- to develop a sense of fair play and cooperation in children and the ability to work in groups, leading to increased cultural understanding
- to provide opportunities for integration of P.E. with other subject areas: language arts, math, social studies, science, health, music, and art

For your convenience, Book 3 in the curriculum is subdivided into seven sections: Introductory Activities, Fitness Activities, Rhythms and Dance, Gymnastics, Games Skills, Special Games, and Closing Activities. This organization allows you to compile complete, well-balanced lesson plans in minutes merely by selecting activities from the various sections, thus saving valuable lesson preparation time.

Each book in the curriculum also provides a special section for you entitled "How to Prepare Lessons Using These P.E. Activities," which explains (a) how to prepare a Yearly/Weekly P.E. Plan, (b) how to prepare a Daily P.E. Plan, and (c) how to record the activities taught. By following the lesson format described in this section, you can use and reuse the program activities in an endless number of combinations with other activities. Moreover, many of the activities contain variations and suggested modifications, thus providing valuable repetition and reinforcement and sufficient material for an entire year of daily physical education.

Other features of the *Complete Physical Education Activities Program* curriculum include the following:

Time Allocation:

Flexibility is a key feature of the program, as the format allows you to select and adapt activities that may be taught within the allotted time.

Indoor-Outdoor:

Activities have been provided for both indoor and outdoor learning stations.

Coeducational:

All of the activities in each level book are suitable for both boys and girls.

Illustrations:

Cartoon-like stick figures supplement the activity directions throughout. All measurements, diagrams, and court markings are written in standard and metric measurement to fit the needs of educators in the United States and Canada.

Basic Equipment:

Most of the program activities can be taught using standard equipment already available in elementary/middle schools. Some enrichment activities may require additional items such as juggling scarves, parachutes, peacock feathers, and scooters.

By presenting K–9 students with a variety of challenging, stimulating activities during each lesson throughout the year, this P.E. program will help you create enjoyable, success-oriented experiences that reach every child. Moreover, the program provides for the mainstreaming of atypical children within the context of the regular physical education lesson. Special attention has been given to (a) social interaction and the improvement of self-concepts, cooperation, and sportsmanship; (b) fitness and skill development; and (c) acquisition of basic fundamentals through conceptual learning.

Interaction of the four "F's"—FUN, FITNESS, and FRIENDSHIP through the FUNDAMENTALS of Physical Education—stimulates children to want to participate in physical activities not only during the school years, but for the rest of their lives.

Joanne Landy
Maxwell J. Landy

Contents

Description of the Activities • xvi

Warm-up Activities (Introductory Activities, Fitness Activities) • *Core Activities (Movement Awareness for K–4, Rhythms and Dance, Gymnastics, Game Skills)* • *Special Games* • *Closing Activities*

Activity Organization • xviii

Number Key • *Descriptive Title* • *Equipment* • *Focus* • *Organization* • *Description of the Activity* • *Variation*

Preparing the Yearly/Weekly Plan • xix

Developing the Yearly/Weekly Unit Plan • *Developing the Daily Lesson Plan* • *Gathering the Equipment* • *Recording the Activities Taught* • *Sample Yearly/Weekly Plan Chart* • *Blank Yearly/Weekly Plan Chart* (**reproducible**) • *Class Record Sheet* (**reproducible**)

Section 1 INTRODUCTORY ACTIVITIES 1

Section 2 FITNESS ACTIVITIES 33

Section 3 RHYTHMS AND DANCE 77

Section 4   GYMNASTICS

SUPPORTING AND BALANCING

Section 5   GAME SKILLS 167

Section 6   SPECIAL GAMES **331**

Section 7 CLOSING ACTIVITIES 373

How to Prepare Lessons Using These P.E. Activities

The following gives you suggestions for using this resource to prepare stimulating, well-balanced physical education activities for your students. Specifically, it provides a description of the different types of activities presented in Sections 1–7, a sample activity illustrating the easy-to-follow organization used for all activities in the program, and directions for creating your own yearly/weekly P.E. teaching plan. Included are a filled-in sample Yearly/Weekly Plan Chart along with a reproducible blank chart, plus a Class Record Sheet to help you evaluate the progress made by each class during the year.

DESCRIPTION OF THE ACTIVITIES

Sections 1 through 7 present a wide range of activities for creating a stimulating variety of daily P.E. lessons.

■ Warm-Up Activities (Sections 1 and 2)

Introductory Activities

The first activity of the lesson is intended to produce a state of physical and mental readiness. This Introductory Activity produces a *general warm-up*, increasing blood flow to the major muscle groups. Mentally, it helps to get children excited about participating in the activities that follow.

Fitness Activities

The Fitness Activity functions as a *specific warm-up* and, when used in combination with an introductory activity, develops overall fitness with emphasis on cardiovascular endurance and muscular strength and endurance.

■ Core Activities (Sections 3–5)

Movement Awareness (K–4)

The activities in this section help to develop the movement principles of space awareness, body awareness, effort awareness, and relationships. Themes are used to set tasks that ask "what, where, how can, and who can?" The children respond to the task or problem by exploring and experimenting at the floor level, on low apparatus, or on large apparatus, with or without equipment.

Rhythms and Dance

The Rhythms and Dance activity is intended to develop creative expression, rhythmic movement, musical appreciation, and active listening skills. Muscular growth and coordination are improved; space awareness, body awareness, effort awareness, and social skills are improved in an atmosphere of fun. Through the rhythms and dance section, specific music suggestions are provided; otherwise, lively popular music is suggested.

Gymnastics

The gymnastics activities progressively develop muscular strength and endurance, flexibility, balance, and overall coordination. The children also develop self-confidence, improved posture, and safety awareness.

Game Skills

Game Skills activities develop the abilities children need to participate in most traditional games, such as soccer, volleyball, basketball, softball, and football as well as more innovative games, such as parachute play, scooter play, Frisbee™ play, and juggling. The Games Skills activities are arranged in units that you could plan to teach over a two- or three-week period.

▪ Special Games (Section 6)

Relays, low-organized games, and tabloid sports activities develop leadership, cooperation, self-esteem, creativity, and a sense of fair play. The emphasis throughout the activities in this section is on fun and team work, not winning or losing.

▪ Closing Activities (Section 7)

After a vigorous physical workout, the Closing Activity serves as a quiet, cool-down activity and leaves children ready to continue with classroom work.

ACTIVITY ORGANIZATION

Each activity in the program is presented in a functional, easy-to-follow format, as illustrated by the following sample:

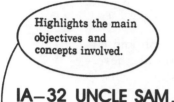

Highlights the main objectives and concepts involved.

Provides a detailed list of all equipment needed for this segment, with some flexibility of choice.

IA—32 UNCLE SAM

FOCUS: Running and dodging

EQUIPMENT: Four cone markers; one pinnie; set of colored flags

■ Organization:

Provides teaching points, safety guidelines, and suggestions on how to organize and teach the activities.

* Mark out the play area. Clearly mark the two endlines. Choose one player to be "Uncle Sam," who stands in the center of the play area wearing the pinnie. All other players tuck a flag in your waistband so that three quarters of it is showing, and stand behind one of the endlines.

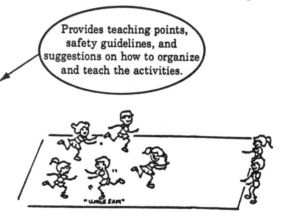

■ Description of the Activity:

1. Endline players start the game by chanting
   "Uncle Sam, Uncle Sam,
   May we cross your ocean dam?"
2. Uncle Sam, you answer by saying, "Yes, if you are wearing red." Players wearing red get a free pass to the other end.

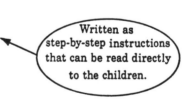

Written as step-by-step instructions that can be read directly to the children.

3. Then on the "Go" signal from Uncle Sam, the rest of the players try to run to the opposite endline without getting your flag pulled. Tagged players become Uncle Sam's helpers.
4. Begin again. This time Uncle Sam, call out another color. Keep going until all players are caught but one. This player becomes the new Uncle Sam for the next game.

■ Variation:

Vary the criteria for a free pass: girls with short hair, wearing glasses, all the boys, all the girls, etc.

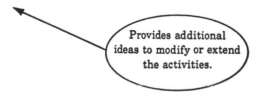

Provides additional ideas to modify or extend the activities.

Preparing the Yearly/Weekly Plan

It is important that the physical education program be planned ahead of time, whether for a two-week unit, a season, or even a year. Yearly planning allows you to meet long-range objectives, to use facilities and equipment to their utmost, and to consider seasonal and special days.

■ Developing the Yearly/Weekly Unit Plan

To develop the yearly/weekly plan, select the activities from the suggestions listed on the Scope and Sequence Chart and the Table of Contents of each section, and then prepare a Weekly Unit Plan Chart. Refer to the Sample Yearly/Weekly Plan Chart for Core Activities, page xxi. The chart shows the school year divided into a sequence of 40 weekly units and, when completed, should give you an outline of the order in which the material will be taught. A blank sample Weekly/Yearly Plan Chart is provided for you on pages xxiii and xxiv.

Although decisions made on the Yearly/Weekly Plan Charts will provide reliable, concrete guidelines, your decisions should never be regarded as irreversible and certainly may be changed as circumstances require.

■ Developing the Daily Lesson Plan

There are five basic steps in preparing a lesson using the *Complete Physical Education Activities Program* system:

STEP 1: Decide how much time is allocated to your lesson. Each part of the lesson can vary in length according to the objectives and focus of the lesson.

STEP 2: Select an activity from the Introductory Activities section, then one or more activities from the Fitness section.

STEP 3: Decide on the Core Unit to be taught by referring to the appropriate week on the Weekly Plan Chart. Then select the appropriate activities from the core sections of Rhythms and Dance, Gymnastics, or Game Skills.

STEP 4: Select a related game from the Game Skills section or the Special Games section.

STEP 5: Select a cool-down activity from the Closing Activities to finish the lesson.

NOTE: It is not necessary that all the material in an activity be taught in one lesson. You may decide to use two or three lessons to cover all of the tasks on that particular activity.

■ Gathering the Equipment

To make a list of all of the equipment needed for each lesson, refer to the Equipment List on the top right-hand corner of each activity. Check that all of the equipment listed is indeed available for use. Prior to the lesson, designate children to bring out and arrange the equipment in the activity area.

▪ Recording the Activities Taught

When all of the tasks or components in an activity have been taught, you can circle the number of the activity on a photocopy of the Class Record Sheet provided on page xxv. By referring to the Record Sheet, you will quickly be able to evaluate the class's progress throughout the year.

Sample for
YEARLY/WEEKLY PLAN CHART
(40 weeks)

SEPTEMBER	OCTOBER	NOVEMBER	DECEMBER	JANUARY
WEEK 1 Date	**WEEK 6** Date	**WEEK 11** Date	**WEEK 16** Date	**WEEK 19** Date
Orientation week I.A. Signals starting positions G.S. Rope play-short S.G. L/o games C.A.	Fit. aerobic routines "measuring" H.R.'s G.S. Football skills & related games Fitness testing	Fit.-Aerobic routines Tummy toners G.S. volleyball skills & related games (serving & reception) C.A.	I.A. Tag-type Fit- "Breaks" G.S. Basketball Skill & related games (defense, rebounding) C.A.	I.A. Warm-ups Fit. Hip Honers G.S. Hockey stick play & related games (handling, passing) C.A.
WEEK 2 Date	**WEEK 7** Date	**WEEK 12** Date	**WEEK 17** Date	**WEEK 20** Date
I.A. Warm-up Activities & Games G.S. Rope Play - Long Rope Skills S.G. · Relays	Fit.- 12 minute workouts #3+4 "Breaks" G.S. Football Skills & lead-up games C.A.	Fit. 12 min. w/o's 5+6 seat shapers G.S. Volleyball Skills (spiking/blocking, defense) lead-up games	G.S. Rope Play Basketball lead-up games Basketball tabloid	R&D: Novelty Dances G.S. Hockey stick Play & lead-up games (goal tending, face-off, defense)
WEEK 3 Date	**WEEK 8** Date	**WEEK 13** Date	**WEEK 18** Date	**WEEK 21** Date
I.A. Tag-type Fit "Breaks" G.S. Juggling Skills S.G. L/o games C.A.	Fit.-limber+loosen aerobic ropes G.S. rope play · formation jump · double dutch S.G. L/o games	I.A. Warm-ups G.S. Basketball skills & related games (ball hand- ling, dribbling) S.G. Relays	G.S. Combative Play Basketball Tourney Volleyball Tourney S.G. L/o games	R&D: Rhythms · Novelty Dances Gym: Supports & Balances S.G. L/o games
WEEK 4 Date	**WEEK 9** Date	**WEEK 14** Date	**WEEK** Date	**WEEK 22** Date
Fit 12 minute workouts #1 #2 · Breaks G.S. Frisbee Play & Related Games C.A.	G.S. Volleyball warm up Fit.-"Breaks" G.S. Volleyball Skills & related games (setting) C.A.	Fit. Aerobics Medicine Ball Fit G.S. B'Ball Skills related games (passing & receiving) C.A. Piano Man	school break	R&D: Folk Dances Gym: Pyramid Building Fitness Testing
WEEK 5 Date	**WEEK 10** Date	**WEEK 15** Date	**WEEK** Date	**WEEK** Date
I.A. Warm-ups · grass drills · astronaut run Fit: muscle & bone signals G.S. Football Skills & related games C.A.	I.A. Exercise hunt Joker's wild Fit.- upper body strengtheners G.S. Volleyball skills & games (bumping, digging) C.A.	Fit- Iron Man Cir #1 G.S. B'Ball Skills & related games (shooting skills) C.A. Stretches	school break	

ABBREVIATION KEY:

I.A. = INTRODUCTORY ACTIVITIES   G.S. = GAME SKILLS
FIT = FITNESS ACTIVITIES   S.G. = SPECIAL GAMES
GYM = GYMNASTICS   (L/O GAMES = LOW-ORGANIZED GAMES)
R&D = RHYTHMS AND DANCE   C.A. = CLOSING ACTIVITIES

FEBRUARY	MARCH	APRIL	MAY	(Sample Continued) JUNE
WEEK 23 Date	**WEEK** 27 Date	**WEEK** 30 Date	**WEEK** 34 Date	**WEEK** 38 Date
R&D: Folk Dances Fit: Bench-step test Gym: Balance Bench & Balance Beam S.G. Yogames	Fit: Iron Man Circuit #2 Gym: Springing & Landing · Climbing Ropes C.A.	R&D: social dances rhythmics G.S: Racquet Play · Badminton Skills & Related Games C.A.	Fit: Prediction run x-country run G.S. soccer skills (punt-volley, Kicking, lead-up games)	F.t: steplechase Limber & loosen G.S. T&F skills Running, Relays Fit: Cool-downs
WEEK 24 Date	**WEEK** 28 Date	**WEEK** 31 Date	**WEEK** 35 Date	**WEEK** 39 Date
RSD: Square Dance Gym: Rotations Games: Day	Fit: Limber & Loosen · Aerobics Gym: Horizontal & parallel bars Station work	Fit. 12min. w/o #7 #8 Design a workout G.S. Racquet Play Badminton Skills & lead-up games Badminton Tourney	Fitness testing RSD: Rhythmics G.S. Softball Play & related games (throwing, fielding) C.A.	Fit: Fit track leg shapers G.S. T&F skills (long, triple, hurdles) high jumping
WEEK 25 Date	**WEEK** 29 Date	**WEEK** 32 Date	**WEEK** 36 Date	**WEEK** 40 Date
RSD: Square Dance Gym: Rotations & shuttles	R.&D: social Dances G.S: Paddle Play & Related Games S.G: L/o games	Fit: Workouts per group G.S. Soccer Skills (dribbling, trapping, passing, Kicking) related games	Fit: Power-walking milk routes I.A.-paper route G.S. softball play (base running, pitching) & related games	G.S. T&F (Throwing events) T&F station work T&F Tabloid
WEEK 26 Date	**WEEK** Date	**WEEK** 33 Date	**WEEK** 37 Date	**WEEK** Date
RSD: Square Dance Dance-Making Gym: Springing & Landing	Easter Break	I.A. Geronimo Cannonball Run milk routes G.S. soccer skills (tackling, goal-keep- ing, throw-in, heading) + related games	R&D · rhythmics G.S.: Softball play (batting) Lead-up games	
WEEK Date	**WEEK** Date	**WEEK** Date	**WEEK** Date	**WEEK** Date

YEARLY/WEEKLY PLAN CHART

SEPTEMBER		OCTOBER		NOVEMBER		DECEMBER		JANUARY	
WEEK 1	Date	WEEK 1	Date	WEEK 1	Date	WEEK 1	Date	WEEK 1	Date
WEEK 2	Date	WEEK 2	Date	WEEK 2	Date	WEEK 2	Date	WEEK 2	Date
WEEK 3	Date	WEEK 3	Date	WEEK 3	Date	WEEK 3	Date	WEEK 3	Date
WEEK 4	Date	WEEK 4	Date	WEEK 4	Date	WEEK 4	Date	WEEK 4	Date
WEEK 5	Date	WEEK 5	Date	WEEK 5	Date	WEEK 5	Date	WEEK 5	Date

YEARLY/WEEKLY PLAN CHART

FEBRUARY		MARCH		APRIL		MAY		JUNE	
WEEK 1	Date	WEEK 1	Date	WEEK 1	Date	WEEK 1	Date	WEEK 1	Date
WEEK 2	Date	WEEK 2	Date	WEEK 2	Date	WEEK 2	Date	WEEK 2	Date
WEEK 3	Date	WEEK 3	Date	WEEK 3	Date	WEEK 3	Date	WEEK 3	Date
WEEK 4	Date	WEEK 4	Date	WEEK 4	Date	WEEK 4	Date	WEEK 4	Date
WEEK 5	Date	WEEK 5	Date	WEEK 5	Date	WEEK 5	Date	WEEK 5	Date

Book 3: Ready-to-Use P.E. Activities for Grades 5–6
Class Record Sheet

Class: _____

Year: _____

Level: _____

Teacher: _____

INTRODUCTORY ACTIVITIES

1	2	3	4	5	6
7	8	9	10	11	12
13	14	15	16	17	18
19	20	21	22	23	24
25	26	27	28	29	30
31	32	33	34	35	36
37	38	39	40	41	42
43	44	45	46	47	48
49	50	51			

GYMNASTICS

1	2	3	4	5	6
7	8	9	10	11	12
13	14	15	16	17	18
19	20	21	22	23	24
25	26	27	28	29	30
31	32	33	34	35	36
37	38	39	40	41	42
43	44	45	46	47	48
49	50	51	52	53	54
55	56	57	58	59	60
61					

FITNESS ACTIVITIES

1	2	3	4	5	6
7	8	9	10	11	12
13	14	15	16	17	18
19	20	21	22	23	24
25	26	27	28	29	30
31	32	33	34	35	36
37	38	39	40	41	42
43	44	45	46	47	

SPECIAL GAMES

1	2	3	4	5	6
7	8	9	10	11	12
13	14	15	16	17	18
19	20	21	22	23	24
25	26	27	28	29	30
31	32	33	34	35	36
37	38	39	40	41	42
43	44	45	46	47	48
49	50	51	52	53	54

RHYTHMS & DANCE

1	2	3	4	5	6
7	8	9	10	11	12
13	14	15	16	17	18
19	20	21	22	23	24
25	26	27	28	29	30
31	32	33	34	35	36
37	38	39	40	41	42
43	44	45	46	47	48
49	50	51	52	53	54
55					

CLOSING ACTIVITIES

1	2	3	4	5	6
7	8	9	10	11	12
13	14	15	16	17	18
19	20	21	22	23	24
25	26	27	28	29	30
31	32	33	34	35	36
37	38	39	40	41	42
43	44	45	46	47	

GAME SKILLS

1	2	3	4	5	6	7	8	9	10	11	12	13	14
15	16	17	18	19	20	21	22	23	24	25	26	27	28
29	30	31	32	33	34	35	36	37	38	39	40	41	42
43	44	45	46	47	48	49	50	51	52	53	54	55	56
57	58	59	60	61	62	63	64	65	66	67	68	69	70
71	72	73	74	75	76	77	78	79	80	81	82	83	84
85	86	87	88	89	90	91	92	93	94	95	96	97	98
99	100	101	102	103	104	105	106	107	108	109	110	111	112
113	114	115	116	117	118	119	120	121	122	123	124	125	126
127	128	129	130	131	132	133	134	135	136	137	138	139	140
141	142	143	144	145	146	147	148	149	150	151	152	153	154
155	156	157	158	159	160	161	162	163	164	165	166	167	168
169	170	171	172	173	174	175	176	177	178	179	180	181	182
183	184	185	186	187	188	189	190	191	192	193	194	195	196
197	198	199	200	201	202	203	204	205					

Introductory Activities

The first activity of the P.E. lesson should help produce a state of physical and mental readiness in children. It provides a general warm-up, increasing blood flow to the major muscle groups, and helps spark excitement about participating in the subsequent activities.

This section offers fifty-one possible Introductory Activities:

IA–1 ORGANIZATION SIGNALS

FOCUS: Class management; formations   **EQUIPMENT:** None

ORGANIZATION:

• Organization Signals mobilize the class, arranging children in various formations quickly and without confusion. Used constantly and spontaneously, these Signals will improve class control. Call out each Organization Signal and use the corresponding hand signal simultaneously. As the children become familiar with the signal's action, simply use the hand signal.

DESCRIPTION OF ACTIVITY:

1. *Listening Circle:* Run quickly to sit cross-legged in a circle near and facing me. (*Hand Signal:* Point with your index finger to the floor near you while circling the other index finger overhead.)

2. *Listening Line:* Run quickly to stand side by side in a line near me. Space yourselves at arm's length and face me. (*Hand Signal:* Point with your index finger to a line near you; then extend your arms sideways at shoulder height.)

3. *Quiet Signal:* Immediately stop what you are doing and raise one hand. Give me your full attention. (*Hand Signal:* Hold one hand overhead. Wait until all are quiet and paying attention.)

4. *Homes:* Run to a free space in the play area and sit cross-legged there, facing me. Check your spot so that you cannot touch anyone or anything. Remember your home. (*Hand Signal:* Make a roof overhead with hands. Mats or hoops could also be used as "Homes.")

5. *Endline:* Run quickly to one end of the play area and stand in a line, equally spaced apart, facing me. (*Hand Signal:* Point with index finger to one end of play area and extend arms sideways at shoulder level.)

IA–2 FORMATION SIGNALS

FOCUS: Class management

EQUIPMENT: Chart paper;
marking pen;
masking tape

ORGANIZATION:

• Formation Signals organize players into partners, small groups, or files. Call out each action and use the accompanying hand signal simultaneously. Establish four (or more) equal teams at the beginning of the year. List the names of the players of each team on chart paper and tape chart to wall. Select a leader and co-leader for each team. Change leaders and co-leaders often throughout the year so that each team member has a turn at both positions.

DESCRIPTION OF ACTIVITY:

1. *Groups:* Quickly sit in a group with the number of players I call; for example, "Groups of 2!" or "Groups of 5!" (*Hand Signal:* Hold up the same number of fingers as players in each group.)

2. *Files:* Leaders, run with your team to the side of the play area and sit cross-legged there, facing me. Other team members, quickly find your leader and cross-leg sit in a file behind him or her. Space yourselves evenly apart. Leader, sit at the front of the file and co-leader, sit at the back. (*Hand Signal:* Extend arms in front, parallel to each other and to the floor.)

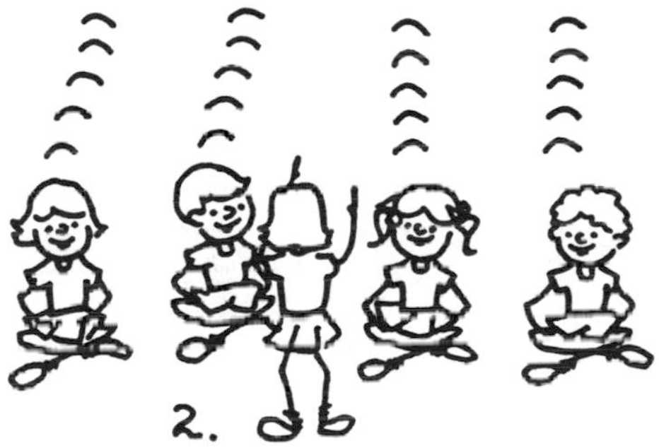

VARIATION:

Waves: Call Files signal and use its hand action; then move to one side of the files and have players turn to face you.

FOCUS: Class management; circle formation

EQUIPMENT: Lively music;
tape or record player

ORGANIZATION:

• Movement Signals quickly get players moving. Call out combinations of formations and locomotor movements such as "Activity Circle, Slide Clockwise!" or "Scrambled Eggs, Run!" Use hand signals as well. Change locomotor movements frequently throughout the activity. Players could jog, skip, hop, slide-step, leap, gallop, or run backward. Motivate players with lively music.

DESCRIPTION OF ACTIVITY:

1. *Scrambled Eggs:* Run helter-skelter in any direction. Remember, don't touch anyone as you move! (*Hand Signal:* Roll hand over hand.)

2. *Activity Circle:* Jog clockwise (or CCW) around play area in single file. Stay in your original order; don't pass anyone. (*Hand Signal:* Circle one arm overhead in a clockwise [or CCW] direction.)

VARIATIONS:

a. Use "Scrambled Eggs" signal with different directions, pathways, and levels (call "Scrambled Eggs, run sideways!" or zigzag, high, and low) or with different walks (call "Scrambled Eggs, crab-walk!" or lame-dog walk and bear-walk); enhance spatial awareness by calling "Scrambled Eggs, jog in a small space," ". . . jog in a smaller space," ". . . jog in an even smaller space."

b. *Switching Sides (Movement Signals Game):* Mark out play area with cone markers. Divide the class into two equal teams. Start with each team standing behind opposite endlines of play area, facing each other. Ensure that players are well spaced along the lines to avoid collisions. Adjust the running distance and the number of runs to class level. Use a variety of locomotor skills such as walking quickly, running with arms in the air, hopping, skipping, galloping, moving on all fours, etc. On signal "Switch Sides," both teams must change sides to sit cross-legged just behind the opposite line; the first team to do so earns one point. Play each game to five points.

— Now divide the class into four equal teams A, B, C, and D. Have each team stand behind an endline or sideline, waiting for the signal to move: A and C, side-step; B and D, skip across. "Go! Watch where you are going!"

IA—4 SIGNALS GAME

FOCUS: Alertness; listening skills   **EQUIPMENT:** None

ORGANIZATION:

- The game of Signals consists of a locomotor movement and a simultaneous verbal and hand signal. Encourage players to respond quickly by issuing a challenge such as "You owe me three jumping jacks (push-ups, or any task) if you are last!"

- Regard the "You owe me three!" challenge as good sportsmanship, not as punishment. Caution children to watch where they are going at all times.

DESCRIPTION OF ACTIVITY:

1. Run quickly. Run slowly. Skip high. Crawl low. Now Clear the Deck! Get off the floor as quickly as possible to stand on a bench, a chair, the climbing frame, and so on. (*Hand Signal:* Open arms overhead.)

2. Gallop in a new direction every time I call "Change!" Now Hit the Deck! Lie face down as quickly as possible on the floor or ground. (*Hand Signal:* Point to the floor with both hands.)

3. Walk like a robot. Waddle like a duck. Crabwalk. Now Corners! Run to any corner of the play area, or where any two lines cross, and sit cross-legged there. (*Hand Signal:* Cross arms overhead.)

4. Walk backward in pairs. Hop in pairs. Skip in pairs. Now Iceberg! Stop immediately and freeze like a statue. (*Hand Signal:* Make a fist overhead.)

VARIATIONS:

a. When playing Signals indoors, use the markings on the play area floor as part of the game. For example, call "Red lines!" and stand on a red line when you want players to sit cross-legged there.

b. Challenge players to keep alert by signaling with hands only.

c. Substitute other previously taught signals such as "Scrambled Eggs!" or "Activity Circle!"

IA–5 STARTING POSITIONS

FOCUS: Class management; personal space awareness

EQUIPMENT: None

ORGANIZATION:

• Starting Positions are used to organize and position the class quickly for any activity. Teach the following positions; then have the children practice the positions by calling them out in random order and in quick succession. Stress correct body posture.

DESCRIPTION OF ACTIVITY:

1. **Long-Sit:** Sit with legs outstretched and together. Lean back on hands for support.

2. **Hook-Sit:** Sit with legs together, knees bent, and feet flat on the floor. Lean back on hands for support.

3. **Wide-Sit:** Sit with legs outstretched and comfortably apart. Lean back on hands for support.

4. **Cross-legged Sit:** Sit with legs crossed and arms resting on knees.

5. **All Fours:** Support your weight on hands and knees.

6. **Front Support:** Support weight on hands and toes, with face down. Hold body straight.

7. **Front-Lying:** Lie face down with legs together and arms at sides, chest level.

8. **Back-Lying:** Lie face up with legs together and arms at sides.

9. **Hook-Lying:** Lie on back with knees bent so that feet are flat on floor. Arms are relaxed at sides.

10. **Back Support:** Sit with legs outstretched and together. Lean back on hands for support, bend elbows slightly, and then raise trunk to take weight on hands and heels. Hold body straight.

11. **Squat:** Stand; bend knees to raise heels from the floor. Place hands between knees and rest them on floor.

12. **Stand Tall:** Stand with feet comfortably apart and toes turned out slightly. Arms are at sides.

VARIATION:

As part of the Signals Game, combine Starting Position signals with Organizational signals; for example, "Scrambled Eggs, skip." "Iceberg, hook-sit!"

IA–6 FORTUNE COOKIE

FOCUS: Warm-up; listening

EQUIPMENT: One bench or table; several 3" × 5" file cards; marking pen

ORGANIZATION:

- Prepare at least twenty "Fortune Cookie" cards (3" × 5" colored cardboard) on which are written aerobic, strength, or flexibility exercises. These cards may be color-coded and laminated for durability and used continually throughout the year. Make the Aerobic ones green; the Strength ones red; and the Flexibility cards yellow. (See examples below.)
- Spread the "Fortune Cookie" cards along the top of a bench, face down. Fortune Cookie cards can be used throughout the year to introduce "breaks" into the lesson. Have the players scatter over the play area.

DESCRIPTION OF ACTIVITY:

1. On the signal "Go," all players run in general space. When I call one of you by name, run to the Fortune Cookie bench, select a card, and read it aloud to the class; then hand it to me.
2. Everyone then perform the Fortune Cookie task. When finished, jog on the spot until everyone else has finished.
3. On "Go!" run again in general space until another player is called to pick a Fortune Cookie card. Continue.

Fortune Cookie Suggestions:

— Touch the middle of each sideline and endline of the play area.

— Crab-walk the width of the play area.

— Do eight Jumping Jacks in each corner with a partner.

— Jog around the boundaries twice: Jog forward on the sidelines and backward on the endlines.

— Touch every circle in the play area with one knee and opposite hand.

— Do eight knee-hugs in each corner.

— Stand, extend arms sideways; circle arms forward ten times; circle arms backward ten times.

— Sit on twelve different lines.

— Do four push-ups in each corner.

— Slide-step around the boundaries.

— Do whatever the teacher does—twice.

— Give "High ten" to eight different people.

— Do a four-body part balance with a partner.

— Do four half jump-turns on the spot; then do two full jump-turns. Jump first in one direction, then in the opposite.

— Step up and down on three different benches, twelve times for each bench.

— Add your own Fortune Cookie exercise!

IA–7 MEET AND GREET WARM-UP

FOCUS: Aerobic warm-up; group interaction; listening

EQUIPMENT: Eight cone markers; music with a steady 4/4 beat; record or tape player

ORGANIZATION:

- Mark out a large circle with cone markers. Have players find a partner and form a double circle around the markers: one player to be part of the outer circle; the other to be in the inner circle. Both partners stand side by side and face in a CCW direction.

DESCRIPTION OF ACTIVITY:

1. When the music starts, jog with your partner around the circle. On the signal "Sprint," the inside partner jog in place while the outside partner, run forward to greet the next person in the circle, saying "Hi Bill," "Hi Mary." Shake hands and carry on a conversation while jogging together to the music.
2. When I call "Sprint 2," outside players run forward to greet the second person on the inside circle in the same way. Listen to the calls. I may also call "Sprint 3, 4, 5, 6." Continue until the music stops.

VARIATIONS:

a. When the music stops, change direction.
b. Instead of jogging, have players skip, hop, slide-step, or use dance steps.

IA–8 RUN–WALK WARM-UP

FOCUS: Aerobic warm-up

EQUIPMENT: See IA-7.

ORGANIZATION:

- Mark out a rectangular running course with cone markers at each corner. Have players scatter evenly around the running course.

DESCRIPTION OF ACTIVITY:

1. When the music starts, travel in a CCW direction around the course, running along the lengths of the track and walking across the widths. Continue this pattern, nonstop, for three minutes.
2. Players may pass each other on the outside after completing one circuit of the course.
3. When I call "Change," this is the signal for you to change direction of travel.
4. Count the number of laps you can do until the music stops, after three minutes. Repeat, using one of the variations.

VARIATIONS:

a. Increase the run–walk time to four minutes as the children get fitter.
b. Place obstacles on the long sides for players to jump over: benches, box horses, ropes, mats, hoops.
c. Substitute "Animal Walks" for walking across the widths.

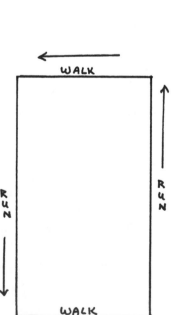

IA–9 COPY CAT

FOCUS: Aerobic endurance; leading and following

EQUIPMENT: Lively music; record or tape player

ORGANIZATION:

• Have players find a partner and move to a free space. Have partners decide who will lead and who will follow.

DESCRIPTION OF ACTIVITY:

1. When the music starts, the Leader, move briskly around in general space over the play area performing a variety of different movements, at different levels, and on different body parts, and moving to the music:
   — running, leaping, rolling, dodging
   — hopping, jumping, slide-stepping
   — twisting, twirling, crawling
   — jumping jacks, knee bends, sit-ups, push-ups
   — finger snapping, hand clapping, arm circling
   — cartwheels, gymnastic stunts
   — dance steps

2. The Follower, stay as close to your Leader as possible, performing identical movements. After one minute and on the signal "Switch," reverse roles with your partner. When the music stops, find a new partner. Continue when the music starts again.

VARIATIONS:

a. *Face to Face:* Have partners face each other about 1 meter (3 feet) apart. One partner, try to outdodge the other.

b. *Mirror Image:* Have partners face each other as they move. One partner, try to do a mirror image of the other.

IA–10 LEADER OF THE PACK

FOCUS: Aerobic warm-up; leadership

EQUIPMENT: See IA-9.

ORGANIZATION:

• Form groups of four to six players. Have each group choose a Leader to start the fun run, and have players stand in a file behind their Leader.

DESCRIPTION OF ACTIVITY:

1. At the start of the music, follow your Leader, doing whatever he or she does. Stay in line and try to keep in time with the music.
2. Leader, think of movements and activities for your followers to do:
   — Running in different ways; crawling, hopping, twisting, rolling, dodging, jumping.
   — Moving forward, backward, sideways, diagonally, zigzag.
   — Trying animal walks such as bear-walks, seal-walks, crab-walks, kangaroo hops.
   — Doing exercises such as sit-ups, push-ups, jumping jacks, knee bends.
   — Doing dance steps that you have learned.
3. On the signal "Change" (after about twenty seconds), the next player in the file, take over as the new Leader to add new tasks to the activity. Try not to repeat tasks that have been done before. Old Leader, join the end of the file.

IA–11 BRITISH BULLDOG

FOCUS: Vigorous warm-up; chasing and dodging

EQUIPMENT: One flag per person; four cone markers

ORGANIZATION:

• Mark out the play area with a safe zone at each end. Make sure that the safe area is large enough to allow for a run-off without hitting a wall. Clear the play area of obstacles. Select one player to be IT, who stands in the middle of the play area. Have all other players tuck a flag in the back of their waistband so that two-thirds of the flag is showing, and stand at one end of the play area.

DESCRIPTION OF ACTIVITY:

1. When IT shouts, "British Bulldog 1, 2, 3!" all players try to run to the safe zone at the opposite end of the play area before IT can pull your flag.

2. Tagged players, you become IT's helpers and join IT in the middle of the play area. Don't forget to return your flag to me. You may change ends only when the "British Bulldog" signal is called.

3. Now all ITs, shout together, "British Bulldog 1, 2, 3!" and players again try to run to the opposite safe zone. Continue in this way until only one player is left. That player becomes IT for the next game.

VARIATIONS:

a. Start with more than one IT.

b. Allow players to start at either end, but they can only change ends when "British Bulldog 1, 2, 3!" is called.

c. Challenge the IT players to lift runners from the floor for a count of "British Bulldog 1, 2, 3!" Any player who is lifted from the floor helps to tag the others.

IA—12 RHYTHM RUNNING

FOCUS: Aerobic endurance; group cooperation

EQUIPMENT: Suitable music; ten cone markers; record or tape player

ORGANIZATION:

- Mark out a circular or oval running track with cone markers. Have players space themselves evenly around the track.

DESCRIPTION OF ACTIVITY:

1. Listen to the music as you walk on the spot and clap your hands in time to the music. Now, snap your fingers in time with the music. This time, walk in a CCW direction as you "snap or clap" to the beat of the music. Pick up the tempo, jogging to the beat.
2. When I call "Twos" or give two blasts of the whistle, without stopping, pair up with a partner as you jog around the track. Can you and your partner keep in step with each other and in time with the music as you run?
3. On the signal "Fours" or four whistle blasts, form groups of four. Continue to run beside each other in time with the music and in step with each other. Form groups of "Six"; "Eight."
4. On the signal "Cool down," slow down to a walk with your group but continue to keep in time with the music.

VARIATIONS:

a. Try other locomotor movements: slide-stepping, skipping, running backward, galloping with the left foot forward.
b. Gradually increase the running time.
c. Change to running in a CW direction.

IA—13 SNOWBALL RUN

FOCUS: Aerobic endurance; friendship; cooperation

EQUIPMENT: Suitable music; record or tape player

ORGANIZATION:

- Have players find a partner, scatter, and stand side by side ready to run.

DESCRIPTION OF ACTIVITY:

1. On the signal "Go," or when the music starts, run in general space beside your partner. When the music stops or on the signal "Snowball," drop hands, split up, and find a new partner. Greet your new partner, "Hi Joey," "Hi Chris." When the music starts, continue to run together. Look for open spaces to run to.
2. Listen for the next "Snowball" signal to find a new partner. Repeat. On our last "Snowball," walk with your partner to cool down, but still keep in time with the music.

VARIATIONS:

a. Have partners skip, hop, slide-step instead of run.
b. Gradually increase the running time.
c. Have players snap their fingers in time with the music as they run.
d. Encourage players to talk to each other as they run.

IA—14 SCORPION TAG

FOCUS: Running and dodging; alertness; fair play   **EQUIPMENT:** Four cone markers

ORGANIZATION:

- Mark out the boundaries of the play area. Choose two pairs of players, consisting of a "Chaser" and a "Runner" in each pair. All others form groups of three players to become "Scorpions," consisting of a head, middle, and a tail. Scorpion players hold on to the waist of the player in front.

DESCRIPTION OF ACTIVITY:

1. On the signal "Go," the Chaser, chase the Runner, who tries to escape being tagged by hooking on to the Tail of one of the Scorpions.

2. Scorpions, try to protect your Tail by running, turning, and twisting away from the Runner. Remember, you must remain joined together throughout the game.

3. If the Runner hooks on to the Scorpion's tail, the head becomes the new Runner to be chased by the Chaser. If the Runner is tagged by the Chaser, you both switch roles.

VARIATION:

Have more than two pairs of Chasers and Runners.

IA—15 PASS 'N STING

FOCUS: Aerobic warm-up; running; dodging and throwing

EQUIPMENT: One beanbag or sponge ball per pair; four cone markers; one whistle; lively music; tape or record player

ORGANIZATION:

- Mark out the boundaries of the play area. Have players find a partner; one player get a beanbag and then scatter over the play area.

DESCRIPTION OF ACTIVITY:

1. When the music starts, or on the signal "Pass," jog around the play area, passing the beanbag back and forth to each other.

2. When you hear the call "Sting" or you hear the whistle, the player holding the beanbag, chase your partner trying to throw the beanbag at him or her to "sting" (hit) him or her below the waist. If you sting your partner, change roles and keep playing until the next "Pass" signal.

3. Continue to play until the music stops.

VARIATION:

Have the chaser hold the beanbag to try and touch the partner with it.

IA-16 BEANBAG AGILITY RUN

FOCUS: Speed; agility; warm-up

EQUIPMENT: Three beanbags per pair; four cone markers

ORGANIZATION:

• Mark out the beanbag course 15 meters (45 feet) long with the cone markers. Have players find a partner, collect three beanbags per pair, and line up one behind the other, behind the starting line. (Use deckrings if there are not enough beanbags.) Have each pair place one beanbag on the starting line in front of them and the other two on the opposite line.

DESCRIPTION OF ACTIVITY:

1. The first partner of each pair, begin in the front-lying position behind the starting line with your forehead on your beanbag.
2. On the signal "Go!" the first partner, quickly spring to your feet and run to the far line; pick up one beanbag, return to your starting line; place the beanbag on the line; grab the beanbag on the starting line; run to the far line again; exchange beanbags once more; and carry it back to the starting line again.
3. Now, the other partner, take your turn to make four crossings, exchanging beanbags each time. The warm-up finishes when each partner has performed three sets.
4. Place, not throw, beanbags on the line. Remember, do not pick up the beanbag on the starting line first, but run to the opposite line to get a beanbag.

VARIATIONS:

a. Set a time limit such as three minutes. Have each pair count the number of beanbag exchanges they can perform in this time by counting the number of crossings made. Have them try to beat their previous score.
b. Shorten or lengthen the distance.

IA-17 JUNK RUN

FOCUS: Agility running

EQUIPMENT: A good supply of small equipment: beanbags, deckrings, balls, rolled-up ropes; six cone markers

ORGANIZATION:

• Mark out the play area with a base at each end and a middle area about 2 meters (6 feet) wide. Divide the class into two equal teams. Have each team line up in its own base behind the opposite end lines. Scatter a variety of "Junk" (small equipment such as beanbags, deckrings, small balls, rolled-up ropes) in the middle of the play area.

DESCRIPTION OF ACTIVITY:

1. On the signal "Go," players run to the middle, pick up a piece of junk (equipment), and take it back to your base.
2. When all the junk is gone from the middle, you can start taking junk from the other team's base, back to your base.
3. Players can carry only one piece of junk at a time. No player can be prevented from getting junk at any time. The "Junk" must be PUT behind the base, not thrown.
4. On the signal "Stop," return with the piece of junk you are carrying, and count the pieces of junk salvaged by your team. The team with more junk wins. The losing team returns all the junk to the containers.

IA—18 FOUR-CORNER WARM-UP

FOCUS: Aerobic warm-up

EQUIPMENT: Four or more cone markers; posterboard and marking pens; lively music; tape or record player

ORGANIZATION:

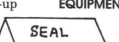

- In Four-Corner Warm-Up, players move continuously around the boundaries of the play area. Each time they turn a corner, they begin a new type of movement. Place a cone marker at each corner of the play area. Write different movements on posterboard to make activity signs. Lean an activity sign against each of the four cone markers. Arrange signs so that players perform quick movements along the long sides and slow movements along the short sides of the play area. Signs must be visible to incoming players. Have players stretch before starting and after the warm-up is completed. Start and stop the activity with music. Adjust the boundaries of the play area to match the players' fitness levels. To begin players scatter evenly around the track.

DESCRIPTION OF ACTIVITY:

1. *Long Side Movements:* jog; skip; slide-step; run backward; grapevine-step; etc.
2. *Short Side Movements:* hop; jump; crab-walk; lame-dog walk; seal-walk; etc.
3. Overtaking players must pass on the outside.

VARIATIONS:

a. *Six- or Eight-Corner Warm-Up:* Place more cone markers and locomotion signs around the perimeter of the play area. Alternate long-quick and short-slower movements.
b. *Reverse Warm-Up:* Repeat circuit in opposite direction.
c. Increase the length of time on the course or the size of the play area as players become fitter.

IA—19 CORNERS

FOCUS: Aerobic warm-up; team work

EQUIPMENT: Music with strong 4/4 beat; tape or record player

ORGANIZATION:

- Divide the class into four equal teams and allocate a corner of the play area to each. Have each team start in their corner.

DESCRIPTION OF ACTIVITY:

1. When I start the music, teams leave your corner and run around in general space. On the signal "Corner—10 Jumping Jacks!" each team, run to one of the other corners of the play area. When everyone on your team is there, do ten Jumping Jacks together; then quickly sit down. No two teams can occupy the same corner.
2. The team that was last to get to its corner and complete the task "owes me three" (that is, the whole team must do three of some task such as three Jump-Turns; three Sit down, stand ups; three Cartwheels).
3. When the music is played again, all teams run in general space. Listen for the next "Corner signal" to be called. Run to another corner, perform the task, and quickly sit down. The game continues in this way.
4. Suggestions for "Corner Tasks": ten Sit-Ups; ten Push-Ups; ten Cross-Over Jumps; ten Crab Kicks (Crab-walk position, kicking each leg out in turn).

IA-20 EXERCISE HUNT

FOCUS: Aerobic warm-up; cooperation   **EQUIPMENT:** One photocopied list of exercises per group; four folding mats; music with a strong 4/4 beat; tape or record player

ORGANIZATION:

- Prepare a list of ten fitness exercises following the suggestions on this card and photocopy the list for each group of five to seven players. Explain that groups may do exercises in any order, as long as they finish all of them. Before anyone in the group can move on to the next exercise task, every player in the group must have completed the immediate task. Play music to start the activity.
- As groups finish the Exercise Hunt, have them stretch out in the middle of the play area.

DESCRIPTION OF ACTIVITY:

Indoor Exercise Hunt:

1. Step up and down eight times at four different benches.
2. Give "High tens" with ten different players who are not a member of your team.
3. Do twenty Cross-over Jumping Jacks.
4. Curl up twenty times.
5. Touch twelve different lines around the play area with your left knee and right elbow.
6. Cross-leg sit in a circle and together recite your favorite Christmas carol or nursery rhyme.
7. Run backward once around the play area, clapping your hands in time to the music.
8. Do twelve bent-knee push-ups.
9. Sit down; stand up. Repeat eight times.
10. Hold hands and slide-step to each corner of the play area.

Outdoor Exercise Hunt:

1. Touch a tree, a fence, and a swing.
2. Squat in file formation. Last player leapfrog over other players; then squat at front of the file. As a group, do a total of twenty leapfrog jumps.
3. Do ten curl-ups at three different trees.
4. Crab-walk greeting to everyone in your group.
5. Crawl under five different playground objects.
6. Run once around the perimeter of your school grounds.
7. Run around three garbage cans located around the school.
8. Touch four benches. Do five push-ups at each.
9. Stretch at a tree or pole or fence.

IA-21 HEART ATTACK GAME_____

FOCUS: Aerobic warm-up; heart disease knowledge; trust

EQUIPMENT: Box of banners; lively music; tape or record player

ORGANIZATION:

• Select three players to be IT. Have each IT wear a banner. Explain that there are five factors that contribute to the risk of having a heart attack: smoking, inactivity, overweight, excessive alcohol, and stress. Discuss the heart attack risk factors. Follow up the topic in health class. Emphasize that players are trusted to keep their own score.

DESCRIPTION OF ACTIVITY:

1. When the music starts, the IT group, try to tag as many players as you can. Use a two-handed tag on the shoulder.
2. Tagged players, run on the spot with arms overhead as a signal to another player to come and free you by doing five Jumping Jacks with you.
3. If tagged once, that player has one risk factor; tagged twice, two risk factors; tagged three times, three risk factors; and so on.
4. When a player is tagged for the fifth time, that player has a "heart attack" and becomes a member of the IT group. Collect and wear a banner and continue to tag the others.

VARIATION:

Have players take a resting pulse before the game begins and take their pulse again when the game ends. Discuss their findings.

IA-22 PARTNER BEANBAG CHASE_____

FOCUS: Running and dodging; cooperation

EQUIPMENT: Four cone markers; three beanbags

ORGANIZATION:

• Mark out the play area. Have the players find a partner, hold hands, and scatter in general space ready to run. Choose one, two, or three pairs to be ITs, depending on the size of the class. Have each IT pair collect a beanbag.

DESCRIPTION OF ACTIVITY:

1. On the signal "Beanbag Chase," the IT pairs, chase the others, trying to tag them with the beanbag. IT partners, you may hand the beanbag to each other with your outside hands to make the tag.
2. If a pair is tagged, you become the new IT, take the beanbag, and continue the chase. See if your pair can go through the game without being tagged.

VARIATION:

Have the IT pair throw the beanbag at the others to hit either partner below the waist.

IA–23 TEAM COLORS TAG

FOCUS: Running and dodging

EQUIPMENT: Four sets of colored flags; stopwatch; one whistle; chalkboard and chalk or chart paper and marking pens

ORGANIZATION:

- Divide the class into four equal teams and have each team choose a captain. Team captains distribute a set of colored flags to their team members, who tuck flags into the back of their waistbands so that most of the flag shows.

DESCRIPTION OF ACTIVITY:

1. Each team, choose an exercise that you can ask the other three teams to do when you tag them, such as sit-ups, push-ups, or jumping jacks.
2. Listen for your team's color. When your color is called, your team is IT and has one minute to "tag" as many of the other players as possible, by pulling a player's flag. The pulled flag is returned to the tagged player and tucked into the front of the waistband.
3. Tagged players and anyone who runs outside the play area, do the exercise the IT team has chosen. Continue to do the exercise until one minute is up.
4. Change the IT team. Listen for another color to be called. When you hear your team's color, remind players of the exercise you want them to do when you tag them. Continue the game until each team has been IT.

VARIATION:

Count the number of players each team tags and record team scores. Which team will earn the best score?

IA–24 NUMBER TAG

FOCUS: Running and dodging; listening

EQUIPMENT: One marking pen; one numbered beanbag per player; basket

ORGANIZATION:

- Number beanbags, one for each player; then have player pick up a beanbag out of the basket and find a free space.

DESCRIPTION OF ACTIVITY:

1. Hold your beanbag so no one can see what number you have. Jog around the play area.
2. On signal "Homes!" find a free space and jog on the spot. I will call out five numbers. When your number is called, you are IT.
3. All ITs, raise your hand so that everyone can see who you are. Now, on the count of five, chase free players and try to hit them below the waist with your beanbag.
4. Tagged players or anyone who runs outside the boundaries of the play area must do jumping jacks on the spot until everyone else is doing them, too.
5. To start a new game, trade your beanbag with another player, check your new number; then jog around the play area again, and listen for the signal "Homes!"

IA—25 SHOES

FOCUS: Running; agility; team work; fun

EQUIPMENT: suitable music;
hoops;
record or tape player

ORGANIZATION:

- Form equal teams of three to four players. Have each team get a hoop and place it to form a circle of hoops, eight meters (25 feet) from the center of the play area.
- Have all players remove shoes and socks and pile all the shoes in the center. Have players decide the order in which they will run.

DESCRIPTION OF ACTIVITY:

1. When the music starts or on the signal "Go," first runners, run to the center to retrieve a shoe and return to place it in your team's hoop and sit down. Second players, jump up and do the same.
2. Continue in turn until you have three shoes in your hoop; then you may take shoes from the center or from other hoops, but may take only one at a time. Players cannot protect shoes from being taken.
3. When the music stops, count the number of shoes in your hoop. The team with the most wins. Who can be the first to retrieve his or her own shoes and socks and put them on?

IA—26 GRAB BAG

FOCUS: Running; quick changes of direction

EQUIPMENT: Every available beanbag; one small mat per pair; one hoop; lively music; tape or record player

ORGANIZATION:

- Place a hoop in the middle of the play area and fill it with beanbags. (If insufficient beanbags, use deckrings, small balls, or rolled-up ropes.) Have players find a partner and get a mat to share. Help players space their mats evenly in a circle around the hoop and about 5 meters (15 feet) away from it. Have pairs sit on their mats and decide which partner will go first. Lengthen the distance that mats are placed from the hoop to increase fitness.

DESCRIPTION OF ACTIVITY:

1. When the music starts, first player run to the hoop, get a beanbag, and return to place, not throw it, on your mat. Then quickly sit on your mat.
2. Now second player, stand and do the same. Continue to take turns at getting a beanbag and bringing it back to your mat. You may pick up only one beanbag at a time.
3. When all the beanbags are gone from the hoop, you may grab a beanbag from any other mat, but only one at a time. One partner must be sitting on the mat at all times, and you cannot prevent others from grabbing a bag from your mat.
4. Continue until the music stops. Count the number of beanbags on your mat. The pair with the most beanbags wins.

IA-27 JOKER'S WILD

FOCUS: General warm-up using fitness parameters

EQUIPMENT: One deck of exercise cards; mats for floor work; one pair of large dice

ORGANIZATION:

- Make up a deck of exercise playing cards on blank index cards: Include the "2" through the "Ace" in "Hearts" and add three Joker cards—these are the "Wild Cards." The cards should include aerobic activity, strength, agility, and flexibility exercises. Make several different exercise cards for each of these fitness parameters. Share your Wild Card ideas with other teachers. Use children's suggestions for exercise cards and how the game will be played. Use the other suites—Spades, Diamonds, Clubs—to increase the number of cards. To begin, have players scatter, find a "home," and sit in their home.

DESCRIPTION OF ACTIVITY:

1. On the signal "Run," all players, run in general space. When I call one of you by name, come forward to draw a card from the deck and read it to the class, who will perform the task.

2. When I call "Sidelines," run to touch the middle of each of the sidelines, return to your home, and perform the task on the card.

3. We will continue the game until we are warmed up.

Sample Wild Cards:

King—thirteen jumping jacks
Queen—twelve wall push-ups
Jack—eleven sit-ups
10—ten side leg raises, each leg
9—nine bench steps
8—eight mountain climbers
7—seven crab-walks forward, seven back
6—six high "tens"
5—five runs—endline to endline
4—four lie down, stand, jump up
3—three different stretches—ten seconds each
2—two minutes of jump rope
Ace—fifteen teacher's choice, girl's choice, or boy's choice
Joker—two speed laps of the play area

VARIATION:

Poker Dice: Have a player select a card, e.g., "King"—Jumping Jacks; then ask another player to roll a pair of dice. Add the numbers on the dice to determine the number of repetitions to be done on that exercise.

IA–28 SLAP AND RUN

FOCUS: Aerobic warm-up; agility; spatial awareness

EQUIPMENT: Lively music; tape or record player

ORGANIZATION:

• Have players find a partner and stand at arm's length facing each other.

DESCRIPTION OF ACTIVITY:

1. When the music starts, or on the signal "Go," partners, try to slap each other on the knee. As soon as one of you hit your partner's knee, you become the Runner and run away as quickly as possible. The partner who was hit, you become the Chaser and try to tag the Runner.

2. As soon as the tag is made, stop, face each other, and begin another knee slap contest. Continue to play in this way until the music stops.

VARIATION:

After thirty seconds, stop play, have the players walk around as a break, then change partners and begin again.

IA–29 DROP 'N RUN

FOCUS: Aerobic warm-up; passing

EQUIPMENT: One ball per player; lively music; record or tape player

ORGANIZATION:

• Have players find a partner; one partner get a ball. Partners scatter around the play area about four paces apart.

DESCRIPTION OF ACTIVITY:

1. On the signal "Pass," partners, run briskly around the play area, passing the ball back and forth to each other.

2. If the ball is dropped while passing, your pair must jog once around the outside of the play area with one partner holding the ball. Then return to the play area to pass and catch once more.

3. When the music stops, exchange partners and continue.

VARIATION:

a. Use a variety of objects such as beanbags, deckrings, utility balls, basketballs, volleyballs, or soccer balls to pass and catch.

b. Use other locomotor movements: skip, gallop, slide-step.

c. Challenge players to move further apart as they throw and catch.

IA–30 HOOP AEROBICS

FOCUS: Aerobic warm-up; strength

EQUIPMENT: One hoop for every player;
suitable music;
record or tape player

ORGANIZATION:

• Have every player get a hoop, find a home, and sit in the hoop. Suggestions follow.

DESCRIPTION OF ACTIVITY:

— Leave your hoop. Can you leap over ten different hoops and return to sit in your own hoop? Who can be the quickest?
— Visit ten hoops, placing your right hand and left foot in each; then return home.
— Hopping on one foot only, land in a hoop; change your hopping foot and hop into another hoop. Continue until you have visited eight hoops; then hop back to your home.
— Crab-Walk (on hands and feet, facing upward) to six different hoops, sitting down in each one. Return home and curl up in your own.
— Jump in and out of your hoop as you move around it. Jump to another hoop and repeat, jumping in the opposite direction around the hoop; then jump home.
— Pick up your hoop in both hands, stand, and stretch upward with it. Then lower it so that you are now inside of it holding the hoop at waist level. Run once around the play area; as you pass me, place your hoop over my arms and sit in the middle of the play area.

VARIATIONS:

a. Vary the number of repetitions to the fitness level of the class.
b. Repeat using different locomotor movements: skipping, sliding, walking, galloping.

IA–31 MATERCISE

FOCUS: Aerobic warm-up; strength; stretching

EQUIPMENT: One mat per player;
lively music;
tape or record player

ORGANIZATION:

• Have players get a mat and hook-sit facing you. Suggestions follow.

DESCRIPTION OF ACTIVITY:

— The mat is your Home. Leave your home and touch ten different mats with your right hand and left foot; then quickly jump Home.
— The mats are now puddles of water. Run and leap over as many mats as you can before I signal "Freeze!" How many mats did you go over? Now skip Home.
— Run to four different mats and do eight sit-up hugs on each mat; then hop home. (To do a sit-up hug, begin in back-lying position with hands stretched overhead. Gently curl up to hug your knees to your chest; then gently curl down to starting position.)
— Run to six different mats and do four knee push-ups on each mat; then walk backward home.
— Long-sit on your mat. Cross your ankles and reach for the toes. Hold for ten seconds; then change the top leg and repeat. Now in back-lying position, stretch in a long narrow shape for ten seconds; roll into back-lying position, and stretch in a wide shape for ten seconds.

IA–32 PARTNER SHUTTLE

FOCUS: Aerobic warm-up; interval training

EQUIPMENT: Lines on the floor; stopwatch

ORGANIZATION:

- Mark four or five parallel lines about 5 meters (15 feet) apart on the floor. Have players find a partner and, one behind the other, stand behind the starting line. Remind players to move in their own path to avoid collisions. Emphasize that players make sure they touch the lines properly. Encourage players to cheer their partner on during the activity.

DESCRIPTION OF ACTIVITY:

1. On the signal "Go," the first player, run to touch the first line with your right foot and left hand, return to tag your partner, who runs to the first line to do the same.
2. Then, taking turns, each touch the second line with your right hand and left foot.
3. Continue until all five lines have been touched with right hand and left foot. When both partners have finished the course, cross-leg sit behind the starting line. Try not to be the last one finished.
4. Run through the course again, touching the lines with different body parts: two hands and two feet; one foot and one elbow; back of head; seat and two hands.

VARIATIONS:

a. Time the partners and record the times. Challenge them to beat their previous times.
b. Perform partner shuttles on scooters.
c. Have players perform sets of exercises at each line: first line—five push-ups; second line—ten jumping jacks; third line—ten sit-ups, etc.
d. Have players crab-walk to the first line; hop to the second line; skip to the third line; slide-step to the fourth line; run to the fifth line.
e. Shorten or lengthen the distance between lines.

IA–33 CIRCLE PARTNER TAG

FOCUS: Aerobic fun run; dodging

EQUIPMENT: Lively music; tape or record player; four cone markers

ORGANIZATION:

- Mark out the play area with the cones. Have players find a partner. Arrange all pairs in a double circle: one player on the inside circle, the other on the outside circle, with both circles facing the center.

DESCRIPTION OF ACTIVITY:

1. When the music starts, or on the signal "Go," the inside circle, slide-step with arms extended sideways at shoulder level in a CW direction; the outer circle, slide-step with arms extended sideways in a CCW direction. Keep in time with the music.
2. When the music stops, the outside players, scatter in all directions while the inside players try to find your partners to tag them. If tagged, players change positions in the circle when the game starts again. Let's play to see who can be the last one tagged.

VARIATION:

Use other ways of moving around the circle: skipping, cross-over step.

IA—34 THREE TIMES THREE

FOCUS: Aerobic warm-up; interval training

EQUIPMENT: One beanbag per three players; one skipping rope per three players; eight cone markers; suitable music; record or tape player

ORGANIZATION:

- Form teams of three players. Mark off four parallel lines, spaced about 3 to 5 meters (10 to 15 feet) apart, in front of each team. Have players in each team stand one behind the other, behind the starting line. Have the players place a beanbag on the first line in front of their team and a skipping rope on the second line.

DESCRIPTION OF ACTIVITY:

1. When the music starts, or on the signal "Go," the first player, run to the first line, place the beanbag between your knees, and do five curl-ups; run to the second line, jump rope ten times; run to the third line, sit down and stand up five times; return to the starting line.
2. The second player, you may go as soon as the first player starts the third stunt.
3. Which team can be the first to finish after three turns each? Sit cross-legged one behind the other behind the starting line.

VARIATIONS:

a. Vary the three assigned stunts. Have the players do a specified number of jumps, ball dribbles, heel clicks, knee dips, jumping jacks—in fact, any previously learned stunt!
b. Allow the losing team to select the stunts for the next race.
c. For a large class, have the players run with a partner to increase participation.
d. How many round trips can each team make in two minutes?

IA—35 PUSH-UP TAG

FOCUS: Running and dodging; arm strength

EQUIPMENT: Four mats; three banners; four cone markers; lively music; tape or record player

ORGANIZATION:

- Mark out the play area. Place a mat outside each sideline of the play area. Choose three players to be IT and have them each wear a banner. All other players scatter.

DESCRIPTION OF ACTIVITY:

1. When the music starts, or on the signal "Go," the IT group, work together to tag as many players as you can in one minute, until the music stops.
2. If tagged, you must go to the nearest mat to do four push-ups before reentering the game.
3. When the music stops, the IT group, count the number of tags made by your group.
4. Then we will choose another IT group. When the music starts, the new ITs, try to tag more players than the last group in one minute. Continue in this way.

VARIATION:

Bench Step Tag: Use benches instead of mats. Have the tagged players do twelve bench steps before reentering the game.

IA–36 WILLIE, BILLIE, MOE, AND JOE

FOCUS: Warm-up activity; agility; alertness   **EQUIPMENT:** None

ORGANIZATION:

- Have players form groups of four. Give each member of each group the name of Willie, Billie, Moe, or Joe: Willie and Billie are a pair; Moe and Joe are the other pair.

DESCRIPTION OF ACTIVITY:

1. Billie, Moe, and Joe join hands to form a circle. Willie, you remain outside the circle and try to tag your partner, Billie, without breaking through the circle of hands.

2. Moe and Joe try to protect Billie by circling either to the right or to the left away from Willie, but you cannot break the hand hold.

3. If Willie tags Billie, you both become part of the new circle with Moe; then Joe tries to tag Moe.

IA–37 ST. GEORGE AND THE DRAGON

FOCUS: Aerobic warm-up; alertness; agility   **EQUIPMENT:** One flag per group of five players

ORGANIZATION:

- Have the class divide into groups of five players. In each group choose one player to be "St. George"; have the other four players, "the Dragon," line up in a file, holding on to the waist of the player in front. Have the last player, "the Dragon's Tail," place a flag in the back of his or her waistband so that two-thirds of it is showing. Scatter the Dragons throughout the play area. Check for good spacing so that groups will not interfere with each other.

DESCRIPTION OF ACTIVITY:

1. On the signal "Go," St. George, try to snatch the "tail" (flag) from the end of your Dragon by dodging and darting to catch the Tail out of position.

2. If successful, St. George joins the front of the Dragon to become the new Dragon's Head; the Dragon's Tail becomes the new St. George; and the next to last player becomes the new Dragon's Tail.

3. Remember, your dragon must stay together and not break up.

VARIATIONS:

a. Have only three players in each Dragon.

b. Allow the Dragon's Head to use his arms to protect the Tail.

IA–38 ASTRONAUT RUN

FOCUS: Aerobic fun run

EQUIPMENT: Eight to ten cone markers; lively music; tape or record player

ORGANIZATION:

- During Astronaut Run, children move continuously around a circle, alternating locomotor movements, which include walking, running, jumping, side-stepping, and skipping. Explain that faster runners can pass, but only on the outside of the circle. Start and stop the activity with music, allowing music to play for three or four minutes in beginning sessions. Gradually increase the duration and intensity of movement as the children's fitness levels improve. Have children space themselves evenly around a large circle. The following are some movement ideas.

DESCRIPTION OF ACTIVITY:

- Jog CW with good posture. Snap fingers overhead as you run.
- Hop, changing feet every three or four hops.
- Walk backward, clapping hands above head, in front, and behind. Repeat clapping pattern.
- Jump from side to side as you move forward.
- Bear-Walk (on hands and feet, moving right arm and leg forward, then left arm and leg).
- Walk with giant cross-over steps.
- Skip with high arm swings.
- Side step facing outward for eight counts; then side-step facing inward for eight counts. Repeat pattern.
- Cool Down: Walk on your toes, heels, and the inside and outside of your feet.

IA–39 GRASS DRILLS

FOCUS: Aerobic warm-up

EQUIPMENT: Popular music; tape or record player

ORGANIZATION:

- Grass drills, commonly used in football training, require players to alternate aerobic or running-type movements with ground exercises. Emphasis is on agility and quickness. Arrange the class in scatter or semicircle formation. Check for good spacing. Start and stop the activity with music, allowing the drill to continue for about two to three minutes at first. Increase the time as fitness levels increase. Alternate any locomotor movement with a grass drill. Select different players to lead the class.
- Following are movement suggestions. Alternate any locomotor movement with a grass drill.

DESCRIPTION OF ACTIVITY:

- On the signal "Jog!" jog in place with knees high and clap for twenty seconds; then on signal "Front!" quickly lie face down.
- On the signal "Rope Jump!" pantomime rope jumping in place for twenty seconds; then on signal "Back!" quickly lie on your back.
- "Jumping Jacks"; "Turtle," lie on back with feet up.
- "Sprint in place"; "Curl-up," hold modified V-sit position.
- "Straddle Jumps"; "Push-up," hold the front-support position.
- "Side-Kicks"; "Seal," in front-support position, raise body and drag feet.
- "Cross-over steps"; "Crab," in back-support position, bend knees and lift hips.
- "Twist-Jumps"; "Bridge," hold the back-support position.

IA–40 THE FRUIT SALAD GAME

FOCUS: Running and dodging; alertness

EQUIPMENT: Four cone markers; several beanbags

ORGANIZATION:

- Mark out the play area with two well-defined safety lines. Choose one player to be IT, to hold a beanbag and to stand in the middle (the "Plantation"). Pick four teams and give each team the name of a tropical fruit, such as Mango, Paw-paw, Kiwi, Avocado. Have all the "fruit" line up in any order behind one of the safety lines.

DESCRIPTION OF ACTIVITY:

1. When IT calls out the name of one of the fruits, e.g., "Mango," players on that team must try to get to the other side of the Plantation without being tagged with the beanbag by IT.
2. If tagged, that player becomes part of the Fruit Salad, gets a beanbag, and helps IT to tag others.
3. If IT calls out "Fruit Salad," everyone must run. Only IT may call out the Fruit to run.
4. The game continues until every Fruit is part of the Fruit Salad.

VARIATION:

Use flags tucked into players' waistbands that must be pulled out in order to be tagged.

IA–41 HOOK-ON TAG

FOCUS: Aerobic warm-up; running and dodging; fair play

EQUIPMENT: Two different colored banners; four cone markers

ORGANIZATION:

- Mark out the boundaries of the play area. Choose one player to be the "Runner" and another to be the "Chaser." The Chaser and Runner each wear a different colored banner. All others find a partner, link elbows, and find a space.

DESCRIPTION OF ACTIVITY:

1. On signal "Go!" everyone run. The Chaser, try to tag the Runner, who may run anywhere in the play area.
2. If the Runner links elbows with one member of a pair, then the outside member of that pair becomes the new Runner.
3. If the Chaser does tag the Runner, the two exchange roles and the game continues.
4. If the Runner steps outside the boundary lines, the Runner immediately becomes the Chaser. Partners cannot assist the Chaser or Runner in any way. Play the game fairly.

VARIATIONS:

a. Have more than one Runner.
b. Increase the size of the play area.

IA—42 AMBLE SCRAMBLE

FOCUS: Aerobic warm-up; partner work

EQUIPMENT: Drum or suitable music; record or tape player

ORGANIZATION:

• Have players find a partner and form a double circle with the inside player facing the outside partner.

DESCRIPTION OF ACTIVITY:

1. When the music starts, hold both hands with your partner, slide-step around the circle in a CW direction, keeping in time with the music or drum.
2. When the music stops and I call "Scramble," the inside players jog on the spot with arms folded.
3. Meanwhile, outside players drop hands and run CW around the circle once. When you return, go past your old partner to the next player, who becomes your new partner. Crawl through your new partner's legs, so that you are now on the inside circle. Both turn and do five Jumping Jacks with your new partner.
4. Hold hands, slide-step around the circle until you hear the next "Scramble" signal; then repeat, taking turns to run around the circle.

VARIATIONS:

a. Instead of jogging on the spot, have the inside players run CCW around the circle while the outside players run CW.
b. Have the outside players leapfrog over the inside players when they return.

IA—43 BEANBAG BENCH PASS

FOCUS: Aerobic warm-up; leg strength

EQUIPMENT: One bench per six players; one beanbag per pair; suitable music in 4/4 time; tape or record player

ORGANIZATION:

• Have players find a partner. Have four pairs get four benches and place them 4 meters (12 feet) apart. Have each pair collect one beanbag only and stand behind opposite benches facing each other; one partner holds the beanbag.

DESCRIPTION OF ACTIVITY:

1. On the signal "Go!" step up and down on your bench at the same time and try to pass a beanbag back and forth. Pass beanbag only when standing on the bench. Check for good spacing on the bench.
2. If one partner drops the beanbag, you and your partner must jog once around the play area; then return to the bench to continue bench-stepping and passing.
3. After one minute, change partners and repeat the activity.

VARIATIONS:

a. Substitute chairs for benches. Adjacent chairs should be about 1 meter (3 feet) from each other.
b. Have each partner throw a beanbag at the same time.

IA–44 GERM BUG

FOCUS: Chasing and dodging

EQUIPMENT: Three beanbags (sponge or tennis balls); four cone markers

ORGANIZATION:

- Define the boundaries of the play area. Choose three players to be the Germ Bugs. Each Germ Bug holds a beanbag in his or her hand and stands in the middle of the play area to start the game. The rest of the players are ordinary "Bugs," who scatter throughout the play area.

DESCRIPTION OF ACTIVITY:

1. On the signal "Go!" Germ Bugs, chase the other "Bugs" anywhere in the play area and try to touch them with the beanbag.

2. Bugs, if you are touched by the Germ Bug you become "Dead Bugs" and must get into the "dead bug position" by lying on your back with hands and feet in the air and wiggling all over!

3. Another Bug may come along and free a "dead bug" by forming a bridge over this player and holding the position for three slow counts.

4. Bugs, you are safe from being tagged as long as you are in the "Stork Stance" by holding one foot with the opposite hand. You may stay in this position as long as you want or until you lose your balance.

5. The fourth ordinary "Bug" to be touched by a Germ Bug becomes the new Germ Bug and the old Germ Bug becomes an ordinary "Bug." The game continues until a warm-up effect has been reached.

IA–45 THE BLOB!

FOCUS: Running and dodging; cooperation

EQUIPMENT: Four cone markers

ORGANIZATION:

- Use the cones to mark out the boundaries of a large rectangular play area. Choose one player to be the Blob, who stands in the middle of the play area; all other players scatter.

DESCRIPTION OF ACTIVITY:

1. On the signal "Go!" Blob, chase free players, trying to tag them with a light one-hand touch.

2. A tagged player must hook onto the Blob by holding hands. Now Blob, try to tag other free players, using only your free hands to make the tag. If the Blob breaks apart, no tagging can happen until it is joined together again.

3. As more players are tagged, the Blob will grow bigger and bigger! Blob players, do not break your hand hold as you give chase. Only the end players may tag with their free hands. Free players may not break through the Blob by running through the arms.

4. The last player to be tagged becomes the Blob for the next game.

VARIATIONS:

a. When the Blob becomes too big, split it into two smaller Blobs.

b. Begin the game with two or three "baby Blobs."

IA–46 SNOWBALL TAG

FOCUS: Running and dodging; accuracy throwing

EQUIPMENT: One folding mat per pair; six small sponge balls; lively music; tape or record player

ORGANIZATION:

- Have players, working in pairs, get folding mats, carry them to free spaces in the play area, and stand them upright in a zigzag position as snow forts. Choose six players to be IT; then have each IT player get a sponge ball, which will be a snowball. IT players go to the middle of the play area; everyone else scatters.

DESCRIPTION OF ACTIVITY:

1. When the music starts, ITs chase the free players and try to hit them below the waist with your snowball.
2. Free players, use the snow forts and duck behind to avoid being hit. Whenever a snowball hits you below the waist, even when you are behind a snow fort, you are tagged.
3. A tagged player, immediately change role with the IT player who hit you, pick up the snowball, and continue the chase.
4. Remember how many times you were hit. Who can be hit the fewest times before the music stops?

VARIATION:

Players choose a partner and take turns trying to hit each other with snowballs.

IA–47 KINGS AND QUEENS

FOCUS: Running and dodging; fair play

EQUIPMENT: Four sets of different colored banners

ORGANIZATION:

- Choose two boys to be Kings and two girls to be Queens; the other players are the Soldiers, who the Kings and Queens will try to "knight," or tag. Give each King and Queen a set of colored banners to wear around their necks. There should be enough banners for all players. Have Kings and Queens then stand in the middle of the play area. Soldiers scatter.

DESCRIPTION OF ACTIVITY:

1. On signal "Go!" Kings and Queens start chasing the Soldiers. Try to tag them with a light, two-handed touch on the shoulder. Knight each tagged player with a banner, placed around the neck. Knights, help your King or Queen tag other Soldiers.
2. When you are tagged by a Knight, jog on the spot until that Knight's King or Queen runs over and officially knights you by placing a banner around your neck.
3. Continue until all players are knighted. The King or Queen with the most Knights wins the game.

IA-48 THE WEAVE WARM-UP

FOCUS: Fun run; warm-up

EQUIPMENT: Lively music;
tape or record player

ORGANIZATION:

• Have players find a partner and form a circle facing their partner. The players facing CW will travel in that direction; the players facing CCW travel in that direction. At first, have players walk through the weave until learned; then change to running. Encourage players to keep in time with the music as they run.

DESCRIPTION OF ACTIVITY:

1. When the music starts and on the signal "Weave," everyone run forward weaving in and out of the oncoming runners: passing the first player by your right shoulder, the next by your left shoulder, the next by your right, and so on.
2. Slap inside hands or give a "high five" to your partner as you pass each other.
3. When the music stops, turn to face the opposite direction and continue. This time "give five" to each person you meet or take their hand in a right-and-left hand-shake grip.

VARIATIONS:

a. Have players carry or dribble a basketball as they run.
b. Gradually increase the running time.
c. Have the players skip or slide-step, or use previously learned dance steps such as the two-step and schottische.

IA-49 JACKAROO TAG

FOCUS: Aerobic warm-up; running and dodging

EQUIPMENT: Chalkboard; chalk; four cone markers; suitable music; record or tape player

ORGANIZATION:

• Mark out the boundaries of the play area. Divide the class into four equal teams. Select one team to be the "Jackaroos" (Australian ranch hands) and to hold hands. All other players are the "Sheep" and scatter in "the Paddock," in the play area.

DESCRIPTION OF ACTIVITY:

1. When the music starts or on the signal "Go," the Jackaroos, try to round up (tag) as many Sheep as you can in one minute. You may stay linked together and the end players only may tag.
2. A Sheep that has been rounded up (tagged) must go to the "Shearing shed" and jog around the outside boundary of the play area until time is up. Any Sheep "straying" outside the boundaries is considered rounded up and must go to the Shearing sheds to run.
3. When the music stops after one minute, stop the activity and count the number of Sheep rounded up and record the number on the chalkboard.
4. Select a new team to be the Jackaroos and continue until each team has had a turn. The team with the highest score are the best Jackaroos for the day.

IA—50 GERONIMO

FOCUS: Fun run; aerobic warm-up

EQUIPMENT: Four cone markers;
lively music;
tape or record player

ORGANIZATION:

- Place one cone marker at each corner of a rectangular race course (about the size of a basketball court). Form four equal teams. Have each team stand in file formation at a different corner of the race course. The player at the front of each file is the leader.

DESCRIPTION OF ACTIVITY:

1. When the music starts, each team, run forward around the race course. Stay in the same order and do not pass each other. Leader, set a steady pace that can be maintained throughout the run.
2. Last runner, sprint forward on the inside of the course, passing all your teammates. As you join the front of your team, yell "Geronimo!" At this signal, the last player in the file will repeat your action and then shout "Geronimo!"
3. Continue this running pattern until the music stops; then walk slowly around the course, inhaling and exhaling deeply. Original leaders, count the number of "Geronimo" yells your team makes, and compare your score with other teams. Which team will be the best "Geronimo team"?

VARIATION:

Increase the time the music plays to improve fitness levels.

IA—51 PAPER ROUTE

FOCUS: Aerobic fun run

EQUIPMENT: Playground equipment;
stopwatch (optional);
wall map (optional)

ORGANIZATION:

- A Paper Route is a jogging route around the block, playground, or nearby park; anywhere that is interesting and challenging. It is a fun alternative to running laps. Gradually lengthen the route so that the children run continuously for at least ten minutes. When out of the school, insist on street safety; use crosswalks and sidewalks.

DESCRIPTION OF ACTIVITY:

Today we're going to run a Paper Route around the playground. We will start with a steady jogging pace. Stay with the rest of the group and follow my directions.

- Run around the swings. Pull yourself across the jungle gym, down the slide, and weave in and out of the goal posts. Keep together!
- Stop at the grass area and do eight sit-ups, eight push-ups, and sixteen arm circles.
- Skip for twenty paces; slide-step for twenty paces right, slide-step for twenty paces left; hop right foot for ten hops, left foot for ten hops; then run backward for twenty paces.
- Repeat the course, or add other activities.
- Run back to the starting point; then slow to a walk for one minute.
- How hard was your heart working? While still walking, hold your fingers to your wrist and count the number of pulse beats. Your target heart range should be thirty to forty beats in fifteen seconds.
- Now do three different stretches, holding each stretch for ten seconds.

Fitness Activities

The daily Fitness Activity serves as a specific warm-up and, used in conjunction with an introductory activity, builds overall fitness, with emphasis on cardiovascular endurance and muscular strength and endurance.

This section presents an assortment of forty-seven Fitness Activities:

FA–1 ORGANIZATIONAL BREAKS

FOCUS: Class organization; listening

EQUIPMENT: Benches;
mats;
balls

ORGANIZATION:

- A "break" is a short informal activity that, when introduced spontaneously throughout lessons, provides for efficiency in class organization and mobilization and in the collection and dispersal of equipment. Breaks can also be used for relief, a change of tempo, alertness training, extra fitness, challenge, and fun. They need not be related to any other part of the lesson.

- Organizational breaks provide transition between lesson segments and efficient mobilization of the class for the next activity. Use these breaks repeatedly throughout the lesson to increase the activity of the class. Try the examples below, but adapt to your own situation.

DESCRIPTION OF ACTIVITY:

1. Slide-step CW around the play area, doing eight jumping jacks in each corner; then fall into your teams. Go!

2. Find a partner and stand back to back. On signal "Go!" race your partner CCW around the play area, touching with your left heel and right elbow the middle of all four walls (or sidelines); then return to your starting place. The slower partner owes you eight sit-ups.

3. On signal "Go!" run to either end of the play area and quickly do any sort of roll, eight push-ups; then crab-walk to my listening circle.

4. Touch a door, a rope, a mat, a bench, and me with a different body part each time. Then quickly hop to the big circle to hook-leg sit in groups of three. Go!

5. Do twelve bench-steps at four different benches. Then stand arm's length apart on this sideline.

6. Serve your volleyball to a wall, catch it; then find your own home space and volley the ball to yourself. Go!

VARIATION:

Make use of the outdoor school environment and playground apparatus and equipment with Organizational Breaks: "Run around four trees, move over one object, under another, and return to my listening circle. Go!"

FA–2 EQUIPMENT BREAKS

FOCUS: Equipment organization; listening

EQUIPMENT: One ball per player; one jump rope per player; two to four benches, two climbing chairs, one bat, softball, and base per group of four; one folding mat per pair; several long jump ropes; two beach balls

ORGANIZATION:

- Equipment Breaks provide time between parts of the lesson for equipment setup, collection, and dispersal. Safety in handling equipment should be emphasized and taught. The fourth break demonstrates how equipment setup can be a group activity with each group responsible for designated equipment. Try these examples, but adapt to your own situation. Divide your class into four equal teams, with a Leader for each team.

DESCRIPTION OF ACTIVITY:

1. Dribble your basketball with your weak hand once around the play area in a CCW direction. Then drop the ball into the cart and sit in your teams, with Leaders sitting on the black line.

2. Touch the endline; then get a jump rope, take it to your home, and skip thirty times in place. Go!

3. Quickly get into groups of four. Two players get a base each; another player get a softball from the basket and the fourth player get a baseball bat from the cart. Find a free space for your group to practice batting, pitching, and retrieving the ball.

4. Number off 1, 2, 3, 4: All number ones collect the folding mats and hook them together at one end of the play area; number twos collect a ball each, put the ball between your ankles, and jump to this sideline. Place all the balls on the line. Number threes carry four benches and two climbing chairs to the middle area; number fours collect the long ropes, two beach balls, and one short rope and place these at this corner of the play area.

5. Each team leader and co-leader collect a bucket of balls and together place the bucket in your designated corner of the play area. The equipment will be later returned to your corner for leaders to collect and put away.

FA-3 TEMPO CHANGE BREAKS

FOCUS: Class organization; listening

EQUIPMENT: Indoor or outdoor play area;
one rope per player;
Joker's Wild exercise cards;
Fortune Cookie cards

ORGANIZATION:

• Tempo Breaks provide a change of pace. Use them to get players moving quickly again after a period of inactivity, or to provide relief or a "rest break" from a vigorous activity, or to ensure that exercising in all the fitness component areas occurs. Reinforce the names of these breaks so that players will remember them to save time explaining when you use them later. Try the following examples, but adapt to your own situation.

DESCRIPTION OF ACTIVITY:

1. On signal "Cricket Jump," jump with both feet together the length of the play area. How many jumps will it take you?

2. Stand about a giant step from a wall. On signal "Splat," fall and catch yourself against the wall with both hands. Push yourself away. Repeat eight times.

3. On signal "Wall Break," quickly run and lean your back against a wall. Slide down the wall until you are in a sitting position. Keep your arms folded, look relaxed, and smile!

4. On signal "Twirl," pivot around and around on the spot five times; then try to balance on one foot for five seconds.

5. On signal "Hang," hang on a piece of climbing apparatus for as long as you can.

6. On signal "Touch 3!" touch the middle of three boundary lines; then quickly return to long-sit in the middle area.

7. On signal "Fortune Cookie" (or "Joker's Wild") pick a card, read the task aloud, and perform it with everyone else. (Refer to IA-6 and IA-27.)

VARIATION:

Use any of the Organizational Signals from IA-1 as "tempo change breaks."

FA—4 PARTNER BREAKS

FOCUS: Class organization; partner work; listening

EQUIPMENT: Four benches; one jump rope per pair; one basketball per pair; one utility ball per pair

ORGANIZATION:

- Use Partner Breaks spontaneously to generate an atmosphere of challenge and fun and to enhance listening skills. Use any previously taught partner activity that can be quickly introduced by name, as a break. Spontaneity will come more easily if you teach players the names of these breaks and repeat them often.

DESCRIPTION OF ACTIVITY:

1. On signal **"Knee Box!"** face your partner and try to touch your partner's knees. Dodge quickly to avoid contact, but stay in a confined area.

2. On signal **"Double Jumps!"** skip rope with a partner. Which pair can skip the longest?

3. On signal **"Body Builders!"** stand facing your partner. Pretend that you are a muscle-bound weight lifter posing in a contest. Copy what your partner does; then change roles.

4. On signal **"Four Benches!"** race your partner to go on and off four benches and return to your starting place. The slower partner owes you eight reps of your choice.

5. On signal **"Toe Wrestle!"** face your partner and, without using your hands, try to step on your partner's toes.

6. On signal **"Hot Passes!"** quickly pass a basketball back and forth to each other twenty-five times.

7. On signal **"Poison Ball!"** partner with the ball, chase the other partner, trying to touch him or her with the ball. If you tag your partner, then he or she becomes the new chaser. Remember to watch where you are going.

8. Add your own idea!

VARIATION:

Refer to Cooperative Stunt Breaks in FA-6 and the Combatives in Section 5 for partner activities that can be used as breaks.

FOCUS: Class organization; listening   **EQUIPMENT:** None

ORGANIZATION:

- Stunts provide excellent breaks and a change of pace. Call out a Stunt Break immediately before changing to the next activity. Teach players the names of these stunts and repeat them often in your future lessons.

DESCRIPTION OF ACTIVITY:

1. *Roll the Log:* In the front-support position, feet apart, roll over and over with a high swing of your arms, moving sideways.

2. *Thread the Needle:* In back-lying position, clasp hands in front and bring one leg through your hands followed by the other. Then reverse the action.

3. *Floor Vault:* From the front-support position, jump your feet forward by lifting the knees and bringing your legs between the arms to finish in a long-sit position.

4. *Heel Click:* Jump up to slap your feet in front of you; then jump to slap your feet behind you. Repeat one more time.

5. *V-Sit Hold:* From hook-sit position, reach forward to grab your toes. Extend your legs upward and try to balance in this position for ten seconds.

6. *Caterpillar:* From front-support position, keep your hands still while you "walk" your feet up to your hands; then keep your feet in place while you walk your hands away from your feet until in the starting position. Move from one sideline to the opposite line in this way.

7. *Rock-Backs:* Sit with legs crossed. Roll backward to touch your feet to the floor behind your head. Hold for five seconds.

8. *Hoppo Boppo:* Hop across the play area by holding your right foot with your left hand and your right hand behind your back, holding your left elbow. Reverse feet and hand positions and hop back.

9. *Mule Kicks:* Take your weight on your hands and gently kick one leg, followed by the other, upward. Repeat four times.

10. Add your own idea!

VARIATION:

Substitute any Animal Walk that you have taught.

FA—6 COOPERATIVE STUNT BREAKS_____

FOCUS: Class organization; partner work; listening

EQUIPMENT: None

ORGANIZATION:

• In these Stunt Breaks partners should be about the same size and well spaced apart from other pairs. Emphasize the importance of safety when doing these stunts. The key to the success of these Breaks is in the spontaneity and unpredictability of their use.

DESCRIPTION OF ACTIVITY:

Backward Get-Up

Log Lift

Stubborn Donkey

Stubborn Driver

Foot Walk

Centipede Walk

Crocodile

Churn the Butter

Piggyback Ride

Pair Bicycling

Fireman's Carry

Bear Hug

BACKWARD GET-UP

LOG LIFT

STUBBORN DONKEY

FOOT WALK

CHURN THE BUTTER

STUBBORN DRIVER

CENTIPEDE WALK

PIGGY BACK RIDE

CROCODILE

PAIR BICYCLING

FIREMAN'S CARRY

BEAR HUG

VARIATION:

Substitute any Gymnastic stunt that players could do in pairs.

FA–7 BONE SIGNALS

FOCUS: Major bones of the body; basic functions

EQUIPMENT: Chart of the Skeletal System; Bone of the Week Chart

ORGANIZATION:

• Teach the names of the major bones of the body, their locations, and their basic functions. Use a large wall chart of the Skeletal System and create a "Bone of the Week" chart, which will focus on one particular bone for that week. Introduce these major bones in your health class. Have players locate the bones on a diagram of the skeleton and discuss their functions. To begin, have players scatter and stand in their own free space.

DESCRIPTION OF ACTIVITY:

1. How many bones do you have in your body? **Your skeleton is composed of 206 bones!** What are the three basic functions of bones? **Bones support and protect the other body systems; store minerals such as calcium and phosphorus; and produce cells for the circulatory system.** Muscles are attached to bones by inelastic cords of tough connective tissue called **tendons**. **Ligaments** are bands of tissue connecting bones or holding organs in place. A tough elastic tissue forming parts of the skeleton (such as nose and ears) is called **cartilage**.

2. **Busy Bones:** Let's learn the names of the major bones. Find a partner and stand beside him or her. I will call out the name of a major bone. Try to touch this bone to your partner's. On signal "Busy Bones," find a new partner and be ready to touch the new bone to your partner's as I call out its name.

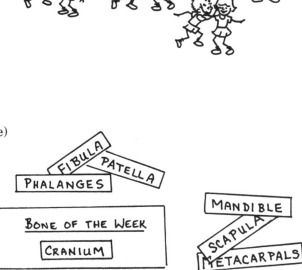

   — Cranium—bones of the head
   — Mandible—jaw bone (the strongest bone)
   — Clavicle—collar bone
   — Scapula—shoulder blade
   — Sternum—breast bone
   — Humerus—upper arm bone
   — Ulna and Radius—lower arm bones
   — Carpal bones—wrist bones
   — Metacarpal bones—bones of the hand
   — Phalanges—finger bones
   — Femur—upper leg bone (the longest bone)
   — Patella—knee cap
   — Fibula—outer bone of lower leg
   — Tibia—inner bone of lower leg
   — Tarsal bones—ankle bones
   — Metatarsal bones—foot bones
   — Phalanges—toe bones
   — Ribs—bones of the chest
   — Vertebrae—bones of the spine

VARIATION:

Bone Charade: Divide the class into groups of three to four players. Write the names of the bones above on pieces of paper, place into a container, and have the Leader of each group draw for a bone. Have each group, in turn, pantomime their bone's actions while the other groups try to guess what the bone is in a twenty-second time limit.

FA-8 MUSCLE SIGNALS _____

FOCUS: Major muscles of the body; basic functions

EQUIPMENT: Chart of the Muscles of the Body; Muscles of the Week Chart; muscle signs

ORGANIZATION:

• In this activity teach twelve major muscles of the body and their location. A large chart depicting the major muscles could be used. Create a "Muscle of the Week" chart and each week highlight one of the muscles. Introduce these major muscles in your health class, locate each muscle on a diagram, and discuss its function. Encourage players to learn to say each muscle's name properly and spell it correctly. To begin, have players stand tall in their own home space.

DESCRIPTION OF ACTIVITY:

1. How many muscles do you have in your body? **600!** What is the strongest muscle? **Your heart is the strongest! It is about the size of your fist and is located in the center of your chest.**

2. Let's learn the names of eleven more major muscles. On signal "Scramble Eggs," run helter-skelter in any direction. On signal (name of the muscle), stop and touch the muscle I name:

   — Biceps—top muscles of the upper arm

   — Triceps—underneath muscles of upper arm

   — Rectus Abdominus—stomach muscles

   — Quadriceps—front muscles of the thigh

   — Hamstrings—back thigh muscles

   — Gastrocnemius—calf muscles

   — Gluteus Maximus—buttock muscles

   — Deltoids—shoulder muscles

   — Trapezius—shoulder blade muscles

   — Pectorals—chest muscles

   — Obliques—diagonal stomach muscles

3. ***Busy Muscles:*** When I call out the name of a major muscle and an object in the play area, quickly run to the object and touch that muscle to it. For example, "Deltoids" to "Bench"!; "Hamstrings" to "Red line"!

VARIATION:

Muscle Charade: Divide the class into ten groups and secretly assign each group a muscle; for example: Group 1, the heart muscle; Group 2, the Biceps; Group 3, the Triceps; Group 4, the Quadriceps, and so on. Have each group pantomime their muscle actions. Have the other groups guess what the muscle is.

FA–9 MEASURING THE HEART RATE

FOCUS: Terminology; monitoring heart rate techniques

EQUIPMENT: One stopwatch or several digital wrist watches

ORGANIZATION:

• Have players sit quietly. Discuss how one's Aerobic Fitness is related to how efficiently the heart works. We can measure this efficiency by recording our Resting Heart Rate (RHR)—the rate at which your heart is beating or pulsing at rest. The pulse is the blood rushing through the arteries after each heartbeat. Explain and demonstrate how to take heart rates. Have players monitor their own heart rates; then take different partners' heart rates. Also have players take their RHR in the classroom as a daily activity; record RHR at home for one week; graph and discuss the results.

DESCRIPTION OF ACTIVITY:

1. **At the Wrist:** Place three middle fingers of one hand on the palm side of the wrist, close to the thumb, to find your Radial Artery. Press gently and listen carefully. On signal "Go!" count the number of beats you hear in fifteen seconds until I say "Stop!" Multiply by four to determine your Resting Heart Rate (RHR) in beats per minute (bpm). The lower this pulse rate is, the better!

2. **At the Neck:** Place three middle fingers on the Carotid Artery located on either side of the neck, just below the chin. Never use your thumb because it has a pulse of its own. Press gently. Count for fifteen seconds; multiply by four to get your RHR.

3. **Maximum Heart Rate (MHR):** Refers to maximum number of times the heart can beat in one minute. Your MHR is estimated to be 220 minus your age in years.

4. **Target Heart Rate (THR) Range:** This is the number of times your heart needs to beat in order for your cardiorespiratory system to become stronger. Your THR is lower than your MHR; therefore, you can exercise longer without stopping. THR range is 60% to 85% of your MHR: (MHR − age) × .6 to (MHR − age) × .85 bpm.

5. Calculate your THR range for your age. By dividing the one-minute THR range you will get the ten-second THR range, which is ideal.

6. Jog around the play area for three minutes. On signal "Stop!" quickly find your pulse and take a ten-second reading. Are you in your THR range? After one minute take another ten-second reading. Is your heart rate returning to your Resting Heart Rate?

$$MHR = 220 - AGE$$

$$THR = (MHR - AGE) \times .6 \text{ b.p.m.}$$
$$to$$
$$(MHR - AGE) \times .85 \text{ b.p.m.}$$

FA–10 TWELVE-MINUTE WORKOUT 1

FOCUS: Leg, arm and shoulder, abdominal strength; hip, back, and groin area mobility

EQUIPMENT: Music with a strong 4/4 beat; tape or record player; one jump rope per player; one mat per player

ORGANIZATION:

• This workout warms, strengthens, and stretches the major muscle groups. To begin, have players get a jump rope, check it for proper length, and find a free space.

DESCRIPTION OF ACTIVITY:

1. *Mat Warm-Up:* On signal "Go!" slide in and out of the mats without touching anyone or any mat. On signal "Jump Ten!" jump over ten different mats; then return to your own and hook-sit. On signal "Touch Ten!" touch ten different mats with a different body part each time; then return to your own to hold a bridge over your mat. On signal "Wall Ten!" touch your mat, then a wall, another mat, then a different wall. Continue for ten touches. End up on your mat in the all-fours position.

2. *Rope Warmer:* Jump rope in place for one minute; then skip around the perimeter of the play area for another minute; return to your starting place and jump rope for one more minute.

3. *Walking Push-Ups:* Begin in front-support position. "Walk" your hands for four counts to the right; four counts back; four counts to the left; four counts back; four counts in toward your feet; four counts back to starting position. Repeat this sequence three times.

4. *Heel-Toe Taps:* In hook-sit position and breathing normally, extend both legs wide apart to touch heels to mat; then draw legs back to touch toes to mat near buttocks. Repeat twenty times.

5. *Sunflower Sit-Ups:* Begin in back-lying position with your arms and legs spread wide apart. Gently sit up to hug your knees for three seconds; then return to starting position. Repeat sixteen times.

6. *Hip Wipers:* Lie on your right side with your head resting on your right hand and the lower arm flat on the floor in front of you for support. Do not lean too far forward or backward, but keep directly on your sides. Keeping your right leg bent, raise your left leg as high as possible; then lower it to touch the floor in front of you. Repeat this action five times. Roll over onto your left side and raise and lower your right leg five times.

7. *Creepers:* Lie on your right side, resting on your right arm, and supporting yourself in front with the left hand. Bending your left leg, touch your left heel to your right thigh. Then extend the left leg straight out in front, making a right angle with your body. Repeat eight times. Roll over onto your left side and do eight more creepers.

8. *Splitz Stretch:* From the long-sit position, spread your legs as wide apart as you can. Gently lean forward from the hips, keeping your back straight, and reach with your arms through the middle. Hold this stretch for ten seconds. Relax; then repeat two more times. Make sure that your back is flat and the head is up. Do not bob or bounce while doing this stretch. Let your legs be slightly bent.

9. *Back Flattener:* In hook-lying position, tighten tummy and seat muscles, and press your back to the mat. Place your hands in between the mat and the small of your back to check if the back is flat. Hold for ten seconds. Repeat three times.

FOCUS: Leg, arm and shoulder, abdominal strength; back and hamstring flexibility

EQUIPMENT: Music with a strong 4/4 beat; tape or record player; one mat per player; four benches

ORGANIZATION:

• This workout warms and strengthens the major muscle groups. The hamstring muscles or muscles of the back of the upper leg (thigh) and the muscles of the lower back are stretched. To begin, divide the class into groups of four. Have each group stand in file formation with a leader at the front, and scatter.

DESCRIPTION OF ACTIVITY:

1. *Follow the Leader:* Follow your leader, who has to "slide-step," "leap," "turn," and "roll" in that order. The next player in the file then takes over as leader, while the former leader goes to the end of the file. Each player, in turn, repeats the sequence twice.

2. *Bench-Step Warm-Up:* Each group go to a bench. Step up and down a bench twelve times in time with the beat of the music. Then jog once around the play area, stopping at the next bench to do another twelve Bench-Steps. Continue until all benches have been visited.

3. *Knee Push-Up Progression:* Get a mat and kneel on all fours with hands directly below your shoulders. Now walk hands forward, keeping your back flat and hips low. Lift feet off the mat and cross your feet at the ankles. Slowly lower chest to mat; then push up to starting position. Repeat twelve times.

4. *Curl-Up Twists:* Begin in hook-lying position, knees slightly bent, heels on mat, and arms overhead. Slowly curl up into a sitting position, sweeping your arms forward and upward. Return to starting position by twisting your body to one side as you slowly curl down and sweeping your arms outward to that side, then back overhead. Repeat curl-up twist on the other side. Do twelve repetitions this way. Remember, do not hold your breath; breathe normally.

5. *Hip Kicks:* Begin in the hook-sit position. Raise your seat off the floor so that your trunk is parallel to the floor. Kick the right leg out, then the left leg out. Alternate kicking legs twelve times.

6. *Fire Hydrants:* Begin in the all-fours position. Bend your right leg and lift it off the floor so that it is at right angles to your body; then extend your lower right foot forward on the right side. Bend your right leg again and return it to starting position. Repeat eight times with the right leg; then eight times with the left leg.

7. *Alternate Leg Stretch:* Long-sit on your mat with your legs wide apart, knees slightly bent. Reach forward to touch your right hand toward your left toes. If unable to reach for toes, try to touch your ankles. Hold for ten seconds; then return to starting position. Reach forward to touch your left hand toward your right toes. Hold for ten seconds. Repeat stretch to each leg two more times.

8. *Hug Stretch:* Begin in hook-lying position. Bend your knees, cross ankles, and grasp feet. Hold for ten seconds. Cross ankles the opposite way and hold another ten seconds. Remember to breathe normally during the stretch.

VARIATION:

Vary the sequence of movements in the Follow the Leader warm-up, such as run–half jump-turn–balance–shrink.

FOCUS: Leg, arm and shoulder, hip and buttock area strength; shoulder and upper back flexibility

EQUIPMENT: Music in 4/4 time; tape or record player; one mat per player

ORGANIZATION:

• This workout warms and strengthens the major muscle groups. The muscles of the shoulders and upper back are gently stretched. Have players stand in a line, side by side, spaced arm's length apart, at one end of the play area.

DESCRIPTION OF ACTIVITY:

1. **Giant Strides:** How many "giant strides" will it take you to cross the play area to the opposite end? How many strides will it take you to come back? Fewer? or more? Count the number of "hops" you will take to move to the other end of the play area. Can you return to your starting line in fewer hops? Repeat, using "jumps"; then "side-steps."

2. **Grinder Warm-Up:** On signal "Go!" run to the opposite sideline, place one palm on the floor, and quickly walk in a complete circle around your hand; then run back to the starting line. Walk around your other hand. Do eight crossings in this way.

3. **Twisters:** Stand tall with elbows high, knees slightly bent, and feet still. Twist upper body from side to side twelve times.

4. **Folded Arms Curl-Ups:** Begin in hook-lying position, hands folded across your chest. Tuck your chin to chest and slowly curl up until your elbows touch your knees; then slowly curl down to starting position. Do sixteen of these curl-ups in this way. Inhale as you curl down; exhale as you curl back up.

5. **Full Push-Ups:** Begin in the front-support position, hands directly below shoulders and fingers pointing forward. Keep your body straight and bend your arms as you lower your chest to the mat; then return to starting position. Repeat ten times.

6. **Seat Lifts:** Get a mat and begin in the hook-lying position, hands at your sides. Raise and lower your hips off the mat twelve times. Keep your upper back in contact with the mat throughout the exercise. Try to squeeze the buttocks together as you raise your hips off the mat.

7. **Sweepers:** Begin in the all-fours position on your mat. Extend your right leg to the side. Gently sweep it as far forward as you can; then swing it as far back and to the opposite side as you can. Sweep forward and back four times; then repeat with the left leg. Now do four more Sweepers with each leg.

8. **Hip Rollers:** Begin in the hook-sit position, back straight and hands at your sides for balance. Keeping your knees together, roll both legs to one side, return to the center, and roll to the other side. Repeat this action ten times.

9. **Shoulder Stretch:** Sit tall on your mat. Bring your right arm across your chest to the opposite shoulder. Gently press your left hand against your right elbow for ten seconds. Reverse arms and repeat.

10. **Wing Stretches:** Stand tall, holding elbows at shoulder level and fingers just touching in front of your chest. Gently press your arms and your shoulders back, squeezing your shoulder blades together; then straighten your arms and press back again. Repeat ten times.

FOCUS: Leg, arm and shoulder, hip, abdominal, buttock area strength; lateral trunk, triceps muscle flexibility

EQUIPMENT: Music with a steady beat; tape or record player; several benches

ORGANIZATION:

• This workout warms and strengthens the major muscle groups. The triceps muscles located underneath of the upper arm are gently strengthened and then stretched. Have players scatter and stand in their home space.

DESCRIPTION OF ACTIVITY:

1. *Steeplechase Warm-Up:* (Position four benches around the play area as shown. Players stand just behind a starting bench so that there are equal numbers at each bench.) On music signal, run around the Steeplechase course and JUMP over each bench in turn until you reach your starting bench. Now VAULT over each bench by placing your hands on the sides of the bench and swinging your legs over to the other side. The third time through the course, CRAWL under each bench; the fourth time, jump ON and OFF each bench.

2. *Karate Kid Warm-Up:* Moving around on the spot, swing your arms out in different directions. Then let your feet take over as you gently kick them out in different directions. Now try to alternate arm and leg movements.

3. *Scissor Kicks:* Stand tall in your home space. Kick one leg upward, then the other. Repeat eight times, alternating the first kicking leg.

4. *Hugging Sit-Ups:* Begin in back-lying position with your arms and legs by your sides. Gently sit up and draw your knees in toward your chest to hug knees for three seconds; then return to starting position. Repeat twelve times. Remember to inhale as you curl down; exhale as you curl up.

5. *Inverted Push-Ups:* In back-support position, gently bend and straighten arms ten times.

6. *Knee Pokes:* Begin in the all-fours position. Keeping the right leg bent, raise sideways parallel to the floor. Now gently straighten and extend this leg backward; then bend knee and gently poke it forward. Do this eight times; then repeat with the left leg. Look downward to avoid any lower back strain.

7. *Bench Push-Ups:* (Players should perform push-ups on either side of bench to ensure that the bench does not move.) Place your hands flat on your starting bench and extend your legs behind you. Keeping your body straight, bend your arms to touch your nose to the bench, then straighten. Repeat ten times.

8. *Triceps Stretch:* Sit tall and bring your right arm across your chest toward the opposite shoulder. Gently press with your left hand against your right elbow for ten seconds. Reverse arms and repeat for another ten-second stretch. Do one more Triceps Stretch for each arm.

9. *Windshield Wipers:* Begin in back-lying position with your arms extended out to the sides, at shoulder level, and your legs together. Raise your right leg upward and across your body to touch the left hand; then return it to center overhead and lower to starting position. Repeat with the left leg. Continue for ten reps.

FOCUS: Leg, arm, abdominal, hip, buttocks strength; forward trunk mobility

EQUIPMENT: Lively music in 4/4 time; tape or record player; one mat per player; one rope per player

ORGANIZATION:

• This workout warms, strengthens, and stretches the major muscle groups. To begin, have players space themselves evenly around a large oval-shaped track, facing CCW.

DESCRIPTION OF ACTIVITY:

1. *Power-Walking:* Walking in a CCW direction, squeeze and open your hands; circle your arms gently forward, then backward; clap your hands in front and behind; snap your fingers above your head; shrug your shoulders; march with high knee lifts and arm swings. Walk as quickly as you can as you do the arm movements. Remember to WALK, not run! On signal "CW," go in the opposite direction.

2. *Roll-Overs:* Begin in a front-support position. Roll to your right, taking your weight on your hands and feet only; then roll to your left.

3. *Heel-Toe Taps:* In hook-sit position, extend legs out to the sides to touch heels to the floor; then draw legs in to touch toes near buttocks.

4. *Cross-Knee Curl-Up:* Begin in hook-lying position on your mat. Rest the heel of your right foot on the knee of the left leg and interlock your fingers behind your head. Curl up to touch your left elbow to your right knee; then curl down to starting position. Repeat twelve times. Rest the heel of the left foot on the right knee and do twelve more curl-ups in this way.

5. *Push-Up Salute:* Begin in the front-support position on your mat. Extend the right arm to the right side. Return to starting position. Extend the left arm to the left side. Return. Repeat this sequence eight times. (Count one for each arm extension.)

6. *Side Scissors:* Lie on your right side and support your upper body on your lower right arm. Place your left hand in front for balance. Raise the left leg as high and straight as you can. Then raise the right leg off the mat to meet the left leg. Return the right leg to the mat. Raise and lower your right leg eight times. Roll over and repeat this exercise eight more times on the left side.

7. *Inner Thigh Lift:* Lie on your right side with your weight supported by the lower arm. Extend your right leg and bend your left leg in front on the floor. Hold the left ankle with your left hand. Raise and lower your right leg ten times. Roll over and repeat the "thigh lifts" with your other leg.

8. *Seat Press:* Begin in the all-fours position on your mat. Raise one leg so that it makes a right angle at the knee. Press the bottom of this foot upward eight times. Return your leg to the starting position and repeat the exercise with the opposite foot.

9. *Splitz Stretch:* In long-sit position on your mat, spread your legs as comfortably apart as you can. Lean forward from the hips, and gently reach with both hands toward your right ankle. Hold stretch for ten seconds; then return to starting position. Reach with both hands toward your left ankle and hold for another ten seconds. Repeat stretch sequence once more.

FOCUS: Leg, arm, abdominal, hip strength; leg stretching; partner work

EQUIPMENT: Music with a strong 4/4 beat; tape or record player; one chair per player; one mat per player

ORGANIZATION:

- This workout warms, strengthens, and stretches the major muscle areas while using a chair. Players perform chair exercises first by themselves, then later with a partner. To begin have players get a chair and a mat, then find a free space.

DESCRIPTION OF ACTIVITY:

1. ***Chairobics:*** Stand behind your chair and clasp the top of the chair with both hands. Keeping in time to the music, do "Heel Kicks" by alternately kicking the heel of each foot toward the buttocks. Now lean on your chair as you do "Pendulum Kicks" by alternately kicking your leg out sideways.

2. ***Chair Bicycle Pumps:*** Sit on the front edge of your chair with your hands on the side edge of the seat for support and lean back against the back of the chair. Now lift your legs and pump them in a bicycle pattern. Repeat twenty-four times.

3. ***Side Leg Swings:*** Stand with your right side closer to the back of the chair and place your right hand on the backrest for support. Keeping your body erect, swing your left leg out and upward in front of you; then return to starting position and swing it sideways and upward, and return to starting position. Keep your swing in one continuous motion. Repeat swing sequence eight times with each leg.

4. ***Chair Push-Ups:*** Find a partner and place your chairs back to back. Now facing the front of your chair, grip the side edges of the seat with your hands and extend your legs behind you, taking your weight on the toes. Gently raise and lower yourself toward the chair's seat ten times. Try to keep your body straight!

5. ***Chair Step-Ups:*** Keeping the same rhythm to the music and to each other, partners step up and down on the seat of your chairs. On the signal "Switch!" partners, run to each other's chairs and begin the "Chair Step-Ups" again. (Repeat this sequence for two minutes.)

6. ***Chair to Mat Push-Ups:*** Begin in the front-support position with your hands flat on the mat and your feet resting on the seat of your chair. Slowly lower and raise yourself toward the mat eight to ten times. Remember to keep your body straight and your back flat.

7. ***Chair Curl-Ups:*** Begin in the back-lying position with your lower legs resting on the seat of your chair and your hands interlocked behind your head. Slowly curl up toward your knees and curl down to the mat until your head touches. Repeat twenty-four times. Don't forget to exhale as you curl up and inhale as you curl down.

8. ***Hamstring Stretch:*** Stand facing the back of your chair and place your right foot on the top of the backrest. Gently lean forward from the hips and reach toward your right ankle with both hands. Hold stretch for ten seconds. Repeat with opposite leg. Slightly bend the raised leg if you cannot reach your ankles.

9. ***Thigh Stretch:*** Begin in the same position as in "Side Leg Swings"; then grasp your right foot with your left hand. Gently press the right heel toward your buttocks and hold for ten seconds. Repeat stretch with other thigh. Repeat this entire stretch once more.

FOCUS: Leg, arm and shoulder, and abdominal strength; lateral and forward trunk mobility

EQUIPMENT: One beanbag per pair; one mat per player; music with a strong 4/4 beat; tape or record player

ORGANIZATION:

- This workout involves working in pairs to warm, strengthen, and stretch the major muscle groups. Have players find a partner about the same size. One partner gets a beanbag; then each pair finds a free space and partners stand facing each other.

DESCRIPTION OF ACTIVITY:

1. **Slide & Toss:** Slide-step in a CW direction, tossing the beanbag back and forth to each other. If the beanbag drops to the floor, pick it up and sprint once around the play area with your partner; then continue to slide and toss. Can you keep going until the music stops?

2. **Partner Leg Push-Ups:** Partner A, lie on your back and lift your legs off the floor. Partner B, face your partner and place your hands against the soles of A's feet. Partner A, bend and straighten your legs while B applies pressure. After ten leg push-ups, change roles and repeat.

3. **Backward Get-Up:** Long-sit back to back with elbows linked. Gently push against each other so that you rise to standing position. Sit down and repeat three times.

4. **Wheelbarrow Walk:** Partner A, get into the all-fours position on one sideline. Partner B, lift Partner A's legs off the floor and hold on to A's upper legs. Partner A, walk forward in this way to the opposite sideline. Reverse positions so that Partner B wheelbarrow walks. Repeat once more for each partner.

5. **Partner Curls:** Each partner collect a mat and place your mat on the floor to face your partner's. Begin in the hook-sit position on your mat, facing your partner, arms folded across your chest. Interlock legs by hooking your feet around your partner's. On signal "Curls!" gently curl up and down together for twenty-four Partner Curls.

6. **Side Winders:** Partners, face in the same direction and stand side by side with inside hands joined and inside feet touching. Now slowly lean away from each other. Hold position for ten seconds. Partners, now turn to face the opposite direction and repeat. With one partner facing in one direction and the other facing in the opposite direction, repeat stretch.

7. **Splits Stretch:** Sit facing your partner, legs wide apart and soles of feet touching. Reach forward from the hips to clasp wrists. You may need to bend your knees slightly. Hold stretch for fifteen seconds. Now stretch for ten seconds away from each other in the back-support position, eyes looking back as far as possible. Repeat each stretch once more.

FOCUS: Agility; leg, arm and shoulder, and abdominal strength; lateral trunk mobility; hamstring-seat stretch

EQUIPMENT: Music with a strong 4/4 beat; tape or record player; twelve cone markers; one mat per player

ORGANIZATION:

• Use cone markers to mark off six sets of lines that are parallel to each other and equally spaced apart. Have players find a partner about the same size and stand one behind the other at one end of the play area.

DESCRIPTION OF ACTIVITY:

1. **Partner Interview:** Jog in a CCW direction around the perimeter of the play area and carry on a conversation. Try to learn as much about your partner as you can. On the signal "Switch," find a new partner and continue the interview.

2. **Shuttle Line Warm-Up:** On signal "Run!" each partner, in turn, run forward to touch two hands to each of the five lines in front of you. Return, by running backward, to touch the starting line before running forward to the next line. Repeat this line shuttle twice.

3. **Bicycle Pumper:** Long-sit facing your partner with the soles of your feet touching. Together lift your legs off the floor and cooperate to pump one leg; then the other as if pedaling a bicycle. Continue until I signal to stop.

4. **Stubborn Donkey:** Partners begin in the same position as for the "Wheelbarrow Walk." (See FA-16.) The standing partner, try to move your partner forward while he or she resists.
   — **Stubborn Driver:** The standing partner, refuse to budge while the other partner tries to walk hands forward.

5. **Spinning Tops:** Stand facing your partner with feet touching. Grasp partner's wrists with both hands and lean back until arms are straight. Circle together, gradually increasing speed by quickening your pivot steps, until you are spinning. Spin CW; then, as soon as you feel dizzy, reverse directions.

6. **Knee Bends:** Stand side by side, placing your inside hands on your partner's shoulder for balance. Each hold the outside foot with your outside hand. Slowly bend and straighten the standing leg eight times. Reverse the leg hold and repeat.

7. **Partner Lateral Stretch:** Partners stand back to back, raise your arms sideways, and clasp your hands together, and spread your legs wide apart. Now both lean to one side, hold for ten seconds; then return to the starting position. Lean to the opposite side and hold for ten seconds. Repeat this sequence twice more.

8. **Partner Seat Stretch:** Begin with one partner in back-lying position on the mat. The other partner, kneel beside your partner and place one hand on his or her knee and the other hand on his or her foot. Gently push the bent leg toward the shoulder. Lying partner, tell your partner when to stop pushing. Repeat with the opposite leg. Reverse roles and repeat stretch.

FA–18 DESIGN A WORKOUT _____

FOCUS: Fitness knowledge; group work;
creating a balanced fitness routine

EQUIPMENT: Paper and pencil per group;
music with a strong 4/4 beat;
tape or record player

ORGANIZATION:

- Discuss the three major health-related fitness components: **Cardiovascular endurance, Muscular strength and endurance, and Flexibility.** Have players give examples or demonstrate an exercise from each of these components.

- Children working in groups of four or five will use these components to design a ten-minute workout. As they put their workouts together, circulate to each group, assisting as necessary. Praise and encourage the children's efforts. Stress the quality of movement and correct exercise technique. Encourage groups to bring in their own music selections to use with their workout. Have children form their groups; one member collects paper and a pencil. Disperse each group to a different area of the play area. Check for good spacing.

DESCRIPTION OF ACTIVITY:

1. Discuss with your group members the fitness exercises we have done in class. Then plan your fitness workout using the following guidelines:

   — a warming-up activity

   — an aerobic activity

   — an upper body strength exercise

   — an abdominal strength exercise

   — a lower body strength exercise

   — a cooling-down stretch activity

   WARM-UP

   AEROBICS

   UPPER BODY STRENGTH

   ABDOMINAL STRENGTH

   LOWER BODY STRENGTH

   COOL-DOWN

   MUSIC ♫

2. Record your fitness workout on paper. Decide how many times to repeat each exercise, using counts of four, eight or sixteen. Vary the body positions to perform the exercises you have selected: standing; back-lying; hook-sitting; front-support; all-fours; and so on.

3. Decide on the music you will use for your workout. Practice your workout together in time to the music's beat. Perform each exercise using correct technique.

4. On successive days, each group will lead the class through its workout.

FOCUS: Large muscle mobilization

EQUIPMENT: Music with a strong 4/4 beat; tape or record player

ORGANIZATION:

- This workout warms the large muscle groups: Head; Forward Trunk; Arms and Shoulders; Back; Lateral Trunk and Legs (H-F-A-B-L-L or HEALTH AND FITNESS ALLOWS BETTER AND LONGER LIFE!). The warm-up phase should last for about four to five minutes to prepare the body for the vigorous aerobic phase to follow, to prevent injury, stress, and strain to the body, and to increase the children's ability to perform movement skills. Each lesson should begin with a proper warm-up! Have players scatter around the play area so that they can see you clearly. They should stand tall with feet comfortably spread apart, tummy muscles tight, pelvis tucked under, back straight, head up, and shoulders relaxed. Knees should be loose throughout the warm-up and players should gently "pulse" them in time to the music.

DESCRIPTION OF ACTIVITY:

1. **Head Swivels:** Drop your head forward; then slowly turn it to the right and left. Repeat four times. Gently move your head forward and back. Repeat four times. Do Head Swivel sequence once more.
2. **Shoulder Shrugs:** Shrug your shoulders four times. Alternate right and left shoulder shrugs eight times. Then roll both shoulders forward four times and backward four times. Do Shoulder Shrug sequence once more.
3. **Traffic Lights:** Hold arms sideways at right angles with one forearm pointing upward and the other forearm pointing downward. Squeeze shoulder blades together two times; then reverse arm positions and squeeze shoulder blades two more times. Repeat for six more times. Do eight alternating arm positions every one count.
4. **Twisters:** With knees slightly bent and feet still, twist upper body from side to side, pushing the opposite hand out to that side. Pulse twice gently to that side. Repeat twelve times.
5. **X-Stretches:** Stand tall with legs apart and knees slightly bent. Stretch right hand upward to left side, then left hand upward to right side. Now extend right hand downward to left side, then left hand downward to right side. Do not bob or jerk. Repeat sequence eight times.
6. **Hip Circles:** Stand, keeping your upper body and feet still and hands on hips. Circle hips CW for four counts; then CCW for four more counts. Repeat sequence once more.
7. **Leg Sways:** Stand with feet wide apart. With hands on hips, lean to each side, bending the knee on that side. Repeat eight times. Now repeat eight Leg Sways each time: (a) Touch elbow to opposite knee, (b) then touch one hand to opposite ankle, (c) touch both hands together to toes of each foot, and (d) finally, touch both hands to the floor between your legs.
8. **Leg Lunge:** Begin with hands on the floor and one foot between the hands so that the knee of that foot is directly over the ankle. Extend the other leg directly back, taking the weight on the toes. Gently pulse the extended leg's knee to the floor eight times. Reverse leg positions and repeat.
9. **Calf Stretch:** From front-support position, raise the hips and push the heel of one foot to the floor, then the heel of the other foot. Repeat eight times.
10. **Back Handclasp:** Standing with knees bent, clasp hands behind your back and raise as far forward as you can while moving your chest toward the knees. Hold for ten seconds; then slowly roll up to starting position.

FA-20 AEROBIC CIRCLE

FOCUS: Cardiorespiratory endurance; leadership   **EQUIPMENT:** Music with a strong 4/4 beat; tape or record player

ORGANIZATION:

- Have players form a large circle and space themselves at arm's length around it, facing the middle. Discuss the meaning of the word *aerobic* ("with oxygen"). Cardiorespiratory endurance activities are aerobic. Ask children to give you examples of aerobic activities: walking, running, rope jumping, biking, swimming, skating, cross-country skiing. Ask each player to think of an aerobic activity. Explain that, when pointed to, each player will come to the middle to lead the class through the activity for sixteen counts. Each Leader then has eight counts to point to the next leader and return to the circle; everyone else jogs in place. At the end of the warm-up, have players take their pulse rate for fifteen seconds.

DESCRIPTION OF ACTIVITY:

- Jog, clapping hands above head; behind; and in front.
- *Sailor Jumps:* Jump with one leg forward and the other back while swinging arms in time to the music.
- *Jumping Jacks:* Jump legs and arms apart, sideways, then together.
- *Combo Jacks:* Alternate Jumping Jacks and Sailor Jumps.
- *Side Kicks:* Kick legs from side to side and wave with hands.

- *Seat Kicks:* Kick buttocks.
- *Mule Kicks:* Kick straight legs behind.
- *Front Kicks:* Kick legs out in front.
- *Skier Jumps:* Jump from side to side.
- *Bell Jumps:* Jump forward and back.
- *X-Jumps:* Jump to cross and uncross ankles.
- Pantomime rope jumping.
- Use any locomotor movements to "move" circle CW or CCW.
- "Cool" dancing!

FA-21 AEROBIC SNAKE

FOCUS: Cardiorespiratory endurance; copying

ORGANIZATION:

- In this aerobic activity, children move through several different movement patterns. Vary the locomotor movements used as the "snake" moves in different patterns around the play area: walk forward, backward; gallop (either foot leading); side-step facing one direction, then the other; skip forward; hop, alternating feet every four counts. Have children stand in file formation at arm's length from each other. Create various running patterns such as moving up and down the length of the play area; back and forth across the width; from one diagonal corner to another; in concentric circular patterns ("Coil the Snake"). Emphasize staying in original order throughout the activity and moving in time to the music. Have children cool down by walking once around the play area and listening to their heartbeats. Discuss the importance of the heart needing regular activity to stay healthy.

DESCRIPTION OF ACTIVITY:

- Clap in time to the music as we walk forward in our long aerobic snake. Let me hear the snake "hissss . . ."
- Jog and snap your fingers to the beat of the music. Let's pretend this is our snake "rattling."
- Follow me around the play area as we move in different patterns. Can you keep all parts of the snake moving together?

FOCUS: Cardiovascular endurance; rhythm sense

EQUIPMENT: Selected music such as the Beach Boys' "Surfin' Safari"; tape or record player

ORGANIZATION:

• This routine provides a fun aerobic activity while enhancing sense of rhythm. Have children find their own home space and face you. Make sure that everyone can see you. Emphasize that children cannot touch others as they move and that they should try to move in time with the music. Have players take their Working Heart Rates for fifteen seconds immediately after stopping the activity.

DESCRIPTION OF ACTIVITY:

1. Let's pretend that our play area is the beach and we are going to go for a swim! On signal "Beach!" jog anywhere around the play area for sixteen counts. Change directions often.

2. On signal "Front Crawl!" stay on the spot while lifting one arm then the other up, forward, and around to eight slow counts, just as if you were swimming in water.

3. On signal "Back Crawl," lift one arm then the other up, back, and around for four slow counts; then repeat for eight quick counts. Now place your hands on hips, and jump with feet together for two counts to the left side, then two counts to the right side. "Push" your hips out to that side each time.

4. On signal "Beach!" jog in free space again for sixteen counts.

5. On signal "Breast Stroke," stay on the spot while bringing straight arms together forward and then opening them to each side for eight slow counts.

6. Repeat the sequence in part 3. Then on signal "Beach!" jog again in free space for sixteen counts.

7. On signal "Sidestroke!" stay on the spot as you roll hand over hand; then extend one arm upward and at the same time the other arm downward. Repeat this action, alternating arms for eight slow counts.

8. Repeat sequence in part 3; then jog in place for another eight counts while you do your own "Swim" stroke, such as the "Dog Paddle," until the music ends.

VARIATION:

Butterfly: Add this swim stroke to the routine in part 8 above by having children jump forward while at the same time throwing their arms back, around, and forward for eight slow counts.

FA-23 SWEAT SHOP ROUTINE

FOCUS: Cardiovascular endurance; routines

EQUIPMENT: Music with a strong 4/4 beat; tape or record player; chalkboard and chalk or chart paper and marking pen

ORGANIZATION:

- This is an aerobic routine consisting of a set of exercises that repeats itself for a desired number of times. Demonstrate the exercises in the routine, then have the children practice each exercise. Put the teaching "cues" on the chalkboard or chart paper to help the participants remember the sequence. Ensure that all can clearly see you. When the music ends, have players take their heart rates for fifteen seconds, and multiply by four to get the beats per minute. To begin have players form four lines or waves of about six to eight per line, equally spaced apart, and facing you so that all can see you clearly.

DESCRIPTION OF ACTIVITY:

1. *Jog in Place:* Jog on the spot sixteen times, keeping in time to the music by clapping your hands.
2. *Jumping Cross-overs:* Place your hands on your hips and continue to jump feet apart; then jump feet to cross each other. Alternate the front foot each time when crossing feet. Keep in time to the music for eight cross-overs.
3. *Twist Hops:* Extend your arms sideways to shoulder level. Keep your feet together as you twist your trunk, from waist down, from side to side eight times.
4. *Elbow-to-Knee Touches:* Hop on the right foot while you lift the knee of the left leg to touch the right elbow. Now hop on the left foot and touch your right knee to the left elbow. Continue eight times.
5. *Rocker Steps:* Hop twice on your left foot while bringing the right knee up and forward. Then hop twice on your right foot while bringing the left foot back. (This is one Rocker Step.) Repeat eight times.
6. *Side Kicks:* Swing right leg to the right side while hopping twice on the left foot; then swing left leg to the left side while hopping twice on the right foot. Repeat eight times.
7. *Sprinter:* Drop down to front-support position with one leg extended back and the other bent forward. Alternate leg positions for eight times.
8. REPEAT SEQUENCE FROM THE BEGINNING UNTIL THE MUSIC STOPS.

FA-24 STING ROUTINE

EQUIPMENT: Music, "The Sting" theme

DESCRIPTION OF ACTIVITY:

1. Skip forward for four steps; then skip back to place, with high arms swings. Repeat twice.
2. Skip clockwise in a circle for eight steps. Skip in the opposite direction for eight steps.
3. Do eight Cross-Jumps with hands on your hips. Alternate the front foot as your legs cross.
4. Do eight Step-Kicks clockwise in a circle, by stepping onto one foot and then kicking out with the other.
5. Side-Shuffle to the right for four steps; then to the left for four steps. Shuffle by keeping your feet parallel and together as you move and wave with your hands together in front of you.
6. REPEAT SEQUENCE FROM THE BEGINNING UNTIL THE MUSIC STOPS.

FA–25 CONTINUOUS AEROBICS

FOCUS: Cardiovascular endurance

EQUIPMENT: Lively music;
tape or record player;
chalkboard and chalk or chart paper
and marking pen

ORGANIZATION:

• In this aerobic routine, several arm and leg movements are combined to give many different aerobic actions. The combinations are limited only to one's imagination! Let the children also contribute their ideas to the development of even more ARM (Arm Rhythmical Movements). Use the chalkboard or chart paper to list the different actions. To begin, have children find their own space, stand tall, and face you. Ensure that everyone can see you clearly. Before, during, and after the aerobic workout, do pulse rate checks.

DESCRIPTION OF ACTIVITY:

Examples:

1. *Seat Kicks:* Keeping hands on hips, kick feet backward toward buttocks for sixteen counts. Then add arm movements: Keeping arms together, move them up and down for eight counts; out to side and back in for eight counts; extend in front and draw back for eight counts. Repeat Seat Kick sequence to four counts; then to two counts.

2. *Break Step:* In place, do eight Step Kicks by hopping on one foot while kicking the other foot forward and swinging opposite arm high.

3. *Twist Hops:* Extending arms sideways, twist and hop eight times in place, then do four Twist Hops while moving to the right; four Twist Hops in place; and four Twist Hops back to starting place. Repeat moving to the left.

4. *Break Step:* Repeat eight Step Kicks.

5. *Front Extended Kicks:* Lean backward as you kick your legs forward eight times; now do eight Back Extended Kicks by leaning forward and kicking legs backward and pulling with hands in and out; and then do eight Side Kicks by kicking each leg in turn to its side while holding arms out to sides at shoulder level. Repeat sequence with four Kicks, then with two Kicks.

6. *Break Step:* Repeat, except swing both arms overhead to clap.

7. *Side Straddles:* Jump feet sideways apart, then together. Now do eight Forward Straddles by jumping one foot forward and the other back; then do eight Combo Straddles. Repeat sequence with four Straddles; then two Straddles.

8. *New Break Step—Cross-Over Step:* Similar to Side Straddles except that hands and feet are crossed instead of bringing feet together. Repeat eight times.

FA—26 AEROBIC MIXER

FOCUS: Cardiovascular endurance; cooperation

EQUIPMENT: Music with a strong 4/4 beat; tape or record player

ORGANIZATION:

- Discuss the FITT Guidelines: **F—Frequency** (How often should we exercise?); **I—Intensity** (How hard should we exercise?); **T—Time** (How long should we exercise?); and **T—Type** (What kind of exercises should we do?). FITNESS USA/CANADA says to maintain a strong, healthy heart and lung system, we need to work out at least three times a week, for at least fifteen minutes of nonstop aerobic activity.

- In this Aerobic Mixer, players participate with many different partners. Demonstrate each partner movement and provide time for pairs to practice. To begin, players pair up and start jogging in place together. When the music starts, partners move in a CW direction around the play area, changing partners or movement on a signal. Call the signals quickly and without stopping the activity. Ensure that the music is not too loud that players cannot hear the signal called. Continue in this way until music ends; then have players quickly take their heart rates for fifteen seconds, and then multiply by four to get the beats per minute.

DESCRIPTION OF ACTIVITY:

1. *Two-Handed Swing:* Take partner's hands and skip in a circle four times in each direction. Repeat.

2. *Elbow Swing:* Hook right elbows and circle your partner four times. Change elbows and do another four swings in the opposite direction. Repeat.

3. *Partner Change:* Release hands and jog to a new partner. (Call "Partner Change" signal frequently and have partners bow to each other before moving on to a new partner.)

4. *Partner Shuffle:* Join hands with new partner and side-step together eight times in each direction. Repeat.

5. *Partner Kicks:* Join hands and face your partner. Hop on one foot while kicking the other foot forward four times. Change legs and repeat.

6. *Promenade:* Walk side by side with your right hands joined over the top of your left hands.

7. *Do-Si-Do:* Face your partner, arms folded, and skip forward four steps to pass right shoulders, back to back, left shoulders, and back in place. Repeat.

8. *Churn-the-Butter:* Face and join hands; then turn under your hands to the right four times, then to the left four times.

9. *Partner Movement:* You and your partner create your own way of moving together to the music.

10. *Pulse Check:* Take each other's heart rates.

FOCUS: Cardiovascular endurance; partner interaction

EQUIPMENT: Lively music in 4/4 time; tape or record player; chalkboard and chalk or chart paper and marking pen

ORGANIZATION:

• To form Waves, divide the class into two equal groups and have each group stand at opposite sides of the play area, facing each other. Opposite players are partners. Put the teaching cues on the chalkboard or chart paper so that players can remember the sequence involved in this routine. Encourage partners to move in time to the music. Have partners take each other's heart rates before and after mixer.

DESCRIPTION OF ACTIVITY:

1. Skip forward for eight counts to meet your partner in the middle; give "High tens," then skip backward to starting place for eight counts. Repeat.

2. Repeat part 1, except swing right elbows with your partner when you meet; repeat again, swinging left elbows with your partner.

3. Slide Step to the opposite line for sixteen counts, facing your partner as you pass on the right. Slide step back to your starting end, passing your partner back to back.

4. Run forward for eight counts to meet your partner in the middle. Once there, do two quarter jump-turns; then push off your partner's hands as you run backward to the opposite line for eight counts. Repeat sequence, ending up at your starting lines.

5. Hop forward for eight counts toward your partner. Change hopping foot every two counts. Do-Si-Do your partner by passing right shoulder, back to back, and left shoulders; then hop backward to your starting line.

VARIATIONS:

a. Incorporate other dance steps the class has learned into this mixer routine.

b. Encourage ideas from the children and implement into the routine.

FA-28 AEROBIC HOOPS

FOCUS: Cardiovascular endurance; strength

EQUIPMENT: One hoop per player; music with a strong 4/4 beat; tape or record player

ORGANIZATION:

- Have players get a hoop, hold it on the sides horizontally overhead in a home space, and face you. When they hear the music, have them gently pulse their knees to the beat. Emphasize the importance of gentle pulsing; not bouncing or bobbing. Have players take their heart rates before and after the workout.

DESCRIPTION OF ACTIVITY:

1. **Hoop Pulses:** Raise hoop overhead and lower it four times. Bend knees in time with the music each time you lower the hoop. Then, raising and lowering hoop, bend to the right, straighten, and bend to the left. Repeat sequence four times, pulsing knees with each repetition.

2. **Hoop Hobbles:** Place your hoop on the floor. Step inside hoop and jog sixteen times. Now hop on your right foot in and out of your hoop in a CW direction eight times. Change hopping foot, and repeat in the opposite direction eight times. Step-Kick around your hoop for eight steps in one direction, then eight steps in the opposite direction.

3. **Hoop Jumps:** Jump four times inside your hoop, then twice outside to the right; twice inside; twice outside to the left; twice inside; twice outside in front of hoop; twice inside hoop; twice outside behind hoop. Repeat jumping sequence once more.

4. **Hoop Tinikling:** Begin by jogging inside your hoop. Then step right foot out to the right side; step left foot inside; then step right foot inside. Now step left foot out to left; then step right foot inside; left foot inside. Step right foot out to right side and continue foot pattern. Repeat sequence eight times. (Each time a foot steps outside the hoop, count one.)

5. **Hoop Stretches:** Hold hoop overhead and stretch to the right; hold for ten seconds. Relax; then stretch to the left for another ten seconds. Repeat sequence once more.

VARIATION:

Have players create a hoop movement of their own and show it to the rest of the class. Add to the routine above.

FOCUS: Cardiovascular endurance; strength; routine

EQUIPMENT: One short rope per player; music with a strong 4/4 beat; tape or record player

ORGANIZATION:

• Have players get a rope, check it for proper length, and find enough space to turn rope freely. Start by having players pulse their knees in time with the music. Ensure players are well spaced so ropes turn easily. Have rope turners take their heart rates before and after workout.

DESCRIPTION OF ACTIVITY:

1. **In Flight:** Holding rope handles in one hand, jog in place, and repeat each of the following rope turns eight times: Circle rope overhead like a helicopter's blade; in front like a propeller; on each side like the wheel of a car; in front in a figure-8 pattern. Change hands and repeat. Remember to keep your feet moving!

2. **Levels:** Pulse knees and continuously circle rope overhead four times at each of the following levels: Sit, lie down, sit up again, and finally stand. Change hands and repeat. Try the same routine with only two repetitions at each level.

3. **Fancy Footwork:**

   — Circle rope overhead and touch alternate heels to the floor eight times; then circle rope in front and do eight jumping jacks.

   — Circle rope on each side while doing eight Pogo Springs (jump one leg forward and the other back).

   — Pulsing knees, swing rope in front in a figure-8 pattern eight times; then add a twist jump while doing eight more figure-8s.

   — Repeat the Fancy Footwork sequence, alternating hands every fourth count.

4. **Break Step:** Hold one rope handle in each hand. With hands together, swing rope to one side; then open hands and jump through rope. Swing rope to the other side; then open hands and jump through rope. Repeat four times.

5. Keep repeating this routine from the beginning until the music stops.

VARIATION:

Add to the routine by adapting other rope tricks from Rope Play in Section 5.

FA—30 ROPERCISE

FOCUS: Cardiovascular endurance; strength

EQUIPMENT: One jump rope per player; music with a strong 4/4 beat; tape or record player

ORGANIZATION:

• This routine consists of rope jumping interspersed with various strength exercises that also use short ropes. Initially, have players repeat rope jumping for thirty seconds and strength exercise task for twenty seconds; then gradually increase the duration to one minute of rope jumping and thirty seconds of strength exercise.

• To begin, have players get a rope and scatter. Check for good spacing.

DESCRIPTION OF ACTIVITY:

1. Jump rope.

2. Stretch rope along floor and do line push-ups. (In full push-up position, place one hand ahead of the rope and the other hand behind the rope. Change hand position after each push-up.)

3. Jump rope again.

4. Drop rope and do crab-kicks. (In crab-walk position, kick alternate legs.)

5. Do a rope stretch. (Double rope, hold overhead while stretching from side to side.)

6. Jump rope.

7. Drop rope and do side leg-lifts.

8. Jump rope again.

9. Holding folded rope in hands, do curl-ups.

10. Jump rope.

11. Do another rope stretch.

VARIATION:

Substitute different jump-rope actions and other strength exercises.

FA–31 TWELVE-MINUTE WALK–RUN TEST

FOCUS: Cardiovascular endurance

EQUIPMENT: Stopwatch or digital watch; recording cards and pencils; measured running track or route

ORGANIZATION:

- Discuss the health-related Physical Fitness Components: Cardiovascular Endurance; Muscular Strength and Endurance; Flexibility; and Body Composition. Cardiovascular Endurance (C/V), which refers to the fitness of the heart, blood vessels, and lungs, is the most significant. The better one's C/V Endurance, the more efficiently the heart and lungs can deliver oxygen and nutrients to the working muscles and remove waste products.

- Discuss the FITT Guidelines: F—Frequency (How often should we exercise?); I—Intensity (How hard should we exercise); T—Time (How long should we exercise?); and T—Type (What kind of exercises should we do?)

- FITNESS USA/CANADA says that we need to work out at least three times a week in an aerobic phase of about fifteen to twenty minutes of continuous vigorous activity, to bring about a training effect of the C/V system.

- For the Twelve-Minute Walk–Run Test, participants should be tested on a measured track, if possible. If no track is available, mark off a 3.3 kilometer (2 mile) distance with the car odometer on a level road or smooth playground area. Emphasize that participants PACE themselves. Have participants pair off. Encourage partners to cheer each other on. Provide a "plan of action" for those participants who need to improve their fitness levels.

DESCRIPTION OF ACTIVITY:

1. One partner is the Runner; the other is the Recorder, who counts the laps and records the number achieved in twelve minutes. Partners then reverse roles and repeat the test.

2. Record the date and the results of your Test, so that on your next Twelve-Minute Walk–Run you should strive to improve your personal best (PB) time.

3. Repeat the Test at regular intervals throughout the year.

FA–32 BENCH-STEP TEST

FOCUS: Cardiovascular endurance; heart-rate monitoring

EQUIPMENT: Several benches; stopwatches or digital watches; paper and pencils

ORGANIZATION:

- Discuss the meaning of ENDURANCE. (Endurance is the ability of your body to do work over a long period of time.) One way to test your cardiovascular and muscular endurance is by performing a two-minute Bench-Step exercise on 30 centimeters (12-inch) high benches. Have players find a partner: one partner is the performer; the other, the timer. The timer will tell the performer when to begin and when to stop for taking pulse rates and performing the bench-step exercise. The timer will also count aloud: "Up, Up, Down, Down." This is one complete cycle. The performer paces himself or herself to complete two cycles every five seconds, or twenty-four cycles every minute.

DESCRIPTION OF ACTIVITY:

1. Timer, take the performer's RESTING HEART RATE for fifteen seconds; then multiply by four to arrive at the pulse for a minute. Record the RHR.

RESTING H.R.

1.

2. Performer, on signal "Go!" bench-step for two minutes: Step up onto the bench, first with one foot, then with the other so that you are standing tall on the bench. Step down with the original leading foot, then with the other, to the floor. Change leading foot every ten step-ups so that both legs lead. Remember to keep a steady step-up rhythm.

3. Performer, quickly sit down on the bench while the timer takes your pulse rate for fifteen seconds, multiplies by four, and records. This is your WORKING HEART RATE.

4. Now performer, rest quietly for one minute in a sitting position. Then timer, take pulse for another fifteen seconds, multiply by four, and record. Take pulse again at the two-minute mark; three-minute mark; four-minute mark; and five-minute mark. These are called RECOVERY HEART RATES. Compare the Recovery Heart Rate to your Resting Heart Rate after five minutes. Are they about the same? (The fitter you become, the quicker your heart will return to its resting heart rate!) Reverse partner roles and repeat.

RECOVERY H.R.

4.

VARIATION:

Perform a three-minute Bench-Step Test.

ENDURANCE

2.

FA–33 MILK ROUTES

FOCUS: Cardiovascular endurance; fun run

EQUIPMENT: Playground area and playing fields; stopwatch or digital wrist watch

ORGANIZATION:

- A "Milk Route" is a jogging route that can be set up around the playground area (football or soccer fields; track or oval), the school block, or the school neighborhood. This is an alternative to running laps, which can become boring. Initially, have the class slowly run around the route so that the children are familiar with the course. Gradually increase the distance until the children can run continuously for at least ten minutes. Ensure that the runs are fun, challenging, and interesting. Stress "street safety" if running in the school neighborhood. Stay on the sidewalks; cross the street only at pedestrian crosswalks. Be aware of children with certain physical problems (asthma, chronic colds, allergies, any physical disability). Modify their running sessions to their ability level, encouraging them to strive to improve. Suggestions that follow can certainly be adapted or modified to your situation.

DESCRIPTION OF ACTIVITY:

1. *Follow-the-Leader:* Run as a whole class in a "follow-the-leader" formation using the playground objects and environment as an obstacle course (swings, slide, jungle gym, goal posts, trees, hills), weaving in and out, around, through, over, under, across, on, and off.

2. *Station Run:* Run as a whole class around a large playing field, pausing at certain stations to perform sets of exercises such as push-ups, arm circles, sit-ups, and stretches. Then continue the run.

3. *Buddy Run:* Run as a class around the school block or neighborhood. Run with a "buddy" (partner) and establish a jogging pace that you can both maintain throughout the run. You may decide to walk-run the route.

4. *Team Run:* Divide the class into teams of six players. Which team can finish the Milk Route in the best accumulated time? (Add together each team member's time.) Cooperation and encouragement are essentials!

VARIATIONS:

For those children who complete the route well before the rest of the class, set up an activity for them to do while the rest of the class is finishing: a "stretch station" where they do several different stretches; throwing a Frisbee™ back and forth; a basketball activity such as shooting from marked positions around the key.

FA–34 PREDICTION RUN

FOCUS: Cardiovascular endurance; fun run

EQUIPMENT: One prediction slip for each player; one stopwatch or digital watch; pencils

ORGANIZATION:

- This is a motivational strategy that takes the emphasis out of winning when running. Set up a running route around the gym, school yard, or nearby park. The distance can be from 400 meters (440 yards) to 3 kilometers (2 miles). Provide slips of paper with spaces for PT (Prediction Time) and AT (Actual Time), for the runners to fill in prior to the run.

DESCRIPTION OF ACTIVITY:

1. Write down on the slip the time you predict you are going to take to run the course (PT). All runners "On your marks"—"Get Set." On the signal "Go!" commence the run. (Start the watch.)
2. At the finish line, remember your time as it is called out at one-second intervals. Record your time and compare your AT with your PT. Subtract one from the other. How close are your scores? Next time, try to predict a faster time and try to match it.

VARIATIONS:

a. Have runners run in groups of two, three, or four. Have each group add their PT scores and their AT scores. Subtract one total from the other and compare with other groups.
b. Vary the running course and the distance to be run.
c. Add obstacles to go over, under, and around.

FA–35 CROSS-COUNTRY RUN

FOCUS: Cardiovascular endurance

EQUIPMENT: Prepared record slips; large wall map

ORGANIZATION:

- Divide each class in the school into four teams. Give each team a name: famous people, explorers, statesmen and women, sportsmen and women, birds, animals, planets, etc. Select the route for the simulated run: across the nation, coast-to-coast, coast to capital, city-to-city. Place a large wall map in a prominent place, to plot the progress of the teams from starting point to destination point. Mark out a measured 400 meter (440 yard) track around the school yard, gym, neighborhood, or nearby park. Photocopy the record slips and have runners complete one after each run. Each run is then added to the team's total distance on the map. Measure all runs in kilometers or miles. Have the runners convert one to the other. Plan to run the cross-country for a month, a term, or a semester. Have volunteers record distances and keep the wall map up to date. Encourage runners to run in out-of-school time if they wish with their recording slip signed by a parent.

Rules:

— Running or jogging is encouraged but walking is allowed in exceptional cases.
— Minimum distance—400 meters or 440 yards
— Record slips must be signed by the runner and a witness and handed to the teacher to be recorded on the map.
— The team whose accumulated time gets them to the destination first wins.

CROSS-COUNTRY RUN
PACIFIC – ATLANTIC
Name: _____
Grade: _____
Date: _____
Distance Run: ____
Runner: _____
Witness: _____
F.I.T.T.

FOCUS: Arm and shoulder strength

EQUIPMENT: One mat per player;
four benches;
music with a strong 4/4 beat;
tape or record player

ORGANIZATION:

- Discuss the major muscles involved when doing upper body exercises: the Biceps (front muscles of upper arm); the Triceps (underneath muscles of lower arm); the Pectorals (chest muscles); the Deltoids (shoulder muscles); and the Trapezius (shoulder blade muscles).

- Discuss the importance of having strong upper body muscles: to carry out daily work and play such as carrying bags of groceries; raking the lawn; snow shoveling in winter; batting a ball; shooting a basketball; and meeting unforeseen emergencies, such as saving a drowning person. Emphasize the importance of breathing rhythmically while performing the exercise: Exhale as you push up and inhale as you lower yourselves to the mat. Check that players' backs are flat and bodies straight during push-ups. Gradually increase the number of repetitions. Have players get a mat and place it in a home space.

DESCRIPTION OF ACTIVITY:

1. *Side Push-Ups:* Lie on one side and wrap lower arm around body. Place free hand on floor in front and push up to raise and lower body from mat. Repeat twelve times each side.

2. *Knee Push-Ups:* Begin on all-fours on your mat. Keeping your hands shoulder-width apart and fingers pointing ahead, lean forward and lower chest to mat; then push up to starting position. Remember to keep your back flat throughout the push-ups. Repeat eight times.

3. *Full Push-Ups:* In front-support position, hands shoulder-width apart and fingers pointing ahead, lower until chest almost touches mat; then push up to starting position. Keep back flat and pelvis tilted forward. Repeat eight times.

4. *Bench Push-Ups 1:* Place hands on bench in full push-up position and bend and straighten elbows to lower body to bench. Repeat sixteen times.

5. *Bench Push-Ups 2:* In the full push-up position, place feet on bench and hands on floor and bend and straighten elbows to lower body to floor. Repeat twelve times.

6. *Triceps Push-Ups:* In back-support position, have players slowly bend and straighten arms to lower body to mat, twelve times.

7. *Upper Arm Stretch:* Standing tall, interlock your fingers behind your back. Now, while straightening your arms, slowly turn your elbows inward. Hold for ten seconds; then repeat stretch with arms extended in front.

FA—37 TUMMY TOUGHENERS

FOCUS: Abdominal strength

EQUIPMENT: One mat per player;
four to five benches;
music with a strong 4/4 beat;
tape or record player

ORGANIZATION:

- Have players get a mat and sit in a long-sit position. Throughout these abdominal exercises, remind children to breathe evenly, exhaling as they curl up and inhaling as they curl down. Encourage them to move smoothly and rhythmically. Increase the number of repetitions as they gain abdominal strength. Discuss the importance of maintaining strong rectus abdominis muscles: to prevent lower back pain and misalignment of the lower back area; to protect the vital organs in that area; and to keep an attractive figure.

DESCRIPTION OF ACTIVITY:

1. *Ankle-Tap Curl-Ups:* Begin in hook-lying position on mat. Lift head and shoulders slightly off mat; then curl forward to touch opposite hand to the inside of the opposite ankle. Slowly curl downward to mat; then curl upward again. Repeat sixteen times.

2. *Curl-Ups:* Begin in hook-lying position, hands resting on thighs. Curl your body upward, tucking chin to chest and rounding back. Continue to slide hands up thighs until wrists are just past your knees. Slowly lower shoulders to mat. Repeat twenty times.

3. *Folded-Arms Curl-Ups:* Begin in hook-lying position with arms folded across chest and hands on the tops of the shoulders. Gently curl up to touch elbows to thighs; then curl down to starting position. Your head should return to touch the mat when curling down and seat should remain in contact with mat throughout the exercise. Repeat sixteen times.

4. *Elbow-Knee Curl-Ups:* Begin in hook-lying position. Raise feet and cross them at ankles, so that your knees are bent at a ninety-degree angle. With fingers at ears, curl up to touch elbows to knees. Repeat sixteen times.

5. *Alternate Elbow-to-Knee Curl-Ups:* Begin in a hook-lying position on the mat. Raise feet so that knees are bent at ninety degrees and hands are clasped behind your neck. Curl up to alternately touch opposite elbow to opposite knee. Repeat sixteen times.

6. *Bench Sit-Ups:* Place your mat on the floor against a bench. Lie in back-lying position on the mat with your lower legs on the bench. Clasp your hands behind the neck. Curl up to touch your elbows to the knees; then curl down to starting position. Keep your back flat against the mat to prevent lower back strain. Repeat sixteen times.

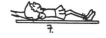

7. *Abdominal Stretch:* In back-lying position, stretch arms overhead and legs straight out. Hold for ten seconds. Pause and repeat.

VARIATION:

Partner Folded-Arms Curl-Ups: Have one partner, in kneeling-sit position with performing partner's feet between his or her knees, securely hold the feet of the performing partner. Curl-ups are done as in Exercise 3.

FOCUS: Mid-body strength

EQUIPMENT: One mat per player;
music with a strong 4/4 beat;
tape or record player

ORGANIZATION:

- Review the name of the buttock muscles (the "Gluteus Maximus" muscles) and why it is important to keep them strong. (These muscles give support to the lower back and hip area.)

- Emphasize that players press lower back to mat and tilt pelvis upward. Have players·get a mat to sit on, facing you.

DESCRIPTION OF ACTIVITY:

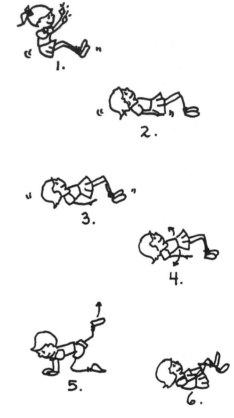

1. *Seat Waddle:* Sitting with legs outstretched and feet together, raise arms in front. Can you snap fingers and move hips forward in time with the music using only your seat muscles? Move backward; sideways.

2. *Hip Tilts:* In hook-lying position, gently squeeze buttocks as you tilt your hips forward and back twelve times. Remember to keep your lower back flat on the mat. Squeeze feet and knees together; then repeat hip tilts another twelve times.

3. *Seat Lifts:* In hook-lying position and knees apart, gently lift and lower your hips off the mat twelve times. Then squeeze your buttocks as you lift hips upward and hold for ten seconds. Repeat with knees together.

4. *Hip Swivels:* Still in hook-lying position, lift hips and gently swing them from side to side. Repeat eight times to each side.

5. *Buttock Press:* In all-fours position, lift one leg at right angles off the mat. Gently press that raised foot upward eight times. Lower leg to starting position and repeat with other leg.

6. *Hugger Stretch:* From hook-lying position, lift legs off the mat, cross your feet right over left, and grasp ankles with opposite hands. Hug knees to chest ten seconds. Relax. Repeat, crossing your feet left over right. Can you feel the stretch in your buttock muscles?

VARIATION:

Straight-Leg Lifts: Same as for Seat Lifts, except that players raise one leg in the air. Change raised leg after six lifts.

FA—39 HIP HONERS

FOCUS: Mid-body strength

EQUIPMENT: One mat per player;
music with a strong 4/4 beat;
tape or record player

ORGANIZATION:

• The following exercises work and tone the muscles of the hip area. Have players get a mat and kneel on all fours. Players should keep head low and distribute weight evenly over hands and knees throughout these exercises.

DESCRIPTION OF ACTIVITY:

1. *Fire Hydrants:* On all fours, with hips square and right knee bent, raise right leg to side. Extend your leg forward and backward, parallel to the floor; then lower it to mat. Move your legs only; upper body should be still. Repeat eight times; then change legs.

2. *Hip Flexors:* Lie on your right side with your head resting on your right hand and your left hand flat on the mat in front of you for support. Do not lean forward. Raise and lower your left leg twelve times. Roll over onto your other side and repeat leg raises. The knee should point ahead, not upward throughout the exercise.

3. *Inner Thigh Flexors:* Lie on your right side with your head resting on your right hand and your left hand flat on the mat in front of you for support. Raise your left leg and hold. Now raise and lower your right leg to meet your left, eight times. Then roll over onto your other side and repeat.

4. *Skyscrapers:* Kneel on all fours, lower weight to forearms, and tighten abdominal muscles. Raise bent right leg behind and push it to ceiling twelve times. At the same time, flex and point foot. Change legs and repeat.

5. *Seat Rollers:* Begin in hook-sit position with your feet flat on the mat. Keeping knees together, roll them to the right side, back to center, then to the left side. Repeat this sequence twelve times.

6. *Sit and Tuck Stretch:* Begin in half-hook, half-long-sit position. Cross the bent leg over the straight leg. Gently press with both hands against the knee of the bent leg, pulling it toward the opposite shoulder. Do not pull your shoulder to the knee. Hold for ten seconds. Change legs and repeat.

FOCUS: Lower body strength

EQUIPMENT: One mat per player; music with a strong 4/4 beat; tape or record player

ORGANIZATION:

- Review the two muscles of the upper leg and their location: the Quadriceps (four muscle bundles of the front thigh) and the Hamstrings (back muscles of the thigh). The back muscles of the lower leg are called the Gastrocnemius.

- Discuss the importance of having strong leg muscles: used for all our daily work and play such as walking, biking, stairclimbing; for kicking a football or soccer ball; skating; cross-country skiing; for meeting unforeseen emergencies. Have players scatter and face you.

DESCRIPTION OF ACTIVITY:

1. *Mountain Climbers:* In front-support position, bring the right knee up under chest and extend the left leg backward. Quickly switch leg positions, keeping in time to the music. Repeat sixteen to twenty-four times.

2. *Straddle Combos:* Combine Side Straddles with Forward Straddles. Stand tall with feet together, hands on hips. Jump feet apart to the sides; then jump feet apart with one foot forward and the other back; now jump feet apart again. Alternate the forward foot each time. The feet do not return to the starting position until the exercise is completed. Repeat sequence eight times.

3. *Thigh Lifts:* Begin in the half-hook, half-long-sit position on your mat. Raise and lower the extended leg eight times. Reverse leg positions and repeat.

4. *Clappers:* Hop on the left foot, kick the right leg up, and clap your hands under the right leg. Hop on the right foot, kick the left leg up, and clap your hands under it. Land on the ball of the foot each time. Repeat sixteen times. Can you turn CW for eight clappers, then CCW for eight clappers?

5. *Half-Knee Bends:* Have players begin by standing tall with the pelvis tilted forward and the feet shoulder-width apart. Bend knees no farther than at right angles, hold, then slowly rise again. Repeat eight times.

6. *Ankle Builders:* In long-sit position on your mat, circle one ankle CW four times; then change direction. Repeat with other ankle. Do this sequence three times. Now flex your ankles by pointing toes toward you; out; away from each other; together, for four counts each direction. Repeat this sequence three times.

FA–41 COOL-DOWN STRETCHES 1

FOCUS: Overall body flexibility

EQUIPMENT: One mat per player;
relaxing music;
tape or record player

ORGANIZATION:

- The cool-down phase is a continuation of activity, but at a slower pace and should never be omitted! This phase should last for at least five minutes to allow the heart rate to return to normal. Stretching and toning activities are included to further improve strength and increase one's flexibility. Discuss the meaning of Flexibility (joint mobility or suppleness): the range of movement around a joint and its muscles. Discuss why it is important to stretch: to warm up the muscles for aerobic activity; to prevent injury; to maintain the elasticity of the muscles. Discuss important tips to remember when stretching: Breathe normally while holding a stretch, don't hold your breath; avoid any bouncing, bobbing, or jerking motions; hold your stretch for at least ten seconds and gradually try to increase the time. Stretch often, daily!

DESCRIPTION OF ACTIVITY:

1. **Head and Eye Rolls:** Rotate eyes as you turn your head gently from side to side. Then keep your head still as your eyes look upward, then downward. Can you make your eyes follow in a circular path?

2. **Face Stretch:** How many different ways can you twist and contort your face in twenty seconds? Then smile to relax your facial muscles. Now altogether, try making these sounds for five seconds each: "Aaah!"; "Eeeh!"; "Oooh!"

3. **Shoulder Stretch:** Standing tall, reach behind your head and down your back as far as you can with your left hand. Try to grab the fingers of your right hand coming up, palm out, behind your back. Hold for ten seconds. Reverse hand hold and repeat stretch.

4. **Sprinter Stretch:** Begin in the all-fours position on a mat. Move one leg forward until the knee of the front leg is directly over the ankle. Extend the other leg back, shifting the weight up onto the toes and ball of the back foot. Hold this stretch for ten seconds. Reverse leg positions and repeat stretch.

5. **Back Stretch:** Begin in the half-hook, half-long-sit position. Cross the bent leg over the straight leg. Gently press the opposite elbow against the outside of the bent knee. Hold this position for ten seconds. Reverse leg and elbow positions and repeat stretch.

VARIATIONS:

a. If players have difficulty getting hands to meet in the Shoulder Stretch, use a folded jump rope to ease the connection. Encourage players to move hands toward each other on the rope until they are touching.

b. In the Sprinter Stretch, have players place both hands on the mat alongside the inside of the front foot and gently pulse the extended leg's knee to the mat.

FOCUS: Overall body flexibility

EQUIPMENT: One mat per player;
several tables or chairs;
relaxing music;
tape or record player

ORGANIZATION:

• Review the stretching tips, emphasizing the importance of stretching safely and frequently.
Homework Stretch: Have players do stretches at home and teach each of the stretches they have learned to their parents, relatives, or friends. These stretches can be performed against a wall when indoors; against a fence, post, or tree when outside; while watching TV; as a break from sitting; at the end of an aerobic activity session!

DESCRIPTION OF ACTIVITY:

1. ***Quad Stretch:*** Using your hands for support and balance, sit with your right leg bent back so that your right heel is near the buttocks. Your left leg is also bent with the sole of the left foot touching the inside of your right thigh. Lean back gently, feeling the stretch in your right quadricep. Hold for twenty seconds; then change legs and repeat. Do this Quad Stretch one more time.

2. ***Calf Stretch:*** Stand near a wall and lean on it with your forearms and with your head resting on your hands. Lean forward with one leg and leave the other leg straight behind you. Press the heel of the back leg to the floor and gently move your hips forward. Both feet should be pointing straight ahead and touching the floor. Hold for twenty seconds; then change leg positions and repeat stretch.

3. ***Soleus-Achilles Tendon Stretch:*** Assume the same position as for the "Calf Stretch," except slightly bend the back knee, still keeping the back foot flat on the floor. Hold for ten seconds. Repeat with other leg.

4. ***Hamstring Stretch:*** Begin in long-sit position. Now rest the sole of your right foot against the inside of your straight left leg. Lean forward slightly from the hips and reach forward toward your toes. If you cannot reach your toes, then reach forward as far as is comfortable. Hold for twenty seconds; then change leg positions and repeat. Remember to not lock your knee and to keep your right foot flexed (upright).

5. ***Groin Stretch:*** Sit with soles of feet together. Heels should be a comfortable distance from your crotch. Lean forward from the hips, grasp toes, and gently press elbows against the lower legs for ten seconds. Relax; then repeat stretch two more times.

6. ***Gluteal Stretch:*** In back-lying position, pull your right knee across your body toward the left shoulder and hold for ten seconds. Press gently with right hand against the outside of the right knee and hold the right ankle with the left hand. Reverse leg positions and repeat stretch. Do this sequence three times.

7. ***Leg Relaxer:*** Elevate your feet by resting them against a wall or chair. Make sure your lower back is flat, not off the floor. Hold this position for one minute at first; then gradually increase the time. This exercise will improve circulation and relax tired legs!

VARIATION:

Hamstring Stretch: Have players stand facing a table. Raise one leg, slightly bent, onto a table. Slowly lean forward from hips until a stretch is felt in the back of the raised leg. Pointing raised foot, grasp ankle with both hands and hold stretch for ten seconds. Change legs and repeat.

FA–43 STEEPLECHASE COURSE

FOCUS: Obstacle course;
cardiovascular endurance

EQUIPMENT: Chart paper, marking pens, masking tape;
chairs, short ropes, cone markers, wands, balance
benches, balance beam, hanging bar, box horse,
folding mats, crash pad, hoops or tire tubes, balls,
jump ropes;
music with a strong 4/4 beat;
tape or record player

ORGANIZATION:

• This obstacle course involves players moving quickly and safely through a variety of obstacles. Upon completing the course, players then perform several stretches that have been previously taught at the "Stretch Tree" located in the center of the play area. Start with about eight stations; then gradually increase their number as players' fitness levels improve. Add other obstacles until the number of stations equals half the number of players in the class. Try to avoid "bottlenecks" (or places where the activity slows down) by ensuring that each obstacle takes about the same time to complete; keep the players moving!

• Begin by "walking" the players through the obstacle course, demonstrating as necessary and emphasizing safety. Have players go through the obstacle course in pairs in fifteen-second interval starts. Use music to start and stop the activity.

DESCRIPTION OF ACTIVITY:

1. Jump over a series of HURDLES (drape short ropes between chairs) or BENCHES (spaced about 4 meters [12 feet] apart).

2. Climb or leap over a box horse, land in a crash pad, and do a forward roll.

3. (Place 8 to 10 hula hoops on the floor, spaced about 30 centimeters [1 foot] apart.) With hands on hips, jump from hoop to hoop.

4. Do three forward rolls along the mats.

5. (Suspend a ladder on a climbing frame.) Grasp the ladder with your hands and swing from rung to rung across the ladder.

6. Walk the length of a balance beam bouncing a ball.

7. Climb up a rope five hand-over-hands to go up; five hand-under-hands to come down, or swing across a large mat to land on the other side.

8. Jump a rope thirty times.

VARIATIONS:

a. Reverse direction of travel and repeat Steeplechase Course twice.

b. Have players create their own Steeplechase Course, or give suggestions for replacing or adding to current activities.

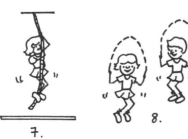

FA-44 OUTDOOR STEEPLECHASE

FOCUS: Cardiovascular endurance; overall strength

EQUIPMENT: Playground equipment and apparatus; school environment

ORGANIZATION:

- Using the playground environment, set up an obstacle course of ten or more stations. "Walk" the players through the course, demonstrating where necessary and emphasizing safety. Have all players in file formation at the starting line; then use staggered starts by having a player go only after the player in front of him or her has completed the first two obstacles. Have players go through the obstacle course a certain number of times, depending on the time available.

DESCRIPTION OF ACTIVITY:

Suggestions:

- Swing on a fixed apparatus.
- Climb over fences, boarded rinks.
- Climb up, across, and down a vertical grid.
- Crawl through a vertical tire.
- Run around the bases of a baseball diamond.
- Run up a slope and roll down.
- Climb up and move down a slide.
- Climb through a jungle gym or pipes.
- Zigzag through a tree line.
- Ladder walk across a climbing apparatus.

FA-45 FITNESS TRACK

EQUIPMENT: Equipment specified for each station; school or park environment; two stopwatches

ORGANIZATION:

- A Fitness Track combines running with doing a set number of exercises at eight to ten fixed apparatus stations, which can be evenly spaced (about 50 to 100 meters or yards apart) around the school grounds or nearby park. If possible, signs illustrating the exercises and repetitions for each should be made and laminated onto posterboard, then permanently fixed to the equipment. Introduce the children to the Fitness Track by walking them through it, stopping them at each station to learn and practice the correct technique of performing the exercise. Then have players find a partner and form a file of pairs at the starting line. Stagger start each pair at ten-second intervals. Record their finishing times.

DESCRIPTION OF ACTIVITY:

Suggestions:

- ***Step-Ups:*** Step up and down on a log, alternating the leading leg.
- ***Hurdles:*** Step onto the hurdle, then over, or leap over the hurdle in one stride.
- ***Climber:*** Carefully climb up and over the wall.
- ***Log Jumps:*** Jump with two feet over each of the log obstacles.
- ***Chin-Ups:*** Grasp the bar with palms facing you. Slowly lift with your arms until the chin is above the bar. Lower yourself. Repeat.
- ***Push-Ups:*** Keeping your body straight, raise and lower your body using arms only.
- ***Horizontal Ladder:*** Using your arms only, move forward along the full length of the ladder.
- ***Curl-Ups:*** Hook your feet under a rope or log and, keeping your legs bent, slowly curl up and down.
- ***Balance Walk:*** Keeping your arms extended sideways for balance, walk from one end of the log to the other and back again.
- ***Sergeant Jump:*** Jump upward to "ring the bell" (touch it).

FA–46 CHARLIE BROWN'S CIRCUIT

FOCUS: Cardiovascular endurance; strength

EQUIPMENT: Posterboard, marking pens, and masking tape; stopwatch; eight cone markers; several mats; two benches; twelve hoops; lively music; tape or record player; Circuit Record cards; pencils

ORGANIZATION:

- Set up a minimum of eight exercise stations around the perimeter of the play area. Make station signs that depict vigorous, continuous exercises and that clearly show the number of the station. Tape cards to walls or lean them against cone markers, positioning them in a circle, oval, rectangle, or square, at least 4 to 6 meters (12 to 18 feet) apart. Try to alternate upper and lower body exercises. Photocopy the Circuit Record card (see FA-47) for each player to record results.
- To begin, explain how to perform each exercise, stressing correct technique. Then have a maximum of four players go to each station. Players will rotate from station to station, in consecutive order, until all stations are completed. Measure pulse rates at the start and at the end of the circuit. Remember to provide a warm-up and a cool-down (stretching). Play popular music for thirty seconds while players exercise; stop music for fifteen seconds while they record their scores and rotate between stations. Gradually increase the exercise time to one minute.

DESCRIPTION OF ACTIVITY:

1. **Lucy's Clover Run:** (Arrange four cone markers so that three markers are the same distance from the center marker and each other [about 5 meters or 15 feet].) Starting at the center marker, run around each of the other three markers, returning to touch the center marker each time. Count one for each time you touch the center marker.
2. **Woodstock's Foot Tracks:** (Arrange four markers in a 3 meter [10 foot] square as shown.) Begin in the full front-support position. Walk your feet around in a circle with your hands, staying in the center area of the square. You may alternate between moving CW and CCW. Count one for each marker passed.
3. **Peppermint Patty's Curl-Ups:** Begin in hook-lying position with your arms folded across your chest. Curl up to touch your elbows to your thighs; then slowly curl down to starting position. Repeat. Remember to breathe in while curling down and breathe out while curling up. Count one for each curl-up.
4. **Linus's Rise 'n Shine:** Stand tall; lie flat on your back with legs straight and feet together; stand up as quickly as you can. Repeat this sequence, counting one point for each time you return to the starting position.
5. **Snoopy's Swimmers:** Begin in the front-support position. Lift your right hand off the floor and reach back to touch the opposite hip. Return to starting position. Repeat using your left hand. Count one each time your right hand touches a hip.
6. **Charlie Brown's Bench-Overs:** (If possible, use two to three benches with two performers to a bench. Ensure that the bench has an immovable base or have partners straddle sit on the ends.) Stand on one side of the bench with your hands clasping the sides of the bench. Keeping your feet together as you jump, jump from side to side over the bench. Count one for each landing.
7. **Marcie's Hoop Hops:** (Arrange six hoops in a file pattern and securely tape to floor. Set up two identical hoop patterns to avoid bottlenecks.) Hop on one foot into each hoop; hop out of the last hoop, change hopping foot, and hop back on that foot into each hoop to the start. Count one for each hop into a hoop.
8. **Schroeder's Paddlers:** Begin in hook-sit position. Clasp your hands and hold firmly on the chest. Lean back so that you can feel your tummy muscles tighten. Keeping this position, twist your trunk from side to side so that your elbows alternately touch the floor. Remember to keep your elbows out to the sides. Count one for each time an elbow touches the floor.

FA–47 CHARLIE BROWN'S CIRCUIT (RECORDING CARD) _____

FOCUS: Circuit Training

EQUIPMENT: Circuit score card;
pencils

ORGANIZATION:

Have players set TARGETS or GOALS for themselves that they must try to reach within a certain time. These targets could be written on the score card. For example, "Within two weeks' time, I will try to improve the number of curl-ups I can perform by ten." Have players continue to work toward their target at home as well as during physical education classes.

DESCRIPTION OF ACTIVITY:

SAMPLE SCORE CARD

CIRCUIT SCORE CARD

NAME _____ GRADE _____ ROOM _____

TARGETS: _____

Date _____

Exercises	*Number of Repetitions*
1. _____	_____
2. _____	_____
3. _____	_____
4. _____	_____
5. _____	_____
6. _____	_____
7. _____	_____
8. _____	_____

IMPROVEMENTS: _____

_____

_____

VARIATION:

Have players graph their results on an individual or class basis using bar or line graphs. Provide a follow-up of each player's performance.

Rhythms and Dance

The Rhythms and Dance activities are meant to develop creative expression, rhythmic movement, musical appreciation, and active listening skills. They improve muscular growth and coordination, space and body and effort awareness, and social skills in an atmosphere of fun. Specific music suggestions are provided through the dance section. Lively popular music is suggested otherwise.

This section presents fifty-five Rhythms and Dance activities:

RD—1 RHYTHMS AND GROUP SHAPES

FOCUS: Body awareness; cooperation   **EQUIPMENT:** Drum

ORGANIZATION:

- The four Basic Body Shapes—wide, narrow, rounded, and twisted—and Basic Body Functions—curling, bending, stretching, and twisting—are explored through individual, partner, and group movement.

DESCRIPTION OF ACTIVITY:

1. In your own space, listen to my drum beats. Now take four counts to stretch high and wide as the wall. Hold for four counts. Now take four counts to fall and spread yourself wide. In four counts make another wide shape at this level. Now curl up into a tight ball for four counts. Can you curl upside down? Curl on one side only? Curl in another way?

2. On the loud drum beat, let your body pierce your space like an arrow in the air; on the floor. On the next drum beat, be narrow and sharp in a different way.

3. Twist yourself like a tangled piece of wire. Twist and tangle. Find a partner. Bend and twist yourself around each other.

4. **Frozen State:** Form groups of five and number yourselves one, two, three, four, and five. First dancer, run to a spot and freeze in a shape. This is the signal for the second dancer to move toward the first dancer and freeze in a different shape. Continue, each following the dancer ahead and adding your own shape. Travel in different ways toward the group shape. Freeze close enough so that body parts are touching. Freeze at high, low, or medium levels. (Provide opportunity for groups to observe each other's "Frozen States.")

5. **Spatial Pockets:** One partner, make a shape and hold it. Second partner, "fill in the spaces" around that partner, creating another shape. Now first partner leave your starting shape, and fill in the spaces around the second partner, creating yet another shape. Second partner, leave your shape, and fill in the "pockets" again.

   — Create three shape changes, each time taking eight counts to move in and out of each other's shapes.

6. **Dance of the Four Seasons:** (Divide the class into four equal groups; have each group select a season: Spring, Summer, Autumn, or Winter; then create a sequence of three movements that represent their season, using even and uneven rhythms and tempo changes.)

   — *Spring:* plants growing, butterflies flitting, thunderstorm roaring

   — *Summer:* sun rising and setting, clouds drifting, beach fun

   — *Autumn:* leaves falling, birds flocking, biking fun

   — *Winter:* snow falling, blizzards, winter fun

RD−2 EXPLORING SYMMETRY AND ASYMMETRY

FOCUS: Body and space awareness   **EQUIPMENT:** Tambourine

ORGANIZATION:

• Explain Symmetry—a condition where half of something is the mirror image of the other half. If a line is drawn down the center of the body, whatever one side of the body does, the other side must do exactly the same. Explain Asymmetry—a condition of unbalance; not symmetrical. One side of the body must not do what the other side is doing. To start, have each dancer find a free space.

DESCRIPTION OF ACTIVITY:

1. Begin standing. Move your arms symmetrically to the beat of my tambourine. Whatever one arm does, the other must do the same.
   — Repeat using a leg.
   — Change level and continue to move symmetrically to my tambourine.
2. Return to standing position and now explore moving asymmetrically to my tambourine. Change levels and body base and continue to explore.
3. Move symmetrically about in general space. Then when you hear the tambourine, change to asymmetrical movement. (Have them change back and forth several times.)
4. Find a partner and stand near each other, face to face. One partner be the leader; the other, the follower. Leader, move symmetrically, very slowly to the shaking of my tambourine. Partner try to copy these movements. Leader change to asymmetrical movements. Partner copy the actions. Reverse roles and repeat.
5. Form groups of four or five. Make up a short sequence using symmetry, asymmetry, levels, and body bases. Do some things in unison; others separately; still others in twos or threes.

RD−3 EXPLORING SYMMETRICAL AND ASYMMETRICAL SHAPES

FOCUS: Body and space awareness   **EQUIPMENT:** Cymbal;
                                                          spooky music;
                                                          tape or record player

ORGANIZATION:

• Symmetrical and Asymmetrical movements are explored through the actions of opening, closing, pulling, and pushing in personal and general space.

DESCRIPTION OF ACTIVITY:

1. Begin in your own space. Curl up on the floor. When you hear the cymbal, slowly open; then close symmetrically. Keep both sides of the body identical. Explore other ways of opening and closing symmetrically.
2. Let one side open asymmetrically, really pushing its way open. Now pull that side back in. Repeat with the other side pushing and pulling. (Use a cymbal to accompany the actions.)
3. Now travel in general space with one side open and the other side closed. When you hear the cymbal, change sides. (Discuss how it feels to use only part of the body in movement.)
4. Listen to the spooky music being played. Does it make you think of grotesque monsters? Create a dance that involves symmetrical and asymmetrical movement in your personal space and general space. Now girls, sit while the boys show us their dance; then girls, your turn.

RD-4 EXPLORING A MIRRORING RELATIONSHIP

FOCUS: Partner relationship; space awareness

EQUIPMENT: Suggested Music: "Childhood Dreams" by Zamfir; tape or record player

ORGANIZATION:

• The "quiet" actions of rising, drifting, turning, and sinking are explored in personal and general space with a partner. Have dancers pair off and each pair find a free space. Provide ample opportunity for partners to develop and practice their Mirror Dance. Have pairs observe each other's dances and look for definite beginning and ending shapes, following and leading changes, and movement changes.

DESCRIPTION OF ACTIVITY:

1. Mirroring is the matching of movements with a partner or group without touching. Listen to the music being played. How does it make you feel? Slow, dreamy. With your partner, decide who will lead and who will follow as you move slowly to the music. Switch roles every sixteen counts.

— Try mirroring only with your arms; legs; whole body. Use parts of the body at times; use the whole body at other times. Move at different levels. Make your movements symmetrical or asymmetrical.

2. Create a Mirror Dance using the actions of rising, drifting, turning, and sinking. When you reach a certain point in your dance, let the other partner take over. Decide on a beginning shape and an ending shape.

— Can one partner take the sequence forward; then the other partner take it in reverse?

RD-5 CONTRASTING BODY ACTIONS

EQUIPMENT: Tambourine

ORGANIZATION:

• Discuss the meaning of Contrasting Actions. Ask dancers for examples of actions that are opposite. Dancers then explore three contrasting actions: floppy/stiff, jerky/smooth, scamper/creep in personal and general space. Have dancers observe each other's Contrast Dances, pointing out the action changes as they occur. Have dancers find a free space to start.

DESCRIPTION OF ACTIVITY:

1. Listen to the quickness of my tambourine's beat. Move quickly, scampering on your feet, to the beat; creeping when you hear the tambourine shake quietly.

2. Move stiffly to the steady beat of the tambourine. When you hear the tambourine shake loudly, change to floppy movements.

3. On the loud irregular beats of the tambourine, make your movements jerky. When the tambourine stops, change to smooth, flowing movements.

4. With a partner, create a Contrast Dance using the three contrasting pairs of action words you have explored. One partner perform an action for sixteen counts; then the other partner take over with the contrasting action for sixteen counts. Decide on a starting action, a middle, and an ending.

RD-6 KARATE!

FOCUS: Effort and space awareness   **EQUIPMENT:** Tambourine

ORGANIZATION:

• The action words *punch*, *slash*, *twirl*, and *collapse* are explored.

DESCRIPTION OF ACTIVITY:

1. How many different body parts can be used to punch? hands, feet, knees, elbows

2. Take four counts to punch one hand forward; punch the other hand forward. (Repeat for three counts; two counts; one count and accompany with loud tambourine beats.) On one count make your punches strong!

   — Instead of extending quickly on each hit, extend very slowly. (Accompany with the shaking of the tambourine.)

3. Slashes are longer, but just as powerful as punches. Explore slashing movements with different body parts. (Shake the tambourine; slow the beat until the slashing is in slow motion.)

4. Twirl in your own space. Twirl quickly; turn slowly. Twirl strongly; twirl gently. Can you twirl and slash at the same time? Now twirl and punch. Repeat, but this time collapse.

5. *Karate Dance:* Find a partner and a free space. Check for good spacing. One partner punch and slash; the other partner react by twirling and collapsing; then switch roles. Remember, there is no body contact!

   — One partner twirl and punch; the other partner, counterpunch with slashes. Switch roles.

RD-7 FIREWORKS!

EQUIPMENT: Tambourine

ORGANIZATION:

• Dancers explore qualities of movement through the action words *flick*, *push*, *jump*, *explode*, *spin*, *shoot*, *leap*, and *scatter*. Discuss the qualities and features of fire and smoke. If possible, play the sounds of fireworks going off and have children perform their dances. Accompany movements with tambourine.

DESCRIPTION OF ACTIVITY:

1. Travel and leap into spaces like sparks shooting from a fire. Make spiky shapes. Now relax your body, moving in soft, flowing, swirling movements like smoke curling upward.

2. *Fireworks Dance:*

   — *Rockets:* Make a small curled shape near the floor, weight on your feet. Push upward through space to a high level, into an explosive jump. As you explode, send your arms and feet out in all directions; then sink slowly and be still. Repeat this sequence: Push–Explode–Scatter–Settle.

   — *Catherine Wheels:* Use different body bases to spin.

   — *Sparklers:* Begin in your own space, hiding your hands. Slowly bring the fingers of one hand out. Make quick flicking movements; then quickly hide them away. Repeat with the other hand. Repeat with both hands together.

   — *Shooters:* Start at a low level. Gradually get higher and higher as you shoot into the sky. Gradually dim, returning to your low level shape.

   — Put these four movements together to make a dance.

RD-8 FOCAL POINT AND GESTURING RHYTHMS

FOCUS: Body and space awareness   **EQUIPMENT:** Tambourine

ORGANIZATION:

* Dancers explore focal point through eye, hand, and foot gestures as they move rhythmically in personal and general space.

DESCRIPTION OF ACTIVITY:

1. Fix your eyes on a certain point, and, as you move in your Home, never let your eyes move from that spot. Change levels and body bases. Now as your eyes stare at a spot in the room, creep toward it with the sound of my tambourine. Freeze for four counts. Pick another spot and repeat.

2. Run to the quick shaking of my tambourine. On the loud beat, freeze low, and slowly gaze around the room moving only your head. Repeat.

3. Travel to your Home space. Look high, look low, look behind you, look between your legs. Each time you hear a loud beat, look in a different place. Look–look–look–gaze–stare.

4. Let your hands be your "eyes." Let them look at a different place each time. Let your hands gaze all around the play area. Look–look–gaze–look–look–gaze. Repeat using one foot, then the other.

5. *Talking Hands:* Let one hand say a big action; other hand reply with a small action. Let one hand say something very quickly; the other reply in slow motion. Let one foot talk and the other reply.

   — Create a "Talking Hands and Feet" conversation with a partner.

RD-9 MEETING, TRAVELING TOGETHER, AND RETREATING

FOCUS: Partner relationships; space awareness   **EQUIPMENT:** Drum or tambourine

ORGANIZATION:

* Partners interact as they explore different ways of meeting, traveling together, and parting in general space. Have dancers choose a partner and find a free space. Observe groups and guide them along as they design their dances. Provide opportunity for pairs to observe each other's dances. Have children name the action words being performed.

DESCRIPTION OF ACTIVITY:

1. To begin, space yourselves about 5 meters (15 feet) apart. Listen to the sound of my tambourine. Very slowly, slither toward each other. When you meet, scurry back to your Home.

2. This time slither toward your partner in another way. Try to move in a different way than your partner (feet first, on your tummy, elbows leading). Can you scurry back Home in a different way? (all fours, quick pitter-patter of your feet, on your back squirming, etc.)

3. Now with your partner, choose a way of quickly traveling together and parting in slow motion.

4. Choose your own meeting, traveling together, and parting action words and create a dance with your partner. Think about meeting in a special way, gesturing with your hands, mirroring an action, traveling in a certain pathway, moving at different levels, using your body or voice sounds to accompany your dance.

RD−10 GROUP RHYTHMS (IN CANON)

FOCUS: Group relationships

EQUIPMENT: Drum; cymbal; music in 4/4 time; tape or record player

ORGANIZATION:

- Dancers move together in canon or one after the other, as they explore the traveling actions of gliding and twirling. They then interact with each other in their group to create a sequence. Dancers get into groups of three and order themselves first, second, and third; then space themselves arm's length apart. If there are one or two children without a group, make groups of four, but have two dancers in those groups travel at the same time.

DESCRIPTION OF ACTIVITY:

1. With the drum, the first dancer glide into an open space and freeze on the loud beat at any level you wish. Now the second dancer, slide toward the first dancer. When you arrive, freeze at a different level. Third dancer, slide toward the other dancers in your group and freeze in yet a different level. Your group should finish in a tight shape.
   — Repeat this sequence using only your drum to communicate traveling and stopping.
2. Now with the cymbal, the first dancer twirl away and freeze. Then the second dancer twirl away and freeze in a different space. Finally, the third dancer twirl away and freeze in yet another space. Is each dancer in your group frozen apart from the others?
3. Now try this sequence:
   — *Coming together:* Glide–Freeze; Glide–Freeze.
   — *Traveling apart:* Twirl–Freeze; Twirl–Freeze.
   — Have dancers in each group change their order and repeat several times. Let groups observe each other. Comment on group shapes created.
4. Each group choose two traveling actions and create your own Group Dance. Let each dancer travel for eight counts, then freeze for four counts, before the next dancer approaches, then later retreats.

RD−11 MOVEMENT CONVERSATIONS AND PHRASES

FOCUS: Group relationships; timing

EQUIPMENT: Drum; cymbal; music in 4/4 time; tape or record player

ORGANIZATION:

- Discuss the term *conversation*. Have children think about a conversation with a friend and how the conversation can be very agreeable, change to another topic, or turn into an argument. Have dancers, interracting with a partner, develop a Movement Conversation. Each partner must decide whether to follow the movement idea or change it to create a new situation. Then introduce Movement Phrases or movement sentences. Phrases may vary in length; a group of phrases may express a thought.

DESCRIPTION OF ACTIVITY:

1. Create a "Stretching Conversation," in which each partner uses a similar or different base of support and stretching direction. While one partner stretches, the other stays still in a starting shape. As soon as the first dancer is still, the second dancer take over.
2. Now each Dancer decide how short or long your part of the conversation will be. This is called a Movement Phrase. Move in counts of four, eight, or sixteen beats.
3. Each create a sequence or three different stretching phrases and, with your partner, create a movement conversation.
4. Create a Movement Conversation with your partner. Include Movement Phrases in your conversation dance.
5. Dancers now work in groups of three or four and develop a "Mood Conversation," depicting happy, sad, angry, peaceful, excited, bored, frightened, courageous.

RD–12 BIRD DANCE

FOCUS: Novelty dance

EQUIPMENT: "Bird Dance" from K-Tel's *Dance, Dance, Dance* album with The Emeralds; tape or record player

ORGANIZATION:

- This popular novelty dance involves the basic steps of skipping and elbow-swinging. Have dancers pair off and form groups of four; each group finds a free space. In each group, one pair of dancers faces the other pair, about 2 meters (6 feet) apart.

DESCRIPTION OF ACTIVITY:

1. **Part A:** Cheep, cheep, cheep, cheep.
   Make "pecking" actions with your fingers.
   — Flap, flap, flap, flap.
   Hook your thumbs under your arms, and make flapping movements.
   — Wiggle, wiggle, wiggle, wiggle.
   Sway hips from side to side.
   — Clap, clap, clap, clap.
   Clap your hands.
   — Repeat Part A three more times.
2. **Part B:** Swing–2–3–4–5–6–7–8.
   Hook right elbows with your partner and skip CW in a circle for eight counts.
   — Swing–2–3–4–5–6–7–8.
   Hook left elbows with your opposite partner and skip CCW in a circle for another eight counts.
   — Repeat Part B once more. But on the last four counts of the left elbow swing, everyone quickly form new groups of four and face each other, ready to begin the dance again.

RD–13 BUNNY HOP

FOCUS: Novelty dance

EQUIPMENT: Any popular music in 4/4 time; tape or record player

ORGANIZATION:

- This American line dance uses kicking and hopping steps. Teach the basic steps of the dance and have dancers practice in their own free space. Then have dancers form groups of six to eight. Each group scatters and stands in file formation, with members placing hands on the hips of the dancer in front.

DESCRIPTION OF ACTIVITY:

1. Kick right, kick right.
   Hop on the left foot and kick right foot twice to the right.
   Kick left, kick left.
   Hop on the right foot and kick left foot twice to the left.
2. Hop forward, hop back. Hop forward, then hop backward.
   Hop forward 3–4. *Hop forward four steps.*
   — Repeat this pattern around the play area.

RD—14 ALLEY CAT

FOCUS: Novelty dance

EQUIPMENT: "Alley Cat" from Dancecraft 73304 or Kimbo Records KIM 503-A;
tape or record player

ORGANIZATION:

• This American dance uses step-touch and jump-turn steps. Have dancers scatter around the play area and face you. Make sure everyone can see you.

DESCRIPTION OF ACTIVITY:

1. Right, touch; right, touch. Left, touch; left, touch.
   Step right foot to the right, then close right to left instep. Repeat. Step left foot to left, then close left foot to right instep. Repeat.
2. Right, back; right, back. Left, back; left, back.
   Reach back with right foot and touch floor behind. Touch right foot to left heel. Repeat. Do again with left foot.
3. Knee, knee; knee, knee.
   Touch right knee to left knee, then touch floor. Repeat. Touch left knee to right, then touch floor. Repeat.
4. Knee, knee, clap, and jump right.
   Raise and lower right knee once. Repeat with left. With weight on both feet, clap hands together once, then do ¼ jump-turn to right as you say "Meow!"
5. Repeat dance seven times, until you have turned completely around twice. On the last time through, repeat each step once only. End with a clap and jump.

RD—15 THE TWIST

FOCUS: Novelty dance

EQUIPMENT: "Let's Twist Again" by Chubby Checker, K-Tel NC 548;
tape or record player

ORGANIZATION:

• Demonstrate and teach the "twisting action." Have dancers practice individually at first, then pair up and have fun exploring different variations. Explain that the "twisting action" is similar to "towelling your backside and rubbing your feet into the ground."

DESCRIPTION OF ACTIVITY:

1. Let's do the Twist! Keeping your knees bent, swivel your body on the balls of your feet. Listen to the music and Twist in time to it. Move your arms freely to help the twisting action. Keep relaxed; loose.
2. Twist from a high level to a low level. How low can you go? Twist from a low to a high level.
3. Twist with your feet together, then gradually "twist" them further and further apart; gradually twist your feet close together again.
4. Twist and move sideways; around in a circle; jump up in the air, land, and keep twisting!
5. Now Twist with a partner. Twist down low; twist up high. One partner twist high; the other low, then reverse. Twist in a circle around each other. Twist in place, turning CW while your partner turns CCW. Change places as you twist. Invent another "Twisting" step with your partner.
   — Create a "Twisting routine" with your partner.

RD—16 THE HUSTLE

FOCUS: Disco dance

EQUIPMENT: "The Hustle" from Dancecraft DC-74528; tape or record player

ORGANIZATION:

- This American line dance involves dancers learning a foot-pattern routine. Any popular 4/4 music with a steady beat can be used. To begin, have dancers stand in waves of about six to ten dancers, all facing the same direction and spaced arm's length apart. When teaching the dance, face the same way as the dancers to avoid confusion.

DESCRIPTION OF ACTIVITY:

1. Back–2–3–4; Forward–2–3–4.
   Beginning on right foot, take three steps backward, swing left foot out in front as you lean back, and clap. Beginning on the left foot, take three steps forward, then place your right heel down in front with the toe up and clap.

2. Repeat Part 1, going backward for four counts; forward for four counts. Now you will move once to your right side and once to your left.

3. Side–Front–Side–Kick; Side–Front–Side–Kick.
   Beginning with right foot, take three steps to right side, crossing left foot in front of right. Place right foot down, and kick left foot to right and clap. Then reverse to the left, beginning with the left foot.

4. Step–Heel; Step–Heel.
   Step right foot in place, put left heel down, toe up; step left foot in place, put right heel down, toe up.

5. Jump forward–Hold; Jump forward–Hold. Jump–Jump–Click–Click.
   Jump forward with feet together, pause; jump backward, pause. Jump forward on two feet, jump backward on two feet; click heels together twice, pivoting on toes.

6. Touch–Forward–Touch–Backward; Touch–Touch–Touch–Turn.
   Touch right toe forward twice; touch right toe backward twice; touch right toe forward, backward, sideways, and pivot quarter turn to left on left foot, keeping right foot off the floor.

7. Repeat entire dance from the beginning, facing this new direction.

RD–17 GRAND MARCH AND VARIATIONS _____

FOCUS: Novelty mixer

EQUIPMENT: Marching music;
tape or record player

ORGANIZATION:

- Dancers learn controlled walking or marching rhythm and marching patterns. Have all the boys stand in a file along one side of the play area, while all the girls stand in a file along the other side of the play area. Everyone in the files faces the "foot" of the play area. You stand in the middle of the endline (the "head") of the play area, facing the files. Emphasize that leaders keep a steady pace, not a race!

DESCRIPTION OF ACTIVITY:

1. *March down the middle in twos.*
   Each file march forward to the foot of the play area, turn the corner, and continue toward the center of the foot. Meet a partner there, join inside hands, and march down the middle toward me, girl on boy's right. (Number odd couples one, three, five, etc., even couples, two, four, six, etc.)

2. *Odd to the left; even to the right.*
   When you reach me, the odd couples go left; even couples go right; and so on. March to the foot of the play area and turn the corner.

3. *March down the middle in fours.*
   Odd and even couples meet and march down the center, four aside.

4. *Couples separate.*
   When you approach me, odd couples go left; even couples go right. Meet again at foot of play area.

5. *Odd couples form arches.*
   Odd couples now form arches; even couples go under. Each couple continue around the sides of the play area to meet at the head.

6. *Even couples form arches.*
   Even couples now form arches; odd couples go under. Each continue around the sides of the play area to meet at the foot.

7. *Make arches and tunnels.*
   First odd couple arch over first even couple; then duck under the arch of the second even couple. Each couple continue to march, going over the first couple and under the next; then couples march around sides to the head of play area.

8. *Pass right through.*
   As you come toward each other, drop your partner's hand hold. One odd-numbered partner walk between two even-numbered partners, and continue walking to the foot of the play area.

9. *March down the center by fours. Four to the left; four to the right.*
   March down the center, four aside. The first four dancers go to the left; the second four go to the right, and so on. Meet at the foot of the play area.

10. *March down the center by eights. Chain together, eight by eight.*
    March down the center, eight aside, joining hands. Keep your hands joined. I will join hands with the dancer at either end of the first line and lead this group around the play area. The other lines of eight dancers, hook on until we form one long chain.

11. *Wind it up; wind it out.*
    I will wind up our long chain in a spiral formation; then when I reach center, turn and march in the opposite direction to unwind until we are in a long chain again.

12. *Back Home you go!*
    Boys go left; girls go right. Finish the way you started.

RD–18 THE CONGA

FOCUS: Novelty dance

EQUIPMENT: Calypso music;
tape or record player

ORGANIZATION:

- This South American party dance involves the basic walk and kick steps. Have dancers practice steps individually; then form groups of four to six dancers. Each group stands in file formation and places hands on hips of the dancer in front of them. As dancers become more confident with the dance steps, form longer files, until the whole class is in a single line.

DESCRIPTION OF ACTIVITY:

1. *Conga Step:*
   — Left, right, left, kick right.
     Walk forward, leading with the left foot (three counts); then kick the right foot to the side (one count).
   — Right, left, right, kick left.
     Walk forward, leading with the right foot (three counts); then kick the left foot to the side (one count).
2. *Dance:* Follow your leader around the play area using the Conga step. Make interesting patterns as you move.

RD–19 THE LIMBO

FOCUS: Novelty dance

EQUIPMENT: "Limbo Rock" by Chubby Checker from K-Tel NC548 or
"Limbo-Lower and Lower" from *Dance, Dance, Dance* album with The Emeralds, K-Tel NC634;
tape or record player;
one long rope or pole per group

ORGANIZATION:

- This challenging dance can be used as a Closing and involves flexibility, particularly of the back area. A long rope or bamboo or plastic pole make ideal "Limbo rods." Have one dancer demonstrate the "limbo action"; then let dancers practice at a suitable height before gradually lowering the pole. Have dancers form groups of six, get a pole, and find a free space. Check for good spacing.

DESCRIPTION OF ACTIVITY:

1. In your group, any two dancers hold the poles between you, at waist height. Other dancers, take turns trying to maneuver under the pole. Keep your "belly button upward"; do not let your hands touch the floor—only your feet! No part of you can touch the pole. Listen to and move with the music.
2. Continue to Limbo in turn, and gradually lower the pole. Who in your group will Limbo the lowest? Challenge another group!
3. *Limbo Contest:* Each group's "Limbo Champ" challenge the other groups' Champs to see who is the "Class Champ girl and boy"!

VARIATION:

Partner Limbo: Have dancers pair off, join inside hands, and limbo together.

FOCUS: Novelty dance

EQUIPMENT: "Salty Dog Rag" from Dancecraft DC-73304;

tape or record player

ORGANIZATION:

• This American foot-pattern dance involves the Brush-kick, Step-hop, and Walking as the basic steps. Demonstrate and have dancers practice the Brush-kick Step: Touch the floor lightly with the ball of the foot while swinging that foot forward. Have dancers pair off and each couple find a free space. Partners stand side by side, holding hands in the Skater's Position (right hand hold over left hand hold).

DESCRIPTION OF ACTIVITY:

1. ***Step–Behind–Step–Brush.***
Beginning with the right foot, step sideways to the right; step on left foot behind right foot; step on right again; then brush-kick left foot forward.

2. Repeat to left, beginning with the left foot.

3. ***Step-hop; step-hop; step-hop; step-hop.***
Take four Step-hops forward.

4. Repeat Parts 1, 2, and 3. On last Step-hop, turn to face partner.

5. ***Right–2–3–Brush; Left–2–3–Brush.***
Circle–Step-hop–Step-hop–Step-hop.
Face your partner and join left hands. Repeat Step 1 while moving away from your partner: step sideways on right foot, step left behind right, step on right again, and brush-kick left foot forward. Repeat to the left, beginning with the left foot and changing to a right hand hold. Then holding your partner's right hand shoulder high, turn in a circle with four Step-hops.

6. Repeat Part 5, changing again to the left hand hold.

7. Quickly pivot round to starting position to begin dance again. Repeat until end of music.

RD-21 JINGLE BELL ROCK

FOCUS: Novelty dance   **EQUIPMENT:** Any popular Christmas music;
                                    tape or record player

ORGANIZATION:

- This American foot dance involves the rocking step, brush-step, step-turn, and kick-step. Have dancers pair off and form a double circle, with partners joining inside hands and facing CCW. Note that the directions are for the outside partners; the inside partners do the reverse.

DESCRIPTION OF ACTIVITY:

1. *Rock forward; rock back; rock forward; rock back.*
   Rock forward onto your outside foot; rock back onto your inside foot. Repeat rocking sequence again.

2. *Walk forward right–left–right, Brush left;*
   Walk backward left–right–left, Brush right.
   Walk forward right foot, left foot, right foot, and brush the left foot forward. Walk backward left foot, right foot, left foot, and brush the right foot forward. Snap your fingers as you walk. Repeat walking sequence again.
   — Repeat Part 1.

3. *Right turn–turn–turn–kick; Left turn–turn–turn–kick.*
   Moving to the right, make three step-turns and kick right, on the fourth count. Moving to the left, do three step-turns and kick left.

4. Repeat from beginning.

RD-22 SLOSH

EQUIPMENT: "Whipped Cream" from Tijuana Brass;
                  tape or record player

ORGANIZATION:

- This American foot dance involves Walking, Foot-swinging, Turning, and Clapping. Have dancers find a free space and face you.

DESCRIPTION OF ACTIVITY:

1. *Step left, step right behind, Step left, swing right and clap.*
   Step left foot to left, step right foot behind left, step on left again, swing right foot in front of left, and clap hands.

2. *Step right, step left behind, Step right, swing left and clap.*
   Step right foot to right, step left foot behind right, step on right again, swing left foot in front of right, and clap hands.
   — Repeat Part 1.

3. Repeat Part 2, except swing left leg back and slap the left heel with right hand behind you.

4. *Elbow-knee touch, quarter-turn right, lift knee, clap.*
   Place your left foot down; lift right knee up and touch left elbow to right knee. Step on right foot and make a quarter-turn to the right. At the same time, lift the left knee and clap hands under it.

5. Repeat foot dance from beginning.

RD-23 POP! GOES THE WEASEL

FOCUS: Folk dance

EQUIPMENT: "Pop! Goes the Weasel" from Folkraft 1329; tape or record player

ORGANIZATION:

• This American Round dance involves Walking, Skipping, and Turning-under steps. Dancers make a circle of sets of threes, with each set facing CCW. Each set forms a triangle with one dancer in front and the other two side by side, behind, and holding inside hands. The front dancer reaches back to hold the outside hands of the back two dancers. Teach the words and encourage dancers to sing along!

DESCRIPTION OF ACTIVITY:

1. *All around the cobbler's bench; The monkey chased the weasel,*
   Each set take four forward skips; then take four backward skips.
2. *In and out and 'round about*
   Back dancers quickly let go of hands, and each back dancer, in turn, skip under the raised hand of the front dancer, who turns in place. Back dancers rejoin hands.
3. *Pop! goes the weasel!*
   Two back dancers raise your inside hands to form an arch; front dancer walk back under the arch releasing hand hold, "wave good-bye," and join hands with the dancers behind.
4. *A penny for a spool of thread; Another for a needle,*
   That's the way the money goes—Pop! goes the weasel!
   Repeat dance sequence in steps 1, 2, and 3 and sing the words.

RD-24 TENNESSEE WIG WALK

FOCUS: Mixer dance

EQUIPMENT: "Tennessee Wig Walk" from Kimbo KEA-1146; tape or record player

ORGANIZATION:

• This American Mixer involves the Side-step and "Boogie-woogie" step. Teach the "Boogie-woogie" step first, and have dancers practice: Pivot on your heels and move both toes left; pivot on your toes and move both heels left; then pivot on your heels and move both toes right; pivot on your toes and move both heels right. Have dancers pair off and form a double circle with partners facing each other. Directions are for outside partner; reverse for inside circle partner.

DESCRIPTION OF ACTIVITY:

1. *Step left, close right, step left, touch right and clap.*
   Step left, close right, step left again, touch right foot to left and clap hands at same time (four counts).
   Step right, close left, step right, touch left and clap.
   Step right, close left, step right again, touch left foot to right and clap hands at same time (4 counts).
   Repeat Part 1.
2. *Boogie-woogie to the left: Boogie-woogie to the right.*
   Do three "Boogie-woogie" steps to the left, pause (four counts); do three "Boogie-woogie" steps to the right, pause (four counts).
3. *Step left, close right, step left, close right.*
   Both partners, take two Side-steps to the left, positioning yourselves in front of a new partner (four counts).
4. *Slap thighs, clap hands together, clap partner's.*
   Slap your thighs, clap your hands together, then clap your partner's hands.
   — Repeat dance from the beginning with your new partner.

RD–25 TROIKA

FOCUS: Folk dance

EQUIPMENT: "Troika" from *Folk Dancing Upper Elementary*, Hoctor Products HLP-4027; tape or record player

ORGANIZATION:

- This traditional Russian Folk dance means "Three Horses" and involves dancers in groups of three, running and stamping. To begin, have the players of each group of three stand side by side around a large circle (like the spokes of a wheel), face CCW, and join inside hands shoulder high; outside hands on hips.

DESCRIPTION OF ACTIVITY:

1. *Run–2–3–4–5– . . . –16*
   Take sixteen running steps forward.

2. *Arch–2–3–4–5–6–7–8*
   Arch–2–3–4–5–6–7–8
   Dancer on the right-hand side, take eight small running steps under the arch formed by the other two dancers, who run in place. Middle dancer, follow the right dancer under the arch, turning in place, to face starting position.

   — Left-hand dancer, repeat.

3. *Circle–2–3–4– . . . –12, Stamp, Stamp, Stamp*
   Circle–2–3–4– . . . –12, Stamp-into line
   Each trio now join hands to make a circle and take twelve small running steps CW; then stamp three times in place. Take twelve running steps CCW, and stamp three more times while changing back to side-by-side formation and switching positions as well.

4. Repeat from the beginning.

VARIATIONS:

a. In Part 1, have trio take four steps diagonally to the right, four steps diagonally to left, then eight steps straight ahead.

b. *Troika Mixer:* On last three stamps, middle dancers run forward to the next group.

RD–26 DANISH FAMILY CIRCLE DANCE

FOCUS: Folk dance

EQUIPMENT: "Danish Family Circle Dance" from Dancecraft, DC-74518; tape or record player

ORGANIZATION:

- This Danish folk dance involves the Buzz-step and the Grand Right and Left pattern. Teach dancers the two different Buzz-steps: sideways or CW (CCW) in a circle. Have dancers pair off and form a large single circle, with partners side by side, hands joined, and everyone facing inward.

DESCRIPTION OF ACTIVITY:

1. *Buzz-Step–2–3–4–5– . . . –16*
   Step right with right foot; push with left, which is slightly behind and close to right.
2. *In 2–3–4; Back–2–3–4*
   In 2–3–4; Back–2–3–4
   Take four brisk walking steps to center, swinging your hands up to shoulder height. Return to place by walking backwards four steps. Repeat.
3. *Grand Right and Left.*
   Swing 2–3–4– . . . –16
   Shake right hands with your partner; then walk CW, passing your partner, to meet the next oncoming dancer, and shake left hands. Continue right and left hand shakes until you meet the seventh dancer. Join hands with this dancer and swing around with sixteen Buzz-steps: turn CW, pivoting on the ball of your right foot, and push with your left, which is just behind and close to right.
4. Repeat parts 2 and 3 to the end of the music.

RD–27 OH SUSANNA

FOCUS: Round Dance mixer

EQUIPMENT: "Oh Susanna" from *Folk Dances from Near and Far*, Merit Audio Visual MAV-1043; tape or record player

ORGANIZATION:

- The Grand Right and Left and the Promenade in the Skater's Position (standing side by side with right hands joined over joined left hands) are reviewed through this popular American dance. Have dancers, in pairs, form a single circle, all facing the center; girl partners stand to the right of their boy partners. Encourage dancers to sing along!

DESCRIPTION OF ACTIVITY:

1. *Forward–2–3–4; Back–2–3–4.*
   While boy partners clap, girl partners walk four steps forward to center; then walk four steps back to place.
   — Boy partners, repeat Part 1 while girls clap.
2. *Grand Right and Left you go!*
   Partners, face each other, shake right hands; then walk forward, passing your partner, to meet the next oncoming dancer and shake left hands. Continue right and left hand shakes around the circle, stopping at the fifth dancer, who becomes your new partner.
3. *Promenade your partner–5–6–7– . . . –16.*
   New partners, walk CCW, side by side, with hands in the Skater's Position, singing "Oh Susanna, don't you cry for me . . ." for sixteen steps. Then promenade your partner for sixteen skipping steps CCW. Turn on the last step to face center and repeat the dance.

RD—28 LA RASPA

FOCUS: Folk dance

EQUIPMENT: "La Raspa" from Folkraft 1188 or *Folk Dances from Near and Far*, Merit Audio Visual MAV-1043; tape or record player

ORGANIZATION:

• This Mexican folk dance means "the rasp" or "the file" in action and involves the Bleking and Step-hop steps and elbow swinging. Review the Bleking Step first. For the dance, have dancers pair off and scatter around the play area.

DESCRIPTION OF ACTIVITY:

1. **The Bleking Step:** Face me and place your hands on your hips. Hop lightly on the left foot, extending the right heel forward to touch the floor; then hop lightly on the right foot, extending the left heel forward. Practice. Now face your partner, turning slightly CCW away so that you are standing right shoulder to right shoulder. Do three fast bleking steps, pause; then clap hands twice. Repeat this sequence standing left shoulder to left shoulder.

2. **Step-Hop:** Step on one foot, hop on the same foot. Practice Step-hopping in place. Step-hop in circle CW for eight steps; CCW for eight.

3. **La Raspa:**

   Part I: Fast–fast–fast; clap–clap:
   Facing diagonally, right shoulder to right shoulder, do three fast bleking steps; pause on the fourth count; and clap hands twice. On the pause, quickly change to face diagonally, left shoulder to left shoulder, and repeat sequence. Do Part I a total of eight times, changing the diagonal direction each time the sequence is repeated.

   — **Part II: Swing–2–3– . . . –7, Clap; Swing–2–3– . . . –7, Clap:**
   Partners hook right elbows, bend left elbows, and point left hands upward. Do right-elbow-swings with seven Step-hops; release hands and clap on the eighth count. Then do left-elbow-swings with seven Step-hops; release hands and clap on the eighth count.

   — Repeat Part II again.

   — Repeat entire dance from the beginning.

VARIATION:

Have couples form a single circle; partners facing. In Part II, do a Left-and-Right Grand around the circle; then repeat Part I with a new partner.

FOCUS: Folk dance

EQUIPMENT: Tambourine;
Mediterranean music in 4/4 time;
tape or record player

ORGANIZATION:

• Review the Grapevine-Step, which is basic to many Mediterranean folk dances. At first, have dancers practice the step individually; then in a line formation; and finally in a circle, with hands joined. Use a tambourine to beat out the rhythm; then have dancers move to the music. Have dancers perform the steps slowly at first, gradually accelerating to dance tempo.

DESCRIPTION OF ACTIVITY:

1. ***Step right, left in front;***
   Step right, left in front.
   Step right foot right, cross left foot in front of right; step right foot right, and cross left foot in front. Practice this foot pattern.

2. ***Step right, left behind;***
   Step right, left behind.
   Step right foot right, then cross left foot behind; step right foot, right, then cross left foot behind. Practice this foot pattern.

3. ***Grapevine-Step*** (Combination of Steps 1 and 2):
   Step right, left in front;
   Step right, left behind.
   Step right foot right, cross left foot in front of right; step right foot right, and cross left foot behind. Practice this foot pattern.

1 – 2.

4.

4. ***Line Dance:*** Stand side by side and join hands to form a long line. Grapevine-step around the play area to the beat of my tambourine; then listen to the music and grapevine-step to its beat.

5. ***Circle Dance:*** Form a single circle, facing inward. Grapevine-step CW to the beat of the music; then grapevine-step CCW.

FOCUS: Folk dance

EQUIPMENT: "Mayim" from Folkraft 1108; tape or record player

ORGANIZATION:

• This Jewish folk dance involves the Grapevine-Step (tscherkessia) and running steps. Mayim means "water." The dance movements express the joy of finding water in a very dry land and emulate the motion of the waves breaking on the shore. Have dancers form a single circle, hands joined and held down; everyone facing inward.

DESCRIPTION OF ACTIVITY:

1. ***Step right, left in front;***
   Step right, left behind. (four times)
   Moving CW, perform four Grapevine-steps. Use a light, springy step, accenting the first step.

2. ***Center–2–3–4; Back–2–3–4.***
   Beginning with your right foot, take four running steps into the center. On the first step, leap lightly, bending the knee. As you move in, gradually raise your joined hands above your heads. Then return to place with four running steps, and gradually lower your joined hands down to sides. Repeat sequence again.

3. ***Run–Toe–Touch–Clap:***

   — Move CW with three running steps, beginning with right foot. Turn to face center.

   — Hop on right foot, touch left across front to right side; hop on right, touch left to side. Repeat hopping sequence three more times.

   — Hop on left foot, touch right foot in front to left side, and clap hands. Hop on left, touch right to side, and swing arms out to sides, shoulder high. Repeat hop-clap-arm swing sequence three more times.

4. Repeat the dance from the beginning.

RD–31 LONGWAYS SET, CASTING OFF, SASHAYS

FOCUS: Folk dance

EQUIPMENT: Music in 4/4 time; tape or record player

ORGANIZATION:

- Dancers review the Longways Set, Casting Off, and Sashay formations. Have dancers each find a partner and then form a set of six pairs. In each set, partners face each other in separate lines, about 3 meters (10 feet) apart. Dancers in each line space themselves arm's length apart. The couple nearest the music is the Head couple; the couple furthest away is at the "foot" of the set.

DESCRIPTION OF ACTIVITY:

1. **Weaving March:** While one line stays still, the leader of the other line, march your file of dancers in and out of the stationary line and back to place. Switch roles and repeat.

2. **Single Casting Off:** Head couple, turn away from your partner and skip outside your file to the foot of the set. Next couple, repeat.

3. **Double Casting Off:** Head couple, join inside hands, turn left, and skip outside the files to the foot of the set. Next couple, repeat, but turn right. Alternate left and right casting off.

4. **Whole Line Casting Off:** Each Head partner turn to the outside and lead your file as you skip to the foot of the set. Meet your partner there, join hands, and skip up the set to your original places.

5. **Sashay Down:** Head couple, holding both hands, side-step between the two lines toward the foot of the set to join the end of your lines. Next couple, repeat.

6. **Sashay Up:** Couple at the foot of the set, hold both hands and side-step between the two lines toward the head couple to join the front of your lines. Next couple at foot of set, repeat.

7. **Passing Through:** The two lines move toward each other and pass through so that the two middle players from one line are between two middle players from the other line. Turn around; then pass back through to original places.

8. Each Longways Set design a routine using three or four of the above formations. After practicing, perform your routine for the class.

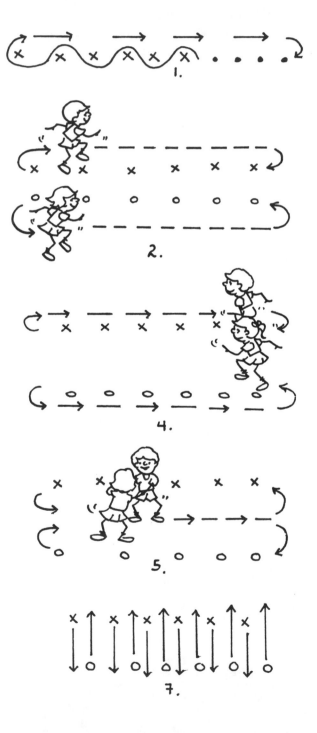

RD-32 VIRGINIA REEL

FOCUS: Folk dance

EQUIPMENT: "Virginia Reel" from *Folk Dancing Upper Elementary*, Hoctor Products, HLP-4027; tape or record player

ORGANIZATION:

- This American folk dance involves skipping, arm swinging, do-si-do, sashay, side-stepping, and casting off. If possible, form longways sets of six pairs per set. Partners face each other across the set, spaced about 3 meters (10 feet) apart from each other and arm's length apart from the dancer on either side. The Head couple is closest to the music. "Walk" couples through the figures at first; then have them listen to the music and perform at the music's tempo. Dancers also learn how to "Reel the Set." Demonstrate the figure and have couples practice slowly at "walking" tempo; then perform the Reel at the music's tempo.

DESCRIPTION OF ACTIVITY:

1. *Forward–2–3–4; Back–6–7–8.*
   Each line take four skipping steps toward the other. Partners greet each other with a "High Ten," then take four skipping steps back to place. Repeat.
2. *Right Elbow-Swing–3–4; Back–6–7–8;*
   Left Elbow-Swing–3–4, Back–6–7–8.
   Skip to the middle, meet your partner, link right elbows, and swing around once; then skip back to place (eight counts). Repeat, linking left elbows and swinging around once.
3. *Two-Hand Swing 3 4; Back–6–7–8.*
   Skip to the middle, meet your partner, join both hands, swing CW around once, and skip back to place.
4. *Do-Si-Do–3–4; Back–6–7–8.*
   Skip toward your partner, pass right shoulder to right shoulder, back to back, and return to place, passing left shoulders.
5. *Head couple, sashay down–3–4– . . . –8; sashay up–3–4– . . . –8.*
   Head couple, join hands and side-step for eight counts down the set; then side-step back up to place. Other couples clap and foot-stomp in time to the music!
6. *Reel the Set:*
   Head couple, skip toward each other, do a right elbow-swing one-and-a-half times around. Then separate and skip toward the opposite line. The "Head boy partner" turn the second girl dancer around once with a left elbow-swing, while the "Head girl partner" do a left elbow-swing with the second boy dancer.
   - Head couple, then meet in the center of the set again for a right elbow-swing. Separate and skip to the opposite third dancer for a left elbow-swing.
   - Continue down the set in this way, swinging partner with a right elbow-swing; swinging opposite dancer with a right elbow-swing.
   - When you have "reeled" all five couples and are now at Foot of set, do a right elbow-swing halfway around (so that you are on your starting sides), join hands, and Sashay back to the Head of the set. Skip back into place.
7. *Cast Off!–3–4–5–6–7–8.*
   Head couple, cast off: Each partner, turn outward and lead your file as you skip down to the foot of the set. Everyone else follow in order.
   - At the foot, Head couple, form an arch by joining hands overhead.
   - Each pair, in order, side-step through the arch and up the set; then separate into your original lines.
8. The second couple now becomes the new Head couple to start the dance again. Repeat the dance until each pair has had a chance to be the Head couple.

RD–33 THE SCHOTTISCHE AND VARIATIONS _____

FOCUS: Folk dance

EQUIPMENT: "Green and Gold Schottische" from *Dance, Dance, Dance* album with The Emeralds, K-Tel NC 634; tape or record player

ORGANIZATION:

• Dancers learn and practice the Schottische and Step-Hop steps, individually, then with a partner, in various combinations. Note that any music with a steady 4/4 beat can be used. To begin, dancers form a large circle, space arm's length apart, and all face CW. Have dancers listen to the music first; then practice the steps without the music, then with the music.

DESCRIPTION OF ACTIVITY:

1. *The Schottische Step:* Beginning with your right foot, step right, step left, step right, and hop on right; step left, step right, step left, and hop on left. Repeat pattern, slowly at first; then pick up the tempo. Now listen to the music. Then with the music do eight Schottische Steps CW; then eight CCW. Repeat.

2. *The Step-Hop Step:* Beginning on your right foot, step then hop on right foot; step then hop on left foot; repeat around the circle for eight Step-Hops. Now in place, do four Step-Hops, circling CW, then four Step-Hops CCW.

3. *The Schottische Pattern:* Moving CW around the circle, do four Schottische steps, followed by four Step-Hops. Repeat.

   — Repeat again, but Step-Hop in place circling CW; next time Step-Hop CCW. Continue in this way.

4. *Partner Schottische Pattern:* Find a partner, join inside hands, and stand side by side around the circle. Check for good spacing. Starting with your inside feet, do four Schottische steps, followed by four Step-Hops in line of direction.

5. *Step-Hop Variations:*

   — One partner step-hop in place, while the other partner step-hops, circling under the stationary partner's raised hand. Switch roles on the next Step-Hop sequence.

   — Both partners circle away from each other while step-hopping.

   — "Wring-the-Dishrag" with partner while step-hopping in place.

6. *Horse and Buggy Schottische* (Folkraft 1166): To dance this popular American Schottische, have dancers pair off, form sets of four, with one couple behind the other, in a double circle. Everyone faces CCW. Each pair joins inside hands and gives outside hands to the other couple, as shown. Have dancers try this dance to popular music with a regular 4/4 beat!

   — *Step, step, step, hop (four times).*
   Starting with the outside foot, and moving forward, do four Schottische steps.

   — *Step-hop, step-hop, step-hop, step-hop.*
   Front couple, drop your inside hands, and step-hop around the outside of the back couple, who step-hop forward. Front couple then rejoin hands behind the other couple, so that your positions are now reversed.

   — Repeat dance from the beginning.

VARIATION:

On Part 2, have the front couple continue to hold hands as they step-hop backward under the upraised hands of the back couple, who step-hop while turning away from each other to untwist and become the front couple.

RD–34 THE TWO-STEP AND POLKA-STEP

FOCUS: Folk dance

EQUIPMENT: *Folk Dances for Everyone,* Merit Audio Visual MAV-1044; tape or record player

ORGANIZATION:

• Review the Two-Step first, then the Polka-Step. Have dancers "walk" through these steps slowly without music, then at the music's tempo. Any bright, lively music with an uneven rhythm can be used to practice the Two-Step and Polka-Step. Dancers are also introduced to the Closed Position. To begin, have each dancer find a free space, facing you.

DESCRIPTION OF ACTIVITY:

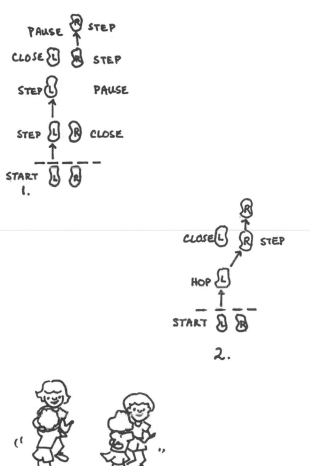

1. ***The Two-Step:*** Stand with feet together. Step forward on left foot, close right foot to left, step left foot forward again, and pause; step right foot forward, close left to right, step right foot forward again, and pause.

   — Practice this step, moving in a forward direction and saying: "Step–Close–Step–Pause; Step–Close–Step–Pause."

2. ***The Polka-Step:*** This is like the Two-Step with a "hop" added to the step sequence: Hop left, step right foot forward, close left to right, step right foot forward. Repeat, beginning with a hop on the right foot.

   — Practice Polka-Step moving in a forward direction and saying: "Hop–Step–Close–Step; Hop–Step–Close–Step."

3. ***Partner Two-Step:*** Find a partner and stand facing each other. The boy partner hold the girl partner's right hand in your left hand out to the side, at about shoulder height, bending your elbows. Then place your right hand on the girl partner's back, just below the left shoulder blade. Girl partner, rest your left arm on the boy's upper arm and your left hand on his shoulder. This is called the Closed Position.

   — Practice the Two-Step to the music being played; practice the Polka-Step.

VARIATION:

Gallop Method of Teaching the Polka-Step: Make two gallops with the left foot leading, then two gallops with the right foot leading. Continue this pattern, but gradually speed up the tempo; then add the Polka-hop.

RD–35 ACE OF DIAMONDS

FOCUS: Folk dance

EQUIPMENT: *Folk Dances for Everyone,* Merit Audio Visual MAV-1044; tape or record player

ORGANIZATION:

• This Danish folk dance involves the Bleking and Polka-Steps. Have dancers form a double circle, with partners facing.

DESCRIPTION OF ACTIVITY:

1. *Clap–Stamp; Walk–2–3–4–5–6*
   Clap–Stamp; Walk–2–3–4–5–6.
   On the first count, clap your own hands. On the second count, stamp your right foot on the floor, and put both hands on your hips. Then hook right elbows with your partner and circle once around to place, using six walking steps. Repeat the above, but stamp your left foot and hook left elbows.
2. *Hop on left; Hop on right; Hop on left.*
   Do three quick Bleking steps by hopping on the left foot and placing the right heel forward; hopping on the right and placing the left heel forward; then hopping again on left foot and placing the right heel forward.
3. *Polka–2–3–4–. . .–16.*
   Do sixteen Polka-Steps around the floor.

VARIATION:

In Part 3, replace the sixteen Polka-Steps with eight Side-Steps CCW, then eight Side-Steps CW.

RD–36 TANTOLI

FOCUS: Folk dance

EQUIPMENT: "Tantoli" from RCA LPM 1621; tape or record player

ORGANIZATION:

• The basic steps used in this Swedish round dance are the Heel-toe, Polka-Step, and Step-hop. Have dancers in pairs form a double circle and face CCW with inside hands joined and outside hands on hips.

DESCRIPTION OF ACTIVITY:

1. *Heel-toe, Polka; Heel-toe, Polka; Heel-toe, Polka.*
   Starting on your outside foot, touch your heel in front, then touch your toe in place, and do one Polka-step. Repeat this sequence three times.
2. *Step-hop; Step-hop; Step-hop; Step-hop.*
   Hook right elbows with your partner and turn with four Step-hops in place. Then hook left elbows and turn with four Step-hops in place.
3. *Step-hop in place–4–5–6–7–8.*
   Partners face each other. Boy partner, put your hands on girl's waist; girl partner, put your hands on boy's shoulders. In this Shoulder-Waist Position, take eight Step-hops turning CCW in place.
4. Repeat dance from the beginning.

VARIATION:

Substitute the Two-Step for the Polka-Step on Part 1.

FOCUS: Folk dance

EQUIPMENT: "Klappdans" from Folkraft 1419 or RCA's *Folk Dance for Fun* LPM 1624; tape or record player

ORGANIZATION:

- This Swedish folk dance involves the Polka-Step and Rhythm-clapping. Have couples form a double circle, standing side by side and facing CCW, with girl partner on the boy's right and inside hands joined.

DESCRIPTION OF ACTIVITY:

1. Everyone take eight Polka-Steps forward, starting on your outside foot. Throughout the eight steps, swing joined hands forward and back while turning your body face to face, then back to back.

2. In Closed Position, take eight Polka-Steps around the circle.

3. Now face your partner, with your own hands on hips. Boys bow as girls curtsy; then both clap own hands three times. Repeat again.

   — Then partners, clap each other's right hand, then own hands, then each other's left hand, then own hands again.

   — Clap your partner's right hand while turning once around to the left; face your partner and stamp three times.

   — Bow to your partner and clap own hands three times. Repeat.

   — With left hand on your hip, shake your right forefinger at your partner; then reverse, shaking your left forefinger.

   — Clap your partner's right hand and take two walking steps to turn left about. Finish facing your partner and stamp three times.

4. Do sixteen Polka-Steps forward, moving CCW. On the last two Polka-Steps, boy partners move forward to new partners, while girl partners move in place. Join inside hands with new partner and repeat the dance from the beginning.

VARIATIONS:

Repeat dance using the Two-Step instead of the Polka-Step.

FOCUS: Basic calls

EQUIPMENT: Square dance or country music; tape or record player

ORGANIZATION:

• Dancers review the basic square dance calls and practice the movements. The Shuffle-Step (a quick walk or half-glide step) is the basic movement step, rather than running or skipping. To begin, have dancers scatter around the play area.

DESCRIPTION OF ACTIVITY:

Move in time to the music by using the Shuffle-Step. Each time you hear a square dance call, find a different partner; then together perform the movement.

— **Hit the Trail:** Shuffle-step in time to the music, moving in different directions.

— **Stop, Clap, and Stomp:** Stop where you are and keep time to the music by clapping and foot stomping.

— **Honor Your Partner; Honor Your Corner:** Bow to a dancer, then bow to another.

— **Allemande Right (Left):** Join right (left) hands with a dancer and shuffle turn in place.

— **Go Forward and Back:** Shuffle-step forward three steps and a touch toward a dancer who is moving toward you in the same way. Then move back to place with three shuffle-steps and a touch.

— **Do-si-do:** Cross arms in front at chest level, pass a dancer right shoulder to right shoulder, back to back, and shuffle-step back to place.

— **Right (Left) Elbow-Swing:** Hook right (left) elbows with a dancer and turn once around in place.

— **Two-Hand Swing:** Partners join both hands, lean away from each other, and circle CW once around.

— **Waist Swing:** Boy partner, place hands on girl partner's waist; girl place hands on boy's shoulder; then turn once around in place.

RD-39 STARS AND CIRCLES

FOCUS: Square dance figures

EQUIPMENT: Square dance or country music; tape or record player

ORGANIZATION:

- Have dancers form groups of four and find a free space. Within each group, have dancers pair off and each pair face the other. Use the terms *right partner* and *left partner,* rather than *boy* and *girl.* If mixed pairs, the girl should be on the boy's right. At any time, use the "Hit the Trail" signal and have dancers separate and form new groups.

DESCRIPTION OF ACTIVITY:

1. *Turns:* Practice the following turns with your partner:

   — Allemande Right, Do-Si-Do, Left-elbow-Swing.

2. *Circle to the (Right) Left:* All join hands and circle once around CCW or CW.

3. *Right-hand Star:* Hold right arms at the wrist, at shoulder level of the dancer in front of you, and shuffle-step CW once around.

   — *Left-hand Star:* Hold left wrist of the dancer in front of you and shuffle-step CCW once around.

4. *Swing your opposite and swing your partner:* Left partner, walk toward the opposite right partner and right-elbow-swing once around. Then both dancers, walk back to your partner and swing once around.

   — *Swing your partner and swing your opposite:* Do the reverse.

5. *Birdie in the cage and three hands round:* One dancer go into the center, stomp feet and clap hands; while the other three dancers join hands and circle CW once around.

   — *Birdie hops out and the crow hops in:* Center dancer, join the circle and another dancer go in.

6. *Go to the middle and come back out; go to the middle and give a little shout:* Each group of four join hands and, raising arms upward, shuffle-step toward center of circle. Lower arms as you shuffle-step back to place. Repeat and add a shout "Ya-hoo!"

RD–40 GREENSLEEVES

FOCUS: Folk dance

EQUIPMENT: "Greensleeves" from *Folk Dances for Beginners*, Merit Audio Visual, MAV-1042;
tape or record player

ORGANIZATION:

- This English folk dance involves the Shuffle-Step and forming Right- and Left-hand Stars and Circles. Have dancers pair off and form a circle of pairs; everyone facing CCW; partners side by side. Then around the circle, combine two pairs to form groups of four. In each group, designate one pair as Couple A; the other pair as Couple B, as shown.

DESCRIPTION OF ACTIVITY:

1. *Shuffle–2–3–4– . . . 16.*
   All couples shuffle briskly forward for sixteen counts.

2. *Right-hand Star–3–4–5–6–7–8;*
   Left-hand Star–3–4–5–6–7–8.
   Couple A turn to face Couple B. Do a Right-hand Star for eight counts. Change to a Left-hand Star for another eight counts. On the last step, Couple A's turn to face CCW again.

3. *Turn the sleeves inside out.*
   Couple B form an arch with raised inside hands; then shuffle forward toward Couple A, who shuffles four steps backward under the arch. Couple A, now form an arch and shuffle forward toward Couple B, who takes four steps backward under the arch. Repeat this figure again.

4. Repeat entire dance from the beginning.

RD–41 BASIC SQUARE DANCE FORMATION

FOCUS: Square dance

EQUIPMENT: Square dance or country music; tape or record player

ORGANIZATION:

Review "Setting the Square," its positions, and a variety of common square dance figures; then practice pattern calls and figures in a routine. Have dancers pair off and form groups of four couples.

DESCRIPTION OF ACTIVITY:

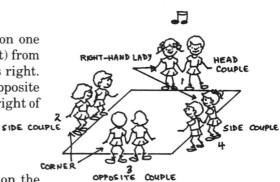

1. *Setting the Square:* Each couple of the group stand on one side of the square, facing inward, about 3 meters (10 feet) from the other pairs. The girl partner is always on the boy's right. Head Couple, with your backs to the music, is 1; the Opposite Couple is 3; Side Couples are 2 and 4. Couple 2 is to the right of the Head Couple.

2. *Positions:*
   — *Partner:* Each member of the pair.
   — *Corner, corner lady, or left-hand lady:* Dancer on the boy's left.
   — *Right-hand lady:* Dancer in the couple to the boy's right.
   — *Opposite or opposite lady:* Dancer directly across the set.
   — *Home:* Each couple's starting position.
   — *Active or leading couple:* The couple designated by the caller to perform an action.

3. *Square Dance Figures:*
   — *Honor your partner:* Bow to your partner.
   — *Honor your corner:* Bow to the corner, who bows back to you.
   — *Swing your partner (corner):* Partner stand side by side, right hip to right hip. Each put your right arm around partner's opposite side at hip. Shuffle once around each other, leaning slightly away.
   — *Allemande left:* Boy partner face your corner, hook left elbows, and shuffle once around the corner, returning to your partner.
   — *Promenade:* Each couple join right hands over left joined hands (skater's position), and walk side by side in a CW direction once around; then return to home position.

4. Practice the following Routine:
   — Honor your partner; Honor your corner; Circle left; Do-si-do partner; Swing your corner; Girls' Star right; Boys' Star left; Allemande left; and Promenade home; Head couples bow; Side couples bow.

VARIATION:

In each set, have girls stand in place while boys move one position right to join a new partner. Combine calls and figures to form another routine.

RD–42 SOLOMON LEVI

FOCUS: Square dance

EQUIPMENT: "Solomon Levi" from MacGregor 007-4A (with calls); tape or record player

ORGANIZATION:

- This square dance uses the Shuffle-Step, Swing, Allemande Left, and Grand Right and Left, and Promenade. Have dancers form Square Dance Sets of four couples, with girls on boys' rights.

DESCRIPTION OF ACTIVITY:

1. ***First couple separate, go 'round the outside track.***
   Head couples, split, turning in opposite directions (boy partner turn left; girl turn right) and shuffle-step around outside the set.

2. ***Keep a-goin' round the set and pass a-comin' back.***
   Head couples, continue shuffling to Home position; then keep going.

3. ***Pass right by your partner; salute your corners all. Everyone swing your honey; swing her high and low.***
   Head couple, pass by each other; then boy partners turn to your corner girls and bow; then swing your partners.

4. ***Allemande left with left hand and around the ring you go. A grand old right and left. Walk on your heel and toe and meet your honey, give her a twirl, and around the ring you go.***
   Boy partner, extend left hand to corner, walk around corner, and face partner. Extend right hand to partner, left to next girl, alternating right and left hands, until you meet your partner. Swing partner; then promenade around the set.

5. Sing chorus as you promenade: ***"Oh, Solomon Levi, tra la la la la la; Oh, Solomon Levi, tra la la la la la."***

6. Repeat dance until each couple has had a turn at being the Head couple.

BOW   CORNER   3. SWING

ALLEMANDE LEFT   GRAND RIGHT & LEFT   PROMENADE

4.

RD-43 RED RIVER VALLEY

FOCUS: Square dance

EQUIPMENT: "Red River Valley" from Folkraft 1056; tape or record player

ORGANIZATION:

- The square dance basics are reinforced through this American square dance, which uses the Shuffle-Step, Swing, and Stars. Have dancers form Square Dance Sets of four couples, with girls on boys' rights.

DESCRIPTION OF ACTIVITY:

1. ***All join hands in the valley.***
   And circle to the left and to the right.
   Everyone in the set join hands and shuffle four steps to the left, then four steps to the right.

2. ***And you swing the girl in the valley.***
   Now swing that Red River Gal.
   Boy partner swing corner, then return to swing your own partner.

SWING

3. ***Now you lead right down the valley,***
   And you circle to the left and to the right.
   Couples 1 and 3 shuffle step to the right, join hands with the couple there, then shuffle four steps around to the left; shuffle back four steps to the right.

4. ***Four ladies star in the valley,***
   Now swing with the Red River Gal.
   Girls do a Right-hand Star, then swing once around with partner.

5. ***Same couples to the left down the valley***
   And you circle to the left and to the right.
   Couples 1 and 3 shuffle step to the left, join hands with the couple there, then shuffle four steps around to the left; shuffle four steps to the right.

6. ***Now two gents star in the valley,***
   And you swing that Red River Gal.
   Boys do a Right-hand Star, then swing your partner.

7. Repeat dance, with Couples 2 and 4 taking the active role.

RD—44 CHAINS AND CURTSY TURNS

FOCUS: Square dance basics

EQUIPMENT: Square dance music; tape or record player

ORGANIZATION:

• Have dancers form Square Dance Sets of four couples, with girls on boys' rights.

DESCRIPTION OF ACTIVITY:

1. *Curtsy Turn:* Boy partner, take the girl's left hand in your left and put your right arm around the girl's waist. Now turn her to your left so that you walk backward, while she walks forward, around in place until you are both facing the center of the square.

2. *Ladies Chain:* The two girls of Couples 1 and 3, cross over the opposite boy partner, touching right hands as you pass each other. Girls, when you reach the opposite boy, join left hands and Curtsy Turn. On "Chain right back," girls, cross back to your partner in the same way. Now the girls of Couples 2 and 4 repeat the Ladies Chain.

3. *Four Ladies Grand Chain:* All four girls form a Right-hand Star and move CW, halfway around the square to the opposite boy, who gives you a Curtsy Turn. On "Four Ladies Chain right back," girls again form a Right-Hand Star and shuffle back to your partner, who gives a Curtsy Turn.

4. *Square Dance Routine:* Together, in your Square Dance Set, make a routine that involves a Curtsy Turn, a Ladies Chain or Grand Chain and Chain right back, a Grand right and left, and an Allemande left your Corner.

RD—45 POP! GOES THE WEASEL

FOCUS: Square dance

EQUIPMENT: "Pop! Goes the Weasel" from Folkraft 1329; tape or record player

ORGANIZATION:

• This American square dance involves the Balance-Step, Circle, and Under the Arch figures. Have dancers form Square Dance Sets of four couples, with girls on boys' rights.

DESCRIPTION OF ACTIVITY:

1. *The Head couple, lead to the right, and balance there so easy.*
   Head couple, turn to the couple on your right, Couple 2. Both couples "balance" by taking a short step forward and back with a slight bow or curtsy.

2. *Now join hands and circle left.*
   Head couple and Couple 2 join hands and circle CW around to place, taking four shuffle steps.

3. *Pop! goes the weasel!*
   Head couple pop under the arch formed by Couple 2, meet Couple 3, and repeat Parts 1 and 2.

4. Head Couple, continue then to Couple 4. Repeat the entire sequence of balancing, circling, and shuffling under the arch.

5. When the Head couple returns to place, Couple 2 then lead off to your right, and so on around the Square until each Couple has had a turn at leading the action.

RD—46 IT'S A SMALL WORLD

FOCUS: Square dance

EQUIPMENT: Walt Disney records;
tape or record player

ORGANIZATION:

• This square dance reinforces the Chain and Curtsy Turn figures learned. Have dancers form Square Dance Sets of four couples, with girls on boys' right.

DESCRIPTION OF ACTIVITY:

1. *Join your hands, make a ring.*
   You circle left and then left allemande that corner girl.
   Your partner then you swing.
   Swing that girl around and then
   Circle left, then boys allemande left your corner, then swing your partner.
   — *Boys Star Left one time around and then*
     Do an Allemande Right with a partner girl.
     Your corners Allemande.
     Boys star left for eight counts, then allemande right with your partner for four counts; allemande left your corner for four counts.
   — *You come back one and promenade, go walking*
     around the town. Though the mountains divide, the oceans
     are wide, It's a small world after all.
     Promenade your partner for sixteen counts.
2. *Four Girls chain across that ring in time,*
   Turn and chain the girls across,
   Go walking back you'll find. Do an allemande that corner girl.
   And Grand Right and Left, go hand in hand around that ring your run,
   Meet your partner Do-Si-Do, go back and then swing that corner girl.
   You promenade that land. Though the mountains
   divide and the oceans are wide. It's a small world after all.

RD—47 DANCE-MAKING

FOCUS: Folk and square dance basics;
creativity; cooperation

EQUIPMENT: Square, folk dance, or popular music;
tape or record player;
recording paper and pencil per group

ORGANIZATION:

• Working in groups of eight, dancers create their own folk and square dances. Ensure groups are well spaced apart. Encourage good participation by everyone in the group. Provide ample time for groups to develop, practice, and refine their dances, and provide opportunity for each group to teach their dance to the other groups. You may wish to list on a card the folk dance and square dance basics taught in this section and provide a copy for each group.

DESCRIPTION OF ACTIVITY:

1. *Folk Dance-Making:* In your group of eight, choose one dancer to be the recorder. Using the basic folk dance steps that you have learned, design a folk dance of your own. You may use folk dance music or music of your choice. Include at least six folk dance steps. Have the recorder write your dance routine on paper. Work in counts of four, eight, or sixteen.
2. *Hoe-Down Time:* Using the square dance pattern calls and figures you have learned, design a square dance that your group can perform to the class. Again work in counts of four, eight, or sixteen. Choose one member of your group to be the Caller for your Square Dance. The recorder should write your dance routine on paper.

FOCUS: Equipment manipulation; rhythmical movement

EQUIPMENT: One rhythm ribbon per player; music with a strong 4/4 beat; tape or record player

ORGANIZATION:

• Make gymnastic ribbons by attaching a 4- to 5-meter (12- to 15-foot) length of plastic, synthetic, or silk ribbon to a 50-centimeter (20-inch) long dowel. Use a fishing line swivel and trace, screw-eye, and about 30 centimeters (12 inches) of fishing line between the two parts, as illustrated. Have each player get a ribbon and scatter facing you. Practice swinging, circling, figure-8, spiral, and snake movements while walking or jogging in place. Experiment using full arm, forearm, and wrist movements.

DESCRIPTION OF ACTIVITY:

1. **Windshield Washers:** Swing ribbon from side to side.
   Traffic Cops: Swing ribbon forward and back.
   Helicopters: Circle ribbon overhead.
   Propellers: Circle ribbon in front.
   Wheels: Circle ribbon at either side.
   Butterflies: Make figure-8s in front.
   Ribbons: Make figure-8s overhead.
   Bows: Make figure-8s on either side.

2. **Coils:** Make bigger and bigger circles; then smaller and smaller circles.
   Zingers: Make spirals from left to right and from right to left.
   Air Snakes: Continuously raise and lower wrist to make snakes in the air.
   Floor Snakes: Lower arm so ribbon snakes along the floor.

VARIATIONS:

a. Challenge players to repeat movements while holding ribbon in nondominant hand.

b. Add footwork that complements ribbon movement.

RD-49 RHYTHM SHAKERS

FOCUS: Cardiovascular endurance; equipment manipulation

EQUIPMENT: Two shakers per player; music with a strong 4/4 beat; tape or record player

ORGANIZATION:

- To make shakers, put 45 milliliters (three tablespoons) of popcorn kernels into a small plastic food container. Punch two holes in the opposite sides of the container near the lid and thread 25 centimeters (10 inches) of elastic through the holes. Knot the ends of the elastic to make a handle that fits children's hands snugly. To begin, have players get two shakers, strap shaker over each hand, and stand in lines of six to eight players, all facing you.

DESCRIPTION OF ACTIVITY:

1. **Polka-Step:** Pretend to strum a guitar while hopping on right foot and lifting left; then hopping on left foot and lifting right. Repeat eight times.

2. **Knee Slaps:** Hop on the left foot, raise right knee, and slap it with both hands. Repeat four times. Then hop on the right foot, raise left knee, and slap it four times.

3. **Diagonal Run:** Run four steps toward the right corner; pivot on the left foot once around while shaking right hand overhead; then run back to where you started. Now shake hands at sides while touching alternate heels to the floor eight times. Then repeat diagonal run to the left.

4. **Cross-Over Pattern:** Shake hands at sides as you step right, step left over right, step right, and kick left leg out to the side. Lean away from the kick. Repeat cross-over step to the left. Continue pattern through once more.

5. **Moon Shake:** With your legs pulsing in time to the music, shake your hands out from your sides upward and cross them in front of you to starting position. Repeat this four times.

6. Repeat routine from the beginning each time until the music stops.

FOCUS: Folk dance

EQUIPMENT: Kimbo KEA-8095 or 9015, or "Bamboo Hop," Hoctor Records; tape or record player; two strikers per group; two crossbars per group

ORGANIZATION

- This Philippine dance mimes the movements of a long-necked, long-legged bird as it steps from one rice paddy to another. Review the Tinikling Strike Rhythm and Basic Step to music in 3/4 time. Have children form groups of four and scatter around the play area. Each group collects two strikers (2 to 3 meters [9 feet] bamboo poles or 4-centimeter [1.5-inch] diameter doweling), and two crossbars (75-centimeter [30-inch] lengths of 5 centimeters by 10 centimeters [2 inches by 4 inches] lumber on which the poles rest). In each group, two dancers kneel at each end of the strikers and rest the poles about 37.5 centimeters (15 inches) apart on the crossbars, which are located about 2.5 meters (7 feet) from each other.

DESCRIPTION OF ACTIVITY:

1. **Tinikling Rhythm:** On signal "Strike, Tap, Tap!" kneeling dancers, slide strikers together along crossbars and strike the poles together; then open strikers about 37.5 centimeters (15 inches) apart and lift about 2.5 centimeters (1 inch) from the crossbars, and tap twice on the crossbars. Take turns practicing the Tinikling Rhythm.

2. **Basic Tinikling Step:** Have each dancer start with right side to the poles and practice in turn. Left out, right in, left in, right out; left in, right in, left out. . .

   "Strike" — step forward on left foot
   "Tap" — step right foot between strikers
   "Tap" — step left foot between strikers
   "Strike" — step right foot outside strikers to dancer's right
   "Tap" — step left foot between strikers
   "Tap" — step right foot between strikers
   "Strike" — step left foot outside to original position

3. **Partner Tinikling:** Two dancers enter and leave toward the same side; enter and leave at opposite end to partner, with right sides to poles.

   — Two dancers face each other, join both hands, and perform the basic tinikling step; then join inside hands and move side by side.

VARIATION:

Use 4/4 rhythm and adjust Tinikling steps to a "close, close, tap, tap rhythm." Basic foot pattern becomes two steps outside poles; two steps inside.

RD-51 MORE TINIKLING STEPS_____

FOCUS: Rhythmical footwork; group work

EQUIPMENT: Music in 3/4 time;
tape or record player;
two strikers per group;
two crossbars per group

ORGANIZATION:

• Have dancers practice the foot patterns with stationary poles before trying steps with the striking action. Ensure that strikers and dancers change roles frequently.

DESCRIPTION OF ACTIVITY:

1. *Straddle-Step:* Dancer, begin by standing between the two poles. On "Strike!" jump feet apart outside the poles. On "Tap! Tap!" jump feet together inside the poles.
2. *Cross-Over-Step:* Dancer, each time you step in and out, use a cross-over-step. Begin with your right foot outside the poles. Cross left foot over the right as you step left foot inside; then step right foot inside.
3. *Over-Step:* Position as for the basic Tinikling step. Step across over both poles with the left foot, while hopping on the right. Then hop twice on the right foot between poles. Then hop on left foot outside the poles to the left.
4. *Rocker-Step:* Dancer, face the poles. Choosing any foot, step in and out (forward and backward) in a "rocking action."
5. *Circling the Poles:* Dancer, position so that your right side is nearer the poles. On "Strike," step forward on the left foot; on "Tap," step right foot between the poles; on "Tap," step left foot between the poles; on "Strike," step with right foot outside the poles to the right; on "Tap, Tap," use light running steps to about-face so that your left side is nearer the poles. On the next "Strike, Tap, Tap" sequence, use the basic tinikling step to return to starting position.

RD-52 ADVANCED TINIKLING POLE PATTERNS_____

EQUIPMENT: See RD-51.

ORGANIZATION:

• Interesting dance sequences can be created by placing the poles in different formations. Three are suggested here.

DESCRIPTION OF ACTIVITY:

1. *Line Formation* (Space three or more sets of poles about 2 meters [6 feet] apart.) Dancers, keeping your right side toward the poles throughout this sequence, step your way down the sets, make a circling movement as in Circling Poles, and return down the line in the opposite direction.
   — Dancer, do a basic tinikling step, finishing on the right side of the first set of poles. Then use three light running steps to get into position to do another tinikling step at the next two sets of poles. When you get to the end, circle with three steps to get into position to go up the sets.
2. *Square Formation* (Place four sets of poles in a square formation. Have one dancer stand with right side toward poles on the inside of each set.) Each dancer, do a tinikling step, crossing to the outside of the square. Then circle with three steps to position for a return tinikling step. Do another tinikling step, returning to the inside of the square. Rotate CCW with three running steps to the next set of poles.
3. *Cross Formation* (Cross one set of poles over another set.) Each dancer, in turn, travel CW, performing the Basic Tinikling Step as you come to each of the four sets of poles.

FOCUS: Rhythm patterns

EQUIPMENT: Two lummi sticks per child;
drum or tambourine;
music in 4/4 time;
tape or record player

ORGANIZATION:

- Progressing from individual, to partners, then to group work, dancers explore rhythm patterns and create rhythm routines using lummi sticks. Have dancers pair up; each partner get two lummi sticks; then find a free space.

DESCRIPTION OF ACTIVITY:

1. *Rhythm Stick Warm-up:* Listen to the music. Keep the tempo as you:
   - Tap sticks under each raised leg, while hopping on the other. Repeat four times.
   - Tap stick to touch alternate opposite foot for four times.
   - Tap sticks overhead as you do four jumping jacks.
   - Roll one stick over the other while twisting from side to side.
   - In turn, flip each stick once and catch; flip both sticks at the same time and catch.
   - Cross your hands, flip sticks, and catch with hands still crossed.
   - Continue with rhythm stick actions of your own!

2. *Partner Rhythm Sticks:* Face your partner in kneel-sit position.
   - Tap sticks on the floor in front of you four times; to the right side; to the left side; tap partner's sticks. Cross hands and tap on floor four times.
   - Tap sticks in the air four times, crossing one stick against the other.
   - Now, with your partner, create a Tapping Routine.

3. *Group Tapping Routine* (Divide the class into four groups and have each group sit in a square formation, all facing inward.)
   - Each member of the group contributes a rhythm pattern of your choice, to form a tapping routine. Each group practice your routine; then teach it to another group. Your routine could even involve exchanges of sticks.

4. *The Pow-Wow:* Everyone cross-leg sit with your group in one large semicircle, all facing the center. Each group should be well spaced apart from the others. Each group will have a different rhythm part to tap out with your sticks. I will sit in the center as your Chief, and, as I point to your group, sound out this pattern—sometimes alone, or in combinations with other groups, or all together.

RD—54 RHYTHM BALLS

FOCUS: Rhythmical bouncing; hand—eye coordination

EQUIPMENT: One utility ball per child; popular music in 4/4 time; tape or record player

ORGANIZATION:

• Children explore rhythmical movements with a ball in personal and general space. Accompany movements by using music with a strong beat and a moderate tempo. To begin, have each child get a ball and find a Home space.

DESCRIPTION OF ACTIVITY:

1. *One-Hand Bounce:*
   — Standing in your home space, bounce the ball with your right hand; then bounce the ball with your left hand to the music being played.
   — Concentrate on coordinating your whole body with the ball.
   — Flex your knees rhythmically.
   — Press the ball to the floor with a hollowed hand that is adjusted to the ball size, firm wrist, relaxed hand action.
   — Keep contact for as long as possible in a flowing smooth movement.

2. *Alternate Hand Bounce:*
   — Cross-bounce the ball from side to side with alternate hands.
   — As ball comes upward, reach out stretching the opposite side, contact the ball from above, turn it over in your palm as the ball rests in your hand, and send it downward to the floor. Let your body flow with the bouncing rhythm.

3. *Arm Swing Bounce:* Bounce your ball in front. Then swing arm at your side forward and backward. Contact the ball as you swing downward. Let your body flow with the movement. Repeat, alternating bouncing hand.

4. *Bounce in L-Sit:* Long-sit with ball in right hand. Bounce ball twice to right side of body; wide sit and bounce ball twice between legs; long-sit and bounce ball twice to left side. Change hands and repeat.

5. *Body Wave Bounce:* Stand with feet together and bounce your ball three times. On third bounce, add a body wave with an arm circle. Bounce the ball two more times; squat on the third count as the ball bounces upward and catch.

6. *Hi-Low Bounce:* Stand with feet together and bounce ball four times. Move down on one knee and do eight quick bounces (twice as fast). On the eighth bounce, stand up and change hands. Repeat sequence.

7. *Cross-Leg Sit Bounce:* Sitting cross-legged, elbows slightly bent, bounce ball in front with two hands. Bounce ball with right hand four times; repeat with other hand. Bounce ball in a semicircle from your left side to the right eight times; then repeat from left to right. Repeat, but change hands at center after four bounces. Push down with whole arm, with no space between hands and ball.

8. *V-Bounce:* Stand with feet wide apart. Bounce ball in center from one hand to other. Lean to the side as you gently catch it.

9. *Locomotion Bounces:*
   — Walk forward with a light springy step, with one bounce for each step, for eight bounces; walk backward.
   — Skip forward with four bounces, turn 180 degrees to face the opposite direction, change hands, and repeat.
   — Side-step to right, bouncing ball with left hand; repeat to left, bouncing ball with right hand.

10. Create a Ball Bounce Routine that has a definite beginning and closing. Select and practice five different ways of bouncing the ball from the above tasks.

FOCUS: Rhythmical throwing; rolling; sequence-making; partner work

EQUIPMENT: One utility ball per child; popular music in 4/4 time; tape or record player

ORGANIZATION:

• Have each child begin with a ball in a Home space.

DESCRIPTION OF ACTIVITY:

1. *Two-Hand Ball Throw:*

— Stand with your feet together and the ball in both hands. Throw the ball diagonally forward and upward. Let your body follow the throw as you stretch your body and arms upward in the direction of the ball's flight, and keep your arms extended. Let the ball roll off your fingertips on its way up; let the ball roll back onto your fingertips, into the palms, on the way down. Arms then drop to original position. Catch the ball without a sound! Let your knees flex with the catch and extend with the throw. Keep the whole movement smooth and rhythmical.

2. *One-Hand Throw:* Repeat throwing action as above, using your right hand, then your left hand. Catch the ball in your throwing hand.

3. *Diagonal Throw:* Stand with feet together and ball in your right hand. Step diagonally forward with your right foot (facing diagonally right) and throw the ball from right hand to left hand. Add a body wave with your throw.

4. *Single-Arm Circle Throw:* Stand with feet together and ball in right hand to start. Circle right arm CW in front of you, throwing ball overhead to right side. Step right and extend arm to catch ball. Repeat to other side.

5. *Ball Throw Routine:* Stand, with feet together and ball in your right hand. Do eight bounces in a semicircle from your right side to your left side. Throw the ball up, body wave, and catch it on the first bounce in your left hand. Throw diagonally forward to right, catch right hand. Single-arm circle throw to left. Repeat this whole sequence again. Add your own throwing action here.

6. *Chest Roll:* Begin in front-lying position, arms stretched sideways, and roll under chest.

7. *Hip Roll:* Roll over to back-lying position, knees bent, and feet close to hips, with arms stretched to side and ball in right hand. Lift your hips off the floor and roll the ball under hips from side to side.

8. *Side-to-Side Roll:* Begin in stride-standing position, with weight on your right foot; left leg and toe stretched; ball in your right hand. Bend down and roll the ball from right to left; left to right.

9. *Ball Roll and Bounce Routine:* Begin in hook-sit position, ball on the floor under your right hand. Roll ball to the left under your lifted straight legs. Do a Hip Roll with ball to the right. Roll over and do a Chest Roll under you to the left. In cross-leg sit position, ball in left hand, do eight bounces in a semicircle to right; catch in right hand and do an arc throw to left. Repeat routine from beginning.

10. *Ball Bounce Routine:* Bounce–Bounce–Quick, Quick–Pass (1–2) (3–4) (1–2) (3–4). Bounce and catch the ball with both hands for two counts. Repeat; then with your right hand, bounce the ball twice just in front of the right foot. On the second bounce send the ball across to your left, catch in both hands, and repeat pattern.

— *Partner Routine:* Stand, facing about 2 meters (6 feet) apart. Repeat ball bouncing pattern, but on "Pass" the ball is bounced with right hand across to partner. Repeat pattern in threes, in fours.

Section **4**

Gymnastics

The Gymnastics activities progressively build muscular strength and endurance, flexibility, balance, and overall coordination. They also develop children's self-confidence and improve their posture and safety awareness.

This section provides sixty-one different activities organized into the following areas: Supporting and Balancing; Rotation Around the Body Axes; Springing and Landing; and Climbing, Hanging, and Swinging.

**SUPPORTING
AND BALANCING**

G–1 Pyramid Building in Twos
G–2 Pyramid Building in Threes
G–3 Pyramid Building in Fours
G–4 Pyramids in Fives and Sixes
G–5 Safety Falls
G–6 Back Bends
G–7 Back Walkovers
G–8 The Splits
G–9 Inverted Balances
G–10 Headstand—Stunts
G–11 The Handstand
G–12 Handstand—Variations
G–13 Balance Bench—Stunts
G–14 Balance Bench—Stations
G–15 Introduction to Balance Beam
G–16 Balance Beam—Mounts and Dismounts
G–17 Balance Beam—Walks
G–18 Balance Beam—Balances
G–19 Balance Beam—Turns
G–20 Balance Beam—Stunts
G–21 Balance Beam—Jumps
G–22 Balance Beam—Routine-Building
G–23 Balance Beam—Designing a Routine

**ROTATION AROUND
THE BODY AXES**

G–24 Introducing Body Axes
G–25 Longitudinal Rotations
G–26 The Forward Roll
G–27 The Backward Roll
G–28 Roll and Balance Combinations
G–29 Roll Combinations
G–30 Forward Rolls on Apparatus
G–31 The Dive Roll
G–32 Partner and Group Rolls
G–33 The Cartwheel
G–34 The Round-Off
G–35 The Front Walkover
G–36 Line Shuttles
G–37 Tumbling Routines

SPRINGING AND LANDING

G–38 The Shoot-Through
G–39 The Headspring
G–40 The Handspring
G–41 Springing Stunts
G–42 Springboard—Running Approach
G–43 Springboard—High Springs
G–44 Springboard—Sequence-Building
G–45 Introduction to Box Horse—Mounts

G–1 PYRAMID BUILDING IN TWOS

FOCUS: Cooperative supporting and balancing

EQUIPMENT: One photocopy of page per group; one mat per group

ORGANIZATION

- Have players form groups of three players of equal size and collect a mat. Give a photocopy of this page to each group. Emphasize the need for a solid base in each partner balance. Players balance only on stronger parts of the body such as shoulders, knees, and hips, and not the neck or lower back. While two players form the balance, the third player assists. Have group members change roles frequently and each pair hold the balance for five seconds. Check for good spacing.

DESCRIPTION OF ACTIVITY:

1. *Knee and Knee*
2. *Swan Balance*
3. *Backward Sitting Balance*
4. *Back and Knee*
5. *Sitting High Chair Balance*
6. *Y-Balance*
7. *Thigh Balance*
8. *Hip and Shoulder*
9. *T-Balance*
10. *Back, Down, and Through*
11. *Invent Your Own Balance*

1.

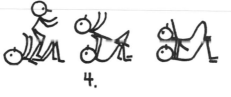

2.   3.

4.

5.

6.

7.

8.   9.

10.

G–2 PYRAMID BUILDING IN THREES

FOCUS: Supporting and balancing in threes

EQUIPMENT: One photocopy of page per group; one large mat per group

ORGANIZATION:

• Form groups of three players of equal size. Give a photocopy of this page to each group and allow time for players to practice together. Emphasize the need for a solid base in each group balance. Players balance only on stronger parts of the body such as shoulders, knees, and hips, and not the neck or lower back. Change roles frequently and hold each balance for five seconds.

DESCRIPTION OF ACTIVITY:

1. *T-Balance*

2. *Knee Stand*

3. *Star Balance*

4. *Thigh Stand*

5. *Handstand on Back*

6. *Handstand on Shoulders*

7. *Supported Thigh Stand*

8. *Goal Post*

9. *Invent Your Own Balance*

G–3 PYRAMID BUILDING IN FOURS

EQUIPMENT: One photocopy of page per group; one large mat per group

ORGANIZATION:

• Form groups of four players of equal size. Give a photocopy of this page to each group and allow time for players to practice together. Emphasize the need for a solid base in each group balance.

DESCRIPTION OF ACTIVITY:

1. *W-Balance*

2. *Supported Handstand*

3. *Head-to-Head*

4. *Leaning Handstand*

5. *Invent Your Own Pyramid*

G–4 PYRAMIDS IN FIVES AND SIXES

FOCUS: Cooperative supporting and balancing

EQUIPMENT: One photocopy of page per group; one large mat per group

ORGANIZATION:

• Form groups of six players of about equal size. Heavier players should be used as bases or supports. Give a photocopy of this page to each group and allow time for players to practice together. Emphasize the need for a solid base in each group balance. While five players form a balance, have the extra player assist. Groups should try to hold pyramids for five seconds, then carefully dismantle.

DESCRIPTION OF ACTIVITY:

1. *Leaning Pyramid*

2. *Supported Headstands*

3. *Supported Handstands*

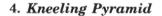

4. *Kneeling Pyramid*

5. *Walking Chair*

6. *Invent Your Own Pyramid*

FOCUS: Safety and body control

EQUIPMENT: One mat per pair; one rope per group of four

ORGANIZATION:

• Learning how to fall with control helps to prevent injury in gymnastics. Use these safety rolls as "breaks" in gymnastics. Have players get a mat and find a free space.

DESCRIPTION OF ACTIVITY:

1. ***Prone Fall from Kneeling:*** Kneel on mat with head up. With your whole body from head to knee in a straight line, fall forward and absorb the force of the fall with your hands all the way down. Finish with chest and shoulders just barely off the mat. Hold position for three seconds.

2. ***Prone Fall from Standing:*** As for Prone Fall from Kneeling; keep body straight throughout the fall. Do not arch your back as you absorb the force of the fall. Finish with chest nearly on mat. Balance on hands and toes only.

3. ***Dominoes:*** (Have players line up alongside each other in the kneeling position along the mats.) On signal "Fall!" first player fall forward, quickly followed in turn by the second, third, and so on down the line. It will look like one player knocking over the next! Repeat in standing position.

4. ***Swedish Fall:*** Stand balanced on toes. As you fall, extend one leg upward and backward with toes pointed. Keep the legs and body straight as you fall. Absorb the body weight with the arms. Finish in the Push-up position with one leg raised in the air.

5. ***Pancake Dive:*** Get in groups of four with two members holding a rope about knee height above one end of the mat. Stand on one side of a rope. Take turns springing over the rope, landing on the hands, and lowering yourself to the Prone Fall position on the mat.

— Partners, hold the rope higher.

6. ***The Judo Roll:*** (This roll is also called the Shoulder Roll and is used as a "safety roll" in gymnastics to learn how to fall and to prevent injury.) Squat down with your feet wide apart and one foot forward. Place one arm forward so the back of your hand is on the mat. The hand should be placed outside the front foot. Tuck your head to your chest, turning your head in the direction of the hand. Hold the other arm out sideways for balance. Roll forward, keeping your chin on your chest, to land on the back of your shoulder. Roll diagonally across your back to finish in the standing position, with one foot behind the other. Slap the mat vigorously with your whole arm and palm of other hand as you roll.

— Start in the standing position; two-foot take-off.

— Walk into the Judo Roll; run into the Judo Roll.

— Place mats end to end and do a series of Judo Rolls.

7. ***Breakfall*** (Used whenever you are forced off balance backward.) Squat with back to mat. Fall back with your back flat, but just before you hit the mat, fling your arms out sideways, slapping backward on the mat with both arms and palms of hands to "break" the fall.

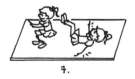

— Continue to backward roll to your feet.

G-6 BACK BENDS

FOCUS: Supporting and balancing

EQUIPMENT: One mat per three players

ORGANIZATION:

- Form groups of three players: One is the performer; the others are spotters. Have each group get a mat to share and place it in a free space.

DESCRIPTION OF ACTIVITY:

1. *Wrestler's Bridge:* Performer, lie on your back on the mat with knees bent and feet flat on floor. Open knees, grasp ankles, and pull feet as close to seat as possible. Point toes outward. Without losing foot position, release hands and stretch arms to side for support. Arch body to balance on feet and top of head. Relax and repeat. Spotters, place hands under performer's hips, ready to help.

2. *Climb Down the Walls:* Performer, stand on mat with your back to wall and heels about one step away from it. Stretch arms overhead; lean back to place palms on the wall. Focus eyes on the wall. Slowly walk your hands down the wall as far as possible. Hold for three seconds and walk hand up again. Spotters, join hands under performer's hips, ready to help.

3. *High Wrestler's Bridge:* From Wrestler's Bridge position, place palms on either side of head, fingers pointing toward shoulders. Lift trunk and straighten elbows to raise head from mat. Spotters, place hands under performer's hips.

4. *Walking Wrestler's Bridge:* Challenge players to walk forward in High Wrestler's Bridge position, alternately stepping with hand and opposite foot.

5. *Assisted Back Bend:* Performer, stand on the mat facing your spotter. Now stretch arms overhead and lean back as far as possible. Place palms on the mat and tilt head back to look at the mat. Bring your hands as close to your heels as you can. Spotters, join hands behind the performer's waist, ready to help.

6. *Back Bend with One Leg Raised:* Performer, lie on mat with knees bent and feet flat on floor. Make a High Wrestler's Bridge; then straighten one leg overhead and point toes. Change legs and repeat. Can you raise both one hand and one leg? Spotters, kneel on either side of performer and join hands under performer's back without touching performer.

G–7 BACK WALKOVERS

FOCUS: Supporting and balancing

EQUIPMENT: One large mat per group; one bench per group

ORGANIZATION:

- Form groups of four players: One is the performer; two players anchor the bench; the other is the spotter. Have each group drape the mat over their bench.

DESCRIPTION OF ACTIVITY:

1. *Back Walkover over a Bench:* Stand on the mat with back to the bench. Lie back so that your back is on top of the bench. Tilt head back, reach back overhead with the hands, and place palms on the mat, fingers pointing toward the mat. Take weight on hands, raise one leg, and push off with the other to a split-leg handstand. Lower front leg, then back leg, with toes pointed to the mat. Push off with hands and stand. Spotters, join hands behind the performer's waist, ready to help.

2. *Assisted Back Walkover:* Stand with arms raised overhead as far as possible. Raise one leg forward as you lean into a back bend. Push off from the other leg, tilt head back, and stretch arms for the mat. Place palms on the mat as close as possible to feet, with fingers pointing toward the feet. Take weight on hands; bring legs over one at a time to the mat. Stand with arms out to side. Spotters, kneel on both sides of the performer, join hands under performer's waist, ready to assist.

— When competent, perform the Back Walkover without spotters.

G–8 THE SPLITS

FOCUS: Supporting; flexibility

EQUIPMENT: One mat per pair; several benches

ORGANIZATION:

- The Splits should be included in the Warm-up and Cool Down in each gymnastic lesson to increase flexibility and reduce the risk of injury. Emphasize that players should stretch to a comfortable position. If pain is felt, they should ease off. Have them hold each split for ten seconds, rest, then repeat. To begin, players find a spot alone, facing you.

DESCRIPTION OF ACTIVITY:

1. *The Middle Splits:* Sit with legs astride and as close to in-line as you can. Point the toes, keep your back straight, and look straight ahead. Lean forward with the hands to touch as far out as possible, hold for ten seconds, then repeat. Try this with your back against a wall.

2. *Straddle Lean:* As for Middle Splits, but grasp ankles, then pull chest to floor. Keep back straight and head up.

3. *Stride Splits with Support:* Support yourself between two benches. Gradually lower yourself to sit with one leg forward and the other back. Keep your hips square, with both legs turned out. Point the toes. Lower yourself to a comfortable position, hold, then stand. Repeat, with the other leg forward.

4. *Stride Splits:* Sit on the floor with one leg forward and the other back, with the hips square and toes pointed. Support yourself on each side with your hands on the floor.

5. *Head to Knees:* Stand, bend forward, and place hands behind thighs. Keep bending forward until your head touches your knees. Who can touch the shins? Rest and repeat.

G–9 INVERTED BALANCES

FOCUS: Supporting and balancing

EQUIPMENT: One mat per pair

ORGANIZATION:

• In these Inverted Balances players learn the progressions to the headstand, with the assistance of a spotter. Remind players to return to starting position or roll forward if they overbalance. Have players find a partner of equal size, get a mat to share, and then scatter around the play area.

DESCRIPTION OF ACTIVITY:

1. **Tripod Balance:** Squat, place hands on mat shoulder-width apart with fingers spread and pointing forward. Bend elbows and lower forehead to mat to form a triangle with the hands. Put weight equally on all three points; then lean forward to lift feet from floor so that the right knee rests on right elbow and the left knee rests on left elbow. Hold balance three seconds.

2. **Frog Stand:** Squat in Tripod Balance position. Bend elbows, lean forward, and press knees against outside of elbows. Continue to lean forward until feet lift. Raise head from the mat to look straight ahead. Hold balance three seconds.

3. **Tucked Frog Stand:** From the Frog Stand, lower forehead to the mat to form a triangle with the hands. Bring the knees together, raise them overhead, and bend them as if you are sitting upside down. Hold for five seconds; then tuck head under, lower weight to shoulders, and push off with hands to a Forward Roll.

   — Spotter, stand directly in front of performer. At first, support hips and then support ankles. Slowly raise legs to position. Remember to move to side when performer rolls forward.

4. **Wall Headstand:** Performer, place mat against wall. Squat 30 centimeters (12 inches) from wall and repeat Tucked Frog Stand. Straighten legs and rest feet against wall. Hold for five seconds. Arch back slightly and point toes; then slowly lower legs to mat.

   — Spotter, kneel at side and support performer at shoulders and just above the knee.

5. **Curl-Up Headstand:** Performer, squat in a Tripod Balance. Slowly raise legs until overhead. Point toes and hold feet together for five seconds; then slowly lower legs to mat.

   — Spotter, stand facing performer. At first, support hips and then ankles.

6. **Kick-Up Headstand:** (Form groups of three players.) Performer, squat in a Tripod Balance and walk feet forward so that the front leg is bent and the rear leg is straight. Now, kick up rear leg and then your forward leg until both are overhead. Point toes and arch your back slightly. Hold for five seconds and return to starting position.

   — Spotters, stand to side and in front of performer. Place lower leg against performer's back. Catch front leg at ankle; then catch the second leg.

FOCUS: Supporting and tumbling

EQUIPMENT: One mat per pair

ORGANIZATION:

- Have players form groups of three, get two mats to share, and then scatter around the play area. One player is the performer; the other two are the spotters.

DESCRIPTION OF ACTIVITY:

1. **Straddle Press to Headstand:** Start in the Push-up position. Draw legs toward your hands, keeping legs apart and straight. Tip your forehead down onto the mat. Keep toes pointed and hips high as you lift your straight legs overhead. Keep the back arched slightly as legs come together. Hold for five seconds. Spot as for Kick-up Headstand.

2. **Forearm Headstand:** Place forearms on mat with elbows wide and palms down so that your thumbs and index fingers are touching. One leg should be forward, the other back. Place forehead in between thumb and index fingers. Kick back leg up; then bring your other leg up to join it overhead. Arch your back as both legs come together. Hold for five seconds. Spot as for Kick-up Headstand.

3. **Backward Roll to a Headstand:** Squat; place hands behind head in Backward Roll position, except that the hands are placed behind the head to form a triangle with the head. As you roll backward, stretch the trunk and legs upward to support yourself on hands and head.

   — Spotters, stand at side of performer. Pull upward on performer's thighs.

4. **Fishflop:** Start in the long-sit position; then do a Backward Roll into a Headstand. At the same time, raise the head slightly and push with hands. Roll smoothly onto the chest and down the tummy, taking your weight on your hands to lie on the mat.

   — Spotters, stand at side and pull up on ankles; then lower to mat.

5. **Forward Belly Roll:** Stand, fall forward, and at the same time arch your body to roll over your knees, tummy, and chest to a Headstand. Hold balance; then do a Forward Roll. Remember to push hard with the hands as they first meet the mat.

   — Spotters, stand at side and pull up on ankles.

6. **Backward Belly Roll:** Stand; then sit to do a Backward Roll to a Headstand. Overbalance, lift your head to raise your chin as high as possible, and arch your entire body. Push up with the hands to roll backward onto chest, tummy, and knees to stand.

   — Spotters, pull up on ankles; then lower ankles and thighs to the mat.

5.   6.

G–11 THE HANDSTAND

FOCUS: Supporting and balancing; handstand technique

EQUIPMENT: One large mat per pair

ORGANIZATION:

• Have players find a partner of equal size, get a mat to share, and then place the mat against the wall.

DESCRIPTION OF ACTIVITY:

1. *Walk the Wall:* Squat on hands and toes with your feet against the wall and head up. Take your weight on your hands and walk your feet up the wall, one at a time. Move hands closer to the wall as your feet go higher. Can you go all the way up to the handstand position and down again?

2. *Donkey Kick:* From the crouch position and with your head up, dive forward to place hands on the floor, shoulder-width apart. Kick upward with both legs at the same time, so that the knees are bent and the hips are high over hands and near the point of balance. Return feet to floor.

3. *Handstand with Safety Twist:* Kick both feet up as in the Donkey Kick. When the balanced position is reached, quickly twist a quarter turn at the waist to rotate your body to one side so that the feet land on the floor to side of hands. Try not to move hands during the Safety Twist.

   — Use the Safety Twist whenever you over-balance during handstands.

4. *The Handstand:* Performer, take the "sprinter's start" position, with hands shoulder-width apart on the floor. Spread and slightly cup the fingers. Move your shoulders over your hands, bring one foot close to the hands, and keep the back leg straight. Kick the back leg up as straight as you can while you push off with the front leg. Arch the back slightly and bring the back leg up to join the straight leg at the point of balance. Hold your head up and stay in balance for three seconds.

5. *Spotter:* Stand in front of performer in the stride position. Have the performer place one shoulder against your knee. As the first leg comes up, catch it at the ankle; then catch the other and hold them in balance. Release the last leg first to allow the performer to come down.

6. *Practice:*

   — Practice on your own: coming down the way you went up; one leg at a time.

   — Practice, using the Safety Twist.

1.

2.

3.

4.

FOCUS: Supporting and balancing

EQUIPMENT: One large mat per pair

ORGANIZATION:

• Once the Handstand has been practiced and the Safety Twist and the Forward Roll have been learned, the following variations should be introduced. Have players find a partner of equal size, get a mat to share, and then scatter around the play area.

DESCRIPTION OF ACTIVITY:

1. ***Handstand with Wall Support:*** Face the wall, then place your hands on the mat about 18 inches (45 centimeters) from the wall and about shoulder-width apart, in the sprinter's start position. Kick up the rear leg to rest the sole of the foot against the wall. Bring the other foot up to join it. Slowly ease both feet away from the wall to hold the handstand. Come down slowly in control.

2. ***Handstand from a Walk-In:*** Take several steps forward to place hands on the floor. Without stopping, use the front leg to push off; then kick the rear leg up to the point of balance. Bring the other leg up to join it. Try not to move your hands as you hold balance for three seconds.

3. ***Handstand to a Forward Roll:*** Kick up into a full Handstand; overbalance slowly; lower your elbows with control; tuck your head under and lower your weight onto the tops of your shoulders and back as you roll. Continue the roll to the standing position.

   — Spotters (Begin by using two spotters: one on either side of performer.): Kneel, place one hand behind the performer's neck, the other under the thigh.

G-13 BALANCE BENCH—STUNTS

FOCUS: Traveling on apparatus

EQUIPMENT: Balance benches; mats; rope (or high-jump bar)

ORGANIZATION:

- Place balance benches in play area with wide surface up and position mats around benches. Have players find a partner of equal size and group with other pairs at benches. One pair straddle-sits the bench to anchor it while the other pairs practice. Have pairs change roles frequently. Use a spotter on either side of performer. Have spotters hold hands of performer. Emphasize that players move slowly and carefully and look ahead.

DESCRIPTION OF ACTIVITY:

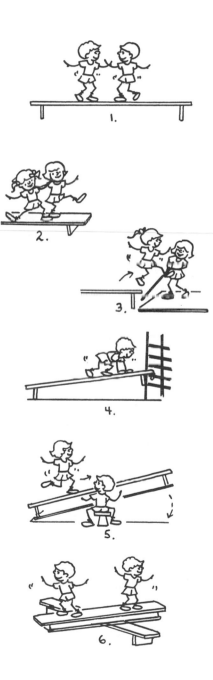

1. **Pass Your Partner:** Partners, start at opposite ends of the bench and walk toward each other, passing at the middle. You may hold each other as you pass.
   - Repeat with hands on head or behind back, without falling off.

2. **Partner Counterbalance:** Partners, stand at one end of bench on opposite sides, facing same direction. Rest foot on bench beside partner's foot, join inside wrists, and raise opposite arm to side. Rise up to balance each other on the bench. How long can you hold the balance? How far can you walk while holding the balance?

3. **Run and Jump:** One partner, stand at the end of bench. Run forward to other end; then jump over a rope or high-jump bar to land softly on mat with knees bent. Other partner, hold rope or bar lightly so it can easily be knocked from your hands if partner bumps it. Raise the rope or bar.

4. **Walk the Inclined Bench:** Incline one bench (narrow side up) by supporting it at one end on another bench or hooking it onto the climbing frame.
   - Walk forward to end, squat, hold bench, spring, and land on mat.
   - Walk sideways to end; "Cat Walk" (in the crouch position).

5. **Walk the Plank:** Support a bench (narrow side up) across another bench at the middle. Use the top bench as a see-saw. Walk forward with arms out sideways, tilt the beam forward, and walk down the other side.
   - Spotters, sit on bottom bench to anchor top bench.
   - Walk sideways; Cat-Walk.

6. **See-Saw:** Balance a bench across another bench, as for Walk the Plank. Step carefully onto the middle of the bench, back to back with your partner; then slowly walk out to the ends of the bench, with arms out sideways, counterbalancing each other as you go.
   - Two spotters, sit on bottom bench to anchor top bench.
   - Two spotters, hold your hands ready under performer's hands.
   - Cat Walk out to the ends.

FOCUS: Station work; partner work; balancing

EQUIPMENT: Mats;
eight balance benches;
one utility ball per pair;
music; tape or record player

ORGANIZATION

• Use the Station Method when reviewing previously learned skills; when teaching large groups of children; when only enough equipment for a small group is available; when you want to individualize instruction and work with small numbers; to provide opportunities for leadership. Any of the activities in this section may be taught by this method. Activities may be selected from the same area (see below) or from four different areas. Select three previously learned tasks and introduce one new task. Closely supervise the new task, but circulate to all four. Form four equal groups and assign each group to set up one of the four stations and arrange equipment. Give group leaders responsibilities: Appoint spotters, arrange equipment, determine order of performance. Explain skills and have leaders, co-leaders, or other players demonstrate the skills at each station. Explain safety procedures at the start. Anchor all benches for performers. Place yourself where you can see all stations at all times. Use music to start and stop activity. Allow three to four minutes at each station. On the stop signal, have groups rotate CW to next station, with the leader in front. Have players arrange pairs of benches side by side and place mats around benches. Players then find a partner and group with other pairs at benches.

DESCRIPTION OF ACTIVITY:

— *Station 1. Ball Support Walk:* Stand on opposite benches facing each other. Both hold the ball between you and walk to end of bench without losing balance.

— *Station 2. Pass the Ball:* Stand on opposite benches facing each other. Pass ball back and forth without losing balance. Return, moving sideways along the bench. Use a bounce pass; a chest pass.

— *Station 3. Ball Balance:* Squat facing partner, with arms raised sideways. Hold the ball between you without using hands (head to head, side to side, chest to chest, and so on), then move up and down, then along the bench while holding the ball in balance.

— *Station 4. Line Passing:* Each group, walk along bench in file formation, passing the ball overhead to the next player behind. Each player, when you reach the end, step off, run to end of file, get back on bench, and continue passing the ball.

  — Repeat these station bench tasks with benches placed upside down so that performers now have to balance on a much narrower edge.

G–15 INTRODUCTION TO BALANCE BEAM

FOCUS: Teaching and safety guidelines

EQUIPMENT: Balance beam;
beat-board or low box;
safety mats;
floor tape;
several 2″ × 4″ lumber studs

ORGANIZATION:

• Mark practice lines on floor, 9 centimeters (4 inches) apart, with floor tape, and arrange the 2″ × 4″ practice beams and the balance beams around the practice area.

• Choose six players to set up the equipment and demonstrate safety guidelines. Choose two spotters, and have one spotter stand on each side of the beam. Spotters should change roles with performers every few minutes. Teach in three steps: individual beam movements; new movements combined with those already learned; and new movements combined with a mount and dismount. Allow players time to practice different balances. Introduce the next movement only after players are confident with the first. Encourage players to develop their own routines.

DESCRIPTION OF ACTIVITY:

1. *Lifting and Carrying the Beam:* Four players, carry the beam as you would a bench: one player at each end; one player at either side; all facing the same direction. Bend knees, keeping back straight, lift together, and then walk in step. Bend knees again as you lower beam to floor.

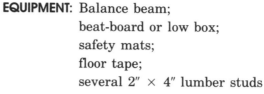
1.

2. *Equipment Setup:* Use a beat-board, or some kind of take-off board, to mount the balance beam. Set it up at one side in middle of balance beam. Place mats on either side, under, and at ends of beam.

   — Practice beams (2″ × 4″) may be laid directly on the floor for some activities and anchored at each end. They may be covered with carpet for a softer surface.

3. *Progressions:* Always work on the beam in bare feet. First, practice all movements on lines taped to floor; then practice on the 2″ × 4″ practice beams. Next, practice on the beam itself.

4. *Safety:* Always use spotters. Tell them the routine you intend to perform before you mount the beam.

5. *Balance Beam Travel:* (Form groups of four to six, each group with a balance beam or bench turned upside down and safety mats placed on sides and ends. Have group members take turns at performing and spotting.)

   — Travel along the beam in different ways: walking forward; walking backward; shuffle-stepping sideways; etc.

   — Balance on the beam in the "push-up" position on toes and hands. Look up as you hold your balance. Walk your feet up to your hands, then your hands forward along the beam away from your feet. Continue along the beam in this way.

   — Find other ways of moving or balancing on the beam.

2.

5.

FOCUS: Mounting and dismounting techniques

EQUIPMENT: Balance beams or balance benches (upturned);
beat-board or low box;
safety mats

ORGANIZATION:

- Form groups of four to six players and have each group find a free space to place balance beam or upturned bench, beat-board, and safety mats on sides, under, and at ends of beam. Have players remove shoes and socks. Designate two spotters to stand one on each side of beam, facing the performer. Check that players focus eyes on end of beam while performing. Remind players to hold balance in each mount position for five seconds.

DESCRIPTION OF ACTIVITY:

1. ***Front-Support Mount:*** Stand at side of beam and place hands on beam shoulder-width apart. Spring up to the front-support position, keeping arms straight and thighs pressed against beam. Hold head high, arch back, and point toes. Start by taking two or three short running steps.

2. ***Straddle Seat Mount:*** Spring to Front Support Mount. Swing left leg over the beam with toes pointed; turn your body so that you sit astride (straddle) the beam. Place hands behind body and sit tall with head up and toes pointed.

3. ***Knee Mount:*** Spring to a Front-Support Mount. Lift one knee to kneel on beam and support weight on hands and knee. Raise other leg behind, hold head high to arch back, and point toes.

4. ***Squat Mount:*** Stand to face side of beam and place both hands on it, shoulder-width apart. Spring up, draw knees to chest, and place toes on the beam between hands. Squat on beam and hold head high.

5. ***Straddle Mount:*** Place both hands on top of beam, shoulder-width apart. At the same time spring up; spread both legs wide to place feet on beam outside the hands in a straddle position.

6. ***Front Dismount:*** From the push-up position on the beam, on hands and toes, kick one leg upward and to one side, and at the same time swing the other leg up to meet it in the air. Drop to the mat and land with both feet together and one hand on the beam. Remember to land softly, bending at hips, knees, and ankles and holding balance three seconds after landing. During all dismounts, look ahead at your own height.

7. ***Straddle Dismount:*** Stand on beam facing the end. Swing both arms upward as you jump forward and upward; straddle your legs, touching your toes with your hands. Bring both legs together for the landing on the mat. Look ahead from start to finish. Bring the feet up to the hands, not the hands down to the feet.

8. ***Knee Scale Dismount:*** From a Knee Scale position (see G-18) on the right knee, swing the left leg down quickly below the beam, then quickly upward above the beam. Push upward from the right knee to join the right leg with the left above the beam. Swing the legs sideways to do a Front Dismount on the left side of the beam. Land softly on the mats.

9. ***V-Sit Swing Dismount:*** Sit in V-sit position on beam with legs apart. Swing legs down and back. As you do, place hands on beam, close to your body. Lean over hands, swing your hips up, and arch your back as you swing your legs over to one side of the beam. Push away from the beam and land on mat. Spotter, stand on landing side. Hold performer's upper arm. When legs have swung back, lift with other hand under tummy to assist off.

G-17 BALANCE BEAM—WALKS

FOCUS: Balancing on apparatus

EQUIPMENT: Balance beams and benches; safety mats; beat-board or low box

ORGANIZATION:

• Have all players remove shoes and socks. Have players set up balance beams or upturned benches, and beat-board, and place mats on either side, under, and at ends of beam. Use extra mats in the landing area. One spotter stands on each side of the beam and faces performer. Have players perform each walk for the length of the beam. In a large class, two players could start at middle of beam and walk toward each end. Suggest that players use a different mount and dismount each time. Remind players to hold arms out sideways for balance and to focus on the end of the beam.

DESCRIPTION OF ACTIVITY:

1. **Toe-Walking Step:** Stand on your toes; then walk along the beam gripping the beam with the toes. Walk backward on your toes. Move the arms naturally. Focus eyes on the end of the beam.

2. **Running Step:** Run carefully along the beam on your toes. Look ahead with arms out sideways for balance. Gradually take higher and longer steps and swing the arms back and forth as you run.

   — Run backward.

3. **Cross-Over Step:** Stand sideways on beam. Now move sideways: Step left foot left; then step right foot across in front of supporting left leg. Repeat.

4. **Cross-Behind Step:** Stand sideways on beam. Step left foot left; then step right foot behind supporting left leg to move sideways. Repeat.

5. **Alternating Cross Step:** Stand sideways on beam. Step left foot left, step right foot in front of supporting left leg, step left foot left, and step right foot behind supporting left leg. Repeat.

6. **Hopping Step:** Hop on one foot, then the other. Hop step to middle of beam, turn on ball of foot, and hop back to end on other foot.

7. **Dip Step:** Stand at end of beam. Bend knee of supporting leg and with each step, swing other leg forward so that the foot is just below the beam. Keep the leg straight and toe pointed. Move arms gracefully as you step forward.

VARIATION:

Routine: Have players create a routine that combines several balance beam travels.

G-18 BALANCE BEAM—BALANCES

FOCUS: Balancing on apparatus

EQUIPMENT: Balance beams and benches; beat-board or low box; safety mats

ORGANIZATION:

• Have players set up balance beams or upturned benches and beat-boards, placing mats on either side, under, and at ends of beam. Designate two spotters to stand one on each side of beam, facing the performer. Have the players practice these balances on the floor first; then have them select one of the mounts learned, use the beat-board to mount the beam, and perform the following balances.

DESCRIPTION OF ACTIVITY:

1. **V-Sit:** Sit on the bar with hands on the beam behind your seat. Bring knees up to chest, lean back at the hips, straighten your legs upward, and point the toes. Hold the "V" position for five seconds. Do not look down, but focus eyes ahead. Now raise hands sideways and upward to balance on seat only.

2. **Knee Scale:** Kneel on the beam with one knee behind the other, holding the beam with both hands in front. As you lean forward, lift the back leg upward and move hands forward. Point toes and hold balance.

3. **Swan Scale:** Place shins of both legs on the beam, one behind the other. Place both hands together and forward on the beam. Lift the arms overhead and raise your upper body so that your head and shoulders are over your hips. Raise arms in a "V" to the sides.

4. **Straddle Hold:** Sit on bar sideways with legs in the straddle position, balancing your weight on your hands between your legs. Lean slightly forward as you support your weight on your straight arms and raise your seat off the beam. Point your toes, look up, and hold balance.

G-19 BALANCE BEAM—TURNS

EQUIPMENT: See G-18.

DESCRIPTION OF ACTIVITY:

1. **Half Turn:** Rise on toes of right foot with right arm raised overhead. Quickly turn right to face opposite direction by throwing the left arm across your body toward the right side. Repeat turn to left.

2. **Full Turn:** Rise on toes and quickly turn right all the way around to face forward again. Repeat turn to left.

3. **Pivot Turn:** Stand with one foot ahead of the other. Rise on balls of feet and, without lifting feet from beam, turn to face opposite direction; then lower heels to beam again.

4. **Pirouette:** Stand on beam on ball of one foot. Hold arms overhead for balance; then swing free leg backward to do a half turn (180 degrees) or a full turn (360 degrees). Return the free foot to beam to maintain balance.

5. **Reverse Pirouette:** Similar to the Pirouette, except that you swing the free leg forward.

6. **Squat Turn:** Squat on toes with one foot ahead of the other and arms out sideways. Without lifting feet from beam, swing around to face opposite direction. Hold balance.

7. **Routine:** Have players create a routine that combines a mount, several balance beam walks and turns, and a dismount.

G-20 BALANCE BEAM—STUNTS

FOCUS: Balancing on apparatus

EQUIPMENT: Balance beams and benches;
safety mats;
beat-board or low box

ORGANIZATION:

• Have players set up balance beams and upturned benches, beat-board or low box, and place mats on either side, under, and at ends of beam. Have spotters stand on both sides of beam facing performer. Have two players practice at the same time on the beam. Suggest that players use a different mount and dismount each time.

DESCRIPTION OF ACTIVITY:

1. **Swedish Fall:** Stand on the beam with one foot in front of the other. Fall forward to place both hands together on the beam, lifting the rear leg upward and bending your arms as you fall. Straighten your arms and raise rear leg as high as possible with toes pointed. Hold balance.

2. **One-Leg Squat:** Stand on beam, taking your weight on one leg. Bend this leg to a full squat position; raise the other leg forward so that it is parallel to the beam. Hold balance. Push upward from squat position to stand.

3. **Body Wave:** Stand on beam and hold your hands down to side. Bend forward slightly at knees and hips and bring your arms backward and upward with a sweeping motion, and, at the same time, move your body in a "wave like" motion; then return to the starting position.

4. **Forward Leap:** Stand on the beam on one foot. Swing the other foot forward and leap on to it. Hold balance.

G-21 BALANCE BEAM—JUMPS

EQUIPMENT: See G-20.

DESCRIPTION OF ACTIVITY:

1. **Upward Jump:** Stand with one foot in front of the other on the beam, with both knees bent. Swing your arms upward and straighten the knees as you leap upward and return to the beam in the same position.

2. **Foot Change Jump:** Do the Upward Jump, but as you jump, change the position of your feet.

3. **Tuck Jump:** Stand on beam on two feet. Bend at the knees and hips, spring upward into the "tuck" position in the air, straighten body, and return to starting position.

4. **Stag Leap:** Move along the bench with a running step. Bend the right knee as you push forward and upward with the left leg. Land on the right foot.

5. **Scissors Jump:** Stand on the beam. Take a step onto the left foot and vigorously swing your right leg up in front to hip level. While in the air, swing the left leg up straight so that both legs pass each other (scissors); then land on the right foot.

VARIATION:

Routine: Have players create a routine that combines a mount, a walk, a turn, a stunt, a jump, and a dismount.

G–22 BALANCE BEAM—ROUTINE BUILDING

FOCUS: Revision; sequence-building

EQUIPMENT: Paper and pen for each player; balance beams and benches; safety mats

ORGANIZATION:

• Routines consist of a mount; combinations of stunts and movements such as steps, turns, jumps, and balances; then a dismount. Have players set up the beam or upturned benches and beat-board and place safety mats. Form groups of four players: One player is the performer; two are spotters and stand on either side of the beam, facing the performer; the other calls out the routine for the performer. Have players take turns.

DESCRIPTION OF ACTIVITY:

Routine:

1. Spring to a Straddle Seat Mount.
2. Lean backward into a V-sit, rock forward onto one foot, stand, and hold a One-Foot Balance.
3. Take four Running Steps: L, R, L, R.
4. Walk for two Dip Steps: L, R, bend the knees, and do two Scissor Jumps.
5. Do a Pirouette Turn, then two Backward Dips.
6. Body Wave, to a Swedish Fall, to a One-Leg Squat.
7. Stand; take three Running Steps to do a Stag Leap.
8. Step to the end for a Straddle Dismount.

VARIATION:

Routine-building: Have players add other stunts and movements to this routine.

G–23 BALANCE BEAM—DESIGNING A ROUTINE

EQUIPMENT: See G-22.

ORGANIZATION:

• Have players collect a piece of paper and pen and create their own routines consisting of (a) a mount; (b) combinations of stunts and movements: steps, turns, jumps, and balances; (c) a dismount.

DESCRIPTION OF ACTIVITY:

1. *Designing a Routine:*
   — plan routine to last 60 to 90 seconds
   — combine stunts so one flows into the next
   — strive for grace and elegance
   — make your routine lively; avoid monotony of rhythm
   — include no more than three held positions
   — try to include different levels: lying, sitting, and upright
   — show confidence and control
2. Perform your routine to the rest of your group.
3. Design and perform a "pair routine."

G–24 INTRODUCING BODY AXES

FOCUS: Teaching and safety guidelines

EQUIPMENT: Chart paper and marking pens; one mat per player

ORGANIZATION:

• Discuss the terms *rotation, axis,* and *center of gravity* or *point of balance.* Use a globe of the earth to show how our planet rotates on its axis. Make a chart with the names of the three body rotational axes—lateral, medial, and longitudinal—so that players become familiar with them. Players should be able to identify each type of rotation. Have different children demonstrate the three types of rotations.

DESCRIPTION OF ACTIVITY:

1. We can rotate around our body's center of gravity in three ways:
   — Rotating Around Lateral Axis: Involves forward and backward rotations along the floor or on apparatus; examples include forward and backward rolls. Lateral rotations are the most common rotations in gymnastics.
   — Rotating Around Medial Axis: Involves rotation to the side; examples include cartwheels.
   — Rotating Around Longitudinal Axis: Involves rotation through the length of the body; examples include spins, half turns or full turns, pivots, pirouettes, and rolls such as log rolls. Longitudinal rotations are often combined with rotations around the other two axes to form more difficult gymnastic stunts.
2. You are going to learn to perform these different rotations. Let's begin with rotations around the Longitudinal Axis.

G–25 LONGITUDINAL ROTATIONS

FOCUS: Longitudinal axis rotations; partner work

EQUIPMENT: One mat per pair

ORGANIZATION:

• Have children find a partner, get a mat, and find a Home space. Arrange mats so that performers are always in view (circular formation). Check for good spacing.

DESCRIPTION OF ACTIVITY:

1. ***Churn-the-Butter Roll:*** Start in the back-support position with legs, body, and arms straight; weight supported on the hands behind and fingers pointing forward. Lift one arm and one leg, reach up, and roll over into the front-support position. Lift other arms and leg, reach up, and roll over again to starting position. Continue rolling smoothly, or "churning the butter" along the mat.
   — Find a partner. With feet touching, "Churn-the-butter" in the same direction; in opposite directions.
2. ***Log Roll in Pairs:*** Lie on your tummies facing each other on the mat. Link hands and roll in the same direction. Try to roll so that your feet do not touch the mat.
3. ***Log Roll with Feet Locked:*** Lie down on the mat on your backs so that your feet are touching; then lock your feet together. Now roll slowly in the same direction with your feet locked.
4. ***Leap the Log Roll:*** (Form groups of six to eight players. Divide into two groups, the "Rollers" and the "Leapers," with each group standing in single file at each end of the mats, facing each other. Have one group demonstrate this activity.) On the signal "Roll," the Rollers, start log rolling down the mat, well spaced apart. At the same time the Leapers leap over the approaching Rollers. Rollers, when you reach the end of the mat, you become Leapers; Leapers, you become the Rollers. Continue.
5. Develop a longitudinal roll with your partner.

G–26 THE FORWARD ROLL

FOCUS: Rotating around lateral axis;
technique; spotting

EQUIPMENT: One mat per pair;
box horses, tables

ORGANIZATION:

• Rotating around the Lateral Axis involves rolling forward or backward. Have players find a partner, get a mat, and find a free space. Move box horses and tables into play area. When practicing the forward roll, players may need spotting assistance. Each player should learn to spot for his or her partner. Remind players to hug their shins as they roll to their feet. The hands contact the mat only once during the roll. The performer should not push off the mat to get to feet. Advise those with long hair to tie it back so that their performance is not hindered.

DESCRIPTION OF ACTIVITY:

1. *Forward Roll Technique:* Begin in squat position, with weight on your toes. Place hands on mat slightly ahead of your toes, shoulder-width apart and fingers facing forward. Round your back by tucking your head between your knees. Your chin should be touching chest. Push off from toes, raising your seat as you roll forward, with chin tucked to chest. Land on the tops of shoulders and push with the hands as you roll forward to the sitting position, keeping heels wide and close to your seat. Hug shins with arms while rolling to your feet. Keep yourself rolled up "like a ball."

2. *Spotting for the Forward Roll:* Kneel on one knee alongside your partner. Place your leading hand on the back of your partner's neck and the other hand under the near ankle. As she or he rolls forward, assist by lifting with the leading hand and pushing forward with the back hand.

3. *Forward Roll with Run:* Take a short run to the mat, and perform a Forward Roll.

4. *Forward Roll to Squat:* Stand, fold arms across chest and squat. Without using hands, roll forward to squatting position.

   — Repeat, forward rolling to standing position.

5. *Forward Roll from a Height:* Lie across the box horse or table. Lean forward, place hands on the mat, shoulder-width apart with fingers pointing straight ahead. Curve back; tuck chin to look at feet. As you roll, keep legs straight and together; tuck knees to chest. Finish in the squat position.

   — Repeat, and finish standing.

6. *Forward Roll Variations:*

   — Squat, hold outside ankles, and forward roll. Do a series.

   — Squat, hold inside ankles, and forward roll. Do a series.

   — Forward roll; then finish with a walk-out (with one leg raised forward, ready to walk forward).

   — Stand on one leg. Forward roll to finish standing on the other leg. Can you hold your balance? Repeat, starting on the other leg. Now do a series, changing the raised leg each time.

   — Create your own forward roll variation!

G–27 THE BACKWARD ROLL

FOCUS: Rotating around lateral axis; technique; spotting

EQUIPMENT: One mat per pair; one ball per pair

ORGANIZATION:

• Have the players find a partner, then get a mat, and take it to a free space. Explain that the partners should take turns at performing and spotting.

DESCRIPTION OF ACTIVITY:

1. *Backward Roll Technique:* Start in the squat position with back to the mat. Place hands pointing back over shoulders with palms up and thumbs near neck. Tuck chin down onto chest. To start the roll, sit on mat and push backward with toes, keeping in the tucked position. As you roll, bring knees to chest and roll onto your back. Push off mat with hands to land in the squat position on toes, not on knees. Make sure your weight is taken equally on both hands and not on the head. Hold balance.

2. *Spotters:* Position yourself at side of partner and kneel on the knee away from her or him. Assist by placing one hand under head at the back of the neck and the other under the hip. Thrust in direction of the roll. Help partner gain enough speed to get the body weight over the hands. Gradually allow performer to roll without your help.

3. *Stand to Stand:* Stand, then squat, keeping feet and knees in as close to body as possible. Roll back, push hard with the hands, bring the legs over quickly to land in a standing position.

4. *Rock into Backward Roll:* Sit, rock back and forth to gain momentum, and then backward roll to squat position.

5. *Backward Roll Series:* How many backward rolls can you do in a row and finish in the squat position?

6. *Backward Roll Variations:*

   — Squat cross-legged, backward roll, and finish in cross-legged position. Do a series of these.

   — Backward roll to finish on one leg only.

   — Start in the straddle position. Do three backward rolls and finish in the straddle position.

   — Backward roll, holding a ball between your knees.

   — Create your own backward roll variation.

1.　　　　2.

6.

G-28 ROLL AND BALANCE COMBINATIONS

FOCUS: Lateral axis rotations; sequence-building

EQUIPMENT: One mat per pair

ORGANIZATION:

• Overbalancing means shifting the body weight away from the base. Children learn how to roll out safely if they overbalance before attempting more difficult roll-balance combinations. Have players pair off, get a mat, and then scatter around the play area. Check for good spacing.

DESCRIPTION OF ACTIVITY:

1. Show me a balance on one hand and one foot; then overbalance into a roll. Repeat using different "point" balances on small body parts (elbows, knees, hands, feet) and overbalance into a roll.

2. Try these Sequences:

   — Do a low balance, to a forward roll, to another low balance.

   — Do a high balance, forward roll, to a high balance, to a different roll.

   — Do a medium balance, forward roll, to a low balance, to a different roll.

3. Squat, forward roll, into a frog stand. Hold the frog stand for five seconds, then overbalance into another forward roll to a stork stand. Repeat.

4. Squat, forward roll to a squat, hold balance, then do a backward roll to a squat, hold balance.

5. Squat, form a high bridge, tuck into a forward roll to a stand. Repeat.

6. Create your own sequence of forward rolls, backward rolls, frog stands, and other balances and demonstrate to the class.

G-29 ROLL COMBINATIONS

EQUIPMENT: One mat per pair

ORGANIZATION:

• Have players find a partner, get a mat, and then scatter around play area. Partners take turns performing and spotting.

DESCRIPTION OF ACTIVITY:

1. *Forward to Backward Roll:* Squat. Forward roll to finish in the squat position; then backward roll to finish in squat position.

   — Forward roll, stand, half turn, backward roll.

2. *Standing Cross-Ankle Roll:* Stand, cross ankles, forward roll, and stand with ankles crossed. Forward roll twice in this position, then backward roll with ankles still crossed.

3. *Straddle-Leg Roll Series:* Standing with feet astride, backward-roll two times to stand in same position; then forward roll two times in straddle position.

4. *Roll to Front Support:* Squat, roll back into the backward roll position. As you roll over, push with the hands against the mat (like doing a push-up), and reach out for the mat with the legs straight. Finish in the front-support position. Now repeat, using a forward roll into a front-support position.

5. *Angel Roll:* Stand; hold arms out to side. Keep heels close to seat as you forward roll to stand on the mat. Thrust arms forward vigorously as you come out of the roll.

G–30 FORWARD ROLLS ON APPARATUS

FOCUS: Rolling over, along, and off apparatus; station work

EQUIPMENT: Mats; springboards; benches; tables; box horse

ORGANIZATION:

• Set up the apparatus in Stations around the play area, spaced well apart. Place mats at sides and ends of apparatus. Form the class into as many groups as there are Stations, and assign each group to a piece of apparatus. While one player performs, the other players act as spotters. After about three minutes at each Station, have the groups rotate clockwise to the next Station. Choose the Station activities from the following, or include previously taught activities.

DESCRIPTION OF ACTIVITY:

1. *Rolling Over a Low Object (Rolled Mat):* Collect a rolled mat and place it on the mat. Place your hands on the other side of the rolled mat, taking most of your weight on your arms. Tuck your chin to your chest. Remain tucked throughout the roll and stand to finish.
   — Use pillows, cushions, benches as low objects.
   — Roll over another player, or a series of players.
2. *Rolling Down an Incline (Springboard):* Place a mat over the springboard. Place both hands on the mat at the high end of the board. Spring high to get started. Remain in the tuck position during the roll down; then stand.
3. *Rolling Up an Incline (Springboard):* Place a mat over the board. Start at the low end of the board. Use a bigger push-off to roll up the springboard. You may have to use a run-in.
4. *Rolling Along a Box Horse, Bench, or Table:* Spring onto the box into the squat position, do a tucked forward roll along the top of the box, to stand on the mat; then roll again on the mat.
5. *Roll into a Height (Bench, Table, or Box Horse):* Stand on the mat. Grasp the end of the box; spring into a forward roll along and off the box. When your feet touch the floor, roll again.

G–31 THE DIVE ROLL

FOCUS: Springing and landing

EQUIPMENT: Two mats per three players; one ball per three players

ORGANIZATION:

• The Dive Roll is a forward roll, but there is a moment when every part of the body is in the air. Form groups of three players. Have them collect two mats and place them one on top of the other, in a free space. While one player performs, the other two act as spotters. Have the spotters kneel alongside the performer, and place one hand under the head and the other under the thigh as the Dive Roll is performed.

DESCRIPTION OF ACTIVITY:

1. *Low Dive Roll Over a Ball:* Performer, squat on one side of the ball. Push off from the toes to land on the hands close to the ball on the other side. Take weight on hands, tuck the head, and lower yourself into the forward roll position to a stand.
2. *Dive Roll:* Start by standing in the half-crouch position. As this dive is higher, more weight has to be absorbed by the arms. Use the arms to cushion the weight and to lower the body into the roll. Keep the head tucked as you continue to roll to stand. Try the Dive Roll with a run.
3. *Dive Roll Over Objects:* Run in and dive over low objects, such as a rolled mat, a held rope, a lying player, or a kneeling player.

FOCUS: Rotating around the lateral axis   **EQUIPMENT:** Two large mats per group

ORGANIZATION:

- Introduce these Rolls only after the Forward Roll and Backward Roll have been mastered. Have players form groups of four, ideally each member about the same size. Each group collects two large mats and joins them end to end in a free space. Check for good spacing.

DESCRIPTION OF ACTIVITY:

1. *Double Forward Roll:* Partner A, lie down on your back with both feet raised in the air. Partner B, stand with a foot on either side of A's head, alongside his or her ears, and firmly hold A's ankles. Partner A, grasp B's ankles firmly with the thumbs on the inside of his or her ankles. Partner B, start by reaching forward to place A's feet on the mat near his or her seat and perform a Forward Roll while holding onto his or her ankles. At the same time A, raise B's feet off the mat; curl up to the sitting position, then to the standing position. At this point the starting positions are reversed. Continue to roll.

   — How many Double Rolls can you and your partner do in a series?

2. *Double Backward Roll:* Start in the Double Forward Roll position. Player B, start by sitting and doing a Backward Roll and at the same time lift A's feet backward and place them on the mat so that he or she can stand to do a Backward Roll. Continue.

   — How many Double Backward Rolls can you both do in a series?

3. *Back-to-Back Roll:* (Two players perform while the other pair are the spotters.) Stand back to back with your partner. Grasp each other's hands with the elbows to the front. Partner A, with your feet astride and knees bent, lean forward and pull your partner over your hips and back. Continue to hold B's hands. At the same time, Partner B, lift your knees to your chest and do a Backward Roll over A's back to land on your feet on the mat. Throw your head back as you roll.

   — Spotters, stand on either side of performer. Hold B's arm with one hand and under the hip with the other.

4. *Porpoise Roll in Threes:* (Form group of three; the other player is the Coach.) Kneel down on the mat about 1 meter (3 feet apart on hands and knees, all facing the same direction. Number off: The center player is No. 1; the player on his or her right is No. 2; the player on his or her left is No. 3. To start, No. 1, Log Roll toward No. 2, who will leap over you to take your position in the center. No. 2, then Log Roll toward No. 3, who will leap over you to become the new center. No. 3, Log Roll toward No. 1, who will leap over you to become the center again. When leaping over, take your weight on your hands first; then lower yourselves to the mat before log rolling.

   — Continue Log Rolling and leaping. Speed it up. How fast can you go?

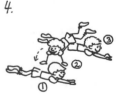

G–33 THE CARTWHEEL

FOCUS: Rotating around medial axis

EQUIPMENT: Several mats; benches; floor tape

ORGANIZATION:

- Arrange several mats end to end. Tape a line down the middle of each row of mats as a guide for performers. Form groups of three or four players and assign each group to a mat area. Have players take turns as performer and spotter. Once learned, have players practice on the lines on the floor.

DESCRIPTION OF ACTIVITY:

1. **Cartwheel—Technique:** Stand sideways to the mat, feet astride and left side toward the mat. Raise left arm overhead and right arm out to the side. Bend to the left side to place the left hand and then right hand in line on the mat. At the same time, throw the right leg overhead, followed by the left leg. The legs should be apart and straight as they pass overhead. Straighten arms and raise your head throughout the Cartwheel. Land on the mat; first with the right foot, then with the left, to stand upright with the feet apart. Spotter, stand behind performer. Hold performer's shorts at waist with a cross-arm grip. As performer cartwheels, the arms will uncross.

2. **Cartwheel on a Large Circle:** Stand facing the center of the circle. Cartwheel around circle, with legs straight and toes pointed. Keep the arms straight and look at your hands. Land on the circle with hands and feet.

3. **Running Cartwheel:** Start with a short run. Just prior to take-off, add a little skip-step on the right foot to take off on the left foot. Do the Cartwheel and finish with a controlled landing. Hold balance.

4. **Series of Cartwheels:** For the first Cartwheel, approach at a slow run. Skip on your right foot with the left leg raised. Perform at least three Cartwheels along a straight line on the mats.

   — Now try the Cartwheels with a little more speed, but don't sacrifice good form for speed. To get more speed, snap the arms down faster and whip the legs over faster.

   — Perform your Cartwheels along the lines marked on the floor.

5. **Spotter:** Move with the performer. Cross your hands and hold the performer's waistband at the hips. Be careful of the performer's legs as they come over.

6. **Cartwheel Along and Off a Bench:**

   — Cartwheel off a bench.

   — Cartwheel along a bench.

G–34 THE ROUND-OFF

FOCUS: Rotating around medial axis

EQUIPMENT: Several mats per pair; several benches

ORGANIZATION:

• Have players learn the Running Cartwheel first and then the Round-Off. Have players find a partner, collect several mats, and arrange them end to end.

DESCRIPTION OF ACTIVITY:

1. **The Round-Off:** The approach is similar to the Running Cartwheel, but your hands are placed closer together in the Round-Off. Do a skip-step before placing your hands on the mat. This increases the momentum. Lift legs high, taking all your weight on your arms. When your feet come overhead, snap them together and make a half turn in the air. Snap the legs down quickly, pushing yourself away from the mat with your hands at the same time. Land on both feet together, facing your take-off point.

2. **Round-Off and Backward Roll:** On completion of the Round-Off, go straight into a Backward Roll. Try not to lose your momentum.

3. **Round-Off from a Bench:** Stand on the bench sideways and about 1 meter (3 feet) from the end. Hold arms above your head. Reach down to do the Round-Off. Dismount onto the mat and finish facing the end of the bench.

4. **One-Hand Round-Off:** Start from the standing position or from a run. Turn sideways and place the left hand down as you would for a normal Round-Off. Fold right arm across chest. Straighten left arm as you push off from the mat. Snap both legs together as you land facing the starting position.

— Left-handed players, do the Round-Off on the right hand.

— Try a One-Hand Round-Off and a Backward Roll.

G–35 THE FRONT WALKOVER

FOCUS: Rotation around the lateral axis

EQUIPMENT: One large mat per group

ORGANIZATION:

• Emphasize that the Front Walkover is done in one continuous movement. Form groups of three players about the same size, collect mats, and find a free work space. Have players take turns at performing and spotting.

DESCRIPTION OF ACTIVITY:

1. **Forward Bridge Stand:** Stand with one foot in front of the other. Rock forward to place both hands on the mat, close to and in front of the front foot. Kick the back leg up straight; then bring the trail leg up to it. Arch your back, bend your knees, and keep your head up as you land on both feet. Support yourself in the high bridge position on hands and feet. Hold the arch; then drop to the mat.

— Spotters, give support under the upper arm and under the lower back.

2. **Front Walkover:** Stand with one foot in front of the other. Rock forward to place both hands on the mat, close to and in front of the front foot. Kick the back leg up straight so that you are momentarily in the split-leg handstand position with your legs straight and the back arched. Keep the arms straight and the head back as the lead foot comes over with the knee bent to land close to the hands. Bring the other leg over straight. Stand with arms outstretched overhead. Keep toes pointed throughout.

— Spotters, lift the performer under the upper back and shoulders.

G—36 LINE SHUTTLES

FOCUS: Tumbling routines; group work

EQUIPMENT: Large folding mats

ORGANIZATION:

- Line Shuttle Tumbling may be used for revision or for a tumbling display act. Form groups of six. Number the players one to six, and have players line up so that the even numbers face the odd numbers. Have each group collect several mats and place them end to end.

DESCRIPTION OF ACTIVITY:

1. *Leap Frog Shuttle:* Player No. 1, run forward to middle to take up the Leap Frog position with a hands-on-knees support.
   No. 2, run forward to leap frog over No. 1; then take up the Leap Frog position in the middle. No. 1, run to end of opposite line.
   No. 3, run forward to leap frog over No. 2; then take up the Leap Frog position in the middle. No. 2, run to end of opposite line. Continue.

2. *Forward Roll Shuttle:* Player No. 1, run to middle to do a Forward Roll, while No. 2 straddle jumps over you as you roll. No. 1 then run to the end of the even number's line. No. 2, run to end of the odd number's line. No. 4, straddle No. 3, and so on. Continue through twice, until you are all back in your original positions.

   — Roller, keep in a tight Tuck Roll, while Straddler, spring high with legs straight and wide apart, and look ahead, not down.

G—37 TUMBLING ROUTINES

FOCUS: Routine-building; tumbling continuity

EQUIPMENT: Line of mats

ORGANIZATION:

- This routine is a revision of selected tumbling stunts done in this section. It may also be used for display purposes. All individual stunts should be learned before attempting the routine. Arrange the mats in a long row. Have the performer move down the mats for the first trip, turn, and return to starting point.

DESCRIPTION OF ACTIVITY:

1. *First Trip:*
   — Stand, rise up on toes, and take a few running steps to a Dive Roll.
   — Do a half-turn with a jump into a Backward Roll, spring to standing position; then do a quarter-turn to either side.
   — Two Cartwheels.

2. *Second Trip:*
   — quarter-turn; take a few running steps into a Headspring.
   — Front Fall Support.
   — Curl-up Headstand for three seconds.
   — Forward Roll to stand and hold balance.

3. Design your own routine, using previously learned stunts, balances, and rolls.

G–38 THE SHOOT-THROUGH

FOCUS: Springing and landing

EQUIPMENT: One mat per player

ORGANIZATION:

• Have players get a mat and take it to a free space.

DESCRIPTION OF ACTIVITY:

1. *Walk-Through:* Start in the front-support position on hands and feet. Without moving hands and using very small steps, walk the feet through your hands until you are in the back-support position with your weight on hands and heels and body extended.

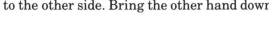

2. *Shoot-Through:* Start in the front-support position. Spring the feet forward in one motion, by lifting your knees and shooting your legs between your hands, to finish in the back-support position. Push upward with the hands to create height. Can you shoot-through in reverse, back to your starting position?

VARIATION:

As a lead-up to the Shoot-Through, have the players lean to one side, taking the weight on that hand. Swing the legs through slightly to the other side. Bring the other hand down quickly for support once the legs have gone through.

G–39 THE HEADSPRING

FOCUS: Springing and landing

EQUIPMENT: One mat per pair

ORGANIZATION:

• Have players find a partner, get a mat, and find a free space.

DESCRIPTION OF ACTIVITY:

Headspring off Stacked Mats: Squat; then swing the hands forward to place them shoulder-width apart on the stacked mat and the head (hairline) on the mat in front of the hands. Spring off both feet into a headstand position with legs straight and piked. Roll forward until you are off-balance forward, and at the same time whip the legs forward and downward, arch the back, and push vigorously off the mat with hands. Land on the mat with legs under body in the squat position; then stand. Spotter, place one hand under upper back and other on the forearm. Lift the performer to the landing.

— Headspring off stacked mats with run-in.

— Standing Headspring from level mat.

G–40 THE HANDSPRING

FOCUS: Springing and landing

EQUIPMENT: Mats; rolled mats

ORGANIZATION:

- Form groups of three players about the same size, collect mats and a rolled mat, and find a free work space. A stack of mats may be substituted for a rolled mat. Have players take turns at performing and spotting.

DESCRIPTION OF ACTIVITY:

1. **Handspring over a Rolled Mat:** Stand; then place your hands on the mat in front of the rolled mat. Look at a spot just in front of your hands. Keep the arms straight as you swing your body and legs up to the Handstand position. Arch your back and push with your hands as you swing both legs over the rolled mat, then forward and down to the mat to a standing position. Keep your head back throughout the handspring.

   — Start with one foot in front of the other.

   — Try this with a short run-in.

   — Spotter, sit on rolled mat, grasp upper arm with one hand, and place the other under shoulders.

2. **Handspring from a Rolled Mat:** Stand, spring to place both hands, shoulder-width apart, on top of rolled mat. Look ahead and swing both legs up straight to the Handstand position. Arch your back and push with your hands as you swing your legs down toward the mat to a standing position.

   — Start with one foot in front of the other.

   — Try this with a short run-in.

   — Spotter, stand alongside performer, grasp upper arm with one hand, and place the other under shoulders. Keep the grasp until performer lands.

3. **Running Handspring:** Stand; run forward for about five steps to do a skip-step from the right foot to the left. Snap the arms down vigorously to place the hands on the mat, about shoulder-width apart and close to the front foot. Throw the right leg up and overhead quickly, followed by the left leg. As the legs move forward and the body is in front of the head, arch the back and push off the mat with the hands to land on both feet in the bent-knee position.

   — Spotters, kneel beside performer, grasp upper arm with one hand, and place the other under shoulders. Move with the performer.

   — Do a Handspring with straight arms.

   — Increase the speed of the run-in.

2.

3.

FOCUS: Springing and landing

EQUIPMENT: Mats; benches

ORGANIZATION:

• Have players get a mat each and find a free space.

DESCRIPTION OF ACTIVITY:

1. *The Upswing:* Kneel on the mat and look ahead. Swing both arms backward, then forward and upward vigorously; at the same time push forcefully with the feet to bring you into the crouch position on your feet.

   — Do the Upswing; then a Forward or Backward Roll.

2. *The Jackknife (Straddle):* Stand with your feet slightly apart; bend at the knees and forward at the waist. Raise your arms backward. Jump, swinging your arms forward and upward vigorously while lifting your legs straight and wide astride in the air. Touch your toes with your fingertips while in the air. Look ahead throughout the jump and bring the feet up to the hands—not the hands down to the feet. Bring your legs down quickly to the mat, bending the knees to cushion the landing. Land as softly as possible.

   — Try this by springing from a low box or bench.

3. *Straddle from a Run:* Run in, take a two-foot take-off with feet parallel; do a Straddle Jump in the air and land softly on the mat.

4. *Straddle Jump from a Bench:* Stand on an anchored bench and do the Jackknife to land softly on the mat. Get as much height as you can.

   — Try this from a chair or box horse.

5. *Split Straddle:* Run in, take a two-foot take-off to straddle jump with one leg forward and the other back while in the air.

6. *Neckspring:* Long-sit; then roll backward onto the neck and shoulders; bring legs overhead in the piked (straight) position. Place your hands alongside your ears with fingertips under shoulders. Roll forward until you are off-balance forward, and at the same time whip the legs forward, arch the back, and push vigorously off the mat with hands and the back of head. Land on the mat in the squat position.

   — Spotter, at first kneel, place one hand under neck and other under shoulder, then lift the performer. Later, place hand under knee, and assist by throwing the legs forward.

   — Perform this first from a stack of mats, then from a level mat.

   — Try the Neckspring from standing position; then roll forward into it.

   — Run in, Dive Roll, into the Neckspring.

G—42 SPRINGBOARD—RUNNING APPROACH

FOCUS: Approach, take-off, springing technique; landing

EQUIPMENT: Springboard, beat-board, or mini-tramp; several mats

ORGANIZATION:

• Review the safety guidelines, the technique of the run-in, springing the springboard, and landing correctly: knees, hips, and ankles bend (give); arms are stretched upward and forward; eyes looking straight ahead. Arrange the class in small groups if you have more than one springboard. Designate three spotters and have them demonstrate the equipment setup and spotting technique.

DESCRIPTION OF ACTIVITY:

1. *Spotting Technique:* Always use three spotters, one on either side of the springboard and the third who stands in front, ready to assist players who overbalance.

   — Spotters, place mats at the sides and in front of the springboard.

   — Performers, have three turns at each task; then change roles with a spotter.

2. *Springing Technique:* Stand on the springboard with your toes slightly over the edge and look straight ahead. Bend at the knees, and take your arms back. Quickly throw your arms forward and upward, spring up, and push off. Cushion your landing by bending at the knees and using arms to balance you. Straighten legs and extend your arms and hands upward. Hold for three seconds.

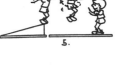

3. *Approach Technique:* Approach the board with short quick running steps; change to a one-foot take-off from the first part of the board (similar to the long jump). Land on both feet at the far end of the board, bringing the arms down and back as you bend at the knees and hips. On the push-off, straighten your body out, stretching vigorously upward with the arms to gain height. Land softly on the mat on two feet, no more than 1 meter (3 feet) ahead of the board. Bend at the hips and knees, take your arms down and back to a safe landing. Stand still and hold your arms out to the side.

4. *Springing Stunts:*

   — *Hand Clap:* Run forward, spring the board. At height of jump, clap hands overhead. Land safely, bending at knees.

   — *Knee Slap:* Run in, spring on the end of the springboard, slap both knees while in the air, and finish with a safe landing. Try to slap your knees twice. Cross your arms then slap your knees.

   — *Heel Slap:* Run in, spring, and slap your heels behind you. Land softly.

   — *Heel Click:* Run in, spring, and "click" your heels in the air. Land properly.

5. *Turning and Rolling Stunts:*

   — *Quarter Turn:* Run in, spring the board, raise left arm overhead, and throw bent arm across body to left, to turn in air. Land and hold balance. Turn to the right ninety degrees; turn to the left ninety degrees.

   — *Half Turn:* Do a 180-degree turn CW in the air to land facing the board. Land softly and hold balance; then do a backward roll to stand. Repeat turning in a CCW direction.

   — *Full Turn:* Do a 360-degree turn to finish facing the mat. Land softly and hold balance. Repeat Full-Turn spring, clap hands while in air, land, do a Forward Roll, then stand.

FOCUS: Springing and landing

EQUIPMENT: Springboard;
safety mats;
one ball; one hoop;
one stocking; one stick

ORGANIZATION:

• At first, teach all springboard activities without the rolls. As ability improves, add the rolls. Designate three spotters. Have them set up the springboard and mats with the long sides of the mats to the end of the springboard and then take up positions: one spotter on each side of the springboard and the third in front ready to assist. Caution the players to land first, count "one, two, three," then proceed with the next stunt; otherwise, they may go into their next stunt directly from the board. Remind the players to look ahead while in mid-air. Explain that if "you look up, you step up; if you look down, you fall down."

DESCRIPTION OF ACTIVITY:

1. *High Spring:* Run in, spring the board, throw arms upward to get as much height as you can. Land on mat in a safe landing no more than 1 meter (3 feet) ahead of the board; then go into a Forward Roll. Stand; hold balance for three seconds with arms out sideways.

2. *Tuck:* Run in, spring high, "tuck" (clasp your knees to your chest), then whip the legs down quickly to land on the mat, do a Forward Roll. Hold balance.

3. *Jackknife or Pike:* Run in, spring the board high. Keep the legs astride and straight as you lean forward and bring feet up to hands to touch your toes. Whip the legs down quickly to land on both feet, Forward Roll, stand, and hold balance.

4. *Touch the Stick:* (Teacher, stand on the box horse or chair holding a wand, hockey stick, or broom handle to challenge players to touch it.) Run in, spring the board, throw arms upward to get as much height as you can. Try to touch the stick with both hands, land on the mat in a safe landing.

   — (Suspend a ball in a stocking.) Try to slap or spike the ball.

   — (Pull a climbing rope up and tie it at a suitable height.) Run in; spring from the floor or from the board to touch the rope.

5. *Land in the Hoop:* (Place a hoop about 45 centimeters [18 inches] in front of the board.) Spring as high as you can to land inside the hoop on the mat.

6. *Dunk:* Get a small ball. Stand on the board, then try to dunk the ball in the basketball basket and land softly on the mat. Try the dunk with a short run-in.

7. *Run In, Spring, Catch a Ball:* While at the height of your spring, catch a ball thrown by a partner, land, do two Forward Rolls over the ball, stand, and hold a balance of your choice. Land, do two Forward Rolls, Half Turn, and a Backward Roll.

G—44 SPRINGBOARD—SEQUENCE-BUILDING

FOCUS: Springing and tumbling

EQUIPMENT: Springboard; safety mats; one large ball per group

ORGANIZATION:

- Designate three spotters. Have them set up the springboard and mats, with the long sides of the mats to the end of the springboard; then take up positions: one spotter on each side of the springboard and the third in front ready to assist players who overbalance. Teach all springboard activities without the rolls, at first. As ability improves, add the rolls. Remind players to look ahead at their own height while in the air. Caution the players to land first, count "one, two, three," then proceed with the next stunt; otherwise, they may go into their next stunt directly from the board.

DESCRIPTION OF ACTIVITY:

1. ***Run in, Spring, Land, Dive Roll, Forward Roll:*** Run in, spring to land on the mat, do a Dive Roll, then a Forward Roll. Hold balance.
   — Spring, land, Dive Roll over a ball, Forward Roll, hold balance.

2.

2. ***Run in, Spring, Seat Kick, Land, Cartwheel:*** Run in, spring the board to do a Seat Kick, land, then run into a Cartwheel, stand, and hold balance.
   — Do a Backward Roll after the Cartwheel, and hold balance.
   — Throw your arms overhead as you do the Seat Kick.

3. ***Run in, Spring, Clap Hands Under Leg:*** Run in, spring the board to clap hands under your left leg, land, do two Crossed-ankle Forward Rolls, stand, and hold balance.
   — Clap under your right leg.

3.

4. ***Run in, Spring, Clap Hands Under Seat:*** Run in, spring, clap your hands under your seat, land, do a Forward Roll, half turn, Backward Roll, stand, and hold balance.

5. ***Run in, Spring, Clap Hands in Front and Back:*** While in the air, clap hands in front and behind your body, land, do two Forward Rolls, stand, and hold balance.

6.

6. ***Backward Tuck:*** Stand on the board with your back to the mat. Spring back to a Tuck (hug your knees to chest); then whip legs down quickly to land on the mat. Do a Backward Roll and stand.

7. ***Backward Pike, Touch Knees:*** Stand on the board with your back to the mat. Spring back to a Pike (touch knees with hands). Land, do a Backward Roll, then stand.

7.

8. ***Turn, Backward Pike, Touch Knees:*** Face the mats, spring, half turn, do a Backward Pike to touch knees. Land, do a Backward Roll, and stand.

9. ***Turn, Backward Pike, Touch Toes:*** Face the mats, spring, half turn, do a Backward Pike to touch the toes. Land, do a Backward Roll, and stand.

G-45 INTRODUCTION TO BOX HORSE—MOUNTS

FOCUS: Vaulting

EQUIPMENT: Box horse;
safety mats;
springboard

ORGANIZATION:

• Choose six players to set up the equipment and two to demonstrate the spotting positions. Spotters generally stand on the far side of the box to prevent falls. Set the box low at first and add sections as ability improves. Arrange a double thickness of mats in the landing area. Explain the terms: The term *Long Box* is used when the length of the box is used. The springboard is placed at one end. The *Short Box* or *Side Box* is used when the box is approached from the side. The springboard is placed at the side of the box.

DESCRIPTION OF ACTIVITY:

1. *Squat Mount* (Long Box): Take a short run, take off from board, place both hands about 30 centimeters (12 inches) from near end of the box. Bring knees up to jump lightly into a squat position on box, landing on both feet. Stand on box. Walk to the end; keep your head up as you jump to a safe landing on mats. Spotter, stand beside performer at the near end, to prevent falling backward. Then walk to the far end to hold an arm to assist with the landing.

2. *Straddle Seat* (Long Box): Run in, spring the board, place hands together as far up the box as you can manage, then bring the legs over straight and apart to sit on the box. Keep legs straight and the toes pointed. Place hands forward to grip one hand on each side of the box. Lean forward, tucking elbows into hips and taking weight on the hands. In one motion, swing both legs back and over to one side of the box to land on the mats.

3. *Forward Roll Mount* (Long Box): Run in, spring the board, grasp the edges of the box about 15 centimeters (6 inches) from the near end, and getting the hips high, do a Forward Roll along the top of box. Spread legs and point toes to sit on the box.

— Spotters, spot as for the Forward Roll.

G-46 BOX HORSE—BASIC VAULTS

EQUIPMENT: See G-45.

DESCRIPTION OF ACTIVITY:

1. *Through Vault Between Two Backs* (Short Box): Two players, sit on box about 30 centimeters (12 inches) apart in an upright position with backs to the vaulter. Place hands behind you to hold the rim of the box. Keep the shoulders firm. Vaulter, run in, spring to place hands lightly on inside shoulders of sitters. Look straight ahead throughout this vault. At the same time, draw the knees up and swing body between the two sitters to land lightly on the mats on far side of box in a safe landing. Spotters, stand in front to prevent overbalancing. Grasp an arm as the vaulter comes over.

2. *Straddle Vault over One Back* (Short Box): One player, sit on box with back to vaulter. Place hands behind you to grasp rim of the box. Draw your chin down to chest. Vaulter, run in, spring the board, and place hands lightly on sitter's upper back to Straddle Vault (Leap Frog) over. Spotters, stand in front to prevent overbalancing.

VARIATION:

After each vault, go into a Forward Roll.

G-47 BOX HORSE—FACE VAULTS

FOCUS: Vaulting

EQUIPMENT: Box horse; safety mats; springboard

ORGANIZATION:

- Choose players to set up the equipment and one to demonstrate the spotting positions. For all these vaults, spotter stands on far side of box. Set the box low at first and add sections as ability improves. Arrange a double thickness of mats in the landing area. For the Courage Vault, explain that the hands are not used during the dismount and to rock back and forth to swing off. For Side Vault, check that players keep both legs together as they lift them over the box. Have performer tell spotter which side the legs will swing over.

DESCRIPTION OF ACTIVITY:

1. *Face Vault* (Short Box): Run in, spring to grasp the edges of box, close to one end (keep the hands parallel). Swing the body and legs over in a straight line to land on the mats on far side of box. Raise hands in air and hold for three seconds. Spotter, grasp closer arm above the elbow and assist over if necessary.

2. *High Face Vault:* As for the Face Vault, except that the body and legs are swung over vertically and the arms are kept straight. Land with a soft landing. Spotter, grasp the closer arm above the elbow.

3. *Courage Vault* (Short Box): Run in, take off on both feet to Knee Mount position on box. Dismount by springing from knees and lower legs, to land on mat on far side of box. Use an upswing of the arms and a forward body lean to lift the body up and forward off the box.

4. *Side Vault* (Short Box): Run in, spring to place the near hand, with arm slightly bent, near one end of box. At the same time swing your body and legs in a straight line over to stand on far side of box. Let spotter know which side your legs will swing over. Try a High Side Vault.

G-48 BOX HORSE—STUNTS

EQUIPMENT: See G-47.

DESCRIPTION OF ACTIVITY:

1. *Backward Roll on the Long Box:* Sit straddling the box on the near end with your back to the box. Roll back to do a Backward Roll. As you roll, grasp the edges of the box to push yourself to a standing position on the mat at the far end of the box. Do another Backward Roll on the mat.

2. *Headstand on the Long Box:* Run in, spring to grasp the edges of the box, to place your head on the box and to raise the body and legs to the vertical Headstand position. Your head and hands should form a triangle. Hold for three seconds, and return legs to mat; Backward Roll on the mat.

3. *Headstand and Forward Roll on the Long Box:* Run in, spring to a Headstand; then overbalance and tuck the chin and the knees to the chest. Let go the edges of the box as you complete the Forward Roll. Land on mat in standing position; Forward Roll on the mat.

4. *Dive Roll over the Short Box:* Run in; take off from both feet to dive over the low box. As the hands are placed on the mat on the far side of the box, take the weight on the arms, draw the knees and chin onto the chest, and do a Forward Roll on the mat on the far side.

G-49 USING THE CLIMBING ROPES

FOCUS: Safety guidelines; climbing technique   **EQUIPMENT:** Climbing ropes; safety mats

ORGANIZATION:

- Train players to arrange the ropes ready for activity; demonstrate and provide practice time for this. Discuss the safety guidelines, and teach the correct procedures for climbing and descending the rope. Form small groups to practice climbing and descending.

DESCRIPTION OF ACTIVITY:

1. *Safety Guidelines:*
   — Use the ropes only when told to do so.
   — Stand well away from the ropes when others are using them, unless spotting.
   — Do not tie knots in the ropes.
   — Do not climb a swinging rope.
   — Climb, hand-over-hand going up and hand-under-hand coming down. Do not slide, as this causes rope burns.
   — Do not interfere with others who are using the ropes.
   — When climbing, look up and hold tight.
   — Always place mats under the climbing ropes when in use.
   — Do not leave a rope swinging after a dismount.
2. Move to a rope and take turns at climbing hand-over-hand. Climb for three pulls; then come down hand-under-hand three times.
3. *Standing Pull-Up:* Stand and hold rope high. Without moving feet, lower yourself hand-under-hand until you are lying on mat; then pull up to stand.
4. *Sitting Pull-Up:* Sit and hold rope high. Brace feet against mat. Raise yourself hand-over-hand, with body straight, to the standing position. Lower yourself and repeat.

G-50 CLIMBING TECHNIQUES

EQUIPMENT: See G–49.

ORGANIZATION:

- Have players stand at rope. Choose one player to demonstrate climbing methods and have everyone practice them. Players may then choose the climbing method they find the most comfortable.

DESCRIPTION OF ACTIVITY:

1. *Climbing Methods:*
   — *Stirrup:* Rope should hang outside left leg, under left foot and over top of right foot. Stand on rope with left foot to lock feet in position.
   — *Foot-Leg Lock:* Rope should hang in front of body and between legs. Hook right leg around rope so that it passes over top of right foot. Stand on rope with left foot to lock rope in position.
   — *Scissors:* Rope should hang inside right knee and outside right foot. Cross left foot behind foot. Press rope between inside of left foot and outside of right foot to lock it in position.
2. *To Climb:* Pull up with arms, allowing rope to slide through feet and knees. Lock feet on rope after each pull, straighten legs, and reach hands up for another pull. Practice locking feet after each pull.
3. *To Descend:* Lock feet in position; move hands down rope hand-under-hand, lowering chest until knees are bent; hold your position and lower legs. Lock feet in new position and lower hands again.

G–51 ROPE CLIMBS

FOCUS: Climbing; arm and shoulder strength

EQUIPMENT: Climbing ropes; safety mats; one ribbon or bell per rope

ORGANIZATION:

• Review the climbing techniques. Set up climbing ropes and mats. Tie a ribbon around each rope about 3 meters (10 feet) to 5 meters (15 feet) from the floor. Divide the class into as many groups as there are ropes. Have groups stand at the ropes.

DESCRIPTION OF ACTIVITY:

1. *Touch the Ribbon:* Stand at rope. Using the Stirrup Method, climb hand-over-hand to touch the ribbon and return to floor hand-under-hand.
   — Climb using the Foot-leg Lock Method.
   — Climb using the Scissors Method.
2. *Speed Climb:* Climb as fast as you can, using the method of your choice, to touch the ribbon. Descend using the same method.
   — Start from the standing position, speed climb using the hand only.
   — Start from the sitting position using the hands only.
3. *Climbing Relays:* Each group, stand in front of your rope. On the signal "Go," run forward and climb to touch the ribbon; then return hand-under-hand to tag the next player in the group. Remember, do not slide down the ropes!

G–52 BASIC ROPE SWINGS

FOCUS: Hanging and swinging

EQUIPMENT: Climbing ropes; safety mats; box horse or benches; one beanbag and hoop per group

ORGANIZATION:

• Place mats under ropes. Explain the Basic Rope Swing positions and have several players demonstrate them. Form groups of three players: one performer and two spotters. Assign each group to a climbing rope and a box (or bench); then have all players practice these swings from the bench.

DESCRIPTION OF ACTIVITY:

1. *Take-Off:* Push back to gather speed.
2. *Sitting Swing:* Swing freely in the sitting position. Do not knot the rope.
3. *Standing Swing:* Climb up, hang freely, and hold elbows in to your sides; then swing.
4. *L-Swing:* Hold the legs in the "L" position. When the legs start to drop, swing again and hold the "L" once more.
5. *Free Hang:* Pull the knees to the chest.
6. *Tarzan Swing:* Stand on the bench, about 2 meters (6 feet) away from the rope. Grasp the rope high, swing forward across the mat three times while sounding like Tarzan, then release.
   — Swing from a bench and land in a hoop.
   — Hold a beanbag between your feet and swing across the mat, drop the beanbag in the hoop, and return to the bench.
   — Swing from the bench, grab the beanbag out of the hoop with your feet, and place it on the bench when you land.

G–53 CLIMBING ROPES—SWINGS AND TURNS

FOCUS: Hanging; swinging and turning

EQUIPMENT: Climbing ropes; safety mats; box horse or benches

ORGANIZATION:

- Place mats under ropes over the entire swinging area. Explain each of these swings and have several players demonstrate them. Form groups of three players: one performer and two spotters. Assign each group to a climbing rope and mat-covered box or bench; then have all players practice these swings from the box.

DESCRIPTION OF ACTIVITY:

1. *The Pirate Swing:* Spring up and back to gain height and momentum, swing out as far as you can, then return to stand on the box.
   - Swing three times shouting "Shazaam!" Place feet in different positions each time. Return to sit on the box.
2. *The Whip Kick:* (Position box horse about 1 meter [3 feet] behind climbing rope.) Push back to gather speed at take-off. On forward swing, whip legs forward and upward to increase speed. Land softly on box. Repeat.
3. *Swing and Turn:* Swing out from the box, do a half turn at the end of the forward swing, and return to stand on the box.
   - Do a full turn at the end of the forward swing. Return to sit on the box.
   - Can you do all these using different leg positions?
4. *Circle Swing:* Stand on the box. Push out sideways at take-off to swing in a circle to return to the box. Return to sit on the box.

G–54 SWINGING GAMES

FOCUS: Hanging and swinging

EQUIPMENT: Climbing ropes; box horses; safety mats; three hoops per group; three beanbags per group; three bowling pins per group

ORGANIZATION:

- Set up the box about 2 meters (6 feet) behind the rope. Place mats all over the swinging area. Have players form groups of three and take turns on the rope. The two spotters stand ready on either side of performer.

DESCRIPTION OF ACTIVITY:

1. *Beanbag Drop:* Place three hoops on the mats in front of the box area and place three beanbags on top of the box. Stand on the box, hold a beanbag between your feet, then swing out to drop the beanbag into a hoop, and return to the box. Can you drop all three beanbags in the hoops?
2. *Rope Bowling:* Place three bowling pins about 5 meters (15 feet) away from the box and give each group a ball. Hold the rope high, place the ball between your feet, and swing forward toward the pins. At the end of forward swing, release ball and try to bowl over the pins.
   - Move the pins farther away.
   - Have a bowling contest between groups.

G—55 TWO CLIMBING ROPES CHALLENGES

FOCUS: Hanging and swinging

EQUIPMENT: two climbing ropes per group;
safety mats;
box horse or bench per group;
one ball per group;
one laundry basket per group

ORGANIZATION:

- For eight climbing ropes, divide the class into four equal groups. Assign each group two climbing ropes and have each group place a mat directly under the climbing rope. Each performer should have a spotter positioned on each side. To begin, each group sits in a file behind the climbing ropes.

DESCRIPTION OF ACTIVITY:

1. Explore different ways of hanging from two ropes.

   — What shapes can you make as you hang from the ropes?

   — Try to climb from one rope to the other, then to the floor.

   — Hang on the two ropes and let your feet "run in the air."

2. *Twister:* Twist yourself into different positions while hanging onto the two ropes.

3. *Hula:* Stand; jump up to grasp the ropes as high as you can. Pull up so that your arms are bent. Can you swing your hips around in a circle to do the "Hula"? Swing your hips the other way.

4. *Still Rope Swing:* Stand holding both ropes as high as you can so that your feet do not touch the mat. Pull up so that your arms are bent and your legs straight. Can you swing your legs forward and backward without swinging the ropes?

5. *L-Sit Hang:* Grasp the ropes as high as you can. Can you raise your legs in the "L" position as you hang?

6. *Inverted Hang:* Grasp the ropes as high as you can, push off, and swing yourself upside down, hooking your feet around the rope. Can you hold this inverted position for five seconds?

7. *Swing and Shoot:* (Place two stacked benches with a mat on top, under the rope.) Stand holding the two ropes as high as you can, well back from the benches. Bend your arms and bring the knees up into your chest as you swing forward over the benches. Just before landing, shoot both legs forward, arch your back, and look up. Land on the mat with a soft landing.

   — Add a Forward Roll after landing. Land in a hoop.

8. *Steal the Hoop:* (Have a partner hold a hoop about 2.5 meters [6 to 8 feet] in front of the ropes.) Swing forward on both ropes to place your feet through the hoop, open your legs to take the hoop out of partner's hands, swing back to stand in the hoop on the mat.

9. *Shoot a Basket:* Stand on the mat about 2 meters (6 feet) behind ropes. Place a ball between your feet. Hold the ropes up high; then swing across to drop the ball into the laundry basket and return.

   — How many times can your group drop the ball in the basket in two minutes?

   — Have your partner catch the ball.

10. *Skin the Cat:* Stand; hold ropes about shoulder height with arms bent. Lift knees to chin; tilt head back so that you roll over backward between your hands to place your feet on the mat. Without changing position of your hands, go back to starting position.

11. Invent your own "Two-Rope Hanging Stunt"!

12. Invent a "Two-Rope Hanging Game"!

G-56 HORIZONTAL BAR—THE GRIPS

FOCUS: Hanging and swinging

EQUIPMENT: Horizontal bar or even or uneven parallel bars; several mats

ORGANIZATION:

• These grips can be taught using the horizontal bar, the parallel bars, or the uneven parallel bars. Arrange the players around the bars. Explain the procedure for carrying, setting up, and using the bars. Explain and have players demonstrate the following five basic grips. For practice, have the players form groups of at least three players: one performer, and two spotters who stand on either side of the performer. Review these Safety Grips often. When moving backward, use the Over Grip; when moving forward, use the Under Grip. Have the players use a low bar at first to gain confidence. Mats should always be used under the horizontal bars. Emphasize that players always use a safe landing: Bend at the knees, hips, and ankles to absorb the shock.

DESCRIPTION OF ACTIVITY:

1. **Over Grip:** When hanging from the bar, place the thumb underneath and the fingers on top. You should be able to see your knuckles.

2. **Under Grip:** Grasp the bar with fingers and thumb pointing toward you.

3. **Mixed Grip:** This is a combination grip: One hand holds the bar with the Over Grip, the other with the Under Grip.

4. **Cross Grip:** Hold the bar with both hands using the Over Grip, but the arms are crossed.

5. **Eagle Grip:** Hang with the arms spread wide and your back to the bar. Your knuckles should be on top of the bar and your thumbs under.

6. **Practice:** Stand by your bar. When I call out the names of the five Grips, I want you to show your group how to do them. They will help you if you have problems.

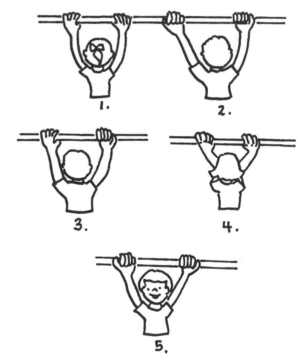

G–57 HORIZONTAL BAR—HANGS AND SWINGS

FOCUS: Hanging; swinging; dismounting

EQUIPMENT: Horizontal bar or even or uneven parallel bars; safety mats

ORGANIZATION:

- Review the Safety Grips. Arrange the players around the bars. Explain and have players demonstrate the following activities. Have the players form groups of at least three players: one performer, and two spotters who stand on either side of the performer.

DESCRIPTION OF ACTIVITY:

1. Stand facing the bar. Jump forward to hang on the bar. Use the Over Grip; use the Under Grip. Swing back and forth each time.

2. *Long Hang or Pencil Hang:* Jump up to grasp the bar with the Over Grip. Hang as straight as a pencil and look ahead. Dismount by dropping straight down to the floor to a safe landing. Finish with arms overhead.

   — Hold your hang for ten seconds.

   — Bring knees to chest. Hold for five seconds.

3. *Inverted Hang in the Tucked Position:* Start in Long Hang position. Draw knees up to chest as you lean backward and hold this position.

   — Spotters, hold the upper arm and give support under the shoulder with the other hand.

4. *Inverted Hang in the Piked Position:* Start in Long Hang position. Draw legs up straight so that they finish parallel to the floor.

   — Can you get your legs close to your face and still hold them straight with toes pointed?

5. *Dismounts:* Swing, gradually come to a still hang, release the bar, and drop gently to a safe landing on the mat.

   — Swing, bend slightly at the hips, and release the grasp at the height of the backswing. Drop straight down onto both feet to a safe landing.

6. Jump up to a Long Hang. Swing forward and backward five times under control.

   — Dismount at the height of the backswing; dismount at the height of the frontswing.

7. *Swing and Arch:* Grasp the bar with the Over Grip while your feet are still on the floor. Push off with one foot as you throw the other forward and upward. Swing under the bar and at the same time pull in with the arms and throw your head back. Stretch the whole body to a slightly arched position with tummy forward. Dismount by releasing the bar at the height of the forward swing to a safe landing.

8. *Kick over the Rope:* Place a rope about 60 centimeters to 1 meter (2 to 3 feet) in front of the bar. Grasp the bar with the Over Grip. Run under the bar, kicking up with one leg, arch the back, throw the head back, and land over the rope. Hold your balance with arms out overhead.

   — Move the rope closer or farther away.

   — Have two players hold the rope loosely about 30 centimeters (12 inches) above the mat.

9. *Knee Hang:* Hang by the Over Grip. Bring the feet up through the hands; hook the knees over the bar. Hang by the knees without using the hands. Return to hold the bar; then dismount.

   — Spotters, hold performer's hands as they hang upside down.

FOCUS: Supporting and hanging

EQUIPMENT: Horizontal bars; safety mats

ORGANIZATION:

- Adjust the bar to head height. Place mats under the bars. Form groups of at least three players: one performer, and two spotters, who stand on either side of the performer. Have spotters support under the arm and back. Advise players to wear sweat pants for all circles. Have spotters stand on either side: Grip one arm and support under the shoulder or back with the other. Insist that all performers be spotted during inverted hangs. Encourage players to finish in good form with toes pointed and head up.

DESCRIPTION OF ACTIVITY:

1. **Skin the Cat:** Hang from bar using the Over Grip. Kick feet up by bringing knees to chest. Bring feet up between your arms. Slowly lower your feet as far as possible. Release bar and drop to floor.

   — Can you return to starting position and then dismount?

   — Spotters, hold arm with one hand and support under shoulder with other hand.

2. **Forward Circle:** Hold bar with the Over Grip. Spring up to the "Front Support" position on bar. Overbalance forward and bend forward at the waist to turn around the bar. Pull bar in close to your tummy. As you roll over, drop to the mat while still holding the bar.

3. **Upward Circle:** Stand facing the bar. Hold bar with the Under Grip. Spring upward with one straight leg to swing it over the bar first. At the same time bring the trailing leg over to join it. Bend arms as your legs go over the bar; pull the bar into your hips as you circle over it. Finish in the front-support position on the bar.

   — Swing both legs over together.

4. **Single Knee Circle Mount:** Hold the bar with the Over Grip. Place one leg over the bar and between the hands (knee over the bar). Raise the free leg up and straight. Pull on the bar, and at the same time swing the free leg down quickly so that the body will rise to sit on the top of the bar.

5. **Hip-Circle Backward:** Mount the bar with an Upward Circle, and hold your balance in the front-support position, with all the body weight on the hands. Swing the legs and thighs upward with a slight bend at the hips, about 20 centimeters (8 inches) away from the bar. Throw the head back and let the momentum circle you around the bar. Stop in the front-support position again on top of the bar. Dismount by slowly dropping to a Long Hang. Release and land on the mat.

6. **Single Knee Circle Backward:** Swing up to a Single Knee Circle Mount. Grasp the bar in the Over Grip, support your weight on your hands, and sit in an upright position. Using the free leg for momentum, swing it forward and upward, and at the same time, let the body fall backward to rotate around the bar to sit once again on top of the bar. Keep a good grasp on the bar throughout.

7. **Double Knee Circle Backward:** Start by sitting on the bar. Grasp with the Over Grip. Sit upright; fall backward absorbing some of the weight by having your knees hooked around the bar. Use the head and shoulders to add momentum to the swing as you come up to sit on top of the bar again. Keep most of the weight on your hands throughout.

G—59 INTRODUCTION TO PARALLEL BARS

FOCUS: Supporting and balancing

EQUIPMENT: Parallel bars; safety mats

ORGANIZATION:

- Many exercises can be mastered on the parallel bars in a very short time. The bars are adjustable for height and width. When beginning, work at the lowest possible height. Bars should be slightly more than shoulder-width apart. Always place mats between, at both sides and at ends of the bars. Spotters should always be used, with safety the first consideration. Have spotters stand on both sides of the bars and hold one arm and support the shoulders or back with the other. Teach the players the names of the exercises so they can be referred to in subsequent lessons. Have players hold all supports and balances for five seconds.

DESCRIPTION OF ACTIVITY:

1. Revise the Under Grip, the Over Grip, and the Mixed Grip. (Refer to G-56).

2. Practice the Outer Grip and the Inner Grip. (See diagram.)

3. *Cross Stand:* Stand at the end or side of the bar facing the length of the bars.

4. *Side Stand:* Stand at the side facing the bar.

5. *Cross Support:* Cross stand, hold bars, spring up, and hold five seconds. Keep arms and body straight, toes pointed, shoulders down, and head up.

6. *Front Support:* Side Stand, grasp bar, spring to straight arm and body position. Hold shoulders down, point toes, look ahead, and hold balance.

7. *Rear Support:* As for the Front Support, but with the back to the bar. Keep your head high, look ahead, and hold balance.

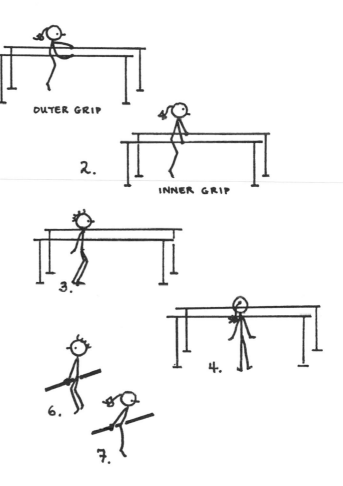

OUTER GRIP

2.

INNER GRIP

3.

4.

6.

7.

G–60 PARALLEL BARS—SUPPORTS AND SWINGS

FOCUS: Supporting and swinging

EQUIPMENT: Parallel bars;
safety mats

ORGANIZATION:

• Adjust the bars for height and width, and arrange mats. Appoint spotters: one on each side of performer, to hold one arm and support under the shoulders or back with the other hand. Have performers hold balances for five seconds.

DESCRIPTION OF ACTIVITY:

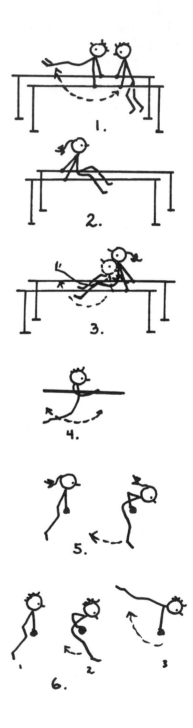

1. *Forward and Backward Swing:* Cross Stand between the bars; then spring up to grasp the bars and straighten the arms. Without moving the arms, swing back and forth so that the body is horizontal above the bars.

2. *Cross Straddle Sit:* Cross Stand, grasp the end of the bars, and in one motion swing the straight legs up between the bars with toes pointed to sit astride the bars.

3. *Swing to Cross Stradde Sit:* Cross Stand with hands on the bar. In one motion, spring upward and swing the legs forward to Straddle Sit on the bar, with arms straight, head up and toes pointed. Make yourself as tall as possible. Regrasp in front, lean forward, raise legs backward; then swing them forward to Straddle Sit again. Repeat one more time.

4. *Under-Arm Support:* Cross Stand between the bars, and in one motion, spring up to grasp the bars and allow the bars to pass under the shoulders. Keep the elbows wide, the body erect, and toes pointed. Prevent the shoulders from sagging.

5. *Front Support with Swing:* Side Stand, spring up to the Front-Support position. While keeping the hips on the bar, swing the legs backward and forward. Bend at the hips on the front swing, and straighten the arms and body on the back swing. Keep the legs straight and toes pointed throughout. Repeat.

6. *Front Support with High Swing:* As for No. 5, but the hips leave the bar on the backswing. On the backswing, raise your hips higher than your elbows and keep the arms straight and toes pointed. As your hips contact the bar on the downswing, lean forward, bend arms, and pike the legs. Repeat.

G–61 GYMNASTIC OBSTACLE COURSE

FOCUS: Review of skills

EQUIPMENT: Mats;
rolled mat;
box horse;
hoops;
crash pad;
table;
climbing rope;
horizontal bar;
springboard

ORGANIZATION:

- Set up name cards and equipment at stations around the play area. Start with about eight stations: The number of stations should equal at least half the number of players in the class. Each station should be a safe distance apart and take about the same time to complete. Select a mixture of traveling; rolling; springing and landing; swinging; vaulting; climbing activities. Select a variety of apparatus and equipment. Use previously learned skills only. Begin by "walking" players through the obstacle course so that they know what to do at each station. Encourage players to move quickly, but safely, through the course. Try to avoid "bottlenecks," or places where the activity slows down; keep the players moving! Therefore, provide duplicate equipment at some stations to allow more players to work at the same time. Have players repeat the course two or three times. Have players pair off and go through the Obstacle Course in fifteen-second intervals.

DESCRIPTION OF ACTIVITY:

Station 1. Angel Roll over Crash Pad: Crash pad, mats.

Station 2. Face Vault over Box, Backward Roll on Mat: Box horse, mats.

Station 3. Dive Roll over Rolled Mat: Double thickness of mats, rolled mat.

Station 4. Two Judo Rolls: Mats in line.

Station 5. Jackknife off Springboard, Land in Hoop, Forward Roll: Springboard, hoop, mats.

Station 6. Spring to Table, Swing out, Land in Hoop: Mat-covered table, climbing rope, hoop, mats.

Station 7. Two Cartwheels, Two Straddle-Leg Backward Rolls: Mats.

Station 8. Upward Circle over the Bar: Horizontal bar, mats. (See G-58.)

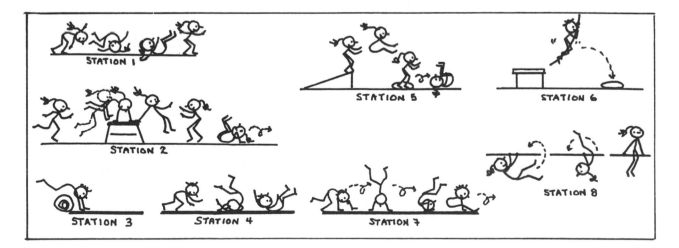

Game Skills

Game Skills activities develop the abilities children need to participate in most traditional games, such as soccer, volleyball, basketball, softball, and football as well as more innovative games, such as parachute play, scooter play, Frisbee™ play, and juggling.

The 205 Game Skills activities in this section are arranged in units that you might teach over a three- or four-week period.

GS–1 HOOP SPINNING FUN

FOCUS: Manipulation; spinning; rolling; partner work

EQUIPMENT: One hoop per player

ORGANIZATION:

• Have players get a hoop and take it to a Home space.

DESCRIPTION OF ACTIVITY:

1. Show me how you can make your hoop spin! Begin by holding your hoop with both hands so that the hoop is standing upright. Place your favorite hand on top of the hoop, grasping it between your thumb and forefinger. Spin the hoop by a quick flick of your wrist in a circular motion.

2. Can you spin your hoop like a top, touch a wall, and then return to grab your hoop before it drops to the floor? Who can spin it, and touch two walls? Touch three walls?

3. Show me how to spin it CW; CCW; with your right hand; with your left hand. Who can keep the hoop spinning the longest?

4. See if you can spin your hoop like an eggbeater; then run around it once and catch it before it falls to the floor. Repeat, running around it in the other direction. How many times can you run around it before it falls?

5. Find a partner. In a free space, stand and face your partner, about 3 meters (10 feet) apart. Spin your hoop in your own space. Can you catch your partner's hoop before it stops spinning?

GS–2 PARTNER HOOP ROLLS AND SPIN TASKS

1. Roll your hoop to your partner while your partner rolls his or her hoop to you. Catch and repeat. Can you do this without moving from your spot?

2. Move across the play area with your partner while rolling hoops back and forth between you.

3. Spin your hoop and then run around your partner's spinning hoop and return to catch your own hoop with your right hand. Repeat, catching with your left hand. Who can make two trips around?

4. Stand 4 meters (12 feet) apart. Spin your hoops at the same time and then run figure-8s around the two hoops. How many times can you pass your hoop before both hoops stop spinning?

5. Roll your hoops toward each other and then run to change places so that you catch your hoop before it stops rolling.

6. Back-spin your hoop and straddle jump over it as the hoop comes toward you; then run and grab your partner's hoop.

7. **Ali-Oop:** Form groups of three and return one of the hoops. Outside players stand facing each other about 5 meters (15 feet) apart. Roll the hoop back and forth to each other while the middle player straddle jumps it. Change roles after every five jumps. Continue until everyone has had a turn in the middle.

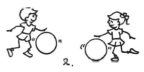

GS–3 HOOP TOSS AND TWIRL FUN

FOCUS: Tossing and catching; rotations; partner work

EQUIPMENT: One hoop per player; one large cone marker or chair

ORGANIZATION:

• Have each child get a hoop, take it to a free space, and hold the hoop vertically. Check for good spacing.

DESCRIPTION OF ACTIVITY:

1. **Hoop Toss and Catch Technique:** Hold your hoop in your favorite hand. Use an underhand toss to send the hoop into the air. By flicking your wrist as you let go, the hoop should spin backward. Keep watching the hoop while it is in flight. Catch it with both hands.
2. **Hoop Tossing Tasks:**
   — Toss the hoop with your favorite hand and catch it with both hands ten times.
   — Toss the hoop with your other hand and catch it with both hands ten times.
   — Toss and catch the hoop with your right hand ten times.
   — Toss and catch the hoop with your left hand ten times.
   — Toss the hoop with one hand and catch it in the other hand.
   — Toss and catch your hoop while walking; while skipping.
   — Toss, clap hands, catch hoop; toss, slap hands to floor, catch hoop.
   — Toss your hoop in the air, spin around, and catch it.
   — From a low position toss hoop overhead. Jump up to catch it in the air.
   — Toss hoop overhead; let hoop drop over your head and shoulders as it lands.
   — Find another way to toss and catch your hoop.
   — Add your own idea!
3. **Partner Hoop Toss:** Find a partner and stand 3 meters (10 feet) apart, facing each other. (As their ability and accuracy improve, have partners step back to increase throwing distance between them.)
   — Using one hoop, can you toss the hoop back and forth to each other and catch?
   — Can you each toss your hoop to the other at the same time and catch?
   — One partner toss the hoop while the other partner rolls it. Change roles after ten tries.
   — Toss high while your partner tosses low.
   — Catch both hoops and toss them back at the same time.
   — Raise your arm in front and have your partner toss hoop over your arm within three tries. Change roles and repeat.
   — Collect a cone marker or a chair (turned upside down). How many times can you toss the hoops over the marker or one of the chair's legs in five tries?
   — Invent a partner tossing trick of your own!
4. **Hula-Hoop Challenge:** Step inside your hoop and hold it around your waist. How long can you keep your hoop twirling around your waist? Now try to do the hula-hoop twirl in the other direction. Try to walk while twirling the hoop around your waist. Now try to toss and catch a ball while twirling the hoop around your waist.
5. **Arm Spinner:** Twirl your hoop around your right arm CW; then CCW. Now twirl it on the other arm. Twirl two hoops at the same time.
   — While rotating the hoop on one arm (wrist), try to move it to other arm without breaking rhythm. Try to twirl the hoop on arm while walking around; while walking across a bench. Toss and catch a ball while twirling hoop on an arm.
   — Share your hoop with a partner. Join hands and keep the hoop twirling on your arms. Which pair can keep two hoops twirling on your arms at the same time?
   — What other body parts can you rotate your hoop around? neck; fingers; legs; ankles
6. **Hoop-Hop Challenge:** Try to twirl your hoop around the ankle of one foot and hop over it with the other foot!

GS-4 JUGGLING SCARVES—CASCADE PATTERN

FOCUS: Hand/eye coordination; concentration

EQUIPMENT: Three juggling scarves of different colors per player

ORGANIZATION:

- Have players get three scarves of different colors before scattering around the play area. Check for good spacing. Have them practice each pattern several times.

DESCRIPTION OF ACTIVITY:

1. Cascade with One Scarf:

— Hold the middle of the scarf between your thumb, pointer, and middle fingers. Hold the scarf with your palm down at waist level.

— Raise your arm as high as you can, across your chest toward the opposite shoulder, and toss your scarf. Reach high with your other hand and catch the scarf straight down as if you were clawing the air. Repeat with the other hand. Repeat this pattern, saying the cues "Toss, grab!"

2. Cascade with Two Scarves:

— Begin with each hand holding the middle of a scarf between your thumb, pointer, and middle fingers.

— Toss the first scarf across your body and above the opposite shoulder. Watch it closely. When this scarf is at the height of the toss, throw the second scarf toward the opposite shoulder.

— Your arms will make an "X" pattern across your chest.

— Let each scarf float down. Catch the scarves at waist level: first scarf in your opposite hand with a clawing action; then catch the second scarf with the other hand. Hands do not cross when catching the two scarves!

— Repeat this pattern, saying the cues "Toss, toss, catch, catch!"

3. Cascade with Three Scarves:

— Hold the first scarf between the thumb, pointer, and middle fingers of your dominant hand. Hold the second scarf in the same way in your nondominant hand. Then hold the third scarf with the bottom two fingers of your dominant hand. Do not stick the scarf between your fingers. Now you are set to juggle!

— Begin with the hand that holds two scarves. Throw the first scarf upward across your body. When it gets to the top of the toss, throw the second scarf from your other hand. As that hand lowers, use it to catch the first scarf. Remember to reach under the first throw when coming across the body.

— When the second scarf reaches the height of the toss, throw the third scarf across your body as you did the first scarf.

— As your hand comes down from throwing the third scarf, use it to catch the second scarf; then throw the first again. Continue this figure-8 pattern, alternating hands and using the cues, "one, two, one two."

— Remember that every time a scarf is as high as it will go, you should throw another scarf; then catch the scarf that is in the air. You cannot have two scarves in a hand at the same time; one scarf must be tossed under the scarf just thrown!

VARIATION:

To learn the throwing order, have players just toss the scarves and let them float to the floor, calling out the colors of the scarves as cues: "Pink, Yellow, Orange!"

GS–5 SCARF JUGGLING VARIATIONS

FOCUS: Hand/eye coordination; concentration

EQUIPMENT: Three juggling scarves of different colors per player; background music in 4/4 time; tape or record player

ORGANIZATION:

• Have players select three scarves of different colors and find a free space. Provide ample time for jugglers to practice these patterns. Have those jugglers who have mastered the patterns demonstrate to the rest of the class and then help others.

DESCRIPTION OF ACTIVITY:

1. **Two–One Juggling Pattern:** Hold the middle of the first scarf between your thumb, pointer, and middle fingers of the dominant hand; hold the second scarf in the same way in your nondominant hand. Then hold the third scarf with the bottom two fingers of your dominant hand. At the same time, toss the first and second scarves out and upward. When these scarves reach the top of their toss, throw the third scarf upward and between the path of the other two scarves. Catch the first and second scarves in their respective hands; then throw upward again and catch the third scarf. Continue in this way.

   — Can you change levels as you juggle in this pattern?

   — Can you slowly move in different directions?

   — Reverse the pattern by tossing the first scarf; then at the peak of the toss, simultaneously throw the second and third scarves upward.

1.

2. **One-Handed Juggling Pattern:** Hold two scarves in your dominant hand. Toss first scarf upward; at the height of toss, throw second scarf upward. To avoid scarves tangling, send the scarves in a circular motion by tossing them upward on the outside and catching them coming down on the inside.

   — Now repeat this pattern using your nondominant hand.

2.

3. **Cascade Overthrow Pattern:** Instead of tossing on the inside and catching on the outside, we are going to toss our scarves on the outside and catch on the inside. Take one scarf and toss it from hand to hand with an overhand throw rather than an underhand throw. Catch the scarf on the inside, and toss it from the outside.

   — Repeat overthrow pattern using two scarves; a scarf in each hand.

   — Repeat pattern using three scarves.

3.

4. **Partner Cascade Steal:** Partners, stand facing each other about 1 meter (3 feet) apart. First partner, begin juggling the scarves in the basic cascade pattern. Second partner, watch the order in which the scarves are being juggled. Choose one colored scarf; for example, orange. When the orange scarf is at the height of the toss, quickly grab it out of the air; grab the next scarf to be sent upward by the first partner; and then the third, to take over the cascade pattern. First partner, when you are ready, "steal" back the cascade pattern!

4.

5. Invent a partner scarf juggling stunt of your own! Teach it to another pair.

GS-6 BEANBAG JUGGLING

FOCUS: Visual tracking; manual dexterity; concentration

EQUIPMENT: Three beanbags of different colors per player; music with a steady 4/4 beat; tape or record player

ORGANIZATION:

• Explain that the basic juggling skill is performed by sending the beanbags in a figure-8 pattern between the waist and the top of the head. Emphasize that players toss with a scooping action from the inside and catch on the outside. Emphasize that players keep their hands and shoulders down and throw with their fingers and wrists. For less distraction, have players face a wall. Have players collect three beanbags of different colors, and find a free space in the play area. Use music with a steady 4/4 beat to help establish juggling rhythm.

DESCRIPTION OF ACTIVITY:

1. One-Bag Toss:

— Hold the beanbag in your dominant hand between your thumb and second and middle fingers.

— Toss your beanbag from hand to hand with underhand tosses in a figure-8 pattern.

— To catch the beanbag, scoop it toward the middle of your body and throw it again. Catch it toward the outside of your body and carry it back to the middle of your body to toss it again.

— Keep your hands down and throw with your wrists and fingers.

2. One-Handed Juggling Pattern:

— Hold two beanbags in the dominant hand. Toss the first beanbag upward. At the height of toss, throw second beanbag upward.

— To avoid collisions, send beanbags in a circular motion by tossing them upward on the outside and catching them coming down on the inside. Perform this pattern using other hand.

3. Two-Bag Toss:

— Hold a beanbag in each hand. First toss the beanbag in your dominant hand and count "One!" When that bag gets to its peak, throw the other beanbag under the first beanbag toward your dominant hand and count "Two!" The first beanbag should go above the opposite shoulder, but no higher than head height, and land in the palm of your nondominant hand. Meanwhile, the second beanbag will land in your dominant hand.

— Practice until you can exchange the beanbags ten times in a row without dropping them.

4. Three-Bag Toss:

— Hold the first and third beanbags in your dominant hand and the second beanbag in your other hand.

— Begin as you did when tossing two beanbags: Toss the first beanbag toward the opposite shoulder and count "One!" Then toss the second beanbag toward the other shoulder and count "Two!" Just as the second beanbag reaches its peak, toss the third beanbag under the second and count "Three!"

— Catch the first beanbag in your nondominant hand. The second beanbag will go over the third and land in your dominant hand, while the third beanbag lands in your other hand.

— Toss the first beanbag from your nondominant hand and count "Four!" just as the third beanbag reaches its peak.

— The third beanbag goes over the first and lands in your nondominant hand, while the first beanbag lands in your dominant hand.

— Practice this pattern, using the cues "One, two, three, four!"

FOCUS: Grip; throwing and catching

EQUIPMENT: One Frisbee™ per pair

ORGANIZATION:

• Explain and demonstrate disc throwing and catching techniques. Have players find a partner and practice together. Encourage them to throw and catch with either hand. Allow time to practice and experiment. Partners should start about 10 meters (30 feet) apart. As throwers become more proficient, have them increase the distance as much as 30 meters (100 feet).

DESCRIPTION OF ACTIVITY:

1. **Grip:** Place thumb on top of the disc and index finger along rim. Other fingers are under the disc and grip is relaxed, as if you were going to use the disc to fan yourself.

2. **Backhand Throw:** Stand sideways to partner and step toward partner on the closer leg. Reach across your body in a full back swing, draw the disc forward across your body again, snap wrist, and release. Try to keep the disc flat as you release it. Aim with your legs, pointing the leading leg toward your partner (the target).

3. **Underhand Throw:** Face your partner and hold the disc close to the side of your body. Step forward with leg opposite throwing arm. At the same time, bring the disc forward, snap wrist, and release, trying to keep the disc flat as you release it.

4. **High Catch:** Watch the disc as it leaves the thrower's hand. If the disc is coming toward you at a height above the waist, catch it with both hands, pointing thumbs down and fingers up. Reach for the disc and close the thumbs and fingers over it.

5. **Low Catch:** If the disc is coming toward you at a height below the waist, point thumbs up and fingers down. Watch the disc, reach for it, and close the hands over it.

6. **Behind-the-Back Catch:** Watch the disc as it comes toward you; then turn your back at the last second to catch it with thumbs up and fingers down.

   — Between-the-Legs Catch: Raise one leg and reach under it to catch the Frisbee™ with thumbs up and fingers down.

GS–8 FRISBEE™ TRICKS

FOCUS: Throwing with control; catching

EQUIPMENT: One Frisbee™ per pair

ORGANIZATION:

• Have players find a partner, get a Frisbee™ to share, and stand about 13 meters (40 feet) apart. Emphasize proper technique and control. Encourage throws and catches with either hand.

DESCRIPTION OF ACTIVITY:

1. **Parallels:** Practice throwing to your partner. Try to get a smooth flight on the Frisbee™ and a good rotation, keeping the disc parallel to the ground when you release. Can you throw so it lands within one step reach of your partner? As you improve, move farther apart.
   — Try catching using various catches: high, low, behind the back, between legs.
2. **360 Degrees:** While practicing Parallels—catcher, after your partner has made the throw, do a full turn (360 degrees) and make the catch. Repeat with the other hand. Catcher, do Heel Clicks, Jumping Jacks, Slap the Ground, Sit then Stand before catching!
3. **Curve:** Try throwing a curve. Take a step toward your partner, tilt the Frisbee™ up or down at the time of release, and follow through. Experiment, throwing to the left, right, upward, slow, fast.
   — Release the disc at different levels: high, low.
   — Experiment with different catches. Try different speeds: fast, slow.
4. **Skip (Bounce Pass):** Stand on a hard surface, such as a gym floor, concrete, or blacktop. Tilt the Frisbee™ at an angle (inside edge down). Using the Backhand Throw, release quickly to bounce the disc about halfway between your partner and yourself. Practice throwing a low fast bounce, then a slow bounce. Throw to catch with either hand.
5. **Throw for Distance:** Move farther apart. Using proper technique, throw for distance. Use the right and the left for throws and catches.

GS–9 FRISBEE™ FUN

FOCUS: Throwing for accuracy; catching

EQUIPMENT: One Frisbee™ per pair; garbage cans (trees or posts)

ORGANIZATION:

• For Target Throw, have pairs get a disc to share and stand 10 to 13 meters (30 to 40 feet) from the target. Outdoor targets may include: garbage cans, trees, posts. Indoor targets may be: garbage cans, basketball backboards, hoops taped to walls, cone markers.

DESCRIPTION OF ACTIVITY:

1. **Target Throw:** Take turns throwing the Frisbee™ at the target. Challenge your partner to see who can hit the target; best out of five throws.
   — Throw with your dominant hand; with your nondominant hand.
   — Shorten or lengthen the throwing distance.
2. **Hand-to-Hand:** Stand 13 meters (40 feet) apart. How many successful throws and catches can you make as a pair in one minute? If the Frisbee™ is dropped, it does not count.
3. **Pepper:** Join another pair and return one Frisbee™. Stand in a square formation. Very quickly pass the Frisbee™ to any other player in the square. Try to surprise someone!
4. **On-the-Move:** Start about 10 meters (30 feet) apart and throw the Frisbee™ with lead passes back and forth to each other while: walking sideways to each other; walking toward each other; away from each other; running sideways to each other.

FOCUS: Technique; visual tracking; right–left dexterity

EQUIPMENT: One scoop per player; one whiffle ball (tennis or small ball) per pair

ORGANIZATION:

• Review these techniques; then have players, working in pairs, practice. Many throwing and catching games from the Game Skills may be attempted using scoops. Emphasize that players should avoid touching the ball with the bare hand when using the scoop.

DESCRIPTION OF ACTIVITY:

1. **Underhand Throw:** This throw is similar to the softball pitch. Hold the scoop with the tip tilted slightly upward so that the ball does not roll out. Bring the scoop back behind the waist; then flick it forward with the arm and wrist, keeping the arm straight. At the same time, step forward on the foot opposite your throwing hand. The scoop should not rise higher than the waist as the ball is delivered.

2. **Overhand Throw:** Place the ball in the scoop; then raise the scoop back and behind the shoulder. Place the foot, opposite the throwing arm, forward. With a straight arm motion, from the shoulder, throw the scoop as if throwing a ball. The ball should fly out when the scoop is vertical. Follow through.

3. **Overhand Snap:** Hold scoop vertically about head high and slightly forward from body. Tilt tip slightly backward. The ball sits in "cup" just above handle. Without moving your arm, snap the wrist to send the ball quickly forward.

4. **Sidearm Throw:** Throw the ball in an overhand, sideward motion. Allow the ball to be delivered as you would for an underhand throw.

5. **Backhand Throw:** Take the scoop across your body; then throw the ball forward with a backhand/sidearm motion.

6. **Overhand Catch:** To catch a high ball, hold the scoop in the vertical position. Let the ball enter the tip and roll along the curve; then cushion impact and smother the spin to prevent the ball from bouncing out.

7. **Underhand Catch:** Use for catching a fly ball. Hold the scoop parallel to the ground. Allow the ball to drop into the scoop; then draw the scoop toward you as the ball enters the scoop.

8. **Cover Retrieve:** To retrieve a "dead" ball, hook the tip of the scoop over the ball. Quickly draw the scoop toward you; twist the scoop toward you as the ball rolls in.

9. **Side Retrieve:** To retrieve a grounder, hold the scoop on its side behind the ball. Quickly hook the scoop toward you to keep the ball in.

10. **Individual Practice:** Stand facing a wall, about 4 meters (12 feet) away. Underhand throw and catch the ball with your scoop to the wall. Flick the ball up and outward. Use either hand.

    — Overhand throw with one hand and catch all with scoop in other hand.

FOCUS: Accuracy throwing; fielding; visual tracking

EQUIPMENT: One scoop per player; two tennis balls (or whiffle balls) per group

ORGANIZATION:

• Have players pair off, get a scoop each and one ball to share, and then find a free space.

DESCRIPTION OF ACTIVITY:

1. **Stationary Passing:** Stand facing a partner, about 4 to 5 meters (12 to 15 feet) away. Throw high, catch high. Throw low, catch low. Use either hand.
   — Explore different follow-throughs. If throwing for distance, use a full follow-through, making sure that the ball leaves the scoop before you start the downward arc. If throwing for accuracy, cut your follow-through short so that your arm is straight up and slightly forward.
   — **One-Step:** Stand facing a partner across the sideline of the play area. Using your scoops, underhand or overhand throw and catch the ball to your partner. Take one step back after every three successful throws and catches.

2. **Passing on the Move:** Pass the ball to each other with your scoops as you move in general space. Remember to look out for others. Keep about 4 meters (12 feet) apart from each other.

3. **Fielding Grounders:** One partner roll the ball toward the other partner, who approaches the ball with the scoop on its side and open to the ball. Let the ball roll into your scoop, lift it up, and throw it back to your partner. Switch roles after ten rolls.

4. **Fielding a "Dead" Ball:** Pick up a ball that has stopped moving by hooking the tip end of your scoop over the ball. Then draw the scoop and ball toward you; quickly twist scoop with a flip of the wrist so that it ends under the ball. Practice.

5. **Split-Vision Drill:** Form groups of three. Stand in a triangle formation about 4 meters (12 feet) apart, facing inward. Two players have a ball each. Pass the ball to the player on your right. At the same time, watch for the ball the player on your left throws to you. Reverse the direction and repeat. Look straight ahead so that you can see both directions at the same time by looking out of the corners of your eyes. This is called peripheral vision.

6. **Circle Scoop Pass:** Form groups of five or six in a circle formation, spaced arm's length apart. On signal "Scoop!" pass the ball to each other. How many throws in a row can you make before the ball touches the ground?

GS–12 SCOOP BUCKET BALL

FOCUS: Lead-up game

EQUIPMENT: One scoop per player;
one tennis ball (or whiffle ball);
one set of pinnies;
six cone markers;
two small plastic buckets

ORGANIZATION:

- For each game, form two equal teams and distribute pinnies to one team. Divide a large rectangular play area in half with cone markers and have teams scatter on opposite sides of the play area. Each team has a goalie, who stands facing his or her team at the opposite end of the play area and holds a bucket. All other players get a scoop. Change goalies every few minutes.

DESCRIPTION OF ACTIVITY:

1. To start the game and to restart it after a point is scored, I will toss the ball in the middle of the play area between two opposing players.
2. The object of the game is to score a goal by throwing the ball into the bucket. Your goalie may move anywhere along the goal line to receive the ball but may not step over it. Any player on your team may throw the ball.
3. Players, you must not touch an opponent with your scoop! Spread out to avoid congestion in the area of the ball.

GS–13 ENDLINE SCOOP-BALL

FOCUS: Passing and receiving while moving

EQUIPMENT: One scoop per player;
one whiffle ball per game;
two sets of pinnies

ORGANIZATION:

- Endline Scoop-Ball is played in a play area about the size of a basketball court. Form two equal teams wearing different colored pinnies. Have each team choose a goalie, who must stay behind the opponent's endline. Change the goalies often. Have players get a scoop and stand beside an opponent to guard, anywhere on the court.

DESCRIPTION OF ACTIVITY:

1. The object of the game is to score points by passing the ball to your teammates and then to your goalie, behind your opponent's goal line. Only the goalie is allowed behind the endline.
2. The game is started with a jump ball at center. A goal may be attempted from your front court only.
3. The Rule of Three is in effect:
   — There must be at least three completed passes before a goal is attempted.
   — You have three seconds to pass the ball.
   — You may take a maximum of three steps with the ball.
4. The first team to score five points wins the game.

VARIATION:

Passes must go to boy, girl, boy, girl alternately before a goal may be scored.

GS–14 SINGLE SCOOTER TASKS

FOCUS: Teaching and safety guidelines   **EQUIPMENT:** One scooter per player

ORGANIZATION:

- Scooters are excellent equipment to use for indoor games. Relays and many other games can be adapted to scooter use if the size of the play area is reduced. One scooter per player is ideal; however, two players may share a scooter for many activities.

DESCRIPTION OF ACTIVITY:

1. *Safety:*
   - Scooters are not skateboards; do not stand on them.
   - Scooters are not missiles: with or without passengers, do not send them crashing into each other.
   - Watch your fingers! Do not drag your hands along the floor.
   - Before using your scooter, check that the casters fit tightly.
2. Practice:
   - Lie face down on your scooter, hold feet off floor, and move forward using hands only; feet only; then both. Can you spin around? Roll onto back and repeat.
   - Kneel on your scooter and pull yourself forward; then push yourself backward and around in a circle.
   - Hold the edges of the scooter. Run in all directions while holding the scooter. When you have gained enough speed, kneel on the scooter on both knees and glide safely as far as you can go.
3. *Wheelbarrow:* (Find a partner and return one scooter.) One partner place hands on scooter in push-up position; other partner lift this partner's legs, holding them above the knees, and push your partner in different directions.
4. *Scooter Tag:* (Choose two or three players to be IT. All other players scatter around the play area.) On signal "Go!" IT players try to tag the others. Tagged players help to tag, until all players are tagged.

GS–15 DOUBLE SCOOTER TASKS

FOCUS: Cooperative activities   **EQUIPMENT:** Scooters

ORGANIZATION:

- Have players get a scooter and find a partner. Have each partner in turn try the following Double Scooter Tasks while the other partner watches for good technique and safety.

DESCRIPTION OF ACTIVITY:

1. Lie face down on both scooters and move in different directions.
   - On all fours, place knees on one scooter and hands on the other. Find a way to move while in this position. How could your partner help you?
   - Now try to move with your feet on one scooter and your hands on the other.
   - Sit on one scooter and place your feet on the other. Can you move forward, backward, and sideways?
   - Show me another way to move while using two scooters.
2. *Partner Races* (Mark off a starting line and a turning line. Have three or four pairs challenge each other to scooter races.)
   - *Elbow-Lock Race:* Partners, sit on your scooters side by side and link your elbows. Race around the turning line and back.
   - *Back-to-Back Race:* Partners, sit on your scooters back to back and link elbows.
   - *Single Push Cart Race:* Put one scooter away. One partner, sit on the scooter. Other partner, push from behind. Change roles at turning line.

GS-16 SCOOTER BALL STUNTS

FOCUS: Scooter and ball control

EQUIPMENT: One scooter per player;
one utility ball per player;
one cone marker per group;
one set of colored pinnies per group

ORGANIZATION:

• Have players get a scooter and a ball before scattering around the play area.

DESCRIPTION OF ACTIVITY:

1. *Partner Stunts:*

   — Sitting on your scooter, dribble the ball with one hand and move forward while pushing with the other hand. Change hands and directions.

   — Sit on your scooter and find a partner. Put one ball away. Pass the ball back and forth while you and your partner move in all directions.

   — Can you and your partner create another stunt that uses two scooters and a ball?

2. *Group Stunts:* Sit on your scooter in file formation with four or five other players. Place feet around the waist of the player in front of you. Leader, pull the group forward with your feet while the rest of the group helps by pushing with their hands. Take turns being the leader; then have the leader dribble a ball while pulling the group forward.

3. *Scooter-Ball Tag:* (Form teams of five or six players and have each team wear different colored pinnies.) On signal "Go!" each team in turn, try to tag with a ball all the other players. When tagged, move around the outside of the play area until the next game. Which team can last the longest in the game?

GS-17 SCOOTER KEEP-AWAY GAMES

FOCUS: Ball control; positional play

EQUIPMENT: One scooter per player;
one utility ball per group;
two cone markers per group;
one set of pinnies per group

ORGANIZATION:

• Have each player get a scooter. Form groups of three and collect one ball per group.

DESCRIPTION OF ACTIVITY:

1. *In the Soup:* (Play in a confined space such as a basketball key. Form groups of three players and have one player sit on a scooter between the other two players, who are about 2 meters [6 feet] apart.) Two outside players, pass the ball back and forth to each other, trying to keep it away from the middle player. If the middle player touches the ball, change places.

2. *Two-on-Two:* (Enlarge the play area. Form groups of four players.) Two players in each group, pass to each other while trying to keep the ball away from the other two players.

3. *Scooter Pin-Ball:* (Divide the class into two teams. Set up a cone marker as a goal at each end of the play area. To begin the game and to restart it after a goal is scored, roll the ball between two opposing players in the middle of the play area.) Pass or roll the ball among the players on your team and try to hit the cone marker. Three players must handle the ball before it hits the cone.

GS-18 SCOOTER RELAYS

FOCUS: Cooperative activities

EQUIPMENT: Two scooters per team;
four cone markers per team;
one baton and ball per team

ORGANIZATION:

• Form equal teams of four to six players. Have each team stand in file formation at one end of the play area. Each of the first two players in each team has a scooter. Place a cone marker 10 meters (30 feet) from each team as a turning point. On the signal "Go!" each player in turn performs the following tasks as they move toward the cone marker, around it, and back to their team. As the first player crosses the starting line, the next player goes. The third player takes the first player's scooter and the first player goes to the end of the file.

DESCRIPTION OF ACTIVITY:

1. *One-Hand Relay:* Place one hand on the scooter, tuck the other hand behind your back, and run forward. Change hands as you pass the cone marker.

2. *Two-Hand, One-Foot Relay:* Place both hands and one foot on the scooter and push forward with your free foot. Change legs as you pass the cone marker.

3. *One-Hand, One-Foot Relay:* Place one hand on one foot on the scooter and push forward with free foot. Change hands and feet as you pass the cone marker.

4. *Kneeling Relay:* Kneel on scooter and move forward using your hands only.

5. *Seat and Feet Relay:* Sit with your feet on your scooter and move forward using your hands only.

6. *Back-to-Back Relay:* First two players, sit on the scooters back to back and link elbows. Move around the cone marker and back to the team to give the scooters to the next pair, and go to the end of the file. Continue until each pair has had two turns.

7. *Link-Up Relay:* Each player sit on a scooter. First player, move forward and around the cone marker, using your feet only. When you return to the team, grip the wrist of the next player and repeat the relay together; then link up with the third player. Continue adding a player until all players on the team are linked.

8. *Horse-and-Cart Relay:* First player, sit on a scooter and have the second player pull you by the legs toward the cone marker. Change roles there and return to your team so the next pair can go. Continue until your team has had a total of six turns.

9. *Shuttle-Scooter Relay:* (All players sit on scooters, half the team facing the other half 10 meters [30 feet] away in shuttle formation. Player at the front of one file gets a baton.) On signal "Go!" player with the baton, move forward, hand the baton to opposite teammate, and go to the end of that file. Player with the baton, repeat relay. Continue until all team members have had a turn.

10. *Zigzag Relay:* (Place four cone markers in a row in front of each team, spacing them about 1 meter [3 feet] apart.) Each player in turn, zigzag through the row of cone markers, circle the last one in the row, and return directly to your team. Repeat.

11. *Partner Ball-Pass Relay:* (Give a ball to each team.) First two players, pass the ball back and forth between you as you move toward the cone marker, around it, and back to the team; then pass the ball to the next pair, who will repeat the relay. Continue until each pair has had two turns.

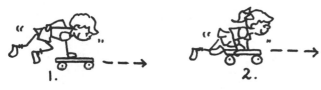

GS–19 SCOOTER DODGEBALL

FOCUS: Team games; passing; catching

EQUIPMENT: One scooter per player;
one Nerf™ or sponge ball per game;
two sets of pinnies per game

ORGANIZATION:

- Form two teams of equal numbers. Have teams wear different colored pinnies and sit on their scooters in their own half of the play area. If there are more players than scooters, the player who is hit out passes the scooter to a player who is reentering the game.

DESCRIPTION OF ACTIVITY:

1. After I toss the ball up between two opposing players at center, to start the game, players, you may go anywhere in the play area. From then on, the object of the game is to hit out the other team first.

2. An opposition player must be hit by a direct hit (the ball does not hit the floor). A ball that hits the floor may be picked up by any player.

3. Players on the same team, you may pass the ball from one to another to gain a better position to hit an opposing player, but you may only use the bounce pass. If you pass directly to a teammate, that player is considered "hit" and must leave the game.

4. A player who is legally hit must leave the game but may reenter when the player who hit him or her is hit out.

5. Players, you must maintain contact with scooter at all times. You must not hold the ball for more than three seconds, or the ball is given to other team.

6. Play until one team runs out of players.

GS–20 SCOOTER VOLLEYBALL

FOCUS: Volleyball skills; team work

EQUIPMENT: One scooter per player;
one volleyball or badminton net;
one beachball per game

ORGANIZATION:

- Divide the class into teams of six to nine players. Set up a low net across the play area, and assign each team to one side of the net. Mark a serving line about 3 meters (10 feet) from the net.

DESCRIPTION OF ACTIVITY:

1. Play regular volleyball positions and rules, with these exceptions:
   - All players, including the server, must sit on the scooter at all times.
   - One help only is allowed on the serve.
2. Set up a Scooter Volleyball Tourney.

GS—21 SCOOTER SOFTBALL

FOCUS: Lead-up game

EQUIPMENT: One scooter per player; two volleyballs; four cone markers

ORGANIZATION:

- Divide the class into two teams. Set up cone markers as a softball diamond, with home plate and the three bases all spaced about 10 meters (30 feet) apart. Have all players sit on a scooter. Pick a number between one and ten to choose the team that will bat first.

DESCRIPTION OF ACTIVITY:

1. Batting team, stand in file formation away from home plate. Fielding team, choose a pitcher for your team, who will stand in the middle of the diamond about 5 meters (15 feet) from home plate. Other players, take up positions at each base and infield.
2. Pitcher, kneeling on your scooter, bounce the ball toward the first batter. Batter, try to hit the ball with the hand or arm; then wheel around the bases, trying to reach base or home plate before the fielding team has a chance to field the ball, pass it around to each base player, and to home plate. If not on a base by the time the ball reaches home plate, you are out.
3. Score one run for every player who gets back to home plate. After each team member has had a turn at bat, batting and fielding teams change roles.

GS—22 SCOOTER BALL

FOCUS: Lead-up game

EQUIPMENT: Two plastic garbage cans; one scooter per pair; one set of pinnies; floor tape

ORGANIZATION:

- Scooter Ball is played according to basic basketball rules. Place garbage-can goals in the middle of each end of the rectangular play area. Form teams of twelve to fourteen players. Give pinnies to one team and have each team scatter on either half of the play area. One player from each team guards its goal and the other players find a partner. One player sits on a scooter; the other pushes that player around the play area. Only the sitting player may handle the ball. Partners change roles each time a goal is scored. Tape a 3-meter (10-foot) foul line in front of each garbage-can goal. Have each pair guard a pair from the opposing team and take a free shot whenever their opposing pair commits a foul.

DESCRIPTION OF ACTIVITY:

1. The game is started and restarted after a goal is scored when I bounce the ball in the middle of the play area between two opposition pairs, who try to tape the ball to a teammate.
2. The object of the game is for each team to pass the ball and throw it so that it hits the garbage can. Score one point each time a goal is scored.
3. You may travel in any direction while dribbling the ball, but you may carry it for only three seconds.
4. No part of the play area is out-of-bounds: You may play the ball off walls.
5. With your teammates positioned behind you, take foul shots from behind the foul line as follows:
   - Take two shots when you are pushed from your scooter.
   - Take two shots when your opposing player holds the ball.
   - Take one shot when the pusher touches the ball.
   - Take one shot when the rider leaves the scooter or stands up to try to score.

GS-23 PARACHUTE FUN

FOCUS: Teaching and safety guidelines   **EQUIPMENT:** One parachute per group

ORGANIZATION:

- Use parachutes indoors or outdoors, on play days, or as part of a lesson. Parachutes require all players, regardless of skill or strength, to cooperate and to be vigorously and continuously involved. Parachutes of 7 meters (24 feet) in diameter are suitable for a class of twenty-five to thirty children. Smaller classes could use a 5-meter (16-foot) diameter parachute, while larger classes could use either one 7-meter (24-foot) diameter parachute or two 5-meter (16-foot) chutes. Have players stand around the edge of the parachute and grip the canopy at the seams.

DESCRIPTION OF ACTIVITY:

1. Hold the chute with both hands and roll the edge toward the center three or four times so that you get a better grip. Avoid long fingernails, as they may cause tears in the material.
2. Use any of the following grips:
   - *Overhand Grip:* Grip the edge of the chute with the palms facing down. The Overhand Grip is the most common parachute grip.
   - *Underhand Grip:* Grip the edge of the chute with palms up.
   - *Cross-Over Grip:* Cross the arms and grip the edge of the chute with the Overhand Grip.
   - *Alternating Grip:* Use the Overhand Grip with one hand and the Underhand Grip with the other hand.

GS-24 INFLATION FUN

FOCUS: Inflation technique and activities   **EQUIPMENT:** One parachute per group

ORGANIZATION:

- Review parachute grips; then demonstrate and explain inflation action, before practice. The inflation action is basic to most parachute activities. Establish definite commands such as "Ready–Begin," or "1, 2, 3–Stretch!" so that everyone responds at the same time.

DESCRIPTION OF ACTIVITY:

1. *Inflation:* Hold the canopy at waist level using the overhand grip. On the signal "Ready–Down!" squat and hold parachute to the floor. On signal "1, 2, 3–Up!" stand and thrust arms overhead to allow as much air under the chute as possible. When the center of the canopy touches the floor, repeat to get an even better inflation.
   - *Inflation Challenge:* Using two chutes, challenge another group to try to keep its chute inflated the longest time.
2. *Tenting:* Inflate parachute; then on the signal "In–1, 2, 3!" walk forward three steps. As the chute settles, on signal "Out–1, 2, 3!" walk backward three steps.
3. *Tent Run:* Inflate the chute as for Tenting, quickly let go of the chute with your right hand, and then run CCW around it. Can you return to your starting positions before the chute touches the floor?
4. *Mushroom:* Inflate chute; then quickly pull the edge to floor to seal in the escaping air and make a mushroom shape. Continue to hold the edges down until canopy settles to floor. Try walking forward three steps before sealing parachute to the floor.

GS–25 MORE INFLATION FUN

FOCUS: Inflation activities

EQUIPMENT: One parachute per group; easy listening music; tape or record player

ORGANIZATION:

• Have players gather around parachute and hold it using the overhand grip. Review the inflation technique; then have players make the following parachute shapes.

DESCRIPTION OF ACTIVITY:

1. *Fly Away:* Inflate the chute until it is totally inflated; then, on signal "Fly Away!" everyone let go at the same time. The chute should remain in the air for a few seconds before it settles down on top of you, but don't move off your spot! How long can you keep the chute in the air?
2. *Igloo:* (Explain that you are now going to make the whole class disappear.) Hold the parachute using the cross-over grip, inflate it, and walk forward three steps. On signal "Turn!" quickly turn and duck under the parachute. Regrasp the inside edge, kneel, and seal edge to floor. Return to the outside when the chute touches your head, and try again.
3. *Peek-a-Boo Igloo:* Make an Igloo, seal the chute to the floor, and lie on the floor on your stomach leaving only your heads outside. Seal the chute to the floor, lying on your backs and poking only your feet outside.
4. *Igloo Crawl:* On signal "Chute Crawl!" everyone crawl under chute across to the opposite side and find a free space to sit and seal the chute to floor.

GS–26 PARACHUTE WORKOUT

FOCUS: Conditioning activities for arms and legs

EQUIPMENT: See GS-25.

DESCRIPTION OF ACTIVITY:

1. *Carousel:* Jog around the chute holding it with the left hand only. Raise and lower the chute as you jog in time with the music. (Change to forward or backward walking, skipping, and hopping; side-stepping; cross-over stepping.) On signal "Jump and Shake!" lightly bounce in place while gently shaking the chute. On signal, "Change!" change hands and direction. Next time, replace bouncing in place with "Jumping Jacks"; or "Side Kicks"; or "Step Kicks"; or "Forward Straddle Jumps."
2. *Modified Squat Thrusts:* Inflate the chute, form a mushroom, and seal the edges to the floor. Squat down and take your weight on your hands on the edge of the chute. on the count of "one" extend your legs straight back; on the count of "two" return to the squat position; on "one" thrust the legs back again. Continue to the count of "one–two." Do five sets of squat thrusts.
3. *Sky-High Pulls:* Stand with feet shoulder width apart and hold parachute at waist level using overhand grip. On signal "1, 2, 3–Up!" slowly raise the chute until your arms are straight overhead. Then, without moving your feet, use your arms and shoulders and pull back, holding the chute tight for ten seconds. Repeat using the underhand grip.
4. *Wrist Roll:* Hold parachute at waist level using the overhand grip with arms fully extended. On signal "Go!" stretch the chute until it is tight and slowly roll the edge toward the middle. When the parachute is completely rolled, it is ready to put away.

FOCUS: Cooperation; team work

EQUIPMENT: One parachute per group;
ten to twelve beanbags per group;
six to eight short ropes per group;
one volleyball per group;
one basketball per group

ORGANIZATION:

• Divide the class into two equal teams and have them stand facing each other on opposite sides of the parachute. Have the players shake the parachute vigorously; then throw ten or twelve beanbags onto the canopy of the chute.

DESCRIPTION OF ACTIVITY:

1. *Popcorn:* (Place all the beanbags on the chute.) How long will it take to "pop" all the popcorn (beanbags) off the chute? Try again. Can you beat your best score?

   — *Spaghetti Boil:* How long will it take to shake the ropes off the chute?

2. *Parachute Volleyball:* Divide into your two teams again and stand on opposite sides of the chute facing each other. When I throw the volleyball into the center of the chute, try to shake it off to touch the floor on the opponent's side of the chute. Score one point each time. Play to five points.

3. *Parachute Basketball:* Hold the edge of the canopy with your left hand using the overhand grip, and hold a basketball in your right hand. On signal "Dribble!" walk forward, slowly dribbling the ball; then gradually increase speed to a run, continuing to dribble. Slow to a walk again. On signal, "Change!" change hands and dribble in the opposite direction.

4. *Speed-Away:* Pull the chute tight. When I place a volleyball on the chute, raise and lower the canopy to roll the ball in a large circle around the parachute. Working together, try to keep the ball circling around the outer edge of the chute. How many times can we get the ball to roll past the same spot?

5. *Number's Exchange:* (Number the players from one to five as they stand around the parachute, holding it at waist level using both hands in the overhand grip. Place mats, balls, jump ropes, and beanbags under the chute.) On signal, inflate the chute. As it reaches the height of inflation, I will call a number from one to five. Players with that number, leave your place on the chute and change places with another player who has the same number.

   — *Challenge:* Perform one of the following tasks, and get to another place before the chute touches your head: Throw and catch a beanbag five times; bounce a ball ten times; do three forward rolls on a mat; jump rope five times.

6. *Running Numbers Game:* Hold the chute in your right hand and run lightly around the chute in a CW direction. When I call your number, quickly release your grip on the chute and run to the vacant spot ahead of you.

   — *Around the World:* Instead of running, everyone walk at a normal pace. When I call your number, run as fast as you can around the chute without touching anyone. Can you be the first back to your place?

7. *Grecian Flurry:* (Form teams of twelve to sixteen players. Arrange teams in shuttle formation: two lines of six or eight players. Place two cone markers in front of each team [one at the starting point; the other, at the turning point] about 20 meters [60 feet] apart. Give each team a parachute.) On signal "Go!" first six players in line, holding the chute high overhead and gripping with one hand at the leading edge, run toward the turning point. Here quickly position the center of the chute over the cone and, holding it taut, run CW around it three times before returning to pass the chute to the second set of six players, who do the same. Continue until your team has made a total of six round trips.

GS–28 BRING HOME THE BACON

FOCUS: Parachute reaction game

EQUIPMENT: One parachute per game; two beanbags (or towels) per game

ORGANIZATION:

- Divide the class into two equal teams, each team facing the other on opposite sides of the parachute. Players hold the chute at waist level using both hands in the overhand grip. Assign each team member a number. Place a beanbag or towel on the floor under the middle of the parachute.

DESCRIPTION OF ACTIVITY:

1. As you inflate the parachute, I will call a number. The two players with that number, duck under the chute, race to grab the beanbag, and try to return to your position before your opponent tags you.
2. Your team scores points as follows:

   — If you return to your position without being tagged by the other player, score one point for your team.
   — If you do not get the beanbag but are able to tag your opponent, you earn one point for your team.
   — If the parachute touches you while you are still under it, you do not score a point.
3. Play to five points or until all numbers have been called.

VARIATION:

For a large class, place two beanbags or towels under the canopy and call two numbers each time.

GS–29 ADVANCED PARACHUTE ACTIVITIES

FOCUS: Challenges using equipment

EQUIPMENT: One parachute per group; two mats per parachute; several balls, ropes, beanbags, and hoop

ORGANIZATION:

- Place equipment around the outside of the parachute area so that it is readily available.

DESCRIPTION OF ACTIVITY:

1. *The Challenge:* (Divide the class into two equal teams and have teams stand facing each other across the parachute, holding edge with both hands in the overhand grip. Each team numbers off consecutively.) On a signal, inflate the parachute; then listen for your number and the challenge I call, such as bounce a ball, jump rope, toss a beanbag, roll a hoop, or do three push-ups. When you hear your number, duck under the chute, perform the challenge quickly, and return to your position.
2. *Tumbling Activities:* (Place two mats under the chute.) On signal, inflate the parachute; then listen for your number and the gymnastic stunt I call, such as perform a forward roll, backward roll, tripod balance, or a cartwheel. Duck under the chute, perform the stunt, and then return to your position before the chute lowers.
3. *Pyramid* (Form groups of five players and have them practice building a pyramid together; then place two mats under the chute, have groups gather around it, and hold the edge in both hands using the overhand grip.) On signal, inflate the parachute. Each group in turn, build your pyramid under the chute before it settles.

GS-30 SHORT ROPE JUMPING

FOCUS: Teaching and safety guidelines; basic form

EQUIPMENT: One short rope per skipper; music; tape or record player

ORGANIZATION:

- Rope Jumping should be taught throughout the school year as a fitness activity or as the main focus of the lesson. Rope Jumping contributes significantly to the development of coordination, rhythm, timing, agility, aerobic endurance, and leg strength. Beaded Ropes should be used for skipping, if possible. Speed Ropes can be introduced when skippers have mastered the Basic Skipping Tricks. Store ropes by hanging them on hooks that can be easily accessed. Use colored tape on the handles to code the different lengths. Wooden floors, indoor/outdoor carpeting, or acrylic rubberized flooring are best as skipping surfaces. Safety: Ensure that skippers have enough space to turn ropes easily and safely. During activity, watch carefully for fatigue. Gradually increase activity time as fitness levels improve. Insist that skippers wear sneakers while skipping; no bare feet or socks!

- Warm up skippers by stretching arm and leg muscles for about five to eight minutes; Cool down for three to five minutes by walking and stretching.

- To develop rhythmical jumping, use appropriate music with a steady beat, increasing tempo as ability improves.

DESCRIPTION OF ACTIVITY:

1. *Size Rope:* Get a rope and check it for proper length by standing in middle of it and drawing ends up to shoulders. Rope ends should not reach higher than shoulders.

2. *Basic Skipping Form:* Stand tall, knees and feet together, head up, knees slightly bent. Hold rope behind heels; handles held loosely. Keep elbows close to sides; point forearms and hands slightly forward and away from body. Turn rope with small, circular wrist movements.

3. *Basic Jump Technique Review:* Keeping feet together, make low jumps that are only 3 to 5 centimeters (1 to two inches) from the floor. Relax as you jump; bend knees slightly, landing softly on the balls of your feet and lower heels to floor (rather than flat-footed). Keep turning rhythm constant, using your wrists rather than your arms to supply the power; jump smoothly.

   — Single or Pogo Jump: turn the rope once, jump once. Practice.

   — Double Jump: Turn the rope once, jump lightly when rope is overhead; then jump when rope passes underneath. Practice.

4. *Rope Limber and Loosen:*

   — Fold your rope in four and hold at arm's length just behind you. Stretch sideways slowly to the right for four counts; then repeat to the left side.

   — Now hold your doubled rope in front and do eight side swings.

   — Standing tall, hold your arms just out from your sides and do eight forward wrist rotations; then eight backward wrist rotations.

   — In wide-sit position, place your folded rope around one foot and gently lean forward from the hips to stretch the hamstrings for ten seconds. Repeat stretch on other leg.

   — Do eight slow ankle rotations with your right foot in a CW direction; then CCW direction. Repeat with your left ankle.

5. *Short Rope Patterns:* Double jump with feet together, turning rope forward, four times; then jump four times on the right foot; four times on left; three times on right; three times on left; two times on right; two times on left; two times with feet together. Repeat, turning rope backward; repeat using single jumps. Create a single-jump pattern of your own.

GS—31 BASIC ROPE TRICKS 1

FOCUS: Mastering basic short rope tricks

EQUIPMENT: One short rope per skipper; music with a strong 4/4 beat; tape or record player

ORGANIZATION:

- Have skippers learn and practice these tricks without the rope at first, then with the rope using double jumps and finally single jumps. Challenge skippers to repeat tricks while turning the rope backward. Skippers get a rope, check that it is the correct length, and then scatter around the play area. Check for good spacing. Remind skippers to jump smoothly, keeping relaxed and in good skipping form. Emphasize turning the rope rhythmically, jumping in time with the music.

DESCRIPTION OF ACTIVITY:

1. *Side Swing Warm-Up:*

   — *Single-Side Swing:* Hold one rope handle in each hand. Swing rope on one side of your body; then open it and jump over it. Swing and jump on the other side. Repeat pattern.

   — *Figure-8 Side Swing and Jump:* Swing rope to right side of body, swing rope to left side; swing rope to right side of body; open it and jump over. Repeat pattern.

2. *Side Straddle:* Start with feet together. As you turn the rope the first time, jump feet shoulder-width apart. As you turn the rope the second time, jump feet back together.

3. *Forward Straddle (Scissors):* Begin with feet together. On the first turn of the rope, jump and spread your feet apart so that the right foot is in front of the left. On the second turn of the rope, switch feet so that the left is in front of the right.

4. *Double Straddle:* Let's try to combine Side and Forward Straddles. On the first turn of the rope, do the side straddle jump; on the second turn of the rope do the forward straddle jump. Your feet do not return to the basic together position.

5. *The "X":* On the first turn of the rope, jump your feet sideways apart. On the second turn of the rope, cross your right foot in front of your left. Straddle feet again on the third turn of the rope; then cross left foot in front of right on the fourth turn of the rope. Repeat pattern.

6. *Rocker:* Start with one foot forward. Jump, taking your weight on the front foot and leaning slightly forward. Then jump, shifting weight to back foot and leaning on it. Repeat Rocker step with the other foot forward.

7. *Boxer:* Jump twice with your right foot, then twice with your left foot. Continue to jump twice on each foot.

8. *Jogger:* Using a running step, step over the rope with first the right foot and then left foot. Continue to alternate footwork, taking one jump for each step.

   — Repeat, stepping over the rope with first the left foot, then the right.

9. Create a routine using these tricks that you have learned.

GS–32 BASIC ROPE TRICKS 2

FOCUS: Mastering basic short rope tricks

EQUIPMENT: One short rope per skipper; music with a steady 4/4 beat; tape or record player

ORGANIZATION:

- Have skippers practice these tricks first without and then with the rope, repeating each trick with both double and single jumps; then challenge skippers to repeat tricks while turning the rope backward. Encourage skippers to jump in time with the music.

DESCRIPTION OF ACTIVITY:

1. **Skier:** Place rope stretched out along the floor and jump with feet together, from side to side, over it. Now add the rope. On the first turn, jump sideways to the right; on the second turn, jump sideways to the left. Imagine you are jumping side to side across a line each time you jump the rope.

2. **Bells:** Practice jumping forward and backward with feet together over your rope. Now add the rope. On the first turn, jump forward; on the second turn, jump backward. Remember, keep your feet together!

3. **Skier-Bell Combo:** Jump two Skiers; then two Bells. Practice pattern. Then jump a One Skier–One Bell pattern.

4. **Twister:** Keeping feet together, jump and twist only the lower part of your body from side to side.

5. **Peek-a-Boo:** Begin in your basic position. As the rope turns overhead, place one foot out sideways about 30 centimeters (12 inches) while the other foot stays in the basic position. On the next turn of the rope, place the other foot out sideways. Repeat this alternate toe-touch sideways, changing feet on each turn of the rope. Keep your feet close to the floor.

6. **Toe-to-Toe:** As the rope swings overhead, tap the toes of your right foot beside and slightly behind the heel of your left foot. Point your right toes downward, bending at the knee. Repeat with the left foot.

7. **Heel-to-Heel:** On every turn of the rope, change the heel that touches the floor about 20 centimeters (8 inches) in front of you. Tap one heel at the same time as you jump with the other foot: jump and touch right heel forward; jump and touch left heel forward.

8. **Heel-to-Toe:** On the first turn of the rope, touch your right heel to the floor about 20 centimeters (8 inches) in front of you. On the second turn, tap your right toe next to your left foot. Repeat on your left foot. Continue to alternate heel-to-toe touches: left hop, right heel; left hop, right toe; then right hop, left heel; right hop, left toe.

9. **Front Leg Kicks:** Alternate kicking your right and left foot in front of you. Do a small forward kick, with heel close to floor for every turn of rope.

10. **Sideway Rockers:** On the first turn of the rope, swing the left leg sideways while jumping twice on the right foot. On the second turn of the rope, swing the right leg sideways while jumping twice on the left foot.

11. Create a routine using the tricks you now know.

GS–33 INTERMEDIATE ROPE TRICKS

FOCUS: Mastering advanced rope tricks; group work; rhythmic jumping; routine-building

EQUIPMENT: One short rope per skipper; recording paper and pencils; music with a strong 4/4 beat; tape or record player

ORGANIZATION:

• Have skippers practice these more difficult tricks without and then with the rope, landing with double jumps and then single jumps.

DESCRIPTION OF ACTIVITY:

1. **Copy-Cat Warm-Up:** (Have skippers form one large circle. Ensure that they are well spaced apart around the circle. If space permits, have two or three jumping circles.) Begin jumping in time to the music using double jumps. As I call out your name, skip forward into the center and do one of the Basic Rope tricks you have learned. Everyone else copy this trick. After sixteen repetitions, center skipper call out another skipper's name; then return to your original place in the circle. New leader skip to the center and perform another basic trick.

2. **Bird Hops:** Set the rope aside and practice Pigeon-toed Hops (toes together and heels apart) and Duck Hops (heels together and toes apart). Alternate Pigeon-toed Hops and Duck Hops as you jump the rope, first with double jumps and then with single jumps.

3. **Front Criss-Cross:** Start in the standing position, feet together, with rope at the back of your heels. Bring the rope slowly overhead, crossing your arms at the elbows, with your elbows touching. Jump through the loop, open arms, and single-jump. As the rope swings overhead, criss-cross your arms again. Keep your hands low. Is your loop large enough to fit your body through? Repeat with your arms staying in the criss-cross position.

4. **Backward Criss-Cross:** Start in standing position, feet together, with the rope in front at your toes. Jumping backward, do the front criss-cross, with your elbows touching.

5. **Double-Unders:** Jump once and try to make two revolutions of the rope. To get the rope to pass under your feet twice during one jump, you need to jump a little higher off the floor, bending slightly at the waist. Whip the rope to rotate it faster!

6. **180-Degree Turn Backward:** Single-jump as you turn the rope forward; then single side-swing the rope to the left, following the rope with a half-turn to the left. Finish the 180-degree turn with a backward jump.

7. **180-Degree Turn Forward:** Single jump as you turn the rope backward; then side-swing left, following the rope with a half-turn to the left. Finish the 180-degree turn with a single forward jump. Repeat 180-Degree Turns with a single side-swing to the right with a half-turn to the right.

8. **Endurance Jumping Challenge:** Jump rope as quickly as you can in thirty seconds. If you stop the rope turning, start again as quickly as possible, and continue until you hear the "Freeze!" signal. Aim for sixty jumps in thirty seconds. (Increase the time to forty-five seconds; sixty seconds; ninety seconds; and so on until a maximum of five minutes is achieved.)

9. **Creating a Short Rope Jump Routine:** (Divide the class into groups of four or five skippers; each group selects a leader and a recorder to write down the routine. Then assign each group to a working area. Ensure groups are well spaced apart.) Design a jump rope routine using the basic tricks that you have learned. Work in counts of four, eight, or sixteen. Decide on the formation for your routine, such as scatter, line, circle, semicircle, waves. Each group, in turn, will lead the other groups through the routine as a warm-up for our gym class. Your routine should last about three minutes.

GS–34 PARTNER JUMPING USING ONE ROPE

FOCUS: Cooperative rope jumping

EQUIPMENT: One short rope per pair;
one ball per pair;
music with a steady 4/4 beat;
tape or record player

ORGANIZATION:

- Have skippers pair up with a partner about the same size and get a rope to share. To check that the rope is the correct length, have partners stand side by side on the rope; the ends should extend to their outer armpits. Pairs then scatter around the play area. Provide opportunity for pairs to perform their tricks for the rest of the class.

DESCRIPTION OF ACTIVITY:

1. **Side-by-Side:** Partners, stand side by side, facing forward, with each partner holding one handle of the rope. You may wish to join inside hands or place an arm around your partner's waist or shoulders. In unison, turn rope forward with your free hands and jump. Turn the rope backward and jump in unison. Now try the following tricks:

   — Skip forward; skip backward; skip sideways together.

   — One partner, move out and back into position while continuing to turn the rope. Other partner, repeat; then both partners move out together and back into position again.

   — One partner, circle the other partner while continuing to turn the rope.

   — Design a routine using the above steps and rotations. Add a new trick of your own!

2. **Side-by-Side, facing opposite:** Partners, face in opposite directions with left hands clasped and right hands turning the rope. One partner is always jumping backward. Repeat the tricks above. Clasp right hands and turn with left hands. Create a new trick!

3. **Face-to-Face:** Start by standing face to face. One partner turn the rope and both jump in unison. Take turns being the rope turner.

   — Together, decide on a basic jump rope trick. While the rope turner performs the trick, partner, run in front door and match steps. How many different tricks can you perform together in this way?

   — Nonturner, get a ball, run in, and bounce the ball while jumping.

   — While jumping in unison, nonturner, try to take over the job of rope turning by placing your hands on the handles to get control. "Steal" the rope-turning back and forth from each other in this way.

   — Nonturner, try to travel around the turner or even under the legs.

   — **Challenge:** Which pair can do a Double-Under in this position?

VARIATIONS:

a. **Invent-a-Trick:** Provide opportunity for pairs to create a new trick in the Side-by-Side and Face-to-Face positions.

b. **Show-Off Time!:** Provide opportunity for pairs to perform their tricks for the rest of the class.

GS-35 MORE PARTNER JUMPING USING ONE ROPE_____

FOCUS: Cooperative rope jumping

EQUIPMENT: One rope per pair;
one ball per pair;
music with a strong beat;
tape or record player

ORGANIZATION:

• Have skippers pair off with someone about the same size; then get a rope, check it for correct length, and find a free space.

DESCRIPTION OF ACTIVITY:

1. ***Front-to-Back:*** Begin by standing one behind the other with the back partner holding the rope in basic position.

   — Back partner turn the rope forward and both jump in unison. Now the front partner turn the rope. Other partner, run in from the back, grasp your partner's shoulders (or waist), and jump in unison.

   — Repeat with the front partner turning the rope backward.

   — One partner do quarter, half, three quarter, and full jump-turns while the other partner turns the rope.

   — Together, decide on a basic jump trick. While the rope turner performs the trick, the other skipper run in from the back and match steps.

   — Nonturner, bounce or toss a ball.

   — Back partner, can you take over the rope turning from the front turner?

   — Try to travel while rope jumping in this front-to-back position.

   — ***Challenge:*** Together, do a Double-Under.

   — Invent a front-to-back jump rope trick with your partner; then teach your trick to another pair.

2. ***Front-to-Back Routine:*** With your partner, create a routine using at least three tricks. Then each pair, in turn, demonstrate your routine.

3. ***Back-to-Back:*** Stand back to back, each holding a handle in your right hands. Turn the rope in one direction; forward for one partner, backward for the other, and jump in unison. Change to left hands and repeat.

VARIATION:

The Three Amigos: Have skipppers form groups of three. One skipper is the turner, who turns the rope forward. The second skipper runs in front door; while the third skipper runs in behind the turner, and all three jump in unison.

GS–36 PARTNER AND GROUP JUMPING

FOCUS: Cooperative rope jumping

EQUIPMENT: One rope per skipper; music with a steady 4/4 beat; tape or record player

ORGANIZATION:

- Have skippers get a rope, check rope for correct length, then find a partner of equal size, and scatter around the play area.

DESCRIPTION OF ACTIVITY:

1. *Two Ropes Side-by-Side:*

   — Stand beside your partner, facing the same direction. Each partner's inside hand turns the other partner's rope, while your outer hands turn your own rope.

   — Practice forward turning both ropes at the same time and jumping in unison.

   — Turn ropes backward and jump together.

   — Jump the Basic Rope Tricks in this position.

   — Repeat tasks in side-by-side position, facing in the opposite direction.

   — Show me how you can travel around the play area while turning and jumping your ropes together.

2. *Two Ropes Face-to-Face:*

   — Face each other, with one partner holding his or her rope behind and the other partner holding his or her rope in front.

   — Turning both ropes at the same time, forward for one partner and backward for the other, jump over both ropes at once.

   — Now turn the ropes alternately, jumping each one in turn.

3. *Chorus Line:* Form groups of four, stand in the side-by-side position, and turn and jump ropes at the same time. *Challenge:* Join up with another group of four and perform the stunt with eight skippers. Can you expand your group of eight skippers to twelve?

4. *The Jumping File:* Form groups of three, standing one behind the other in a file. Each turn your rope forward at the same time and jump in unison. Change position in your file and repeat.

   — Join with another group to form a file of six and repeat.

5. *The Jumping Circle:* Form a circle of twelve skippers, holding ropes in the side-by-side position. Can you turn and jump ropes in unison to the music? *Challenge:* All skippers form one large jumping circle!

GS-37 LONG ROPE JUMPING

FOCUS: Long rope turning and jumping
technique

EQUIPMENT: One long rope per group;
one hoop per group;
music with a steady 4/4 beat;
tape or record player

ORGANIZATION:

• Form groups of four skippers: Two skippers turn while the other two skippers jump. Change ropes frequently so that everyone turns the rope. Use ropes that are 3 to 5 meters (10 to 15 feet) long. Ensure groups are well spaced around the play area. Using music in 4/4 time will encourage skippers to turn the ropes rhythmically and smoothly.

DESCRIPTION OF ACTIVITY:

1. *Technique:* Turners, holding a rope handle each, let the rope dangle between you. With elbow at your side, turn the rope with your forearm, in toward the body. Let the rope touch the floor at the bottom of each swing. Listen to the rhythm of the rope as it hits the floor each time. Turn rope with a high arch. Switch hands after every ten rotations. Repeat four times. Change turners and repeat above.

   — Challenge: Can one pair take over the rope turning without stopping the rope's rhythm?

2. *Jump the Bridge:* Turners, hold long rope at knee height. Gradually raise the height of the rope off the floor. Each skipper, in turn, jump each of the raised heights, traveling in a figure-8 pattern. Which skipper in your group can jump the highest?

3. *Rope Exchange Challenge:* Begin with one jumper near each turner. Left jumper, change places with the right turner after your jump. Try not to stop the rhythm of the rope's turning. Right jumper, change places with the left turner. Continue this pattern of opposite jumpers and turners exchanging places.

4. *Jumping Challenge:* Each jumper take a turn and jump the turning rope as many times as you can without stopping it. Which member of your group will jump the most times?

5. *Hoop Capture:* (Have each group stand in a circle and space themselves evenly apart. The leader stands in the center, holding a long rope with a hoop securely attached to one end.) Leader, gently swing the outstretched rope CW around the circle and along the floor. Jumpers, try to jump in the hoop as it comes near you. If successful, you become the new turner. Repeat with turner swinging the rope in CCW direction.

GS–38 FRONT AND BACK DOOR PATTERNS

FOCUS: Entering and exiting technique

EQUIPMENT: One long rope per group; music with a strong 4/4 beat; tape or record player

ORGANIZATION:

• Form groups of four skippers and have each group get a long rope before scattering around the play area. Review and demonstrate the basic Front Door technique of turning the rope toward incoming jumper; Back door technique of turning rope away from incoming jumper. Emphasize smooth, rhythmical rope turning.

DESCRIPTION OF ACTIVITY:

1. *Front Door Entry-Run-Exit Pattern:* Each jumper stand near left rope turner's right shoulder. Watch the rope as turners turn it toward you, down, and away. As rope passes your nose, enter and run through to exit near the right turner's right shoulder. Reenter front door near the right turner's left shoulder. Remember, run through—do not jump the rope! Repeat this until each skipper has gone four times.

2. *Front Door Figure-8 Pattern:* Jumper, stand near the left turner's right shoulder. Watch the rope as it swings toward you, down, and away. As the rope passes your nose, enter and jump three times; then exit rope by right turner's right shoulder. Reenter Front Door near right turner's left shoulder. Remember to jump into the middle! Repeat this figure-8 pattern four times.

3. *Window Tag:* First jumper, enter and exit as in the Front Door Figure-8 Pattern. Second jumper, enter and exit after the first jumper exits, trying to tag the first jumper. Once tagged, the first jumper becomes the chaser.

4. *Back Door Entry-Run-Exit Pattern:* Jumper, stand near the left turner's right shoulder. Watch the rope as it hits the floor and rises upward, away from you. When the rope is at the top, run through the open window; exit near the right turner's left shoulder. Reenter near right turner's right shoulder; then run through again, exiting near left turner's left shoulder, around that turner, ready to go again. Remember to run through; do not jump the rope! Repeat this pattern until each skipper has gone twice. Reverse the pattern by having Jumper start near right turner's left shoulder.

5. *Back Door Figure-8 Pattern:* Each jumper start near the left turner's right shoulder. Watch the rope as it hits the floor and rises upward, away from you. When the rope is at the top, run in, jump three times, and exit near the right turner's right shoulder. Reenter Back Door near the right turner's left shoulder. Repeat this pattern until each skipper has gone four times. Repeat Back Door Pattern, jumping five times in the middle before exiting.

— Play Window Tag.

6. *Call-In Game:* Turners, turn rope toward jumpers in the Front Door Pattern; then first jumper, run in the Front Door and begin jumping. At random, call the name of another jumper, who will run in and join hands with you so that you jump together three times. First jumper, run out, and second jumper, call another jumper's name at random. Hold hands and jump together three times. Continue until all skippers have called in another jumper. Change rope turners and repeat.

GS-39 LONG ROPE STUNTS

FOCUS: Cooperation; hand/eye coordination

EQUIPMENT: One long rope per group; one hoop per group; one large utility or basketball per group; one short rope per group; two deckrings per group; music with a strong 4/4 beat; tape or record player

ORGANIZATION:

- Form groups of four or five skippers. Have each group collect a long rope, short rope, ball and hoop, and two deckrings, and then scatter around the play area. Ensure that groups are well spaced.

DESCRIPTION OF ACTIVITY:

1. *Basic Tricks in a Long Rope:* Jumpers, in turn, run in Front Door and perform a short rope trick; then run out Back Door or Front Door.
   - Rocker; Jogger; Boxer; Bell-Skier Combo; Jump-Turns
   - Forward, Side, and Double Straddle Jumps, The "X"
   - Bird Hops, Twister, Peek-a-Boos, Toe-to-Toe, Heel-to-Heel
   - Heel-to-Toe, Front Leg Kicks, Sideway Rockers
2. *Ball Bounce and Jump Stunt:* While jumping in the middle, each jumper, in turn, bounce a large ball.
3. *Long and Short Stunt:* Each jumper, start in the middle with a short rope held behind your heels and face one of the turners. As the turners turn the rope at a constant speed, turn your short rope at the same speed and jump inside the long rope.
   - Jumper, hold your short rope behind you, run in Front Door, and turn and jump your short rope inside the long rope. (Now you are facing sideways to the turners.) Try your favorite Short Rope trick.
   - Repeat, jumping in the center with a hoop.
4. *Copy Cat:* Two skippers, enter front door together, perform a stunt; then exit together. Explore different ways of jumping together:
   - Jump and clap partner's hands; jump and touch the floor.
   - Jump side by side, holding on at the waist; link elbows and jump around.
   - Jump-turn away from each other so that you are sideways, back to back, then facing your partner; Wring-the-Dishrag.
   - Invent a partner trick of your own!
5. *Outside Pass and Jump:* While one partner jumps in the middle the other partner stand just out of range of the turning rope and hold a ball. Partners toss the ball back and forth to each other. Continue until everyone has had a turn at being a jumper, a tosser, and a turner.
6. *Shoot and Jump:* Perform as for Stunt 2, except that jumper runs in front door, tries to catch the ball thrown by the outside skipper and then shoot it into the basket. After three tries, another jumper takes a turn. Continue until everyone has been a turner, tosser and retriever, and a jumper.
7. *Inside Pass and Jump:* Both partners, one holding the ball, enter front door and begin jumping. How many different ways can you and your partner toss and catch the ball while jumping? Repeat using a deckring. Repeat using two deckrings, one for each partner.
8. *Jumping "W":* Two jumpers, standing side by side and facing in the same direction, hold short ropes in the "W" position (hold own rope handle with outside hand and partner's rope handle with inside hand). Now try to jump in unison inside the long rope.

GS-40 LONG ROPE CHALLENGES

FOCUS: Jumping stunts; cooperation

EQUIPMENT: One long rope per group; one 10-meter (30-foot) long rope per large group; music with a strong 4/4 beat; tape or record player

ORGANIZATION:

- Form groups of four or five skippers. Have leaders get a long rope; then groups scatter around the play area. Ensure groups are well spaced.

DESCRIPTION OF ACTIVITY:

1. ***Hot Pepper Challenge:*** Turners, begin by turning the rope slowly. Jumper, enter front door, and jump the rope; on your signal "Pepper!" turners will turn the rope quickly. How many times can you jump without stopping the rope? Repeat until everyone has had a turn at jumping. Who will be your group's "Hot Pepper Champ"? Challenge another group's.

2. ***High-Lo Water Challenge:*** Turners, at first turn the rope so that it hits the floor; jumper, enter front door and jump in the middle. Now turners, gradually turn the rope higher, until quite high; then gradually turn the rope lower, until it touches the floor. Jumper, can you keep jumping without stopping the rope? Repeat until everyone has had a turn.

3. ***Revolving Doors:*** Each jumper, in turn, try the following ways of entering and exiting:
   — Run in Front Door, exit Front Door.
   — Run in Front Door, exit Back Door.
   — Run in Back Door, exit Front Door.
   — Run in Back Door, exit Back Door.

4. ***Pop-Ups (Double-Unders):*** Turners, begin by turning the long rope slowly. Skipper, enter and jump. On your signal, "Fast!" turners turn the rope very fast. Skipper, jump high so that rope will pass twice under your feet!

5. ***Spinning Wheel:*** Each jumper, in turn, jump in the center of the rope as the Turners turn the long rope while traveling CW. Repeat for eight jumps; then reverse direction for another eight jumps. Turners, try to keep jumper centered.

6. ***Double Decker:*** Turners, turn a long rope in place. Two jumpers, enter Front Door, each holding the handles of a second long rope. On signal, "Turn!" jumpers turn your rope and jump inside the turner's rope while jumping outside your rope. Both ropes should turn in unison.

7. ***Jump-a-Long Challenge:*** (Combine two groups together to form large groups of eight to ten skippers. Give one 10-meter [30-foot] long rope to each group. Select two tall players from each group to be the rope turners.) Each jumper, in turn, run in Front Door and continue to jump the rope. Add skippers until someone stops the rope. Change turners, and repeat the challenge. Which group can collect the most skippers jumping in one rope? Which group can collect the most consecutive jumps by a fixed number of skippers in your group?

GS—41 FORMATION JUMPING STUNTS

FOCUS: Cooperation; rhythmic jumping

EQUIPMENT: Four long ropes per group; one short rope per group; music with a strong 4/4 beat; tape or record player

ORGANIZATION:

- Divide the class into groups of six to eight skippers. Have each group collect four long ropes and find a free space. Ensure that groups are well spaced.

DESCRIPTION OF ACTIVITY:

1. **Square:** Four rope turners, hold the handles of two ropes, one handle in each hand. Turn the four ropes up and away from center in unison. Four jumpers, run in Front Door and jump several times; then run out the same side you entered. Jumpers and turners change roles and repeat.

   — Turn ropes down and away from center in unison; jumper enter through Back Door.

2. **Wheel Jump:** (Combine two groups for this stunt.) Four pairs of turners, each pair with a long rope, position in a wheel formation as shown. Jumpers, stand in a file formation, facing one of the turning ropes. On signal, "Turn!" rope turners turn the long ropes in unison. Each jumper, run in Front Door, jump once, then exit toward the next long rope. As soon as the jumper just ahead of you has entered the next rope, you may go. Continue in a CCW direction around the "wheel." Turners and jumpers change roles and repeat Wheel Jump in a CW direction.

3. **Loop Run:** (Combine two groups for this stunt.) Four pairs of turners stand in a file. Each pair face inward and hold a long rope between you. Jumpers, stand in a file near one end turner. On signal "Turn!" turners turn long ropes. Each jumper, in turn, run a loop pattern as shown, until all have completed the Loop Run. As soon as the Jumper ahead of you has entered the next rope, you may go. Change roles and repeat the "Loop Run." Repeat in the reverse direction.

4. **Egg Beater:** (Four skippers of each group stand in a square formation, with turners 1 and 3 holding the handles of a long rope so that it crosses over the rope held by turners 2 and 4. Refer to illustration.) Turners, turn ropes in unison so that they meet at the bottom at the same time. Each jumper, in turn, enter the ropes at an angle, jump in the center five times, then exit. Repeat until everyone has had a turn at being a turner and a jumper.

VARIATIONS:

a. **Parachute:** Three pairs of turners turn three long ropes in unison. The ropes must all turn in the same direction and touch the floor at the same time. Each jumper, in turn, try to jump five or more times in the center of the ropes.

b. **Egg Beater:** Have jumper turn a short rope.

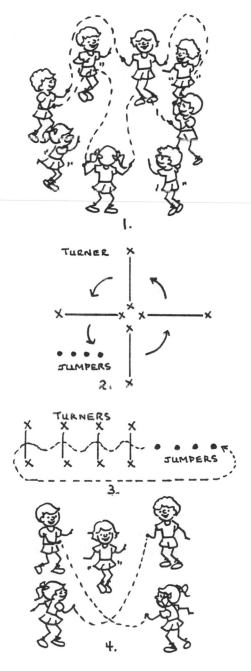

FOCUS: Turning technique; entering; exiting; basic tricks

EQUIPMENT: Two long ropes per group

ORGANIZATION:

• First teach skippers the Double-Dutch turning technique, then the entering, jumping, and exiting techniques. Have one pair demonstrate Double-Dutch turning so that skippers can observe how ropes turn alternately toward each other. Emphasize that turners turn rope rhythmically and smoothly and that turners center jumper in ropes and focus on jumper's feet. Remind jumpers to focus on the rope farther away and enter as it nears the floor. Divide the class into groups of four or five. Have each group get two long ropes and then find a free space.

DESCRIPTION OF ACTIVITY:

1. **Double-Dutch Rope Turning Technique:**
   — Two turners, hold a handle of each long rope, and move apart until the ropes are taut.
   — Keeping your elbows at your sides, turn the ropes alternately toward the midline of your body, with your wrists, in small circles.
   — As your Double-Dutch turning improves, move forward toward each other until the ropes are alternately touching the surface. Note when rope A is at the top of the turn, rope B is at the bottom.
   — Practice for three minutes until everyone has had a turn.
   — Practice changing the speed at which the ropes turn.

2. **Window Jumping:**
   — Turners, hold the long ropes to make a window: rope A on top; rope B touching the floor. Keep your ropes in the window position. Do not let them move!
   — Jumper, stand by the right shoulder of the left turner. Enter the window, jump the rope, and exit by the right shoulder of the right turner.
   — Reenter by the left shoulder of the right turner, jump rope B, and exit by the left turner's left shoulder. Repeat this figure-8 pattern twice.
   — Continue until everyone has had a turn being a turner and a jumper.

3. **Window Run:**
   — Turners, turn long ropes Double-Dutch rhythmically.
   — Jumper, start as in Window Jumping. Watch the ropes carefully, looking for the "window." Jump through open window when the rope farther away is at the bottom; exit by right shoulder of right turner. Reenter by right turner's left shoulder. Repeat figure-8 pattern twice. Remember to jump through the ropes without touching!
   — Continue until everyone has had a turn jumping and turning.

4. **Pogo Jump:** Turners, rhythmically turn ropes Double-Dutch. Jumper, enter by right shoulder of left turner, jump five times, and exit by right turner's right shoulder. Jump with feet together, in the middle of the ropes. Complete the figure-8 pattern. Take turns being jumpers and turners. Repeat jumping only once in the middle, in a figure-8 pattern.

5. **Pogo Jump-Turns:** Turners, turn long ropes Double-Dutch. Each jumper, in turn, enter rope by right shoulder of left turner, facing right turner. Jumping with feet together, complete a full turn by doing quarter jump-turns until you again face right turner. Try to complete four full turns in this way.

6. **Skier:** Turners, turn long ropes Double-Dutch. Each jumper, in turn, jump in center and, keeping feet together, jump from side to side on each turn of the rope.

GS–43 MORE DOUBLE-DUTCH TRICKS

FOCUS: Rhythmical jumping; group work

EQUIPMENT: Two long ropes per group; one short rope per group; one basketball and hoop per group

ORGANIZATION:

• Divide the class into groups of four or five. Have each group get two long ropes and then find a free space.

DESCRIPTION OF ACTIVITY:

1. *Side Straddle:* Each jumper, in turn, enter Double-Dutch ropes and jump feet together on first turn; feet shoulder-width apart on second turn. Change feet position every turn of the rope.

2. *Scissors:* Jumper, enter Double-Dutch ropes, and jump Pogo. When ready, jump one foot in front of the other. Switch feet on each turn of rope.

3. *The "X":* Jumper, enter Double-Dutch ropes and jump Pogo. When ready, jump Side Straddle on the first turn, cross feet on second turn, side straddle on third turn, cross alternate feet on fourth turn. Continue this jumping pattern.

4. *Pogo Kicks:* Jumper, enter Double-Dutch ropes and jump Pogo on first turn of rope. On second turn, jump on right foot, kicking left leg straight outwards; on third turn, jump Pogo; on fourth turn jump on left foot, kicking right leg outward. Continue this pattern. Can you kick your leg higher and touch the knee or toes of that leg with the opposite hand as you double-dutch jump?

5. *Jogger:* Jumper, enter Double-Dutch ropes and jump Pogo. When ready, jump over rope with left foot on first turn; jump over rope with right foot on second turn. Do sixteen Jogger steps in this way.

6. *Prancer:* Perform Jogger step in Double-Dutch ropes, but lift knees up as high as possible.

7. *Speed Jumps:* Start jumping with Jogger steps. As turners gradually speed up Double-Dutch turning, jumper match speed with "Running Steps." How long can you keep jumping before stopping the ropes?

8. *Pop-Ups:* Jumper, enter Double-Dutch ropes and jump Pogo. On signal, "Pop!" turners speed up ropes as Jumper jumps high so that both ropes pass under.

9. *Partner Stunts:* Two jumpers, enter Double-Dutch ropes in the middle. Take turns matching each other's tricks. Invent a trick of your own!

10. *Short and Double-Dutch:* Jumper, enter Double-Dutch ropes with a short rope. Match the speed of the Double-Dutch ropes while turning and jumping your own short rope. Try short rope tricks that you have learned!

GS-44 ROPE JUMPING CIRCUIT

FOCUS: Long and short rope jumping

EQUIPMENT: Several short ropes; several long ropes; two hoops; four utility balls; four beanbags or deckrings; four scoops; posterboard, marking pen, masking tape; lively music with a strong 4/4 beat; tape or record player

ORGANIZATION:

• Set up five or six skipping stations around the play area in a circuit. Post signs (and posters, if available) to designate each station. Put strong and weak skippers together in groups of four or six, to promote peer teaching. Every five to eight minutes, have skippers rotate from station to station in a CW direction. If possible, write to your state or national Heart Foundation for jump rope posters. Provide opportunity for skippers to "show off" their routines they have developed or new tricks they have created. Following are suggestions for jump rope stations.

DESCRIPTION OF ACTIVITY:

1. **Short Rope Routine:** Create a short rope routine using the tricks you have learned. Work in counts of four, eight, and sixteen.

2. **Skill-Builder Idea:** Using the short rope tricks you have learned, combine them to create new tricks. Give your new trick a name!

3. **Partner Routine:** With a partner, develop a routine using one or two ropes.

4. **Long Rope Stunts:** Using equipment such as balls, beanbags or deckrings, hoops, scoops, short ropes, and other members of your group, invent long rope stunts. Teach them to other members of your group.

5. **Double-Dutch:** Practice double-dutch turning and jumping at this station. Perform single rope tricks while double-dutching, such as Skier, Twister, Straddles, Boxer, Jogger, and Speed Jumps.

6. **Rope Challenger:** (Post posters of tricks the skippers have not as yet learned.) Choose a trick, read the description or helpful hints to go with the illustration, and try to learn it. You may get help from other skippers in your group and from me.

GS–45 PLAY WRESTLING

FOCUS: Leg, arm, and shoulder strength   **EQUIPMENT:** One mat per pair

ORGANIZATION:

• Explain that combatives can be a lot of fun, provided that players play fairly and safely. Have players find a partner of equal size, get a mat to share, and stand together in free space.

DESCRIPTION OF ACTIVITY:

1. *Stubborn Donkey:* One player, the Donkey, place your hands on the mat in "wheelbarrow" position, with legs supported by your partner. Partner, hold the legs of the Donkey and gently try to push him or her forward. Donkey, refuse to budge off the spot. Exchange roles and repeat.

2. *Stubborn Driver:* Donkey try to move forward while the driver (partner holding your legs) resists!

3. *Arm Wrestling:* Lie face down, head to head with your partner. Interlock your partner's right thumb and close your right hand around it. Pressing your right elbow to the mat, reach your left hand under your right elbow and join hands. Now force your partner's right hand to the mat. Change hands and repeat. Find a new partner and repeat.

4. *Leg Wrestling:* Facing opposite directions, sit side by side with hips touching. Lie back with your knees bent and lock your inside elbows; then raise your inside legs three times. On the third time, hook your partner's leg at the knee or ankle so that you pull your partner over. Repeat with the other leg; then challenge someone else.

5. *Back-to-Back Wrestling:* Sit with your backs touching and your legs spread. Interlock elbows with your partner; then try to force one of your partner's elbows to the mat. Challenge someone else and repeat.

6. *Shoulder Wrestle:* Get a mat and face your partner while kneeling on all-fours on the mat. Touch right shoulders and try to drive your partner off the mat. Repeat, pushing with left shoulders.

7. *Neck Pull:* Stand facing each other, on the mat. Both players, place your right hand around your partner's neck; then try to pull your partner off the mat. Change, to pull with your left hands, and repeat.

8. With your partner, invent a "play wrestle" and teach it to another pair.

FOCUS: Leg, arm, and shoulder strength; balance

EQUIPMENT: One mat per pair; one sponge ball per pair

ORGANIZATION:

- Have players find a partner of equal size and ability. Partners get a mat and a sponge ball to share and find a free space. Use sponge balls for Ball Wrestle, as they are safe to fall on.

DESCRIPTION OF ACTIVITY:

1. ***Ball Wrestle:*** Both partners, hold the ball firmly. On the signal "Go!" try to wrestle the ball from each other.

2. ***Turn the Turtle:*** Put the ball away; then kneel on all fours facing your partner. Try to turn your partner over onto his or her back. Change roles and repeat; then challenge another player and try again.

3. ***Turn the Eagle:*** One partner lie face down on your mat with your arms and legs spread while your partner kneels alongside you. Challenge your partner to try to turn you over onto your back. Change roles and repeat; then challenge others!

4. ***Squat Tug:*** Both partners, squat facing each other, holding each other's arms by the wrist grip. On the signal "Go!" try to wrestle each other to force your partner off balance.

5. ***Rooster Fighting:*** Squat facing your partner and clasp your hands behind your knees. Now bump your partner with shoulders only, so that he or she releases the clasped hands. Repeat, holding your heels with your hands.

6. ***Hoppo Bumpo:*** Stand on your left leg and hold your right ankle with your left hand behind your back. Grasp your left arm behind your back with your right hand. Now try to gently bump your opponent off the mat so that he or she touches the floor with one or both feet. Reverse leg/hand positions and repeat. Challenge your partner to best two out of three tries.

7. Invent a Dual contest with your partner and challenge other pairs!

VARIATION:

Team Hoppo Bumpo: Have players hook four mats together to form one large mat area. Team of four players challenge each other to see who is last still standing on the mats.

GS-47 PARTNER TUGS AND REACTION CHALLENGES _____

FOCUS: Arm, shoulder, and leg strength; quickness

EQUIPMENT: One short rope per pair; mats; one beanbag per pair; flags

ORGANIZATION:

• Have players find a partner of equal size and stand facing each other on either side of a line or short rope.

DESCRIPTION OF ACTIVITY:

1. *One-Hand Tug:* Grip your partner's right wrist, turn sideways, and try to pull each other across the line. Best two out of three tries. Repeat using a left wrist hold; then challenge a new partner and repeat.

2. *Two-Hand Tug:* Gripping the fingers of both hands, try to pull your partner across the line. Best two out of three tries. Challenge a new partner and repeat.

3. *Elbow Tug:* Lock elbows with your partner and stand on opposite sides of the line. Now try to pull your partner across the line. Best two out of three tries with each elbow. Challenge a new partner and repeat.

4. *Hopping Tug:* Hopping on only one foot and gripping right index fingers, try to pull each other across the line. Repeat with a left finger grip while hopping on the other foot.

5. *Rope Tug:* Together, get a short rope and hold onto it with both hands. Now try to pull each other across the line; then hold the rope with first only your right hands and then only your left hands. Try pulling with your backs to each other and the rope between your legs.

6. *Floor Touch Pull:* Double the short rope and then double it again. Grasping the rope in your right hands, lean away from each other and try to be the first to touch your free hand to the floor. Repeat, holding the rope with left hands. Can you be the first to touch one hand and one knee to the floor?

7. *Knee Boxing:* Stand facing your partner in a semicrouch position, holding your hands out in front. Try to slap your partner's knees while protecting your own with your hands and arms and quick, short steps. No body contact is allowed. Score one point for each successful tap on your partner's knee. Play to three points; then challenge someone else.

8. *Tiger Tail Wrestle:* Get a flag and tuck it into the back of your waistband so that most of the flag shows. Kneel on the mat facing each other. While remaining in the kneeling position, try to grab your partner's flag while protecting your own. Repeat three times; then challenge a new partner.

VARIATIONS:

a. *Beanbag Tug:* In Hopping Tug, Rope Tug, and Floor Touch Pull, have partners try to pick up a beanbag placed on the floor behind them.

b. *Hand-Knee Boxing:* Have partners grasp right hands and knee box with the open free hand. They then repeat, grasping left hands.

c. *Team Tiger Tails:* Form two groups of three and issue pinnies to each team. Place three mats together to form one large mat. Have all players start on all-fours on the mat, with teams facing each other head to head. Each partner has a flag tucked into the back of his or her waistband. Players, try to grab the other team's flags while staying in the all-fours position. Can your team grab all the other team's flags?

FOCUS: Arm, leg, and shoulder strength

EQUIPMENT: One hoop per group; one beanbag per player; one short rope per player

ORGANIZATION:

- Have each player get a short rope and a beanbag; then form groups of three players, collect a hoop for the group, and find a free space.

DESCRIPTION OF ACTIVITY:

1. *Poison Hoops:* Place the hoop on the floor and stand around it, holding hands. Try to force each other to step on the hoop itself. You may step inside the hoop, but not on it! Who will be the last player to touch the hoop?

2. *Triangle Tug-o-War:* Tie three short ropes together with figure-8 knots, in which you knot right over left and then left over right. Space yourself evenly around the rope, pulling it taut to form a triangle. Now place a beanbag one meter (3 feet) behind you and try to grab your beanbag with your free hand while pulling on the rope to prevent the other players from reaching their beanbags.

3. *Tug-o-Peace:* Stand facing another team on the other side of a line. Join hands with the two players who are directly opposite you using a finger or a wrist grip. The end players will have a free hand. On signal "Pull!" try to pull the other team over the line.

4. *Bumper-to-Bumper:* Stand back to back with a partner on either side of a line. Reach forward between your legs to grab your partner's wrists. Try to pull each other over the line.

5. *Line Bumper-to-Bumper:* Divide into two equal groups and stand back to back. One line, take a step to the right while the other line stands still so that you are each covering a gap. Reach down between your legs, cross your arms, and hold the hand of the player behind you on the right and on the left. On the signal "Pull!" try to pull the other line forward. You may not get very far, but it's fun trying!

6. *Bull in the Ring:* Form groups of four players. Three players join hands to form a circle around the fourth player, the "Bull." On signal "Go!" circle players try to stop the Bull from breaking out of the circle. Change roles until each player has had a turn at being the Bull. Bull, you may go under, over, or through the circle players' hand holds, but no roughness is allowed.

7. *Krazy Glue:* (Form teams of about six to eight players, and have one team sit tightly together, with arms and legs linked, on a large mat. The challenging team stands off the mat.) On signal "Krazy Glue!" the mat team, try to resist being dragged off the mat by the standing team. Mat players, you are still in the game as long as any part of your body is in contact with the mat. Once you lose contact with the mat, you sit out and cheer for your teammates who are still in the game. When the last player is off the mat, time is up and another team takes up the challenge! Which team will last the longest? Remember, no rough play!

GS—49 FOOTBALL FOOTWORK

FOCUS: Running and faking strategy; ball-carrying technique

EQUIPMENT: One junior-sized or sponge football per player;
several hoops and cone markers;
one flag per pair

ORGANIZATION:

- *Faking*: Explain to players that, when changing directions to the left, they should push off with the inside of the right foot; to move to the right, they should push off with the inside of the left foot, leading with their arms and shoulders. Have each player get a football and stand in a free space to start.

DESCRIPTION OF ACTIVITY:

1. ***Running Without the Ball:***

   — Run, changing direction often. Rise on the balls of the feet to increase speed as you change direction.

   — Run slowly, sprint three seconds, and then run slowly again. Repeat.

   — Run using short, quick steps; then repeat using long, slow steps.

2. ***Faking Without the Ball:***

   — Run as if you are going to go straight ahead; then suddenly turn arms and shoulders to one side and change direction. Continue to run, changing direction to the other side.

   — (Scatter hoops around the play area.) Run toward the hoop; then suddenly change direction to the right side. Repeat, changing direction to the left.

3. ***Open Field Carrying Technique:*** Carry the ball against the side of your body with your arm along and under the ball and your hand around the front end. The other end of the ball is nestled between the crook of your elbow and your chest. Find a partner and check each other's technique by hitting the ball with your hand to make sure it is held tightly.

4. ***Switch Drill:*** (Place cone markers at opposite ends as turning points in one half of the play area; then, in the other half, set up several cone markers in a row for the Zigzag Run.) One player, carry the ball as you sprint across the play area around the cone and back. As you round the cone, switch the ball to the side away from the cone. When you return, have your partner comment on and correct your technique. Change roles. Change the ball to the other arm and repeat.

5. ***Faking with the Ball:*** Tuck the ball under one arm. Run as if you are going to go straight ahead; then suddenly turn arms and shoulders to one side and change direction. Continue to run, changing direction to the other side.

   — (Scatter hoops around the play area.) Run toward the hoop; then suddenly push off with the inside of the right foot and change direction to the left. To fake to the right, push off with the inside of the left foot.

6. ***Zigzag Run:*** Have both activities going on at the same time. While your partner observes, carry the ball as you run through a row of cone markers and back again. Change roles.

   — Switch the ball to the side away from the cone as you pass each cone. Repeat.

7. ***Dodge and Mark:*** One partner, tuck a flag into your waistband and carry the ball. On the signal "Go!" try to run away from your partner, with quick fakes and changes of direction, while your partner tries to steal your flag. Change roles when your flag is stolen.

FOCUS: Running; faking

EQUIPMENT: One football per group; cone markers

ORGANIZATION:

- For each game, form two teams of six to eight players. Have the two teams line up facing each other about 23 meters (25 yards) apart, and place a football in the middle. Number off each member of each team (one to eight).

DESCRIPTION OF ACTIVITY:

1. **Steal the Football:** When your number is called, the two opposing players with that number, sprint to the middle to get the football. Score one point for your team if you can return to your line with the football without being tagged. After all players have had a turn, the team with the highest number of points wins.

2. **Touchdown Run:** (Form three teams of four to eight players. Have the teams line up on one end and two sides of the rectangular field, as shown. First player on team C, get a football.) On the signal "Go!" No. 1 player on team C, try to run downfield to score a touchdown at the other end.

   — At the same time, the No. 1 players from teams A and B, come forward to try and tag the runner. Score six points for a touchdown, if not tagged at all. Score three points if tagged by one player, and no points if tagged by both. Team leaders, keep the score for your team. Teams, rotate CW until all three teams have had a turn.

3. **No-Ball Football:** (This game is best played across half a regular football or soccer field or similar area. Mark the fields with cones. Form two teams of six to ten players; then designate one team as offense and the other team as defense. Have players tuck flags into the back of their waistbands so that most of the flag shows.) Offensive team, stand side by side along the goal line. Defensive team, scatter throughout the field. On signal "Go!" offensive players, try to run through the defensive players to the opposite goal line. Defensive players, try to snatch as many flags as you can and tuck them into your own waistband. Defensive players, count the number of flags your team has gathered, return all flags; then change roles with the offensive team. The team that can snatch the most flags wins the game.

4. **Ball Carrying Shuttle:** (Form groups of four to eight players. Have half of each group stand in file or shuttle formation facing the other half 10 meters [30 feet] apart. Leader of one file holds a football in carrying position.) On the signal "Go!" the ball carrier, run to the opposite side and hand the ball to the leader of the other file; then join the end of the file. New ball carrier, repeat. Continue until all players have had a turn.

VARIATIONS:

a. To increase participation in the "Touchdown Run" game, have two runners run for a touchdown against two defenders; against four defenders. Only the player with the ball may be tagged.

b. **No-Ball Football:** If an offensive player loses a flag, that player becomes a moving obstacle and may block the path of defensive players.

c. **Thirty Carries:** Challenge other groups to count the number of times they carry the ball back and forth. First team to reach thirty carries wins. If a team drops the ball, they start counting from zero again.

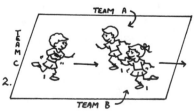

GS–51 FORWARD PASSING AND CATCHING

FOCUS: Forward passing and catching techniques

EQUIPMENT: One football per player

ORGANIZATION:

• Have each player get a football and find a free space.

DESCRIPTION OF ACTIVITY:

1. *Forward Pass Technique:*

   — Grip the football behind the middle, with fingers on the lace at one side of the ball and the thumb on the other side. Relax the fingers.

   — Point the opposite foot toward the target and turn the body sideways.

   — Raise the football back and over the shoulder. To deliver the ball, extend the arm forward, throw your index finger toward the target, and snap the wrist downward on the follow-through as the ball leaves your hand.

2. *Catching Technique:*

   — Position yourself under the ball and keep your eyes on it.

   — For a low pass, cradle the hands so that the fingers are spread and pointing down, with little fingers together and fingers relaxed.

   — For a high pass, spread the fingers with the fingers pointing up and thumbs together. Relax the hands.

   — Let the ball fall into the cradle of your hands. "Give" with the hands, elbows, wrists, and knees by drawing the ball toward the body to absorb the impact.

   — After catching the ball, tuck it into the carrying position at your side.

3. *Practice:* (Have players find a partner and get a football to share; then scatter around the play area facing each other about 6 meters [2 feet] apart.)

   — Stand and throw the ball to each other, making sure that you grip the football behind the middle with fingers on the lace.

   — Kneel on one knee; then throw the ball back and forth so that your partner does not have to move.

   — Throw the ball to your partner while he or she is moving backward; moving to the left; moving to the right; moving toward the ball.

4. *Star:* Pass the ball to your partner, counting the passes. When you have caught the ball three times in a row, you get an "S." After three more consecutive passes you get a "T." Continue play until you spell "STAR." Play fairly and give your partner good passes.

5. *Receiver:* Play as for Star, but you get one letter for each successful catch. Who can be "RECEIVER" first?

6. *Points:* Pass to your partner about 9 meters (30 feet) apart, for three minutes. You may both run to receive the ball. Count one point for each successful catch. Who can get the most points? Change partners and repeat.

VARIATIONS:

a. Repeat Star, Receiver, and Points while the receiver is moving.

b. Increase the distance that the ball is thrown.

GS–52 HOOP FOOTBALL

FOCUS: Forward passing; lead-up game

EQUIPMENT: Two footballs per group;
one hoop (or beachball) per team;
cone markers

ORGANIZATION:

- Review the forward pass and catching techniques before playing Hoop Ball. Form teams of four to six players and choose a leader for each team. For each game have two teams stand opposite and facing each other, in a line, about 10 meters (30 feet) apart. Mark each team's starting line with cones. The leader collects a hoop and stands in the middle and tosses the hoop into the air.

DESCRIPTION OF ACTIVITY:

1. Leader, hold the hoop vertical and as high as you can. The line player with the ball, try to throw the football through the hoop using the forward pass.

2. Any player on the opposite team can catch the ball by calling "Mine!" Then try to throw it again through the hoop.

3. Continue alternating until all players on both sides have had a turn. Exchange leader in the middle and play another game.

4. Score two points for your team if the ball goes through the hoop without touching it. Score one point if the ball touches the hoop. Score one point if the catching team catches the ball before it touches the ground. Team leaders, keep score for your team.

VARIATIONS:

a. Have leader toss the hoop upward.

b. Use a beachball instead of a hoop.

GS–53 END-ZONE PASSING GAME

FOCUS: Forward passing; lead-up game

EQUIPMENT: Four footballs per game;
cone markers

ORGANIZATION:

- Mark out the playing field with cone markers, identifying the end zones. Review the correct forward pass technique before the game; then divide the class into two equal teams. Have each team get two or more footballs. Allocate half the field to each team. Each team must stay within the boundaries of its own half of the field. Adjust the length of the field to the player's throwing ability.

DESCRIPTION OF ACTIVITY:

1. On the signal "Go!" players, throw the footballs into the other team's end zone from anywhere on your team's side of the field. You may run up to the center line, but not over it.

2. Players on the opposite side, try to catch the balls and throw them back.

3. Score two points if the ball lands in the end zone without first touching the ground. Score one point if the ball bounces or rolls into the end zone.

4. Play for about ten minutes or any agreed length of time.

VARIATION:

Increase the number of balls used for a large class.

GS–54 INTERCEPTION

FOCUS: Passing, catching; pass interception; offense and defense

EQUIPMENT: Two or more footballs per game; two sets of pinnies per game; cone markers

ORGANIZATION:

- Mark out the playing field and the "No Man's Land" with cone markers. Review the correct Forward Pass technique; then divide the class into two equal teams. Both teams have half their players on either side of "No Man's Land." Explain that no player may cross into the other half of the field. Team leaders, toss to see who has first throw with the football. Adjust the length of the field to the player's throwing ability. Encourage players to play "man-to-man" defense. Emphasize good sportsmanship and fair play.

DESCRIPTION OF ACTIVITY:

1. On the signal "Go!" the team with the ball, try to throw the football to a teammate on the other side of No Man's Land.
2. Opposition players, you may intercept the ball or knock it away. No blocking or tackling is allowed. Any player may pick up a ball that is lying on the ground.
3. The non-offending team, throw the ball in after it has gone out-of-bounds. From out-of-bounds, the ball cannot be thrown directly over No Man's Land.
4. Score one point for a completed pass over No Man's Land. Team leaders, keep score for your team.

NO MAN'S LAND

GS–55 LATERAL PASSING AND CATCHING

FOCUS: Lateral passing and catching techniques

EQUIPMENT: One football per pair

ORGANIZATION:

- Have players pair up, get a football per pair, and then scatter into free spaces. Explain and demonstrate the lateral pass technique; then have players practice.

DESCRIPTION OF ACTIVITY:

1. *Lateral Pass Technique:* In the lateral pass the ball is passed sideways or backward (not forward).
   - Cradle the hands around and behind the ball.
   - Point the nearer foot toward the receiver and adopt a wide stance.
   - Swing the ball with an easy motion across the body, and release the ball about waist high.
   - Pass in front of a running receiver.

2. *Catching Technique:* The receiver, you must be behind or to the side of the passer.
   - Turn at the waist to face the passer, and keep your eyes on the ball.
   - Reach out to the ball so that the fingers are spread and relaxed.
   - Gather the ball into your chest with both hands.
   - After catching the ball, tuck it into the carrying position at your side.

3. *Practice:* Find a partner and stand 3 meters (10 feet) apart.
   - Pass the football back and forth. Pass to the left, then to the right.
   - One player, stand to pass to the running receiver. Pass slightly in front. Practice passes to the left and to the right.
   - Both players, run and pass continuously. Pass left, then right.

FOCUS: Lateral and forward passing; catching; offense-defense play

EQUIPMENT: One football per group; one set of pinnies

ORGANIZATION:

• Review the technique of the Lateral Pass. Explain the games and allow the teams to practice before playing the games.

DESCRIPTION OF ACTIVITY:

1. *Running Circle Pass:* (Form circles of six to eight players, and have them stand facing in a CW direction. The leader stands with the football in the center.) On the signal "Go!" circle players, jog slowly around the circle, while the leader lateral passes to each player in turn. Players, as soon as you have caught the ball, pass it back to the leader. When each player has had a turn, a new leader takes over in the center; reverse the direction and continue, so that you receive passes from either side. Leader, pass the ball slightly in front of the running players. Receivers, reach out with both hands; then gather the ball into your chest.

2. *30-Up:* Challenge other teams to see which one can make thirty consecutive passes without dropping the ball. If the ball is dropped, start counting again from zero. The first team sitting down after thirty catches wins.

3. *Follow That Pass:* (Have all players stand in a circle, pointing the nearest foot across the circle.) On the signal "Go!" pass to any teammate across the circle, except the players on either side of you; then follow your pass across the circle to take the receiver's place.

   — *30-Up:* Continue passing and following your pass, trying to make thirty consecutive catches before the other teams. The first team sitting down after thirty catches wins.

4. *Five Passes:* (Form two teams of six to ten players and have each player get a pinnie and stand beside an opposing player. To start the game, call a jump ball at the center between the smallest players on each team; then have players try to pass the ball to teammates. They must make five consecutive passes to five different players without dropping the ball or having it intercepted. Teams score one point for each five-pass sequence. Encourage players to move to an empty space to receive a pass. Have the whole team count aloud the number of passes made. Explain the following rules to the players.)

   — *Rule of Three:* Players may not take more than three steps with the ball or hold the ball for more than three seconds. No personal contact is allowed.

   — The ball is awarded to the opposing team at the nearest boundary line if: the Rule of Three is broken; a point is scored; the ball goes out-of-bounds; the ball touches the ground.

   — Two opposing players holding the football results in a jump ball at the spot.

   — The first team to gain five points wins.

1.

3.

4.

GS–57 FLICKER BALL

FOCUS: Positional play; passing and catching; offense and defense

EQUIPMENT: One football per game; two sets of pinnies; basketball court

ORGANIZATION:

• Flicker Ball is played on a basketball court, with no boundaries. Form two teams of six to twelve players and have each player get a pinnie and stand beside an opposing player. Start the game with a jump ball at the center; the players then try to pass the ball to teammates to score two points by shooting the ball through the basket, or one point if the ball touches the top of the hoop but does not go in. Explain the following rules to the players.

DESCRIPTION OF ACTIVITY:

1. *Rule of Three:* Players may not take more than three steps with the ball or hold the ball for more than three seconds.

2. *Contact:* No personal contact is allowed, and the ball may be intercepted. For any breach of the rules, the opposing team is awarded the ball at the point of the infraction.

3. *Tagging:* After three seconds a player holding the ball can be tagged by a light two-handed touch. The tagged player must then release the ball immediately and move back 1 meter (3 feet) to allow the opposition player making the tag to throw the ball.

4. *Jump Ball:* Players jump for the ball if two opposing players are holding it.

5. *Scoring:* Players may attempt to score only when in the opposition's court. After a score, the ball is still "alive" and play continues. If you just scored, you may score again and again. The team with the most points after an agreed time limit wins.

GS–58 SNAPPING THE BALL

FOCUS: Centering the ball

EQUIPMENT: One football per pair

ORGANIZATION:

• Have players find a partner, get a ball to share, and stand one behind the other about 30 centimeters (1 foot) apart. The front player with the ball is the Center; the back player is the Quarterback.

DESCRIPTION OF ACTIVITY:

1. *Center Position:* Front player (the Center), place the ball on the ground. Stand behind the ball about an arm's length from it. Lean forward with knees bent in the wide astride position. Grasp the ball with your dominant hand around the lace and nondominant hand on the other side of the ball.

2. *Short Snap Technique:* Center, lift the ball and turn it sideways into the Quarterback's hands. Quarterback, spread your fingers to receive the ball in the throwing position by placing your throwing hand on top of the ball with palm down, while the other hand mirrors this position underneath.

3. *Long Snap Technique (Hiking the Ball):* (Have the Center and Quarterback stand about 5 meters [16 feet] apart.) Center, to snap the ball, look for the Quarterback, pass it back low to the ground, through the legs with both hands, releasing the ball with a flick of the wrists off the fingertips. Quarterback, watch the ball and extend both hands forward to receive it.

4. *Long Snap Practice:*

   — On the Quarterback's signal "1, 2, 3, Hike!" Center, pass the ball behind you. Repeat for ten passes; then change positions.

   — After hiking the ball, Center, run forward to receive a forward pass from the Quarterback. After ten passes, change positions and repeat.

5. *Center the Circle:* (Form equal teams of six to eight players and form a circle about 4 meters [12 feet] apart, all facing in a CCW direction.) On signal "Go!" the leader, center the ball to the player behind. That player will center to the player behind and so on until the football comes back to you.

   — Challenge other teams to Five Times Around the Circle.

6. *Hike 'n Pass Game:* (Form groups of three with one football per group. Each group find a free space. Check for good spacing.) In your group, one player is the Hiker; another, the Quarterback-Passer; and the third, the Receiver. Receiver starts in line with Hiker. On Quarterback's signal, the football is hiked, then passed to the receiver, who runs forward in a right or left pattern. After three "Hike-Pass-Receive" sets, exchange roles. Repeat until each player has had a turn at each position.

GS-59 PUNTING

FOCUS: Technique and practice   **EQUIPMENT:** One football per pair

ORGANIZATION:

- The punt is used in many football games. Explain and have players demonstrate the punting technique and review the catching technique. To practice, have players find a partner, have one player get a ball, and partners stand about 14 meters (15 yards) apart.

DESCRIPTION OF ACTIVITY:

1. *Punting Technique:*

   — *The Grip:* Point the ball downward, with the hands down both sides and the thumbs almost touching on top. Center the ball over the kicking leg.

   — *The Drop:* Take a step forward with the kicking leg, then a step with the other leg. As the second step is taken, lean forward, drop the ball, swing the kicking leg forward, and straighten the knee. The ball should be almost vertical as contact is made with the instep of the foot.

   — *The Follow-Through:* Follow through with the kicking leg with toe pointed in a line toward the target. Throw both arms out sideways for balance. Keep your eyes on the ball throughout the punt and the catch.

2. *Practice:* Punt directly to your partner. Punt the ball high; then low. Punt to your partner over objects: goal posts, baseball backstops, trees.

3. *Forcing Back:* Stand facing your partner about 20 meters (22 yards) apart. Punt the ball back and forth to each other; however, the ball must be kicked from the spot where it was caught or fielded. Try to force your partner back.

4. *Triangle Punting:* (Form groups of four players; one player gets a ball. Have the players form a triangle, with A and B at one corner, and C and D at the other two corners, about 18 to 27 meters [20 to 30 yards] apart.) Player A, run forward a few steps and punt to C. C catch the ball and punt to D. After punting to C, player A, run forward to take C's place. After each kick, players move to the next corner. How many catches can your group make in a row before the ball touches the ground?

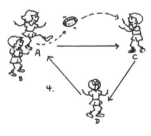

5. *Centering, Punting, and Receiving:* (Divide the class into groups of four players: a Center, Punter, and two Receivers. Have the Center get a ball; then have the players adopt the positions as illustrated. The Center crouches in the hiking position; the Punter stands about 5 meters [16 feet] behind, and the two Receivers wait upfield, about 15 meters [15 yards] in front of the Center.)

   — Center, look back between your legs; then "hike" the ball to the Punter, who catches it and punts it up field to each of the Receivers in turn.

   — Punter, watch the ball all the way into your hands; then kick the ball to a Receiver upfield.

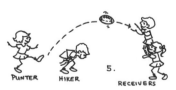

   — Receivers, as soon as the ball is "hiked," break free to position yourselves under the ball. Watch the ball all the way into your hands; hold your hands out ready to receive the ball; then pull the ball in to your body to bring it under control.

   — After six punts, all players move in a CW direction to a new position; Center to Punter; Punter to Receiver; Receiver to Receiver; Receiver to Center.

GS–60 GOAL LINE FOOTBALL

FOCUS: Forward passing; punting; catching

EQUIPMENT: Four footballs per game; cone markers

ORGANIZATION:

• Mark out the playing field with cone markers, identifying the goal lines. Review the correct punting, catching, and forward pass techniques before the game; then divide the class into two equal teams. Have each team get two or more footballs. Allocate half the field to each team. Each team must stay within the boundaries of its own half of the field.

DESCRIPTION OF ACTIVITY:

1. On the signal "Go!" players, try to punt or throw the footballs across the other team's goal line, from anywhere on your team's side of the field. You may run up to the center line, but not over it.
2. Players on the opposite side, catch or field the balls; then kick or throw them back.
3. Score two points if the ball lands in the end zone without first touching the ground. Score one point if the ball bounces or rolls into the end zone.

VARIATIONS:

a. The player who catches or fields the ball must kick or throw it from that spot and may not pass or kick to a teammate.
b. For a large class, divide the class into two games and play across the field and increase the number of balls used.

GS–61 KICK-OFF RETURN

FOCUS: Punting, lateral passing; catching

EQUIPMENT: One football per game; two sets of pinnies; cone markers

ORGANIZATION:

• Mark out a field about the size of half a regular football field. Form two teams of six to ten players. Issue each team with a set of pinnies; then assign each team to their own side of the field. Toss a coin to see who kicks off first.

DESCRIPTION OF ACTIVITY:

1. After the kick-off, the receiving team, try to run the ball as far upfield as possible before being tagged by an opposing player. You may lateral pass the ball to each other to prevent being tagged, but you cannot use the forward pass. When you are tagged, the ball is dead.
2. Now a member of the receiving team kicks off from this spot. The team that gains more yards is the winner.

VARIATIONS:

a. Have five kick-offs each; then add all the yards gained to determine the winner.
b. A two-handed tag must be used.
c. A punt or place kick may be used for the kick-off.

GS—62 THE HAND-OFF

FOCUS: Ball exchange (hand-off technique)   **EQUIPMENT:** One football per pair

ORGANIZATION:

- This technique is used when a "reverse" is required. That is when the ball is moved in one direction and is then given to another player moving in the opposite direction. The ball may be exchanged backward or forward. The ball carrier makes the exchange with the inside hand (the one closer to the receiver).

DESCRIPTION OF ACTIVITY:

1. *Technique:*
   - Ball carrier, hold the ball in two hands to begin. As the receiver approaches, move the ball across to that side with the hand under the ball and elbow bent. The ball should be held out from the body slightly.
   - Receiver, as you approach the ball carrier, hold your inside arm bent and high out in front of your chest, with your palms down. As the exchange takes place, clasp the ball from above with the top arm and from below with the other arm. Do not stop, but run "through" the ball as it is handed to you (not thrown). When you have received the ball, shift it to your regular carrying position.

2. *Practice:* (Have players find a partner, and get a ball to share. Partners then take turns being the ball carrier and the receiver.)
   - Player A, stand with the ball, then hand-off to player B, who walks past you on your right side. Repeat on your left side.
   - Player A stand. Player B, run past player A on the right side, then on the left.

   - Both players, walk toward each other for the exchange.
   - Both players, run toward each other for the hand-off.

GS—63 THE THREE-POINT STANCE

FOCUS: Technique of the three-point stance   **EQUIPMENT:** None

ORGANIZATION:

- The Three-Point Stance is used in flag football and other football games.

DESCRIPTION OF ACTIVITY:

1. *Technique of the Three-Point Stance:* Place your feet about shoulder width apart with one foot slightly ahead of the other. Place the hand (on the same side as the foot that is farther back) on the ground for support. Rest the fingers and thumb on the ground. Keep your head up and look straight ahead. Your seat should be down and your body weight forward.

2. *Four-Point Stance:* (Some players prefer this to the Three-Point Stance.) Place both hands on the ground. The placement is similar to the Three-Point Stance. Keep your seat down and your weight forward.

3. *Practice:* Players, line up alongside each other in the line in the Three-Point Stance. On the signal "One," "Two," "Hike!" sprint forward. Return and repeat. Repeat in the Four-Point Stance. Which do you prefer?

GS-64 NAME THE POSITIONS

FOCUS: Football field positions

EQUIPMENT: One football per eleven players

ORGANIZATION:

• Players should be familiar with the field positions of offense. Teach these positions and have players learn them by name.

DESCRIPTION OF ACTIVITY:

1. **The Front Line,** which includes the Center, the Guards, the Tackles, and the Ends; use the Three- or Four-Point Stance.
   — The Center, line up in front of the ball. On the snap, hike the ball to the Quarterback.
   — The Right and Left Guards, position yourselves on either side of the Center.
   — The Right and Left Tackles, line up outside the Guards.
   — The two Ends, line up on the ends of the line, outside the Tackles. You receive passes from the Quarterback.

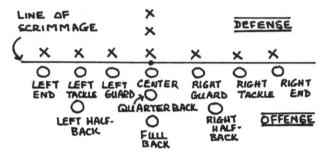

2. **The Backs** usually pass or run with the ball and include the Quarterback, the Half Backs, and the Full Back.

   — The Quarterback, position yourself directly behind the Center to receive the ball. You may run or pass the ball.
   — The two Halfbacks, stand behind and on either side of the Quarterback. You usually run with the ball.
   — The Fullback, stand behind the Quarterback. You also run with the ball.

GS-65 LINE-UP

FOCUS: Offensive field positions; passing; kicking; catching

EQUIPMENT: One football per game; football field or large open area

ORGANIZATION:

• Form two teams of eleven players. Give each player a field position. If there are insufficient players for a full team, eliminate the Tackle positions. Have both teams line up on opposite sides of the field, facing each other about 14 meters (15 yards) apart in scatter formation.

DESCRIPTION OF ACTIVITY:

1. One team, start by kicking or throwing the football to the other team. Receiving team, place the ball on the ground at that spot. Both teams, then line up in your positions on each side of the ball.
2. The team that lines up first in the correct positions earns one point. Both teams, then go back to your starting positions and the other team throws the ball or kicks off.
3. The first team to score five points is the winner.

GS–66 BLOCKING

FOCUS: Technique of blocking

EQUIPMENT: None

ORGANIZATION:

- Blocking means obstructing an opposing player by contacting his or her upper body only. Blocking is not generally suitable for coed classes. Girls may wish to practice in a different part of the field, or the rules of games may be changed to exclude such body contact. *Note:* Blocking from the rear is illegal in football and may result in serious injury.

DESCRIPTION OF ACTIVITY:

1. ***Pass Blocking Technique:*** Make the block by charging the opponent's upper body with your forearms or shoulder. Your objective is to hinder the opponent's progress, not to hurt the player. Start in a Three-Point Stance. Stutter-step on the spot to allow movement in any direction. At the same time, close your hands and bring the arms up in front of the chest with elbows out wide.

2. ***Break Through Game:*** (Form teams of six to eight players; one team is the "Chargers" and the other, the "Blockers." Both teams line up facing each other on either side of a line, about 1 meter [3 feet] apart.) On the signal "Snap!" the Chargers, dodge and fake to try to break through the opposing line while the Blockers try to prevent you from charging through. Blockers, stay squarely in front of your opposing player. Continue until you hear the "Stop!" signal (five seconds). Chargers, you get one point for each player who breaks through the Blockers' line. Repeat two more times; then reverse the roles. The team with the largest number of breakthroughs wins.

GS–67 SIX-SECOND FOOTBALL

FOCUS: Passing and receiving; dodging and tagging

EQUIPMENT: One football per game; one set of pinnies per team

ORGANIZATION:

- Form two equal teams of six to eight players and give each player a position to play. Have each team get a set of pinnies and be ready to start in its own half of the field. The team that wins the toss gets a football and places the ball on the center-line with both teams on side.

DESCRIPTION OF ACTIVITY:

1. The Center for the team that won the toss, put the ball into play by centering to the Quarterback, who may run or pass to any teammate. All players are eligible to receive a pass. Receivers may also run, pass forward, or lateral pass to each other.

2. The team with the ball, you have four downs to score a touchdown. After a touchdown, the other team puts the ball into play at center field. A "down" is 5 meters (5 yards) or more. Each team has four downs (tries) to make the yardage; then the downs start over again!

3. If no touchdown is scored after four downs, the other team takes over the ball where the ball was last played. The ball is also turned over if it is intercepted.

4. The play ends when the ball carrier has been tagged with one hand or fumbles the ball. No blocking is permitted.

5. ***Six-Second Rule:*** The Quarterback may be rushed by the defending team only after they have counted "one second," "two seconds," "three seconds," . . . "six seconds." However, if the Quarterback runs with the ball, he or she may be rushed immediately.

6. Score six points for a touchdown. Play is restarted by a center snap by the team that was scored upon.

GS–68 BORDENBALL

FOCUS: Passing; catching; offense and defense

EQUIPMENT: One football per game; one set of pinnies per team; open field

ORGANIZATION:

• Mark out the field and the goal crease with a 6-meter (20-foot) radius, as shown. Divide into two teams of six players: one goalie, two defensive players, and three forwards. Have each team get a set of pinnies and stand in its own half of the field. A player from the team that won the toss gets a football and stands on the center-line.

DESCRIPTION OF ACTIVITY:

1. The team that won the toss, start play by a pass to a teammate, after which players may pass the football until a pass can be made to the goalie to score a "touchdown" for six points.
2. Only the goalie may be inside the goal crease.
3. After a team has scored, the other team restarts the game by a pass at center field. After an unsuccessful shot at goal, the goalie puts the ball into play by a pass to a teammate.
4. Defensive players, you may "guard" an opponent, but no body contact is allowed. You may intercept the ball, after which play continues.
5. The non-offending team gains possession of the ball, where the infraction occurred, for the following violations:
   — taking more than three steps with the ball
   — holding the ball for more than three seconds
   — an offensive player in the goal crease
   — stepping out of bounds with the ball
   — an incomplete pass, or the ball is knocked down
6. A Penalty Shot is awarded for a body contact foul, tripping, pushing, holding, or a defensive player in the goal crease. The penalty throw must be taken outside the goal crease. Both feet must be in contact with the ground until the goal is scored or missed.
7. A basketball-style Jump Ball is taken at the spot of infringement when two opposing players simultaneously hold the ball, or two opponents cause the ball to go out-of-bounds.

VARIATIONS:

a. Increase the number of players to eight or ten per team.
b. Use floor hockey goals or cone markers as goals.

GS—69 FLAG FOOTBALL _____

FOCUS: Passing; catching; punting; offense and defense

EQUIPMENT: One football per game;
one set of pinnies per team;
one flag per player;
referee's whistle;
open field

ORGANIZATION:

- Flag Football is a modified version of regulation football. Mark out the field, as shown, or play on a regular football field. The field is divided into four equal zones. The offensive team has four downs (attempts) to advance the ball from one zone to the next. Divide into two teams of eight to eleven players, with at least five players on the line of scrimmage. Have players get a pinnie and a 50-centimeter × 6-centimeter (20-inch × 2-inch) flag to tuck into the back of the belt, with most of it showing; then stand in their own half of the field. The team winning the toss has the option of which end it will defend, or choose to kick or receive. The decision is reversed at the start of the second half.

DESCRIPTION OF ACTIVITY:

Rules:

1. *Length of Game:*
   - Four quarters of ten minutes, with five minutes at half time. An overtime of an extra five minutes will be played if necessary.
   - A team has four downs to advance the ball to the next zone. On the line is considered in the next zone.
   - Forward and lateral passes are the best way of advancing the ball. All players are eligible to receive passes.
   - Teams may substitute when the whistle is blown.
   - Only twenty seconds for a huddle is permitted.
   - Time-outs are permitted for injuries, after a score, when the ball goes out-of-bounds, or at the referee's discretion.

2. *The Kick-Off:* This is taken from the center line. All players must be on side. The kick-off must cross the center line or is rekicked. The kick-off receiver must be allowed 5-meters (5-yards). The kick-off may be recovered by the kicking team only if the receiver fumbles the ball.

3. *Scoring:*
   - Score six points for a touchdown. A conversion attempt is then given. One point is awarded for a conversion, when the scoring team is allowed one additional play only to score from the 5-meter (5-yard) line.
   - Two points for a safety touch: when the ball bounces in the end zone and then bounces out, or a player receives the ball in the end zone and fails to run it out.
   - One point is scored for a single: when the ball goes over the end zone, or outside the end zone within the sideline. The ball is then brought out and scrimmaged on the first zone line by the defending team.

4. *Dead Ball:*
   - When the ball is fumbled, it is declared "dead" at that spot. The first player to touch the ball after a fumble is awarded the ball.
   - A player carrying the ball, whose flag is pulled, is considered "downed" and the ball is dead at that spot.

(continued)

5. *Passing:*

— All forward passes must be thrown from behind the line of scrimmage, and all offensive players are eligible to receive a pass.

— The ball may be intercepted by any defensive player.

6. *Punts:*

— A team must declare its intention to punt. Teams must remain on side until the ball is kicked. The player receiving the punt may run with the ball or lateral pass. The ball may not be passed forward.

7. *Tackling:*

— Tackling, holding, or contacting the ball carrier is not permitted. Blocking on any player is also illegal.

— The ball carrier is not allowed to fend off, push, or charge a defensive player. Also, the carrier may not protect his or her flag with the arms.

8. *Penalties:* A 5-meter or 5-yard Penalty is awarded for:

— off side, before the ball is put into play

— forward passing from in front of the line of scrimmage

— failing to declare the intention to punt

— using the straight arm, chop, or push off by the ball carrier or charging an opponent

— insufficient flag showing

9. A 15-meter or 15-yard Penalty is awarded for:

— tackling, tripping, holding, pushing, or roughing an opponent

— blocking

— unsportsmanlike conduct

VARIATION:

Touch Football: This game is another modified version of the regular game of football. The rules for Touch Football are similar to Flag Football with the following exceptions: All the rules for Flag Football apply except that no flags are worn; the ball carrier is downed; and the ball is "dead" when the carrier is tagged with both hands simultaneously by a defensive player.

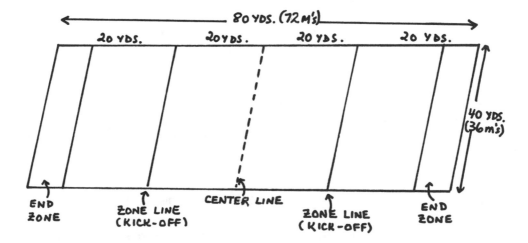

GS-70 DOUBLE ELIMINATION TOURNAMENTS

FOCUS: Tournament draws

EQUIPMENT: None

ORGANIZATION:

- Once the various skills have been practiced and learned, tournaments may be set up that further stimulate interest in games, contests, and other physical education activities. The players should have the opportunity to participate also as team captains, referees, umpires, timekeepers, and scorekeepers. When selecting a draw, consider the number of teams, the time available, the facilities, and equipment. With the exception of the Single Elimination Draw, the following draws are suitable for school tournaments, because they offer each team two or more games.

DESCRIPTION OF ACTIVITY:

Championship Consolation

Unseeded Draw: If the previous record of the teams is not known, the teams may be entered on the unseeded draw in any order. (Figure 1 in GS-71.)

Seeded Draw: To avoid having the top teams meeting in the first round, the teams should be seeded (ranked in ability from 1 to 8) and entered on the draw as in Figure 2 in GS-71.

GS-71 SINGLE ELIMINATION TOURNAMENT

ORGANIZATION:

- In this tournament, each entry is eliminated after only one loss; therefore, it is not the most suitable for school tournaments. However, if there are limitations on time and facilities or the tournament has to be over quickly, this alternative should be considered.

DESCRIPTION OF ACTIVITY:

1. **Single Elimination Tournament:** If the number of entries is four, eight, sixteen, or any power of two, the entries are grouped in twos, and then after each round, the winners are grouped until a champion is declared. (See Diagram A.)

2. **Byes:** When a number of teams is not a power of two, teams are given a "bye," that is, they are automatically advanced into the next round without playing. For example: For a single elimination with seven teams, determine the number of byes by going to the next highest power of two, which is eight; then subtract the number of teams. $8 - 7 = 1$ bye (See Diagram B.)

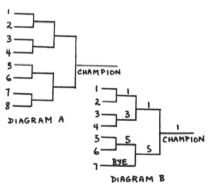

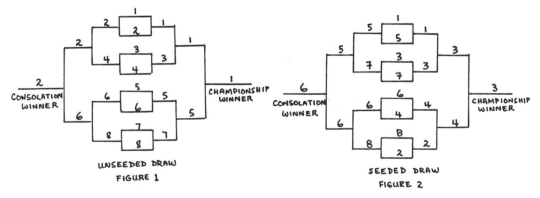

UNSEEDED DRAW
FIGURE 1

SEEDED DRAW
FIGURE 2

GS–72 ROUND ROBIN TOURNAMENT

FOCUS: Tournament draws

EQUIPMENT: None

ORGANIZATION:

• A Round Robin Tournament provides maximum participation, because every team plays every other team. The example below is for up to eight teams. If there are a large number of entries, set up two leagues and have the winners playoff. Substitute the numbers with the team names on the draw. If there is an uneven number of teams, add a "bye" to make an even number.

DESCRIPTION OF ACTIVITY:

1. To determine the number of games to be played, use the following formula:

$$\frac{n(n - 1)}{2} \qquad n = \text{number of teams.}$$

For example: If eight teams enter a single Round Robin tournament, the number of games played will be 28: $\frac{8(8 - 1)}{2} = \frac{8(7)}{2} = \frac{56}{2} = 28$ games.

2. The number of rounds to be played will be $n - 1 = 8 - 1 = 7$ rounds. The number of games each team will play will be $n - 1 = 8 - 1 = 7$ games.

3. *Round Robin Draw:* Substitute names for numbers:

Round 1	Round 2	Round 3	Round 4	Round 5	Round 6	Round 7
1 v 2	1 v 3	1 v 4	1 v 5	1 v 6	1 v 7	1 v 8
8 v 3	2 v 4	3 v 5	4 v 6	5 v 7	6 v 8	7 v 2
7 v 4	8 v 5	2 v 6	3 v 7	4 v 8	5 v 2	6 v 3
6 v 5	7 v 6	8 v 7	2 v 8	3 v 2	4 v 3	5 v 4

Note: If only seven teams enter, substitute a "bye" for the number eight.

GS–73 LADDER AND PYRAMID TOURNAMENTS

ORGANIZATION:

• Both the Ladder Tournament and the Pyramid Tournament provide a continuous and challenging series of games. They also provide the opportunity to rate players or teams on levels of ability. These draws are usually used for individual or partner sports such as paddle tennis, badminton, tennis, or table tennis, which may be conducted during lunch time or after school.

DESCRIPTION OF ACTIVITY:

1. *Ladder Tournament:* (Players draw numbers for their starting place on the ladder. The names are then listed on easily moved separate tags and placed on the rungs of the ladder. The more skilled players should be listed at the bottom. If there are a large number of entries, divide the ladder into A, B, and C flights to provide an incentive for poorer players.) The object is to move up the ladder by challenging and defeating either of the two players directly above you. Challenger, if you win, you both exchange places on the ladder. If the challenged player wins, no change is made. A player must accept the challenge within two days or forfeit the game.

2. *Pyramid Draw:* (This draw is similar to the Ladder, but the format is that of a pyramid.) Players, you may challenge any player on your line first; then, after winning, you may challenge any player on the next line. If you win, you both change places. As a variation, players may challenge their own line or the line above.

1. Mary	A. 1
2. Joe	B. 2 3
3. Bill	C. 4 5 6
4. Jane	D. 7 8 9 10
5. Max	E. 11 12 13 14 15
6. Jill	F. 16 17 18 19 20 21
7. Nikki	*Pyramid Draw*
8. Mark	
Ladder Draw	

GS–74 READY POSITION

FOCUS: Footwork; alertness; partner work   **EQUIPMENT:** Whistle

ORGANIZATION:

- Explain and demonstrate the "ready position" for receiving the volleyball. Note that the wide position of the feet gives stability; keeping the weight forward allows quick movement in any direction to get under the ball. Have players find a free space where they can all see you.

DESCRIPTION OF ACTIVITY:

1. ***Ready Position Technique:*** Stand with your feet slightly wider than shoulder-width apart; step one foot slightly ahead of the other, bend your knees comfortably, and bring your weight forward onto the balls of your feet. Hold hands at chest level in a relaxed position with palms facing forward.
2. ***Heads-Up Drill:*** Stand in the Ready Position and watch me for directions. Whatever direction I point, shuffle-step in that direction; to the left, to the right, forward, backward! Continue for one minute.
   — Whenever I blow the whistle, "pitter patter" (small quick steps) on the spot.
3. ***Outlining the Court:*** Find a partner. One partner, stand on the boundary of the court facing your partner, who stands inside the court, 1 meter (3 feet) away; both in the Ready Position. Lead your partner CW around the boundary of the volleyball court.
   — When you hear one whistle blast, "pitter patter."
   — When you hear two whistles, find a new partner and shuffle CCW around the court.

GS–75 MEMORY DRILL CIRCUIT

FOCUS: Volleyball warm-up   **EQUIPMENT:** Volleyball net and poles;
lively music;
tape or record player

ORGANIZATION:

- Use the Memory Drill Circuit as a warm-up for your volleyball lessons. First review the Ready Position and the shuffle-step; then form groups of four to six players and have each group stand in file formation at one corner of the volleyball court. Use both sides of the court simultaneously.

DESCRIPTION OF ACTIVITY:

1. When the music starts, first player in each group, lead the other players through the following action:
   - Run forward to the net.
   - Block at the net by facing it and jumping straight up, arms extended high overhead with your thumbs touching.
   - Shuffle-step to the opposite corner while facing the net.
   - Block at the opposite corner.
   - Run backward to the next corner.
   - Shuffle-step to the corner your group started at.
2. Leader, after the first time through, run to the end of your file so that the next player in line can lead the group through the circuit. Continue until your group has gone through the Circuit five times.

GS–76 OVERHEAD PASS (THE SET) _____

FOCUS: Volleying technique; body positioning   **EQUIPMENT:** One volleyball per player

ORGANIZATION:

• The Overhead Pass, also known as the Volley, Set, or Face Pass, is used to pass the ball among teammates during a game. To teach the set, have players get a volleyball and scatter.

DESCRIPTION OF ACTIVITY:

1. *Body and Hand Position:* Stand in the ready position. Spread fingers of both hands in a cupped position with thumbs and index fingers forming a triangle above your face. Look through the "little window" made by your hands.

2. *Movement:* Position directly under the ball as it comes toward you, with knees and elbows bent and hands in front of your face. Watch the ball constantly and distribute your weight evenly on both feet.

3. *Making Contact:* Contact the ball with the pads of your fingers and thumbs, relaxing your fingers so that you cushion the ball's impact with the cupped fingers, bent arms and legs. After contact, extend your arms and legs upward and flick your wrists out in the line of direction of the ball.

4. *Practice:*

   — Put the ball on the floor. Spread your fingers in the cupped position, place them on the ball, and pick it up. Repeat, several times, checking the hand position each time.

   — Toss the ball into the air and catch it just in front of your forehead. Pause and check your hand positioning; then repeat the toss and catch several times. Gradually reduce the amount of time you pause while holding the ball so that you are continuously volleying the ball.

   — Toss the ball up; squat to touch the floor before catching the ball in the ready position. Repeat using the set.

   — Toss the ball so that you must move quickly to get position under the ball to set it. Repeat, tossing in a different direction each time.

5. *Setting Tasks:*

   — Toss the ball, set the ball once, and catch again.

   — Toss the ball, set twice, and catch again.

   — Can you set three times before catching the ball?

   — How many times can you do it in a row?

   — Toss the ball, set, let the ball bounce once, set again, and then catch it. Repeat this set–bounce, set–bounce pattern.

6. *Wall Set:* Toss the ball against the wall, let it bounce on the floor, and then set it back to the wall. Let the ball bounce and set again. Do continuous wall sets to yourself, setting the ball above head level each time.

7. *Partner Set:* Find a partner, stand about 3 meters (10 feet) apart, and set the ball back and forth. At first, pause slightly after catching the ball; then gradually eliminate the pause so that you are continuously setting the ball to each other.

GS-77 PARTNER SETTING TASKS

FOCUS: Setting accuracy; body positioning; partner work

EQUIPMENT: One volleyball per pair; square wall targets

ORGANIZATION:

• Tape square targets to the wall, about 3 meters (10 feet) up the wall, and a setting line about 4 meters (12 feet) from the wall. Have players find a partner, get a volleyball, and stand about four or five steps apart. Remind players to Face Pass (or Set) and catch the ball while in the Ready Position.

DESCRIPTION OF ACTIVITY:

1. ***Partner Pass:*** Player with the ball, toss the ball to yourself; then set to your partner's head. Partner, position yourself to catch the ball with the correct finger position, about 5 centimeters (2 inches) in front of your forehead. Repeat, setting back and forth.

   — Gradually eliminate the catch, and immediately set the ball back to your partner.

2. ***Target Passing:*** Set the ball to the target ten times from the setting line. Partner, retrieve the ball. Change roles and repeat.

   — How many times can you hit the target in one minute?

3. ***Basket Volley:*** Stand at the free-throw line on the basketball court. Set the ball to yourself; then try to set the ball into the basket. Take ten sets and change roles.

4. ***Sit 'n Volley:*** (Have partners sit about 4 meters [12 feet] apart, facing each other.) From the sitting position, partner A, with the ball, toss the ball up and volley the ball to partner B; then roll back and do a sit-up. Partner B, volley the ball to yourself; then volley back to A and do one sit-up. Continue this pattern.

5. ***Reaction Volley:*** Partner A, stand with your back to partner B, who has the ball. Partner B, set the ball to A and at the same time shout "Go!" A must quickly turn around, get position under the ball, and volley it back to B. Change roles and repeat ten times each.

6. ***Pass and Go, One Line:*** Partner A, stand with your back to a line on the floor, facing partner B, 4 meters (12 feet) away. Partner A, volley the ball to B, turn, and run and touch the line and back to volley the ball back again. Continue for 1½ minutes; then switch roles. Use short strides and avoid crossing your feet. As you improve, move farther away from the line.

7. ***Pass and Go, Two Lines:*** Partners, stand about 2 meters (6 feet) from your respective sidelines and face each other. Volley the ball back and forth to each other, touching the line behind you after each volley.

8. ***Three-Line Volley:*** Form groups of three and form a line about 1 meter (3 feet) apart. Player A, volley to B. Player B, volley back to A, who volleys a long pass over to player C; C volley a short pass to B, who volleys back to C, and so on. Exchange positions and continue.

VARIATION:

Hopscotch Volley: (Replace the square target in Target Passing with a hopscotch chart. The squares should be about 30 centimeters [12 feet] square.) Have partners take turns to hit each square in order, moving from number one to eight.

FOCUS: Setting accuracy; positioning; cooperation

EQUIPMENT: One volleyball per group of four players; volleyball court and net

ORGANIZATION:

- Form groups of four players and have each group get one volleyball. Remind players to volley (or set) the ball while in the ready position.

DESCRIPTION OF ACTIVITY:

1. *Square Volley:* (Have players position themselves at the corners of a 3-meter square.) Set the ball to each other from one corner to the next in a CCW direction. How many passes can you make without a miss?

   — Set in a CW direction.

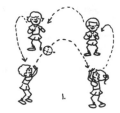

2. *Keep the Ball Up:* Set the ball to each other to keep it in the air as long as possible. Start over when the ball hits the floor. Call "Mine" for the ball, to avoid confusion.

   — Challenge other groups to see who can keep the ball up for the most consecutive volleys.

3. *Wheel Game:* (Form groups of five to eight players; each group form a circle with players about an arm's length apart. Have one player go to the middle with the ball.) Each player in turn, volley the ball back to the center player. Continue until all have had a turn in the center. Challenge other groups to a competition.

4. *Circle Pass:* (As for the Wheel Game, without the player in the center.) Volley the ball to any other player across the circle. Keep alert and move into position as the ball comes to you. Call "Mine" if you are going to receive the pass. Challenge other groups.

5. *Battle Ball:* (Divide the class into two equal teams, and position each team on one side of the net. Give each team at least three volleyballs; with one team having an extra volleyball. Explain that the game is divided into four quarters of two minutes each.) On the signal "Battle Ball!" players with a ball, toss the ball up; then face pass it over the net so that after each quarter of two minutes, the other team will have more balls on its side of the net than your team does. The set must be made quickly from the spot it was caught or retrieved. You may then pass it directly over the net, or to a teammate to pass over. Both teams, count the number of balls on your side after each quarter. The team with the lower score at the end of the fourth quarter wins. Exchange sides at halftime. Look for vacant spots in the opposition's court to pass the ball.

GS–79 THE FOREARM PASS (THE BUMP)

FOCUS: Bumping (forearm passing) technique; positioning

EQUIPMENT: One volleyball per player

ORGANIZATION:

- Emphasize that players move to the ball while in the ready position; watch the ball at all times; keep the arms extended and together when preparing to bump the ball; follow through with the arms and lift with the legs after the bump. Have players get a volleyball and scatter. Ensure that players can see you and hear your instructions.

DESCRIPTION OF ACTIVITY:

1. ***Body and Arm Position:*** Place the ball on the floor beside you and show me your ready position. Good! Now place the knuckles of one hand into the palm of your other hand. Thumbs should be side by side with knuckles up, resting on top of your index fingers.
   - Try to rotate your forearms forward so that your elbows almost touch. Look at the flat surface formed by the fleshy insides of your forearms, that soft, round area just above your wrists and below your elbows. This is where we contact the ball.
   - Find a partner and show each other your body, hand, and arm positions. Check each other for correct technique.

2. ***Making Contact:*** Now pretend that a low ball is coming toward you. Move toward the ball, bending your knees to get under it. Watch the ball! Follow the flight of the ball and watch its contact.
   - Keep the arms together and extended, with the elbows straight. Drop the wrists to absorb the force of the ball on the inside of your forearms.
   - Now lift with your legs and follow through with your arms in the direction of the flight of the ball. Keep the motion smooth and continuous.

3. ***Practice:***
   - Mime the action of bumping the ball, using the correct body, hand, and arm positions. Start in the ready position. Move your body and arms in the direction I call. On signal "Bump Right!" pretend to bump a ball on your right. Continue for "Bump Left!" "Bump Forward!" and "Bump Backward!" Repeat in any order.

4. ***Moving to the Ball:*** Get a volleyball, scatter in free space, and do these Bumping tasks:
   - Toss the ball in the air and move into position under it with your arms in the bumping position. Let the ball contact your forearms, bounce off, and then bounce onto the floor.
   - Toss the ball again and try to bump the ball twice in a row before tossing it again.
   - Toss the ball into the air some distance away from you. How quickly can you move into position under it with your forearms in the bumping position?
   - Toss the ball overhead, let it bounce on the floor, bump it with your forearms, and catch it again.
   - Bounce the ball on the floor, bump it overhead, let it bounce again, bump it again, and then catch the ball.
   - Continue this pattern: throw–bump–catch; throw–bump–bump–catch; throw–bump–bump–bump–catch.
   - Bump the ball overhead for as long as possible.

GS–80 INDIVIDUAL AND PARTNER BUMPING TASKS

FOCUS: Contact awareness; positioning; partner work

EQUIPMENT: One volleyball per player; wall targets

ORGANIZATION:

- Tape 1-meter (3-foot) square targets to the wall, 2 meters (6.5 feet) above the floor. Encourage players to concentrate and to watch the ball at all times; anticipate and be ready to move to the ball. Emphasize that the ball is hit high and softly, in a continuous motion. Contact is made on the bellies of the forearms, with the arms straight. Have each player get a volleyball and find a free space on a wall.

DESCRIPTION OF ACTIVITY:

1. **Individual Practice:**
   - Toss the ball up above your head; then bump it to the wall and catch. Repeat.
   - Throw the ball high against the wall, bump it back high to the wall, and catch. Repeat.
   - Set the ball to the wall; then bump it back and catch the rebound.
   - **Keep It Up:** How many times can you bump the ball to the wall in a row without the ball touching the floor? Follow through, and lift with your legs and body, with your arms straight. Send the ball high.

2. **Partner Practice:**
   - Find a partner. One player, toss the ball to the wall; then the other player, bump the ball and continue bumping as long as you can. Take turns.
   - Now partners, take turns bumping the ball to hit the target on the wall.
   - Bump the volleyball back and forth to each other off the wall.

3. Now one partner knee-sit about 3 meters (10 feet) away from the other and hold your arms in the bumping position. Standing partner, toss the volleyball to your kneeling partner so that he or she can bump it back to you. Change roles after ten bumps.

4. Step back so that you are standing 4 meters to 5 meters (13 feet to 16 feet) apart. Toss the ball to your partner, who will bump it back to you. Catch the ball and toss it again. Repeat ten times; then change roles.

5. Toss the ball to one side of your partner so that he or she must quickly move into position under it in order to bump the ball back to you. Your partner then returns to his or her original spot. Change roles after five bumps; then toss the ball to your partner's other side.

6. Toss the ball to your partner, who will bump it to himself or herself once, then bump it back to you; then try to bump it back and forth as long as you can. Change roles after five tosses.

7. Toss the ball to your partner, who will bump it back to you. Bump the ball back to your partner. How many times can you bump it back and forth before the ball touches the floor?

GS–81 BUMPING IN SMALL GROUPS

FOCUS: Bump-passing the ball; group work   **EQUIPMENT:** One volleyball per group of six

ORGANIZATION:

• Review the Forearm Bumping technique. Have players form groups of six, elect a leader, and stand in semicircular formation, arm's length apart, facing the leader with the ball.

DESCRIPTION OF ACTIVITY:

1. *Leader Ball:* Leader, toss the ball to the first player, who bumps it back to you. Catch the ball and toss it to the second player, who bumps it back to you, and so on until each player has bumped the ball. Change leaders and continue until each player has been leader.

2. *Shuttle Bump:* (Have the players get into shuttle formation, with a file of three players facing the other three.) Player 1, toss the ball to 2, who bumps to 3, who bumps to 4, and so on. Run to the right and join the end of the opposite file after bumping the ball. How long can you bump without the ball touching the floor?

3. *Donkey:* Stand in file formation facing a wall. Leader, bump the ball high onto the wall; then move to the end of the file. As the ball rebounds off the wall, the second player, bump to the wall. Continue taking turns bumping to the wall. For each time you miss, take a letter of the word *Donkey*. The game is over when one player gets all the letters.

4. *Bump and Over:* (Stand three players on one side of the net and the other three on the opposite side.) See how many times your group can bump the ball back and forth over the net in one minute. Repeat, but remember your best score.

GS–82 BUMPING AND SETTING TASKS

FOCUS: Bump-passing and setting to a partner   **EQUIPMENT:** One volleyball per pair; volleyball net

ORGANIZATION:

• Have players find a partner, get a ball, and stand facing each other in a free space.

DESCRIPTION OF ACTIVITY:

1. Player A, toss the ball to partner B at waist level. Player B, bump the ball back to A, who volleys it back to you. B, bump back to A again, and so on. Begin again, reversing the roles.

2. Player A, bump the ball to yourself; then volley to your partner. Partner B, bump to yourself, then volley to A. Continue this bump-volley pattern.

   — Reverse the pattern: volley to yourself; then bump to your partner.

3. One player, toss the ball to your partner; sometimes high, sometimes low. Your partner must decide whether to volley or bump it back. Change roles and repeat.

4. Player A, pass to B; then do a 360-degree turn. Partner B, volley or bump to A; then do a 360-degree turn. Continue.

5. Partners, stand on opposite sides of the net. Pass the ball back and forth over the net. Decide whether to volley or bump the ball. How many times can you pass the ball back and forth before it hits the floor?

GS—83 SETTING UP THE BALL

FOCUS: Setting sequence; group work

EQUIPMENT: One volleyball per group; one square floor target per group; floor tape

ORGANIZATION:

• Form groups of three or four players. Have the Leader get a ball and position behind a 1 meter by 1 meter (3 feet by 3 feet) square, taped on the floor. Have the remainder of the group stand in a file about 3 meters (10 feet) away, facing the leader.

DESCRIPTION OF ACTIVITY:

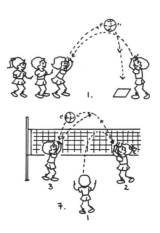

1. **Set the Square:** Leader, toss the ball high to the first player, who will try to set the ball in a high arc into the square. Continue tossing to the file players until each player has had three turns, after which the first player becomes the new Leader. Continue the task until all players have been the Leader.

2. **Net Setup:** (Form groups of five or six players. Have them position themselves at the net as shown.) Player No. 1, toss a high ball to No. 2, who sets up the ball for No. 3. Player No. 3, try to volley the ball over the net to a receiver. When completed, retriever go to the end of the file and all other players move up one position. Continue in this way.

   — Now Player No. 1, set the ball to yourself; then set to No. 2.

   — Receiver, volley or bump the ball to yourself; then change positions.

GS—84 COURT POSITIONS

FOCUS: Rotations and service

EQUIPMENT: Volleyball net and poles; whistle

ORGANIZATION:

• Form teams of six players and have each team take up the following court positions: Right Forward (RF), Right Back (RB), Center Back (CB), Left Back (LB), Left Forward (LF), Center Forward (CF).

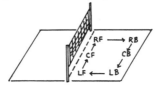

DESCRIPTION OF ACTIVITY:

Court Positions:

— When you hear the whistle, rotate CW from one position to the next until you are back in your starting positions.

— During volleyball games, you will rotate one court position CW each time your team wins the serve.

— As you rotate from one position to the next, shuffle-step in the ready position while facing the net. Check the location of the players on either side, in front, and behind you; know where the boundary lines are in relation to your court position.

— During volleyball games, cover the area around your court position. The other players will cover their areas also!

— Players at the back of the court, if the ball comes at or above your shoulder, let it go! It is on its way out-of-bounds!

GS–85 UNDERHAND SERVE

FOCUS: Underhand serving technique; partner work

EQUIPMENT: One volleyball per player; volleyball net and poles; one hoop per pair; floor tape

ORGANIZATION:

• Have players get a volleyball and experiment with different ways of striking it: with the heel of the open hand, a semiclosed hand, or a closed fist. Have them decide which hand position they prefer; then explain and demonstrate the Underhand Serve.

DESCRIPTION OF ACTIVITY:

1. **Stance:** Stand with feet shoulder-width apart facing the net. Step forward on the foot opposite your serving hand. Bend your knees slightly, and lean forward. Hold the ball at waist level in the palm and fingers of your nonserving hand.

2. **Movement:** Open your hand, straighten your serving arm, swing it back and then forward to contact the ball. Shift your weight onto the front foot as your arm swings forward to hit the ball slightly below center with the heel of your serving hand, as the other hand drops away. Swing your serving hand up and forward to follow-through. Step forward to complete the movement.

3. **Individual Practice:**

— Take the ball and find a free space at the wall. Serve the ball to the wall so that it hits above a line that is 3 meters (10 feet) from the floor. Gradually step farther away from the wall as you continue to serve the ball.

— Remember to contact the ball slightly below center with the heel of the hand; drop your nonserving hand away as contact is made with the ball; watch the ball during contact.

— Free serving over the net. Serve short at first; then gradually move back.

4. **Partner Serve:**

— Find a partner, return one ball, and serve the ball so your partner can catch it. Coach each other in the correct serving technique.

— Serve the ball over the net to your partner. Stand 3 meters (10 feet) away from the net; then gradually step back to increase the distance between you and your partner.

— Now partners, stand on your endline, on your own side of the net. Serve the ball back and forth to your partner, who catches the ball and serves it back.

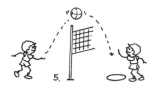

5. **Hoop Serve:** Place a hoop about 3 meters (10 feet) from the net on each side of the net. Serve the ball back and forth into your partner's hoop from behind your hoop, using the Underhand Serve. Gradually move both hoops back one step at a time until you are serving from the back line. Serve over the net so that the ball lands in the hoop on the first bounce.

6. **Serve, Bump, or Set:** Stand facing each other without the net. Partner A with the ball, serve to Partner B, who bumps the ball back to Partner A to catch. Reverse roles after ten serves. Then have your partner set the ball back to you. Repeat, over the net.

GS-86 UNDERHAND ACCURACY SERVING

FOCUS: Accuracy serving; partner work

EQUIPMENT: Three to five volleyballs per team; volleyball courts and nets

ORGANIZATION:

• Adjust the height of the net to the ability of the players. Remind players to use the correct serving technique.

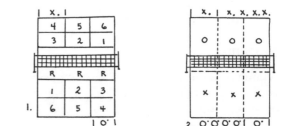

DESCRIPTION OF ACTIVITY:

1. *Serving Accuracy:* (Mark out the court as in the diagram.) From the service area, at the back of the court, serve the ball into area No. 1 in the opposite court; then 2, 3, 4, 5, and 6. You are allowed two tries to serve into each area. Score two points for each successful serve; one point for landing in the area next to the target area.
   — Retrievers, field the balls and return them to the servers by rolling them under the net. Change roles, and repeat.

2. *Corridor Serving:* (Divide the court on both sides of the net, into three equal parts as shown. Form two teams of about five or six players with a team at one end and the other team at the other end. Have a retriever from each team in each of the three corridors on the opposite side of the net. Have each of the other players on both teams get a ball and line up, in the serving area at the right side of their endline, ready to serve.) Each player has three serves from the serving area, to serve a ball into each of the three corridors on the opposite side of the court. Retrievers, catch or field the balls and return them, by rolling under the net, to your own team. After each player has three serves, rotate to the retriever's position.

GS-87 SERVE RECEPTION

FOCUS: Accuracy serving; serve-bump-volley sequence

EQUIPMENT: One volleyball per pair; volleyball net and poles; two mats per pair; wall targets

ORGANIZATION:

• Tape targets on the wall about 3 meters (10 feet) from the floor. Have players find a partner, get a volleyball, and stand facing each other, about 4 meters (12 feet) apart, without a net.

DESCRIPTION OF ACTIVITY:

1. *Partner Wall Serve:* (Have partners stand about 4 meters [12 feet] from a wall, facing a target.) Partner A, serve the ball at the target on the wall. Partner B, bump or volley the ball back to the wall, for the server to catch and Partner A serve again. Switch roles after every five serves. Each keep track of the number of times you serve into the target area.

2. *Serve and Bump:* (Place a mat on each side of the net, near the center of the net. Have the server stand toward the endline, on one side of the net, and the receiver near mid-court on the other side.) Server, serve the ball to the receiver. Receiver, bump the ball to the mat on your side of the net. Change server after ten serves.

3. *Serve-Bump-Set Sequence:* Get in groups of three: server, receiver-bumper, and setter. Server, on opposite side of net, underhand serve ball to receiver, who bumps ball upward to a setter near the net. Setter, set the ball along your net side. Collect ball; then roll it under net to serve. Change roles after every five serves. (Allow server to serve ball from inside the endline if having difficulty getting the serve over the net.)

GS-88 OVERHAND SERVE

FOCUS: Overhand serve technique

EQUIPMENT: One volleyball per server

ORGANIZATION:

- The Overhead Serve is for advanced players, after having mastered the Underhand Serve. It is a more difficult serve for the receiving team to receive and play. The server has to master two difficult skills: tossing and hitting the ball.

DESCRIPTION OF ACTIVITY:

1. *Technique:*
   - *Stance:* (For a right-handed player.) Stand with the left side of your body facing the net, with your feet shoulder-width apart. Place your left foot slightly in front of the right, so that your body weight is on both feet. Keep your eyes on the ball.
   - *Hand Position:* Hold the ball in your left hand, directly in front of your face. Toss the ball straight up just above your head and in front of your right shoulder.
   - *Movement:* As the ball is tossed, shift your weight to your rear foot. Swing your right arm, with elbow slightly bent, upward and backward; then forward to hit the ball hard in the center, with the heel of the hand, about 30 centimeters (1 foot) above the shoulder. Follow through as you transfer your weight from the back to the front foot and take a step forward toward your target.
2. *Wall Serve Practice:* Get a ball each and stand facing a wall. Serve the ball to the wall, catch, and repeat. Gradually move farther away from the wall as you strive for control and accuracy.
3. *One-Step Serve:* Put one ball away, and stand 5 meters (15 feet) apart. Player with the ball, serve to partner, who catches the ball and serves it back. Continue. For each successful serve and catch, both players, take a step back. If an error occurs, or the receiver has to move his or her feet to make the catch, re-serve from that spot.
   - On the serve reception, volley or bump the ball to yourself before catching and serving back.
   - Serve to partner over the net, playing One-Step Serve.

GS-89 SERVE AND BUMP GAME

FOCUS: Overhand or underhand serving; bumping; setting

EQUIPMENT: Five to six volleyballs per game; volleyball courts, nets, poles

ORGANIZATION:

- Form teams of six to eight players. For each game, appoint two teams to a court: one team to serve, the other to receive.

DESCRIPTION OF ACTIVITY:

1. Serving team, you must serve from the serving zone and continue to serve until each player has had three serves. Look for open spaces to which to serve, and follow the serve onto the court.
2. Receiving team, in "ready position," try to bump or set the ball up high so that it can be played by a teammate, and returned over the net, to earn one point. The ball may be played by three players before going over the net. Remember to watch the ball at all times.

3. Serving team, you earn one point for each successful serve that is not returned over the net. At the end of the game, tally up the scores and play again.

GS-90 SPIKING

FOCUS: Spiking and blocking techniques; group practice

EQUIPMENT: One volleyball per player; volleyball nets, poles, courts; one chair per group

ORGANIZATION:

- Spiking is the attacking action of forcefully hitting the ball over the net to score a point or regain the serve. It is the last stage of the serve reception sequence: Bump–Set–Spike! Players must not make contact with the net or land in the opponent's court. Spiking may only take place by a player in the front zone.

DESCRIPTION OF ACTIVITY:

1. *The Hitting Action:* The ball should be struck while the striking arm is bent, with the elbow leading. Hit on top of the ball with the butt or heel of the hand, to drive the ball downward. Keep the hand relaxed, but just before contact, the fingers become rigid and slightly bent to form a solid unit. As the ball is hit, snap the wrist forward to add power to the spike. To execute the spike, jump straight up and hit the ball above the net while at the height of your jump. Once the hitting action has been learned, have players take a short run-in to coordinate the jump with the spike.

2. *Practice:*
   - Hold the ball in your nonhitting hand, at shoulder level. Now, hit the ball out of your hand to the floor.
   - Go to a wall, hold the ball in your nonhitting hand, high in front of your hitting shoulder. Spike it down to the floor. Catch the rebound and repeat.
   - Now toss the ball upward, watch it carefully to time your jump, and hit the ball downward toward the wall.
   - Form groups of six to eight and each group line up on the left side of center near a lowered volleyball net. One player stand on a chair and hold the volleyball in one hand above the net. Take turns to time your jump and spike the ball over the net!

GS-91 BLOCKING

EQUIPMENT: See GS-90.

ORGANIZATION:

- Blocking is the action of one or more players, who are close to the net, intercepting the ball coming over the net with the hands or arms and deflecting the ball back into the opponent's court. Teach individual blocking at the elementary level, and multiple blocking, with two or more blockers, in the upper levels. Explain the technique and have two players demonstrate; then have the class practice. Adjust the net height to the jumping ability of the class.

DESCRIPTION OF ACTIVITY:

Blocking Technique:
- *The Jump:* To be effective, the blocker's jump must be timed to that of the spiker. The jump must be high enough so that the wrists will be slightly above the net. For maximum height, keep your arms in front or close to the sides of your body when jumping. You must not touch the net when blocking.
- *Body Position:* As you jump vertically, thrust your arms upward, straighten the elbows, and stretch the arms overhead, palms facing the ball. Spread your fingers and tilt them slightly backward, with the thumbs almost touching, to form a rigid block. Deflect the ball downward off the hands and arms, contacting the ball with the heel of the hand; then snap the wrists downward.
- *Landing:* Land in the "ready position," on the balls of the feet, with your knees bent, ready to play the next ball.

GS-92 DEFENSIVE FORMATIONS

FOCUS: Serve reception; serving practice

EQUIPMENT: Volleyball court and net; three volleyballs per team

ORGANIZATION:

• *"M" Formation*: This is most commonly used at the elementary level. *"W" Formation*: Used for receiving hard serves or to cover for a weaker backcourt player. Use a shallow "W" for a high serve. (Refer to illustrations.) Teach these defensive formations, and have players practice the positions and rotations. Form two teams of six players per court; one team serving, the other receiving, using first the "M" Formation, then the "W" Formation.

DESCRIPTION OF ACTIVITY:

1. Members of the serving team, serve in turn from the serving area until each player has served three times.

2. Receiving team, get in the "ready position" in your defensive formation and when the serve comes over the net, try to set up the bump–set–attack sequence. After every three serves, rotate one team position in a CW direction.

— Remember to attack by volleying deep into the opposition's court or spiking!

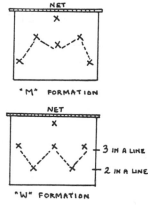

GS-93 STATION VOLLEYBALL

FOCUS: Serving; setting; bumping; blocking; spiking review

EQUIPMENT: One volleyball per player; volleyball nets and poles; station cards and wall tape; whistle or selected music

ORGANIZATION:

• Review volleyball skills that have been previously taught through station work. Explain the activity and the procedure for practice at each station. Divide the class into six groups and assign each team to a station to begin. Decide how long teams should spend at each station, and inform teams. Use music, or the whistle, to start and finish each activity; then have groups rotate CW to the next station. Circulate to each group in turn, correcting poor technique and praising good performance. Refer to Sample Volleyball Station below.

DESCRIPTION OF ACTIVITY:

See illustration.

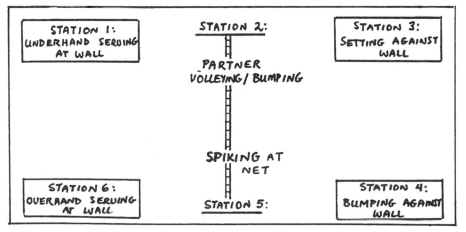

FOCUS: Lead-up game; serving; catching; volleying

EQUIPMENT: One volleyball per game; volleyball net and posts; one coin

ORGANIZATION:

- Divide the class into teams of six to eight players. Each team positions itself on one side of the net, with players in their court positions. Adjust the height of the net to suit the player's ability. Toss a coin to determine which team starts with the ball.

DESCRIPTION OF ACTIVITY:

1. The team with the ball, start the game by serving the ball over the net from the serving area.

2. Players on the receiving team, try to catch the ball before it touches the floor. After catching the ball, without moving from the spot, volley the ball up to three times on your side before volleying it over the net on the third try.

3. *Faults:* A team scores one point if:

   — an opposition player tries to catch the ball but drops it, or the ball touches the floor

   — the server fails to serve the ball over the net

   — more than three passes are made on one side

4. The receiving team scores one point if the server serves the ball out-of-bounds or into the net, causing the ball to hit the floor on his or her side of the net. The boundary lines of the court are considered in-bounds.

5. Both teams, rotate one court position every three points. The game continues until one team has fifteen points. A team must win by two points.

6. Remember to:

   — crouch in the ready position when catching the ball

   — play their court positions and call "Mine!" when they intend to catch the ball

   — try to serve to open spaces in the opposition team's court

   — roll the ball under the net to the server

VARIATIONS:

a. The ball must be passed three times on one side before going over the net.

b. Use the serve–bump–catch sequence instead of the serve and catch.

c. Set up a tournament between teams.

d. Throw a ball back and forth over the net. Throwing team scores a point if an opposition player fails to catch the ball. Receiver must throw ball from the spot where he or she caught it.

GS–95 REGULATION VOLLEYBALL

FOCUS: Applying volleyball skills; positional play

EQUIPMENT: One volleyball per game; volleyball court and net

ORGANIZATION:

• For each game, form two teams of six players a side: a team on each side of the net. For a class of twenty or more players, use two courts if available. Adjust the height of the net according to the ability level of the class. Teach the court positions and the rotational order.

DESCRIPTION OF ACTIVITY:

Basic Rules:

1. The team who wins the toss of a coin decides to take the service or court side.

2. The server must stay behind the back right corner of the endline while serving the ball. After the serve, the server should move into his or her position on the court.

3. Only the serving team may score points. The serving team scores a point when the receiving team fails to return the ball to the server's court. The receiving team gets the serve when the opposing team fails to return the ball over the net, or the served ball touches or goes into the net or out-of-bounds. This is called "Side Out!"

4. A team gaining the serve must rotate CW one position before serving.

5. The ball may not be carried or held.

6. Players may not reach over or touch the net.

7. The ball may be played a maximum of three times by a team before going over the net; however, the same player may not touch the ball twice in succession.

8. A ball touching the boundary line is considered in-bounds.

9. A team wins when it scores fifteen points and has a two-point lead; otherwise, play continues until the two-point advantage is obtained.

10. At the end of each game, teams exchange sides. The losing team begins the new game.

11. Blocking on the service is not allowed. A blocked ball is not considered a hit.

12. The ball may only be "spiked" within the 10-foot spiking zone.

13. A point or "side out" occurs when:
    — the ball touches the floor
    — a team plays the ball more than three times
    — the ball is held or pushed
    — a player touches the ball twice consecutively, except when blocking
    — a player touches the net
    — a team is out of position for the service
    — a player lands in the opponent's court during play
    — the ball passes outside the vertical markers
    — the server is out of rotational order
    — the server has served incorrectly
    — the server steps into the court before the ball has left his or her hand
    — a backline player, while in the attack area, hits the ball into the opponent's court, from above the net

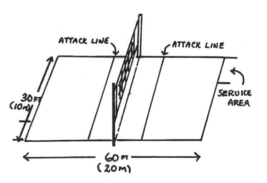

GS-96 MODIFIED VOLLEYBALL

FOCUS: Positional play; rotations; team work

EQUIPMENT: One volleyball per game; volleyball court and net; whistle

ORGANIZATION:

- Form two teams of nine to twelve players per team. Have one team on each side of the net. Adjust the height of the net according to the ability level of the class. Teach the court positions and the rotational order; then play regulation volleyball with any or all of the following modifications.

DESCRIPTION OF ACTIVITY:

1. The server serves from a mark in the center of the court.
2. The server is allowed two attempts to serve the ball over the net.
3. One "help over" is allowed on the serve.
4. The ball may be hit twice in succession by the same player before going over the net.
5. A team may hit the ball any number of times before going over the net.
6. The ball may be played in the air or after one bounce.
7. Server calls out the score before serving.
8. The game is played to fifteen points, or for an agreed time limit.

GS-97 BLINDMAN'S VOLLEYBALL

FOCUS: Positional play; court awareness; team work

EQUIPMENT: One volleyball or beachball per game; volleyball court and net (or long rope); several bed sheets or parachutes; several clothespins; whistle

ORGANIZATION:

- Form teams of six to nine players a side, with each team on one side of the net or long rope. Hang the sheets over the rope, using the clothespins, so that only the opposition's feet can be seen. Play regulation volleyball rules. Have players roll the ball under the sheets to the serving team. Explain that there should be "no peeking" under or around the sheets. Have players call out the score before serving. Remind players to call "Mine!" if going to play the ball. Emphasize that players should be in the "ready position" and to move to the ball. Encourage teamwork: A ball taken in the back court should be passed to the front line, instead of trying to hit it directly over the net.

DESCRIPTION OF ACTIVITY:

See illustration.

VARIATIONS:

a. **Three-and-Over:** The ball must be played three times by each team before going over the net. The team loses the serve or the point if the ball is not played three times.

b. Set up a tournament.

GS–98 SIDELINE VOLLEYBALL

FOCUS: Serving; bumping; setting; team work

EQUIPMENT: One volleyball per game; volleyball court and net; whistle

ORGANIZATION:

- Form two teams of eight to ten players per team. Arrange the players as shown in the diagram in GS-99, with four players from each team inside the court and four along the sidelines and endline. The game is played as in regulation volleyball but includes the extra sideline players in the game.

DESCRIPTION OF ACTIVITY:

1. Sideline players, you must stay in your positions and cannot enter the court area, but may bump or set any loose ball from either team back into your team's court, as long as the ball has not touched the floor.

2. Sideline players, you may not pass the ball to each other. A hit by a sideline player does not count as one of the team hits.

3. After every five points, sideline players, exchange places with the court players. Continue the game until one team scores fifteen points.

VARIATIONS:

a. Restrict sideline play to either a set or a bump.

b. Count sideline hits as team hits.

GS–99 FOUR-SQUARE VOLLEYBALL

EQUIPMENT: Two volleyball courts; one volleyball or beachball; two long ropes; volleyball standards

ORGANIZATION:

- Using two long ropes and standards, set up a rope at right angles to the second rope, to divide the two volleyball courts into four equal half-courts. Divide the class into four equal teams and assign each to a court: team A, team B, team C, and team D.

DESCRIPTION OF ACTIVITY:

1. Each team begins with ten points. The object of the game is to finish with the best score, after a certain time or when one team has no points.

2. One team, start by serving the ball from the serving area into any of the other three courts. From then on, play regulation volleyball rules.

3. Each team, try to force one of the other teams to make an error. When a team makes an error, a point is deducted from your score. The ball is given to the next team in order, upon loss of service.

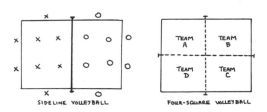

SIDELINE VOLLEYBALL   FOUR-SQUARE VOLLEYBALL

FOCUS: Ball familiarization; ball control   **EQUIPMENT:** One basketball per player; music

ORGANIZATION:

• Have players get a basketball and scatter. Play music to establish a lively atmosphere. Allow ample time to practice these activities. Encourage players not to look at the ball.

DESCRIPTION OF ACTIVITY:

1. **Slap-the-Ball Drill:** Hold the ball in front of your chest with your elbows slightly bent. Pass the ball back and forth from hand to hand using a slapping motion. Try this while walking.

2. **Fingertip Drill:** Hold the ball overhead using only your fingertips. Pass the ball from the fingertips of one hand to those of the other hand. Try to pass the ball in time to the music. Can you pass the ball overhead without watching it? Try this while walking.

3. **Butterfly Drill:** Stand with feet wide apart; hold the ball between your legs with one hand in front of your body and the other behind. Quickly change hands and grasp the ball again before it drops to the floor. Repeat as many times as you can.

4. **Circling:** Pass the ball from hand to hand, circling the ball around your waist.

   — **Circling on the Run:** Form teams of four or five players, get one ball per team, and get into file formation behind your leader behind a sideline. Leader, circle the ball around your waist while running the width of the court and back to give the ball to the next player. Continue until each player has run twice. Challenge other teams.

5. **Figure-8 Drill:** Stand with your feet wide apart and crouch slightly as you lean forward. Pass the ball under and around one leg and then under and around the other leg in a figure-8. Try not to move your feet as you pass the ball. How many times can you make a figure-8 without looking at or dropping the ball? Repeat, making the figure-8 while walking forward, slowly.

6. **Monkey Walk:** Form teams of four or five players and line up as for Circling on the Run. Each player performs the Monkey Walk by passing the ball between each leg in the figure-8 pattern while fast walking the width of the court and back. Continue until each player has run twice. Challenge other teams.

7. **Roller Ball:** Roll the ball down your back, catch it behind you, and then bounce the ball through your legs so that you catch it in front.

GS-101 DRIBBLING

FOCUS: Dribbling technique; ball manipulation and control

EQUIPMENT: One basketball per player

ORGANIZATION:

- Explain and demonstrate the dribbling technique; then have players get a basketball and scatter. Players practice dribbling technique and the Control Dribbling Drills using first one hand and then the other.

DESCRIPTION OF ACTIVITY:

1. *Technique:* Lean forward and bend your knees slightly, keeping your weight evenly distributed on the balls of both feet. Push the ball toward the floor with the fingers and wrist of one hand, not palms. Do not slap the ball! Your wrist and fingerpads should be relaxed and your hand cupped, with fingers spread. Keep the ball close to your body and low to the floor as you dribble. Look beyond the ball rather than directly at it.

2. *Pocket Dribble (Protection Dribble):* Bend your knees and place opposite foot to dribbling hand forward. Keeping low and bending over the ball, dribble your basketball in the triangular space, the "pocket" formed by your feet and body. The ball should bounce beside the back leg. Keep your free arm up; protect the ball with your body and this free hand. The top of the ball should not rise higher than your knees. Practice. Switch hands and forward foot. Remember, heads up—do not watch the ball while you dribble!

3. *Low Dribble:* Place your left hand on your knee and bend both knees slightly. Dribble the ball rapidly with your right hand so that the ball stays below knee level. Now low dribble with your left hand. Can you low dribble with your eyes closed?

4. *Control Dribbling Drills:*

   — Place one hand on your knee, dribble the ball low rapidly with one hand, then the other.

   — Dribble the ball low under your legs. Dribble around your legs.

   — Dribble the ball around your body without moving your feet.

   — Dribble the ball in place while you travel around the ball.

   — Dribble the ball with one hand and touch the floor with the other. Change hands and try again.

5. *Stunts:*

   — Bounce yourself up and down on both feet while dribbling the ball. Change hands and repeat; then dribble the ball from one hand to the other while you are jumping up and down.

   — Hold one ankle. Dribble the ball on the spot with your free hand; then change hands and ankles and repeat. Try this while walking.

   — Place one foot out in front and dribble around it; then around the other foot. Can you make a figure-8 pattern around your legs? Now dribble in the other direction. Repeat walking forward.

   — Stand while dribbling the ball; then kneel on one knee, kneel on both knees, then sit, without stopping your dribble. Kneel, and stand again, still dribbling the ball.

6. *Greetings:* Dribble the ball with your left hand; then continue to dribble, shake hands with as many players as you can. Greet each player by name. Change hands and repeat.

FOCUS: Ball control; use of right and left hands   **EQUIPMENT:** One basketball per player

ORGANIZATION:

• Explain and demonstrate the following dribbling techniques, one at a time; then have players get a basketball and scatter. Players practice these dribbling techniques, using first one hand and then the other.

DESCRIPTION OF ACTIVITY:

1. **Shuffle-Step Dribble:** Dribble the ball with the hand that is opposite to the direction in which you shuffle-step. When you shuffle-step to the left, use your right hand to dribble; when you shuffle-step to the right, the left hand becomes the dribbling hand. Practice this at a low level; a medium level.

2. **Cross-Over Dribble:** Cross the ball from one hand to the other as you dribble around the court. Keep the ball low, knees bent, feet spread, and your head up. Do not look directly at the ball.

3. **Yo-Yo Dribble:** Stand with your feet apart and your knees slightly bent. Dribble the ball below knee level from one hand to the other in a "V" pattern. Now move forward, yo-yo dribbling with your right hand. Move backward, still yo-yo dribbling with your right hand.

— Repeat Yo-Yo Dribble with your left hand while moving forward and backward.

4. **Power Dribble:** This is used when dribbling around an opponent or driving to the basket. Lean your body toward the opponent, with the nondribbling arm hanging low to protect the ball. Place your body between the ball and your opponent.

5. **Heads-Up Dribble:** (Used to practice all of the above dribbles. Have players stand about 2 meters [6 feet] apart in a free space facing you.) On the signal "Dribble!" watch me all the time and, using the shuffle-step, dribble the ball low, in the direction I point. When I point to your right, dribble sideways to the right. When I point to the left, change hands and dribble in that direction. When I point behind me, dribble the ball forward. When I point to the back of you, dribble backward. When I point up in the air, yo-yo dribble quickly on the spot. Do not watch the ball. Remember to change hands each time the direction changes.

— Increase the time spent, each time this activity is practiced, to improve endurance.

GS-103 DRIBBLING ON THE RUN

FOCUS: Control dribbling

EQUIPMENT: One basketball per player;
five cone markers per team;
one stopwatch or digital watch;
lively music (optional);
tape or record player

ORGANIZATION:

- In performing these tasks, have players strive for control; keep the ball low; keep the head up and not look at the ball; execute a quick cross-over; keep the nondribbling arm low to protect the ball; and keep the body facing in the direction of travel. To start, have players get a basketball and dribble anywhere in the play area.

DESCRIPTION OF ACTIVITY:

1. *Jog and Dribble:* Dribble slowly around the play area; then change to different speeds: quickly, normal speed, walk, run, on the spot. Change your dribbling hand often. Dribble high and slow; then dribble low and fast. Dribble at a medium height.
   — Repeat using other locomotion movements: skipping, side-stepping, walking backward.
   — Dribble to the music. When the music stops, yo-yo dribble in place.
2. *Line Dribble:* Stand on any line on the floor. On signal "Go!" dribble your ball along the floor lines in any direction. When you come to a corner, or where two lines cross, change hands and direction. If you meet another player, pass each other right shoulder to right shoulder and dribble with your left hands.
3. *In and Out Relay:* (Form teams of four to five players. Have each team stand in file formation behind a starting line, place a row of five cones in front of each team as in the diagram, and have the leader of each team get a basketball.) On the signal "Dribble!" Leader, dribble the ball to the right of the first cone with your right hand. As you approach the second cone, do a cross-over dribble by crossing the ball over to the left hand. Continue switching hands so that your body is always between the cone and the ball. When around the last cone, dribble and pass off the dribble to the next player in line. Continue until everyone has had two turns.
   — Give each team two or three basketballs. How many times can each team dribble the In and Out course in two minutes?
   — Dribble slowly around the cones, and fast between the cones.
4. *Copy Cat:* (Divide into teams of five or six players, and have them line up behind their leaders. Make suggestions only if leaders cannot think of a ball movement. Encourage players to establish control without looking directly at the ball.) On the signal "Copy Cat!" follow your leader around the play area, doing whatever your leader does with his or her ball. Leader, when you run out of ideas, move to the back of the line and allow the next player to take over as leader.
   Possible Dribble Suggestions:
   — use right and left hands
   — along lines
   — anywhere but on the lines
   — around the circles on the floor
   — forward, backward, and sideways (right and left hands)
   — on the spot, around the ball
   — under the legs, in a figure-8
   — high, low, behind the back
   — on, over, under, and around obstacles
   — shake hands with another team while dribbling
   — skipping, hopping while dribbling
   — with both feet off the floor
   — "dance" dribble
   — invent your own dribble action

3.

FOCUS: Technique; ball control

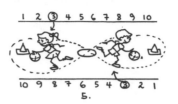

EQUIPMENT: One basketball per player;
one cone marker per team;
one hoop per team;
one stopwatch;
three hoops per team

ORGANIZATION:

• When players show control in dribbling, Speed Dribbling should be introduced. Explain the technique; then have players get a basketball and practice fast dribbles on their own.

DESCRIPTION OF ACTIVITY:

1. *Technique:* Push the ball farther out in front of your body, at waist height, as the speed increases. Rather than looking directly at the ball, "feel" for the ball with your fingertips. Practice with either hand.

2. *Speed Dribbling in Waves:* (Form groups of five or six players and have them line up in "waves" alongside each other, one wave behind the other, just behind an endline.) In waves, dribble low with control until you get to the center line; then speed dribble to the opposite endline. Move to either sideline and dribble off the court and back to the starting point. When a wave reaches the center line, the next wave may go.

3. *Circle Dribble Relay:* (Divide the class into two equal teams and have both teams number off consecutively. Teams then form one large circle. The leader of each team gets a basketball.) On signal "Dribble!" leaders, dribble the ball in a CCW direction around the outside of the circle, return to your starting position, and pass the ball to the second player on your team, who does the same. Continue until all players have had a turn.

4. *Speed-Dribble Relay:* (Form teams of four to five players and have each team stand in file formation at one end of the play area, facing a cone marker at the opposite end. Leaders of each team get a basketball.) On signal "Dribble!" leaders, dribble toward the cone marker using your right hand; then dribble back to the team using your left hand. Pass the ball to the next player and join the end of the file. Continue until each player has had four turns.

   — *Challenge Speed-Dribble Relay:* How many times can each team repeat the relay in ninety seconds?

5. *Figure-8 Scramble:* (Divide the class into two equal teams and have teams stand side by side, facing each other on opposite sides of the play area as shown. Have teams number off; then set a hoop on the floor between the teams and place two basketballs in the hoop. Place a cone marker at each end between the two teams. Keep the score on the chalkboard for all to see.) Listen for your number. When it is called, run quickly toward the hoop, grab a basketball, and dribble it in a figure-8 pattern around the two cone markers. Return the ball to the hoop and run back to your starting position. Your team scores one point if you are the first to return to your starting position. Continue until everyone has had a turn.

6. *Hoop Dribble Game:* (Form teams of three players. Have each team collect three hoops and three balls, lay the hoops on the floor in a file, about 5 meters [15 feet] apart, and place a ball in each hoop. Team members stand in a file behind a starting line facing their hoops.) On signal "Go!" each player in turn run to the first hoop, pick up ball, and dribble it to the second hoop. Put first ball in this hoop, grab the other ball in the hoop, and dribble to the third hoop. Put the second ball in the third hoop, grab the third ball, and dribble back to the first hoop, placing this ball in the first hoop. Then return to "give five" to the next player, who repeats the task. Game finishes when everyone has gone twice and team is cross-leg sitting in its file.

GS–105 DRIBBLE GAMES

FOCUS: Ball control; alertness

EQUIPMENT: One junior basketball per pair; several cone markers; one banner per player

ORGANIZATION:

- Play these dribbling games in a confined space. Emphasize that players may dribble the ball with either hand but not both; otherwise, it is Double-Dribbling. Remind the dribblers to keep low with feet spread and focus their eyes on their partner as they dribble rather than on the ball. Have players find a partner, get a basketball, and run to a free space.

DESCRIPTION OF ACTIVITY:

1. *Ball Touch:* The player holding the ball is on offense; the other is on defense. On signal "Ball Touch!" players on offense, try to dribble the ball so that the player on defense cannot touch it. Protect the ball by positioning yourself between the ball and your partner.

   — Defensive players, stay close to your partner. Try to touch the ball with an upward flick of the hand without touching your partner. Stay low with your feet spread and hold one hand out in front and the other out to the side, ready to touch the ball.

   — Change roles whenever the ball is touched or when the dribbler dribbles with two hands.

2. *Dribble Tag:* Each player get a ball. The taller partner is IT. Both players, dribble your ball as the IT player tries to tag the other partner with the free hand. Remember to watch where you are going.

3. *Knock Away:* On signal "Knock Away!" continuously dribble the ball within the play area while attempting to knock away someone else's ball with your free hand. At the same time, try to protect your ball by positioning yourself between the ball and other players. You may dribble the ball with either hand but not both. Try to knock away the ball with an upward flick of your free hand without touching anyone. Stay low with your feet spread. After your ball has been knocked away, retrieve your ball, do five push-ups, and rejoin the game. Give yourself one point for each knock-away. Play again. Can you beat your previous score?

4. *Steal the Tails:* (Have players get a banner each and tuck it into the back of their waistband so that most of it shows.) On the signal "Steal the Tails!" continuously dribble the ball within the play area while trying to steal as many banners as possible from other players. When you steal a banner, tuck it into the back of your waistband. If your banner is stolen, you are still "alive" and may continue stealing banners. The player with the most banners after two minutes is the winner. The ball must be dribbled at all times, even while putting banners in your waistband.

VARIATION:

To increase the difficulty and the fun, confine the space even further.

FOCUS: Basic body and footwork skills; terminology

EQUIPMENT: One basketball per player

ORGANIZATION:

- The ready position in basketball is introduced, followed by the fundamental body and footwork movements and a Signals game to reinforce these skills.

DESCRIPTION OF ACTIVITY:

1. ***Triple-Threat Position:*** (The "ready position" in basketball.) With both feet planted, hold the ball close to your body at waist level, pull your elbows in, bend your knees, crouch, and lean forward over the ball. Now you are ready to pass, shoot, or dribble.

2. ***Cutting:*** To change direction quickly, plant one foot firmly, bend your knees and lower your body; then push off the planted foot to take a step in the new direction with your other foot.

3. ***Jump Stop:*** To do this two-foot stop, jump off either left or right foot so that you land with both feet together at the same time. Plant feet about shoulder-width apart, bending at the knees to absorb any forward movement and to keep balance. Keep head up and eyes forward. Your hands should be up in the ready position to receive the ball; otherwise, protect the ball in the triple-threat position.

4. ***Stride Stop:*** Run in a slightly crouched position. Stop suddenly with one foot contacting the floor first; then land the other foot to ensure stopping and good balance. Feet should be spread about shoulder-width apart, knees bent. The first foot to touch the floor becomes the "pivot" foot and must remain in contact with the floor. Use this one-foot stop to receive a pass while running or to finish a dribble. Remember to keep head up, eyes forward, and hands in the ready position.

5. ***Pivoting:*** Do a Jump Stop. Pivot on the ball of one foot (for good body balance) while the other foot (stepping foot) moves in any direction by taking short steps to the right, to the left, forward, or back. Keep the pivot foot in contact with the floor; knees bent, body crouched low, and feet about shoulder-width apart. Keep head and eyes up and protect the ball with your body. Use this fundamental footwork to protect the ball, passing, faking, driving to the basket, and getting good rebounding position.

6. ***Jumping:*** Keep head and eyes on target. Bend your knees just before take-off, use your arms to swing forward and upward, and extend your body upward. Jump off both feet. Land on the balls of your feet, bending knees to absorb the impact. Both feet should hit the floor at the same time.

   — Toss a ball overhead; jump straight up to catch the ball at the top of your jump; land in a Jump Stop; then crouch with the ball close to your body in the Triple-Threat position. Do this five times; then repeat using the Stride Stop.

7. ***Footwork Signals:*** On signal "Dribble!" dribble the ball in general space with good technique. On signal "Stop!" catch the ball and Jump Stop. On Signal "Triple Threat!" hold the ball in the Triple-Threat position. On signal "Right Pivot!" plant on the ball of your right foot and pivot around on the left foot. On signal "Jump!" toss ball upward, jump up, and catch it at the top of your jump before your feet touch the floor; land in Triple-Threat position.

   — Other signals: "Left Pivot!"; "Stride Stop!"; "Cutting!"

FOCUS: Chest pass and catch technique; peripheral vision; partner work

EQUIPMENT: One basketball per player

ORGANIZATION:

- The Chest Pass is the most frequently used basketball pass and is mainly used to pass over short distances. The ready position or "Triple-Threat Position" is introduced in order to execute the pass. Have each player get a basketball, explain and demonstrate the technique, and then have players scatter to practice.

DESCRIPTION OF ACTIVITY:

1. ***Chest Passing:*** Begin by holding ball close to chest, with elbows into the sides of your body. Stand with one foot slightly ahead of the other, knees bent, and body crouched low. This is called the Triple-Threat Position (to pass, shoot, or dribble). Hold ball with hands on the side of the ball, keeping your fingers relaxed and spread. Your thumbs should be pointing upward, in line behind the ball; the palms should not touch the ball. Step toward the target (for power) and thrust your arms forward. As you release the ball, snap your wrists; follow through with thumbs pointing to floor and fingers pointing to the target—the receiver's chest. Keep your head up, eyes on the target.

2. ***Receiving:*** Position feet about shoulder-width apart, knees bent, body crouched low (weight evenly distributed on both feet). Give a hand target for the passer. Step toward the ball in flight. Keep your eyes on the ball all the way into your hands. The "target hand" acts like a glove while the other hand tucks the ball into the glove or blocking hand. Reach for the ball, bending your elbows upon contact. "Give" with your fingers, wrist, and arms to absorb the force. Keep balanced and ready for triple-threat position upon receiving the ball.

3. ***Wall Practice:*** Stand about 3 meters (10 feet) from a wall. Chest pass the ball to the wall and receive it as it comes off the wall, with good technique.

4. ***Partner Chest Passing:*** Stand facing a partner about three or four giant steps apart from each other. Practice chest passing and receiving with good technique.

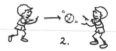

5. ***Split-Vision Challenge:*** (Form groups of three players: A, B, and C. Have each group collect two utility balls and stand side by side.) Player B, holding one ball, step forward three meters (10 feet) and turn to face the other two players. Players A and C, stand 3 meters (10 feet) apart, facing B. Player A hold the second ball. Player B signal "Pass!" and chest pass to C; at the same time, A pass to B. Continue with C chest passing back to B, while B passes back to A. Throw at the same time, calling out in unison "Pass," "Pass." Throw slowly at first; then gradually increase speed.

6. ***Corner Spry:*** (Form teams of five to seven players. Teams line up in a semicircle with the leader in the middle facing the team and holding the basketball.) On signal "Go!" Leader, pass to No. 1, who passes it back. Leader, then pass to 2, then 3, 4, and 5, in turn. No. 5, when you receive the ball, run to the middle to become the new leader, and the former leader joins the semicircle in No. 1's position; the other players move over one place.

— Challenge other teams.

FOCUS: Chest passing and catching; team work   **EQUIPMENT:** One basketball per team

ORGANIZATION:

- Review the Chest Passing and catching technique. Form teams of five to eight players. Have each team choose a Captain, get a basketball, and line up in file formation behind the line with the Captain in front, holding the ball and facing the rest of the team.

DESCRIPTION OF ACTIVITY:

1. ***Captain Ball:*** On signal "Go!" Captain, pass to the first player, who passes it back and then squats down; then pass to the second player, who squats down; then to the third player, and so on down the file until the ball is passed to the last player. Last player, when you catch the ball, run to the front to become the new Captain. Former Captain, join the file in first player's position, and the other players move back one place. Continue until the Captain is back in his or her original position.

   — Challenge other teams.

2. ***Circle Pass and Follow:*** (Have the players of each team form a circle, collect one ball, and stand about 1 meter [3 feet] apart.) On signal "Go!" Leader, pass to any player across the circle, except the player next to you. Follow your pass across the circle to take that player's position in the circle. By the time you get there, that player will have passed to someone else across the circle. Players, continue passing and following your passes.

   — Which team can complete thirty passes the quickest and sit cross-legged in your circle?

3. ***Triangle Pass and Follow:*** Get into position as in the diagram. Player No. 1 at the head of the file, pass to No. 2; then follow your pass to take No. 2's place. No. 2, pass to No. 3, follow your pass, and take No. 3's place. No. 3, pass to No. 4 (at the head of the file), follow your pass, and join the end of the file. Continue.

   — Increase the distance between players.

4. ***Dribble, Pivot, and Pass:*** Find a partner, put one ball away, and stand facing each other about 3 meters (10 feet) apart. Player with the ball, No. 1, Chest Pass to No. 2; then run to take 2's position. No. 2, dribble to No. 1's old position, pivot, and pass back to No. 1. Continue.

   — Change the pivot foot and the direction of the pivot each time.

   — Change the dribble hand each time.

   — Use the Bounce Pass.

5. ***Star Pass and Follow:*** (Form groups of ten to fifteen players per group. Have each group set up in a "star" formation as shown.) The passing pattern goes from Line 1 to Line 2 to Line 3 to Line 4 to Line 5. After a player has chest passed to the opposite Line, that player follows the pass and joins the end of this line.

   — ***Challenge:*** Which "Star" can complete fifty passes the quickest?

GS–109 THE BOUNCE PASS AND THE PUSH PASS

FOCUS: Bounce and push pass technique; partner work

EQUIPMENT: One basketball per player; one bowling pin or bleach bottle per group; stopwatch

ORGANIZATION:

• Have players find a partner, get a ball to share, and stand about 3 meters (10 feet) apart. Players practice the Bounce Pass and Push Pass.

DESCRIPTION OF ACTIVITY:

1. **Bounce Pass:** This pass is similar to the Chest Pass, except that the ball is bounced off the floor before it reaches the receiver. Hold the ball in the Triple-Threat position as for the Chest Pass. Step toward your target and thrust your arms forward and down. Snap your wrists as you release the ball. The target area for the bounce pass is about waist level. Aim your ball to hit the floor two thirds of the distance toward the receiver.

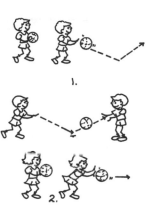

2. **One-Handed Push Pass:** This pass is similar to the Chest Pass in footwork. For a right-handed player, hold the ball in both hands with the right hand more to the back of the ball and the left hand supporting the ball on the side. Move your weight from the back right foot to the front left foot; push the ball forward with the right hand with a downward flick of the wrist, putting a slight backspin on the ball.

3. **Wall Practice:** Stand facing the wall about 2 meters (6 feet) away.

   — Bounce Pass the ball to the wall twenty times; move forward each time to catch the ball.

   — Push Pass the ball to the wall twenty times, let the ball bounce once, and catch.

   — Using the Push Pass, count the number of passes that you can make in thirty seconds. In forty-five seconds. Repeat using the Chest Pass.

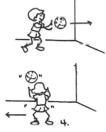

4. **Wall Shuffle:** Stand about 1 meter (3 feet) from a wall at one end of the court. Side-step (shuffle) along the length of the wall as you Chest Pass to the wall, rebounding as you go. Putting a little top-spin on the ball will make the ball rebound at the correct height. Pass the ball slightly ahead to the wall to allow for your speed.

   — Repeat using the Push Pass and the Bounce Pass.

5. **Guard the Pin:** (Form groups of six to eight players and have each group find a space and form a circle around a bowling pin. Have one player stand in the circle to guard the pin.) Circle players, pass the ball around and across the circle until you get a chance to knock down the pin. You must be outside the circle to throw at the pin. Circle players, when you hit the pin, trade places with the center guard.

GS–110 PARTNER AND GROUP PASSING

FOCUS: Chest, Bounce, and Push passing; partner and group work

EQUIPMENT: One basketball per pair

ORGANIZATION:

• Have players find a partner and get one ball to share.

DESCRIPTION OF ACTIVITY:

1. ***Slide Stepping:*** (Have partners stand facing each other 3 meters [10 feet] apart at one end of the basketball court.) Slide-step (shuffle sideways) to the other end of the court, chest passing the ball back and forth. When you reach the end, run back to the start, change sides, and repeat.

   — Repeat using the Push Pass, then the Bounce Pass.

2. ***Ten-Times-Three:*** (Form teams of three players, collect a ball for your group, and stand in a triangle formation about 3 meters (10 feet) apart.) On signal "Pass!" player A, with the ball, chest pass to B. B pass back to A. A pass to C, C pass back to A, and so on until A handles the ball ten times. Change positions until each of the three players have had a turn in the middle.

   — Repeat using the Push Pass and the Bounce Pass.

3. ***Continuous Split Vision Drill:*** (As for Ten-Times-Three, except that A and B start with a ball each.) Player A, call "Go!" and Chest Pass to C. At the same time B, pass to A. Continue with A passing to B; C passing back to A and so on until A handles the ball twenty times; then change positions in the middle.

   — Repeat using the Push Pass and the Bounce Pass.

   — Challenge other groups.

4. ***Circle Keep Away:*** (Form Circles of seven to ten players. Have one or two players stand in the center of the circle.) The circle players, try to pass the ball across the circle without having the ball touched or intercepted. Do not pass to the player on your immediate left or right or to the previous passer. Center player, if you touch the ball, change places with the circle player who passed the ball. Use Chest, Push, or Bounce passes.

5. ***Run the Gauntlet:*** (Form groups of six to eight players: Three of the players stand about 5 meters [15 feet] apart in a zigzag formation without a ball; the others form a file facing the three stationary players, each with a ball.) First player with the ball, Chest Pass to the No. 1 stationary player and continue running to receive a return pass from No. 1; then pass to No. 2 without dribbling. Continue in the same manner to No. 3. When you receive the return pass from No. 3, reverse direction, passing back to No. 3, 2, and 1 as you return to the file, so that the second player may go. Change roles so that all players have a turn at being a stationary player.

   — Repeat using the Bounce Pass, then the Push Pass.

6. ***Partner-On-the-Run Pass:*** (Form pairs and have one partner get a ball.) Using the Chest Pass, Bounce Pass, or Push Pass, pass the ball back and forth to each other as you move around the play area. To receive the ball, run to open spaces and hold your hands ready. The ball should not be dribbled. Be careful to avoid other players.

7. ***Two-on-Two:*** (Play each game in a confined area. Have players join with another pair and return one ball.) One pair, start the game by passing the ball to each other using the Chest Pass, Bounce Pass, or Push Pass. The other pair, try to intercept the ball. If you are successful, you take over the ball and the game continues.

   — Play three-on-three, four-on-four, five-on-five.

GS-111 PASSING OFF THE DRIBBLE

FOCUS: Dribbling and passing

EQUIPMENT: One basketball per team of six players

ORGANIZATION:

• Form teams of six players. Have each team collect one basketball and line up in file formation behind the starting line.

DESCRIPTION OF ACTIVITY:

1. ***Dribble and Pass Back Relay:*** On signal "Go!" Leader, dribble to a line 4 meters (12 feet) away, turn (pivot) on one foot, and Bounce Pass the ball back to the second player, who dribbles to the line, turns, and passes back to the third player, and so on. After passing the ball, return to the end of the file. Continue until you are back in your original positions.
   — Repeat using the Chest Pass; the Push Pass.
2. ***Shuttle Dribble and Pass:*** (Form groups of six players and have one half of the group face the other half about 3 meters [10 feet] apart.) On the signal "Go!" player No. 1, dribble the ball once without looking at the ball and Chest Pass to No. 2; then run and join the end of the opposite file. On receiving the ball No. 2, dribble once; then pass to No. 3 and join the end of the opposite file. Continue the pattern. Players, cut to the right after passing the ball; then go to the end of the opposite file. Passers, aim for the receiver's outstretched hands. Receivers, do a little jump in the air to receive the ball.
   — Use the Bounce Pass and the Push Pass.
   — Increase the distance as ability improves.
   — Receiver, move toward the ball to catch it in two hands, dribble, and pass.
   — ***Thirty-Up:*** Challenge the other groups to be the first group to make thirty passes without dropping the ball. If the ball is dropped, start counting from zero again. Call out aloud the number as each pass is made.

GS-112 LEAD PASSING

EQUIPMENT: See GS-111.

ORGANIZATION:

• A Lead Pass is a pass thrown just ahead of another player, who is on the run. Have players find a partner, get a ball to share, and stand on the endline of the basketball court about 3 meters (10 feet) apart, facing their partner. Have players move slowly at first; then increase speed as skill improves.

DESCRIPTION OF ACTIVITY:

1. ***Lead-Pass Drill:*** Player with the ball, Chest Pass the ball just ahead of your partner, who will run forward to catch it with a Jump Stop; then run down the court ahead of your partner. Jump-Stop as you catch your partner's pass. Continue until you reach the end of the court and return.
   — Repeat, using the Stride Stop.
2. ***Three-Passes Game:*** (For each game, form two teams of six to eight players. One team wears pinnies. The game is started by a jump ball at the center.) The object of the game is for a team to complete three consecutive passes to three different players in order to score one point. When the ball touches the floor or is intercepted, the other team gets the ball. Pivoting is allowed, but dribbling or running with the ball is not. You may not hold the ball for more than three seconds.
3. ***Four Corners:*** (Form groups of twelve players. Divide the twelve players into four smaller groups of three players: groups A, B, C, and D. Each smaller group stands in file formation in each corner of a 5-meter [16-foot] square, facing inward.) First player in groups A and B, get a ball. On signal "Go!" Chest Pass the ball to the opposite corner; then run CCW to the end of the next file. Continue.

GS–113 BASEBALL PASS

FOCUS: Passing and catching technique

EQUIPMENT: One basketball per player

ORGANIZATION:

- The Baseball Pass is used to pass over long distances. Have each player get a basketball and gather around. Explain and demonstrate the passing technique. Review catching technique; then have players scatter.

DESCRIPTION OF ACTIVITY:

1. *Technique* (for a right-handed player; reverse positions for a left-hander): Stand with the left foot ahead of the right with knees bent and the weight evenly distributed on both feet. Bring the ball back over the right shoulder and behind the ear. The right hand should be behind the ball with the left hand supporting the ball in front and to the side, as the weight shifts to the back foot. As the right arm is brought forward to make the throw, the weight shifts to the front foot. Release the left hand from the ball. The wrist should follow straight through so that there will be spin on the ball.

2. *Wall Ball:* Stand about 5 meters (15 feet) from a wall in your own space. Using the Baseball Pass, pass to the wall, higher than your own height. Try to hit a certain spot on the wall. Let the ball bounce once; then catch it. Repeat.

3. *Throwing to a Moving Partner:* Find a partner and stand about 6 meters (20 feet) apart in the play area. Get a ball to share. One player, stand with the ball; then using the Baseball Pass, throw the ball slightly ahead of your partner, who cuts toward the ball, away from the ball, sideways to the ball, in a circle, in a zigzag pattern. Take turns at being the receiver after each pass. Watch where you are going and avoid other players. Continue.

   — Move farther apart and still make the catch.

GS–114 OVERHEAD PASS

FOCUS: Technique and practice

EQUIPMENT: One basketball per player

ORGANIZATION:

- The Two-Handed Overhand Pass is effective when throwing a short, high pass above the reach of an opponent, for instance a pass to the Center. It is usually accompanied by a fake.

DESCRIPTION OF ACTIVITY:

1. *Technique:* Stand tall with your feet parallel and the weight evenly balanced on both feet. Hold the ball up over the head with the elbows slightly bent and the fingers spread around both sides of the ball as for the Chest Pass. Step toward the target and thrust your arms forward. Snap your wrists as you release the ball. Aim for your receiver's face. Try not to telegraph your pass. Hold ball overhead, not behind.

2. *Individual Practice:* Stand facing a wall, about 3 meters (9 feet) away. Throw an Overhead Pass to the wall, catch the rebound of the first bounce, and continue. Try catching the ball directly off the wall.

3. *Partner Practice:* Find a partner and stand about 3 meters (9 feet) apart. Pass the ball back and forth to each other. Receiver, establish a target by extending the arms toward the ball.

4. *Practice in Threes:* Stand in threes, as above, but neither receiver should know who is going to receive the ball. Passer, try to keep them guessing by faking with the ball.

GS—115 THREE-PERSON PASSING WEAVE

FOCUS: Lead chest passing and catching on the run

EQUIPMENT: One basketball per three players

```
x x x x |2  x
·x·x·x x |1 ·
x x x x |3 ·x
```

ORGANIZATION:

• Form groups of three players. Have them collect a ball and stand about 3 meters (10 feet) apart, at one end of the court in a shallow "V" formation, with the center player (No. 1) holding the ball. Have players "walk through" the drill at first, then jog, and finally at game speed. Remind all players that they must say to themselves "Pass and go behind" the player you pass to.

DESCRIPTION OF ACTIVITY:

1. No. 1 player, start by passing to either side player, for example, No. 2, as they both move up the court. No. 2, as soon as you receive the ball, pass across to No. 3.
2. No. 1, after passing to No. 2, run behind No. 2 to receive the pass from No. 3, and the drill continues with players running diagonally across the floor as they proceed up the court. Remember to pass and go behind.
3. No traveling (running with the ball) is allowed. Pass the ball as soon as you receive it. The ball must not be dribbled.
4. When finished at the other end of the court, move off to the sideline to return to the starting point to repeat.

GS—116 BOMBARDMENTS

FOCUS: Baseball pass; team work

EQUIPMENT: Twelve cone markers; 6 to 8 sponge balls per game; basketball court

ORGANIZATION:

• Stand six markers on each endline of the basketball court, evenly spaced apart. Adjust the throwing distance to the ability level of the players by moving the cones closer or farther away. Form teams of six to twenty players. Have each team collect three or four sponge balls and stand on opposite sides of the basketball court facing each other.

DESCRIPTION OF ACTIVITY:

1. On the signal "Go!" using the Baseball Pass, throw the balls into the opposite half of the court to try and knock down the cones behind your opponent's endline; at the same time try to stop your cones from being hit.
2. All players, you must stay in your own half of the court and must not cross the center line. Be alert and try to catch balls thrown into your court. Only one player can guard a cone at a time.
3. You may throw the ball from anywhere in your half of the court, or bounce, chest, push, or overhead pass to teammates in your court area.
4. Remove markers that have been knocked down. The team that knocks down all the cones or hits the most in two minutes wins.

VARIATIONS:

a. Use bleach bottles, milk cartons, tin cans, or wooden blocks instead of cones.
b. Have players throw the ball from the spot where the ball was caught.

FOCUS: Lay-up and Set Shot techniques; hand and foot work; listening

EQUIPMENT: One basketball per player

ORGANIZATION:

• A lay-up shot is the basic basketball shot taken directly in front of or to either side of the basket. It is generally made after a player dribbles the ball to the basket or receives a pass near it. Players should learn to perform a lay-up with either hand. The Set Shot is the basic outside shot. Explain and demonstrate the right-hand lay-up and set shot; then have players get a ball and practice.

DESCRIPTION OF ACTIVITY:

1. ***The Overhand Lay-Up Technique:*** (for a right-hander)
   — Begin by holding the ball in both hands, Triple-Threat position, feet parallel and shoulder-width apart. Step forward with the left foot and let the ball bounce once near this foot. Catch the ball in both hands off the dribble, step right foot, then left foot, keeping the ball to the right side of your body. Now push upward off your left foot, driving the right knee up to increase the height of your jump.
   — For right-hand lay-up, when ball is picked up in two hands, the right hand is on top of the ball, the left hand on the side for support. Keep both hands on the ball until you reach the height of your jump, bringing the ball up to a shooting position. Now your right-hand wrist should be cocked back to release the ball off your fingers. "Lay-up" the ball softly against the backboard, with the target being the top right corner of the rectangle on the backboard. Eyes stay on target, fingers follow through, and left hand comes off the ball but stays in the air to protect the shot.

2. ***Lay-Up Progressions:***
   — Pantomime the footwork and arm action "bounce–2–3–up."
   — Now stand about two giant steps from a wall. Check for good spacing. Practice pushing off with the left foot, driving the right knee upward, and laying-up the ball against the wall.
   — Now stand in front of and to the right of the basket and about 1.5 meters (5 feet) away from it. Push upward on your left foot and carry the ball upward as high as possible with both hands. Lay the ball softly against the "target" on the backboard so that the ball falls softly into the basket. Remember to take off with your inside foot and shoot with your outside hand.
   — "Walk through" the "bounce–2–3–up!" pattern using your basketball. Practice several times.
   — Now practice the whole sequence at a controlled speed. (Equally distribute players to a basket, depending on the number of baskets available.)

3. ***Underhand Lay-Up:*** (This shot is used when approaching the basket from the front.) Position your shooting hand under the ball and place your other hand on the other side of the ball to steady it. Lift the ball to the basket with both hands; then remove the nonthrowing hand as your shooting hand carries the ball up and over the rim of the basket. Allow the ball to roll off your fingertips. It is not necessary to use the backboard for the underhand lay-up shot.
   — ***Practice:*** Do Overhand and Underhand Lay-ups in your own time at the baskets.

4. ***Lay-Up—Rhythm Method:*** (This alternative method of teaching the lay-up, created by the author, involves the establishment of a rhythm of steps, rather than the use of the terms *right* and *left*. Have each player get a basketball.) Stand on the free-throw line with your back to the basket and hold the ball in both hands, waist high. From this position, the lay-up is made to the count of "One," "Two," "Three."
   — To do a lay-up on the right side of the basket: On the count of "One," take a step backward toward the basket onto the toes of your left foot and pivot on your left to face the basket.
   — As you do, a dribble is made with the right hand. Catch the dribble in both hands, and on "Two" take a second step with the right foot toward the basket; on "Three," take the final step with the left foot to jump up to the basket off that left foot and lay the ball up on the backboard for the shot.
   — Repeat on the left side. Whichever side the lay-up is done, the foot on that side moves first. There is no need to mention "lefts" and "rights"!

GS—118 LAY-UP DRILLS

FOCUS: Overhand and underhand lay-ups; rebounding

EQUIPMENT: One basketball per player

ORGANIZATION:

- Have players get a basketball and form files of four or five players. Have files stand on the right-hand side, about 5 meters (16 feet) away from the basket, at a 45-degree angle to the baseline.

DESCRIPTION OF ACTIVITY:

1. ***Overhand Lay-Up from the Right:*** Dribble to the basket with your right hand, watching the basket all the time. When close to the basket, take off with your left foot and push the ball against the backboard, off the fingertips of your right hand; follow through with a snap of the wrist. Catch the ball on the rebound and return to the end of the file.

2. ***Overhand Lay-Up from the Left:*** Dribble to the basket with your left hand, take off on your right foot, carry the ball up with both hands, and, at the height of your jump, release the ball off the fingertips of the left hand. Rebound the ball and join the end of your file.

3. ***Underhand Lay-Up:*** Stand in file formation directly in front of the basket. Dribble to the basket with your right hand, take off on your left foot, and lay the ball over the front rim of the basket with your right hand. Taking turns, try dribbling with your left hand, taking off on your right foot and shooting with your left hand. Rebound your own shot and join the end of your file.

4. ***Individual Practice:*** In your groups, practice the different types of lay-ups on your own.

5. ***V-formation Lay-Up Drill:*** (Form two teams of four or five players at each basket. One team, the Shooters, get one basketball and stand in file formation facing the basket on the right side of the keyhole and about 10 meters [30 feet] from the basket. Have the first player hold the basketball. The other team, the Rebounders, stand in a similar formation on the other side of the court, so that both teams form a "V" formation, facing the basket.) On the signal "Go!" the first player on the shooting team, dribble the ball to the basket, do a right-hand overhand lay-up, and continue around the outside of the rebounding team to the end of that team. Meanwhile, first player on the rebounding team, run in to catch the first shooter's rebound; then pass the ball to second shooter, who will dribble in for a lay-up, then join the end of the shooting team. Continue shooting from the right side of the court and rebounding from the left.

   — Change, so that the lay-ups are taken from the left side and the rebound from the right.

6. ***Lay-Up Relay:*** (Form teams of five or six players at each basket. Have each player get a ball and get into file formation on the right side of the keyhole about 10 meters [30 feet] from the basket.) On the signal "Go!" the first player, dribble in and take a right-hand lay-up from the right side of the basket, rebound your own shot, and dribble back to the end of your team. Continue. The first team to score fifteen points is the winner. Shout out your group's score whenever you make a basket.

   — Repeat the relay from the left side; down the middle; along the right baseline, and then along the left baseline.

FOCUS: Lay-up off the pass and dribble; team work

EQUIPMENT: Six chairs or cones per group; one ball per player

ORGANIZATION:

• These drills now involve the skills of passing, dribbling, and lay-up shooting. Explain and demonstrate each one. Have groups perform them slowly at first; then gradually pick up the speed.

DESCRIPTION OF ACTIVITY:

1. *Dribble Weave and Lay-Up Drill:* (Place a line of three cones or chairs at a 45-degree angle on each side of the baskets. Cones or chairs should be about 1.2 meters [4 feet] apart. Form groups of five or six players and have them stand in a file just behind a starting line, facing the cones or chairs. Have each player get a ball.) Dribble through each set of chairs to score three lay-ups at each basket. Take your time; dribble the ball low for good control. Move the ball to the outside hand as you dribble around a chair, lay-up the ball with your left and right hands, take your own rebound, and continue. Keep your head up; look out for other players, and be courteous. Keep moving, and look for empty baskets.

2. *Pass and Lay-Up Drill:* In your groups, stand about 3 meters (10 feet) apart in files, facing the basket, behind the center line. The two leaders, pass the ball back and forth to each other as you move up court. When you near the basket, one player take a lay-up, either player rebound, then return to the end of the opposite file. Continue taking turns performing lay-ups.

3. *Tandem Drill:* Find a partner and get a ball to share; then line up in files, alongside each other parallel to a backcourt sideline. Player A, on the inside, hold the ball. On the signal "Go!" both players move; player A, dribble the ball to the center circle; then pass to player B, who cuts at a 45-degree angle to the basket and attempts a lay-up. Player A, rebound the ball and repeat the drill to the other end of the court: player A dribble to the center circle; player B run to the other basket in a wide arc, then cut to the basket for the pass from player A. Rebound the ball and join the end of the opposite file. The inside player holds the ball for the next turn.

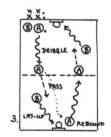

4. *Three-Person Weave with Lay-Up:* Refer to GS-115 for description of drill. Finish drill with one player making a lay-up. Basket must be made before group retires.

5. *Lead-Pass Lay-Up Drill:* (Review the Lead Pass and the Baseball Pass; then explain and demonstrate the drill. Form two teams of five to six players and have them line up in file formation behind the halfway line. Have players on Team A get a basketball each.) The first player on Team B, run in toward the basket. The first player on Team A, throw a Baseball Pass (lead pass) to a spot just ahead of the runner, who will catch the ball and go to the basket for a shot. Player A follow B to the basket, rebound the ball, and make another Baseball Pass back to B as he or she continues to run up court to join the end of Team A. Player A, join the end of Team B, and the next pair will have a turn. After a certain time, Team B will start with the basketballs and pass to Team A.

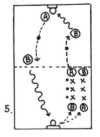

GS-120 FREE THROW, SET SHOT

FOCUS: Technique; practice; related games   **EQUIPMENT:** One basketball per player

ORGANIZATION:

- An unhindered shot at goal, awarded from the free-throw line, is called a Free Throw or Foul Shot. The same shot taken farther from the basket is called a Set Shot.

DESCRIPTION OF ACTIVITY:

1. *Technique of the Free Throw and the Set Shot:*

   — *Stance:* The Free Throw and the One-handed Set Shot are performed by positioning feet about shoulder-width apart with the foot under the shooting hand slightly ahead of the other foot. The knees should be slightly bent and the body should be square to the basket.

   — *Hand Position:* Position the ball with both hands level with your chin and over the leading foot. Place the shooting hand under and behind the ball, supporting it on the finger pads. (There should be a slight space between the ball and the palm of the hand.) Place the nonshooting hand under and to the side of the ball for balance and control. Your shooting arm should be at a right angle with elbow and arm in straight line with the basket and your wrist cocked back. Keep your back straight and elbows in.

   — *Head Position:* Keep your head up and eyes on the ring. During the shot, your eyes should follow your shot all the way to the ring.

   — *Execution:* Look at the leading edge of the basket, and bring the ball up just above your forehead but not behind your hairline. Release the ball with a straightening of the knees, a push with the arm, a flick of the wrist, and a follow-through in which the arm reaches for the ceiling, to impart a high arc and a slight backspin to the ball for a nice soft shot. Stand perfectly still after the shot is taken. If you move forward after the shot, you should shoot the ball higher.

2. *Practice:*

   — Find a spot alone and lie down on your back. Hold the ball in the shooting position with the index finger in front of your nose; then shoot the ball straight up. Flick your wrist upward and forward as you straighten your arm. If the ball goes straight up and down, you have applied the correct amount of backspin to the ball.

   — Stand facing a wall about 3 meters (10 feet) away. Practice Set Shooting to the wall at a height of about 3 meters (10 feet).

   — Practice Free Throws from the free-throw line. Practice Set Shots from any comfortable distance from the basket.

   — Stand on the free-throw line. Shoot Set Shots from this position. Follow the ball, rebound, and shoot a lay-up.

3. *Shooting Games:*

   — Play "GOTCHA!" with a partner around the basketball key. Partner A shoots; if successful, Partner B must make the same shot; otherwise, B missing the shot is given a letter. Partner A gets to shoot from another spot. If Partner A misses the shot, B need not take the same shot and becomes the leader. First one to "gotcha!" loses.

   — *"Around-the-World Shoot-Out":* Each partner must make the shot at each of the seven designated spots on the basketball key lines before moving to the next spot. Which partner will complete the shoot-out the quickest?

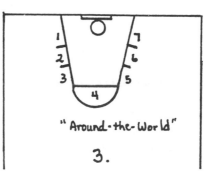

"Around-the-World"

3.

GS-121 THE JUMP SHOT

FOCUS: Technique and practice; shooting games   **EQUIPMENT:** One basketball per player; floor tape

ORGANIZATION:

• The Jump Shot is essentially the same shot as the Set Shot or Free Throw, except that the shot is taken in the air after a jump off the floor.

DESCRIPTION OF ACTIVITY:

1. *Technique of the Jump Shot:* Position your feet comfortably, with the lead foot slightly ahead of the pivot foot or, if you prefer, with both feet parallel and shoulder-width apart. Hold the ball in both hands in exactly the same position as in the Set Shot, square your shoulders to the basket, and bend your knees. There are two movements in the Jump Shot; call out to yourself as you make these moves:

   — On the count of "one," jump upward; bring the ball upward vigorously to a position in front of and above the head with the elbow underneath the ball and pointed at the basket.
   — On the count of "two," release the ball at the height of your jump: As the ball is shot, release the supporting hand, and with the shooting hand push the ball to the basket with a high arc in a similar manner to that of the Set Shot. The jump is made straight up so that you land back in the same spot. Follow through by reaching for the ceiling with the shooting hand.

2. *Practice:*
   — Collect a ball and stand 2 meters (5 to 6 feet) from a wall, aiming for a spot on the wall about 3 meters (10 feet) high. Practice your jump shots to the count of "one"–"two." Repeat. If you are having difficulty with the timing, shoot the ball (count of "two") when you "think" you are coming down. The higher the jump, the more time there is to shoot.
   — Move to a position 2 meters (6 feet) from the basket. Without taking a dribble, shoot a soft Jump Shot, aiming to place the ball over the leading edge of the basket. Retrieve the ball and repeat.

3. *Pivot and Shoot:* Pivot to face the basket, shoot a Jump Shot, or Set Shot. Retrieve the ball and dribble to a similar spot on the other side of the basket. Pivot and shoot from there and continue.
   — Gradually increase the distance from the basket.

4. *Dribble and Shoot:* Stand at the top of the keyhole. Dribble the ball to a position on the baseline. As you pick up the ball, square your shoulders to the basket and do a Set or Jump Shot with both feet parallel to the basket. Rebound the ball, dribble to the top of the keyhole, and repeat from the other side.

5. *Basketball Golf:* (Place numbers one to nine on the floor, around the keyhole as in the diagram, with masking tape. Form groups of nine players and have each take up a position around the basket on a number. Players may then use the Set Shot, or the Jump Shot to score.) Players, shoot a shot and rebound the ball, starting at position No. 1. Keep shooting until you score a basket. If successful, on your next turn, you will begin at the next hole. You must play and finish a hole before moving on to the next. Count the total number of shots taken to complete the nine-hole course. The lowest number of shots wins.

   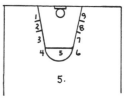

   — Establish a "par" for the course and have players try to beat par.

FOCUS: Defensive foot and body work; practice drills; partner work

EQUIPMENT: One basketball per pair

ORGANIZATION:

- During the game of basketball, both teams spend approximately half the time on offense and the other half on defense; therefore, the fundamentals of Man-to-Man Defense should be learned early and emphasized while the offensive skills are being taught. Have players find a partner, collect a basketball between them, and scatter in free space.

DESCRIPTION OF ACTIVITY:

1. **Man-to-Man Defense—The Boxer's Stance:**

   — Take a position between the offensive player and the basket.

   — Keep the weight evenly distributed on both feet—feet shoulder-width apart, with one foot forward; knees bent.

   — Keep your seat low and your back upright.

   — Keep one hand up and the other hand down.

   Focus your eyes on your opponent's waistband and hips. Watch everything else out of the corner of your eye.

   — Keep your feet moving all the time and rarely leave the floor.

   — Never cross your feet, but use the slide-step to move from side to side and the shuffle-step to go back and forward.

   — Don't leap in the air on a fake pass or shot.

   — Rush your opponent when the dribble is finished.

   — Don't try to steal the ball; force bad passes instead.

2. **Hands-Up Drill:** Find a spot alone in a free space, facing me in the Boxer's Stance, with both hands up. When I point and give a direction (forward, back, right side, left side) I want you to move in that direction. When I point to the floor, I want you to do the Stutter-Step (run quickly on the spot).

3. **Line Shuffle Drill:** (Have the class line up across the basketball court, behind the endline, standing in the defensive stance and facing one side wall.) On the signal "Go!" using the defensive shuffle-step (slide-step sideways), shuffle to the first line, touch it with one hand, and shuffle back to the starting line, touch it with one hand, then shuffle to the next line, and so on until you reach the other end line. Rest; then shuffle back to the starting line again, one line at a time.

4. **Corridor Drill:** (Divide the basketball court into three or four corridors. Have players pair off; one player is an offensive player; the other defensive. Assign pairs to a corridor.)

   — Offensive player, maneuver your way from the starting end of the corridor to the opposite end. Defensive player, strive to keep good defensive position as you "defend" your partner. Once at opposite end, switch roles.

   — Offensive player, now control-dribble a basketball to opposite end while defensive player keeps good position.

   — Offensive player, now try to dribble past defensive player.

5. **Two-on-Two:** (Form groups of four players: Two players stand about 3 meters [10 feet] apart, with the ball. The other two players stand in the middle.) Outside players, pass the ball back and forth to each other without being intercepted by the middle players. You may pivot or use fakes but may not dribble. If intercepted, the middle players, change places with the outside players.

GS–123 BLOCKING OUT AND REBOUNDING

FOCUS: Defensive techniques under the basket; partner work

EQUIPMENT: One basketball per player

ORGANIZATION:

• A rebound occurs when a ball comes off the backboard after a missed shot. Explain and demonstrate the blocking and rebounding positions. Emphasize that most important to rebounding is to get an inside position on your opposition player. Have players each get a basketball and find a free space.

DESCRIPTION OF ACTIVITY:

1. **Blocking Out Technique:** Keep your eyes on the player you are guarding and the ball. When a shot is taken, you should first try to "block out" your offensive player off the boards by pivoting on one foot to step into his or her path. As you turn your back on him or her to face the basket, make body contact. Arms should be up and fingers spread ready to grab the ball. Bending at the knees, position your feet in a low, wide stance, with your rear end sticking out toward your opponent.

2. **Rebounding:** After blocking out your opponent and getting the "inside" position, go for the rebound. Jump into the air with both hands reaching up to catch the ball as it rebounds downward. Try to grab the ball in two hands at the height of your jump. After catching the ball, bring it into your chest with elbows out and lean over the ball for protection. Spread-eagle your legs as you land back on the floor. Immediately look for an "outlet," a teammate to pass the ball to.

3. **Air Rebounding:** Pantomime the blocking out and rebounding positions. Repeat.

   — Now toss your ball upward in your space. Try to grab it in both hands at the height of your jump. Land in good rebounding position. Repeat.

4. **Rebounding Off the Wall:** Get a ball each and stand at a wall. Throw the ball high on the wall; then jump up, with your arms fully extended, to catch the ball at the top of your jump with both hands.

5. **Rebounding with a Partner:** (Have players take a partner and stand 3 to 4 meters [10 to 12 feet] apart, and get one basketball to share.) Player with the ball, lob the ball to your partner, who will jump up with arms outstretched to catch the ball at the peak of the jump, land and protect the ball; then lob-pass back to you.

6. **Rebounding in Pairs:** One partner with the ball face the wall; other partner stand with your back to the wall. Player with the ball, call "Rebound!" and toss the ball high on the wall. Other Partner, pivot on one foot to face the ball; jump as high as you can to take the rebound. Land in good rebounding position. After five turns, change roles.

7. **Rebounding at the Basket:** (Have partners stand inside the keyhole.) The defensive player, hold the ball and stand with your back to the basket facing the offensive player. Defensive player, hand the ball to the offensive player, who immediately shoots. As soon as the shot is taken, defensive player, quickly pivot, turn your back on the offensive player, and face the basket to block out and prevent the offensive player from taking the rebound. Try to get the "inside" position to take an easy rebound. After five shots, change positions.

GS–124 SIDELINE HOOP BASKETBALL

FOCUS: Offense; defense; passing; shooting; team play

EQUIPMENT: Two sets of pinnies per game; one basketball per game; several hoops and cones

ORGANIZATION:

* For each game, have two teams of eight to ten players with one team wearing the colored pinnies. Each team has five players on the court and the remaining players standing in hoops on the sidelines, as shown in the diagram.

DESCRIPTION OF ACTIVITY:

1. The game begins with a jump ball at center by two opposing players. Try to move the ball down the court to the opposition's end to score a point by shooting a basket.
2. Court players, you are not allowed to dribble the ball but may only pivot and pass the ball inside the court, or outside to teammates in the sideline hoops. Move to open spaces to get a good position for a pass.
3. Sideline players, you must keep at least one foot inside your hoop. Defensive players, play Man-to-Man Defense; that is, each player guards an opposition player.
4. After each goal, court and sideline players exchange places. Restart the game at center with a jump ball.

GS–125 THREE PASSES

FOCUS: Offense; defense; passing; positional play; team play

EQUIPMENT: See GS-124.

ORGANIZATION:

* Mark out the courts with cones. For each game use one half of a basketball court, have two equal teams of five or six players, and give one team a set of pinnies. Have all players pick out an opposition player to "guard." To begin, players stand next to their opposition player just outside the jump ball circle, with the two smallest opposition players to jump for the ball inside the circle.

DESCRIPTION OF ACTIVITY:

1. The two smallest players, stand inside the circle for a "Jump Ball." (The ball is tossed up between the two players, who jump to tap it to a member of their own team.) The team who wins the ball, try to pass it back and forth between your players for three consecutive passes before your team is allowed to take a shot at a goal. The ball cannot be passed back to the same player from whom it was received. Count out loud as each pass is made.
2. The defensive team may intercept the ball but cannot touch a player who has the ball. If this happens, the team with the ball is awarded a free pass.
3. Passers, if you dribble or drop the ball, hold it for more than three seconds, or run with the ball, the ball is awarded to the other team behind the sideline near where the infraction occurred.
4. Score one point every time your team completes three consecutive passes. If still in possession of the ball, try to complete another three passes!
5. Remember to get into open spaces for a pass; play Man-to-Man defense; use the defensive stance to intercept the ball; pass to all your players, not just a few!

GS-126 BASKETBALL RULES

FOCUS: Knowledge of the game

ORGANIZATION:

• Teach the following information in the classroom. A knowledge of the rules of the game will allow players to understand the need for proper skill development and the necessity of avoiding bad habits. Teachers should modify these rules to the ability level of their classes. Lowering the baskets, playing with a smaller or lighter ball, reducing the size of the court, increasing the number of players on a team, and limiting the number of dribbles are but a few ways of adapting the rules to meet the needs of the players.

DESCRIPTION OF ACTIVITY:

1. ***Team Positions:*** A team consists of five players, namely: one center, two forwards, and two guards. Players are not restricted to any part of the court, and all positions are interchangeable.

2. ***The Game:*** To start the game, an official tosses the ball up (Jump Ball) between two opponents, who stand in the smaller center circle. All other players may take any position they wish, outside the larger center circle. The two opposition players jump to tap the ball to a teammate; then each team tries to advance the ball toward the opponent's goal to score by shooting it through their goal. A Jump Ball is also called when two opposing players are holding the ball.

   — The game can be divided into quarters or two halves. The length of each quarter to be decided upon by both teams; usually five-minute quarters or twenty-minute halves for elementary schools.

3. ***Scoring:*** A successful goal from the field is worth two points. One point is awarded for a successful free throw. After a score the ball is put back into play at the end of the court by the nonscoring team.

4. ***Violations:*** A violation is a minor infraction of the rules, and the penalty is that the ball be given to the opponents outside the sideline, opposite the spot where the infraction occurred. Violations occur for:

   — traveling—taking more than one step while in possession of the ball (sometimes called "carrying the ball")

   — double dribbling—dribbling the ball, stopping, then dribbling again; or dribbling with two hands instead of one

   — out-of-bounds—causing the ball to go out-of-bounds by stepping on or over the boundary line while in possession, or by passing or knocking the ball out

   — kicking the ball—kicking the ball intentionally

   — three seconds in the keyhole—offensive player staying in the offensive keyhole for three seconds or more while that team has possession of the ball

5. ***Fouls:***

   — A Personal Foul occurs when a player holds, trips, blocks, pushes, kicks, or charges an opponent or engages in rough or unsportsmanlike play. If the referee feels the foul was intentional, the player being fouled is awarded two free throws from the foul line.

   — If a foul occurs while a player is shooting or in his or her steps toward the basket for a lay-up, the shooter is awarded a free-throw situation. If the shot was successful, the shooter is awarded one foul shot. If the field goal was missed, two foul shots are awarded. If the second free throw is successful, the defending team throws the ball into play from outside the endline. If the ball touches the rim but does not go in, play continues. If the ball fails to touch the rim, the ball is given to the defending team on the sideline.

   — Five personal fouls on any one player results in disqualification from the game.

   — A Technical Foul occurs when a player or coach acts in an unsportsmanlike way; when a substitute fails to report to the officials; for delaying the game; or for leaving the court. The opposition team is awarded two free throws at the foul line and ball possession afterward.

GS–127 HALF-COURT BASKETBALL

FOCUS: All basketball skills; team play

EQUIPMENT: Two sets pinnies per game;
one basketball per game;
one whistle

ORGANIZATION:

• The game is played like regulation basketball, except that it is played in half a court and only one basket is used. This allows two games to be played on one court at the same time. Have players play Man-to-Man Defense. Remind players of the rules regarding fouling. Encourage substitute players to act as referees to reinforce the rules. For each game, form two teams of three to five players, and have teams wear different colored pinnies. Before the game, have players pick an opposition player to guard.

DESCRIPTION OF ACTIVITY:

1. **Rules:** The game starts with a Jump Ball at center. After that, regulation basketball rules will apply, except for the following modifications:

   — If the offensive team scores a basket, they retain possession of the ball and restart the game from the other side of the center line.

   — If the defensive team gets possession of the ball, they must pass or dribble it over the center-line before they become the offensive team.

2. Play three-on-three; four-on-four; five-on-five.

3. Play a half-court tournament. (Refer to GS-70 through GS 73.)

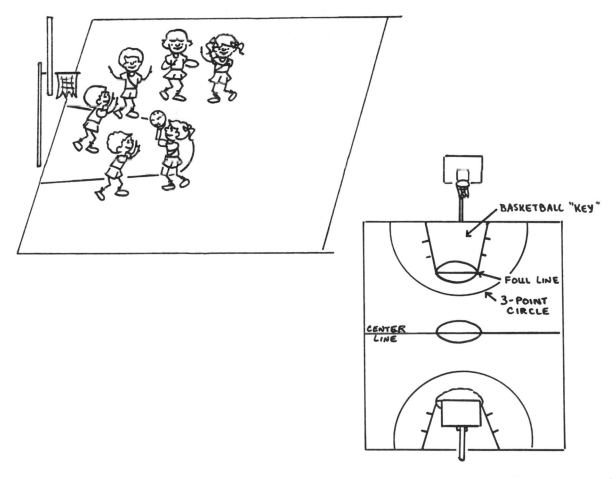

BASKETBALL "KEY"

FOUL LINE

3-POINT CIRCLE

CENTER LINE

GS-128 STICK-HANDLING SKILLS

FOCUS: Stick and puck manipulation; control; footwork

EQUIPMENT: One hockey stick per player; one plastic puck per player; one whistle; several cone markers; hoops; several chairs; 1 to 2 benches

ORGANIZATION:

- Review and demonstrate the grip, ready position, carrying the stick, dribbling, and stick-handling technique. Allow players time to practice; then set up obstacles in the play area. To start, have players get a floor hockey stick and a puck before scattering around the play area.

DESCRIPTION OF ACTIVITY:

1. *Grip Technique:* Place one hand at the top of your stick and the other hand 15 centimeters to 20 centimeters (6 inches to 8 inches) below it. Now reverse hands and repeat. Which position feels the most comfortable to you?

2. *Ready Position:* Holding the stick with both hands, let the edge of the blade of the stick rest on the floor. Bend your knees slightly.

   — When on the move, hold your stick in both hands with the blade low to the floor. Keep your stick below hip level and run "heads up!"

3. *Carrying the Puck:* Move the puck along the floor so that it always stays in contact with the blade, on one side only.

4. *Dribbling Technique:* Dribble by moving the puck forward out in front of you with short taps or pushes, rather than continuous carrying. The blade should be slightly tilted over the puck for better control. Keep the puck in the middle of the blade. Hold your head up as you move and only glance at the puck when necessary. Try to "feel" the puck on your stick.

5. *Stick-Handling Technique:* Use this technique to control the puck when you change direction. Move the puck in front of you rather than to the side. Keep your head up and try to "feel" the puck on your stick by using short taps. Move forward quickly, pushing the puck from side to side in the middle of the blade.

6. *Practice:*

   — Can you carry the puck on your forehand going forward and pull the puck toward you with your backhand as you go backward?

   — Dribble your puck along the lines on the floor with good control.

   — Stick-handle the puck as you move around the play area. Change direction frequently, keeping the blade of your stick on the floor at all times.

   — When the whistle blows once, stop in ready position. The puck should be touching the blade of your stick. When the whistle blows twice, continue dribbling the puck in general space.

7. *Obstacle Field:* (Scatter several cones, chairs, benches, and hoops throughout the play area.) Carry, dribble, or stick-handle the puck in and around the obstacles: around the benches or chairs; in and out of cone markers or hoops; along the lines; through the chair legs.

8. *Zigzag Relay:* (Form teams of four players and have each team stand in a file behind a starting line facing a row of four cones spaced 2 meters [6 feet] apart.) On GO signal, each player in turn stick-handle a puck through the cones, around the end cone, and directly back to the file to give the puck to the next player in line. Relay ends when everyone has had three turns.

   — Repeat Zigzag Relay in shuttle formation.

GS-129 SHOOTING THE PUCK

FOCUS: Wrist and slap shots; forehand and backhand technique

EQUIPMENT: One floor hockey stick per player; one plastic puck or soft ball; wall targets; floor tape; ten cone markers

ORGANIZATION:

- Explain and demonstrate the Wrist and Slap shots. The Slap Shot is used to shoot at a goal over moderate to long distances; the Wrist Shot is used for shorter distances and quick execution. For practicing these shots, tape several 1-meter (3-foot) wall targets, 15 centimeters (6 inches) from the floor. Tape a shooting line 4 meters (12 feet) from each wall target. Players get a floor hockey stick and a puck and stand behind the shooting line, facing the target.

DESCRIPTION OF ACTIVITY:

1. **The Wrist Shot Technique:** Check the puck; then concentrate on the target. Be sure that the blade and the puck are touching before shooting. Shoot with the right hand lower than the left hand on the stick. Allow the lower hand to guide the stick down and "through" the puck. Do not raise the stick higher than your hips on the follow-through.

   - **Forehand Shooting:** The right hand pushes the puck from the right side, with the nonhitting shoulder facing the wall. With elbows slightly bent, snap your wrists and point your stick at the target to follow-through. Keep your eyes on the target.

   - **Backhand Shooting:** The shooting shoulder faces the wall. The right hand pulls the shot from the left side.

   - **Alternate Hand Positioning:** Repeat the Forehand and Backhand shots with the left hand lower than the right on the stick.

2. **The Slap Shot Technique:** Approach the puck, drop your lower hand down the shaft a little for better control, and keep your eyes on the puck. Swing the stick behind you to about waist level and in line with the target. Now swing the stick quickly forward and hit through the puck. Follow through with the stick no higher than the waist. Finish with all your weight on your front foot.

3. **Practice:**

   - Shoot the puck at the wall. Use the Wrist Shot, with forehand and backhand shooting. Repeat ten times.

   - Now use the Slap Shot to send the puck to the wall. Repeat ten times.

   - **Target Shooting:** Shoot the puck at the hoop ten times. Recover the puck each time and repeat. Gradually move farther away from the wall and repeat.

4. **Target Hockey:** (For each game mark out a middle line in a rectangular play area [10 meters by 10 meters or 30 feet by 30 feet]; then divide the class into teams of six to eight players. On each court have a team take up position on one side of the middle line. Equally space five cone markers on each endline of the play area and give each team an equal number of pucks.) On signal "Shoot!" each team try to shoot as many pucks into the opponent's half of the play area as possible. Try to hit the opponent's cone markers as well. You may not enter your opponent's half of the play area. On the signal "Stop!" each team count one point for each puck in your team's play area. Count two points each time a cone marker was hit. The team with the lowest score wins. Play fairly. (You may wish to keep score or have a player who is unable to participate keep score.) Remember, sticks must not be raised above hip level and pucks must travel low to the floor!

FOCUS: Stick-handling control; defense; shooting; alertness

EQUIPMENT: One hockey stick per player; one puck or ball for two thirds of class; floor tape; chalkboard, chalk, brush

ORGANIZATION:

• These action games reinforce the stick-handling skills and teach players the concept of playing defense.

DESCRIPTION OF ACTIVITY:

1. *Hockey Pirates:* (Select one third of the class to be the Hockey Pirates, who each have a stick and stand in the center of the play area to start. Have the remaining two thirds of the class, the Free Players, each get a stick and ball, then scatter throughout the play area.) On the signal "Pirates are coming!" Hockey Pirates, try to stick-handle the puck or ball away from the Free Players. Free Player, as soon as you are without a puck or ball, you become a Pirate and must now try to get the puck away from any free player. Who will still have their puck or ball at the end of the game? Remember to keep your head up and sticks down as you move around! No body contact is allowed. Play fairly— you cannot step on the puck or pin it against a wall.

2. *Square-Box Hockey:* (Form four teams with an even number of players on each team. Have each team stand on one side of a 10-meter [30-foot] square. Each team numbers off. Mark a 30-centimeter [1-foot] circle in the middle of the floor and place four pucks inside it. Record team scores on the chalkboard.) When a number is called, all players with that number, run to the middle, dribble a puck out of the circle, through the spot just vacated, CCW around the square, back through your vacant spot to place the puck back in the circle. The first player back scores four points for the team; the second player scores three points; and so on. Which team will score the most points by the time all numbers have been called? Players on the square, cheer for your teammates but do not interfere with the puck dribblers.

— Repeat game, but when a number is called, the two players with that number run to the middle, try to gain possession of the puck, then try to score a goal by shooting the puck past the opposition team.

VARIATION:

Hockey Team Pirates: Divide the class into two teams, identified by the color of stick each team player has. Players of one team each have a puck. Players of the other team try to "capture" as many pucks as they can before the whistle blows to signal stoppage of play. The number of captured pucks are counted and a score recorded. The two teams switch roles and the game continues.

GS-131 PASSING THE PUCK

FOCUS: Passing and receiving on the run; partner work

EQUIPMENT: One floor hockey stick per player; one plastic puck per pair; one soft ball per pair; one hoop per pair

ORGANIZATION:

- Have players find a partner. Each pair gets two floor hockey sticks and one puck and stands 5 meters (15 feet) apart.

DESCRIPTION OF ACTIVITY:

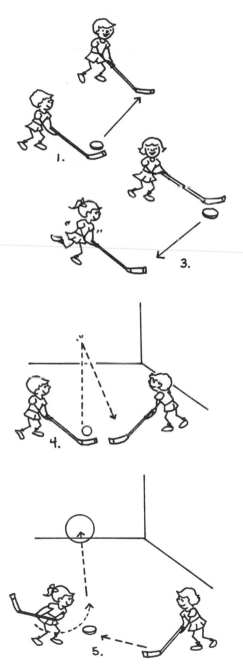

1. **Passing Technique:** Keep your stick blade upright and use a smooth, sweeping motion. Try not to raise the stick above your waist in the backswing or when swinging it forward. Pass slightly ahead of your receiver on his or her stick side. This is called a "lead pass." You will have to judge how fast the receiver is moving so that you know where to place the puck.

2. **Receiving Technique:** Watch the puck. Tilt your stick blade over the puck to trap it. Cushion the pass by allowing your stick blade to "give" at the moment of impact.

3. **Partner Passing Tasks:**

   - While both of you are stationary, pass the puck quickly back and forth. Trap the puck correctly and immediately pass back to your partner.

   - Partner standing still, pass the puck to your partner who is on the move. Partner on the move, stop, trap the puck, and pass it back to your standing partner. After five passes, change roles and repeat.

   - Pass the puck back and forth while you are both moving. Make short passes; make long passes.

   - How many passes can you and your partner complete to each other on the move in two minutes?

   - Collect another puck. Pass the two pucks to each other at the same time, while stationary; while on the move.

4. **Power Passing:** Taking turns with your partner, hit a ball continually against the wall. One partner, hit the ball hard; the second partner, receive the rebound and hit the ball back again. Begin close to the wall; then gradually move farther away as your power increases.

5. **Pass and Shoot:** One player, pass to your partner, who shoots quickly at a hoop against the wall, using the Wrist Shot or the Slap Shot. Take ten shots, change roles, and continue.

   - Start farther away from the wall target. Pass back and forth to each other until close enough to take a shot at the hoop.

GS-132 PARTNER AND GROUP PASSING TASKS_____

FOCUS: Passing and receiving; partner and group work

EQUIPMENT: One hockey stick per player; one plastic puck or soft ball per player; cone markers

ORGANIZATION:

- Have players find a partner and get a floor hockey stick each. Partners share a puck and a hoop. Explain that a "Drop Pass" is a pass to a player behind.

DESCRIPTION OF ACTIVITY:

1. *Truck 'n Trailer:* Stand behind your partner; the player in front with the puck is the Truck and the player behind is the Trailer. Truck, stick-handle the puck while your Trailer follows close behind; then softly tap the puck backward, or "Drop Pass," to your Trailer and continue to travel forward. Trailer, receive the puck and shoot it against the wall. Change roles after four shots.

2. *Pig in the Middle:* (Form groups of three players in a marked area, with one puck.) One player, stand in the middle between the other two players. Middle player, while the two outside players pass the puck to each other, try to intercept it. If successful, swap places with the last player to pass the puck. Continue.

3. *Give and Go:* (Form equal teams of four to six players and have each team stand in shuttle formation, with each half of the team facing the other half, 10 meters [30 feet] away.) The first player in line, pass the puck across to the first player on the other side, who fields the puck and repeats the action. After passing, run across to join the end of the opposite line. The first team to make thirty passes is the winner.

GS-133 GOALTENDING_____

FOCUS: Shot blocking technique

EQUIPMENT: One floor hockey stick per player; three soft pucks or balls per group; three cone markers and three hoops per group

ORGANIZATION:

- Form groups of three players and have each player get a stick and puck. Each group gets two cone markers. Have each group set up the cones as goals 2 meters (6 feet) apart and 1 meter (3 feet) from the wall.

DESCRIPTION OF ACTIVITY:

1. *Goalie Ready Position:*
   — Crouch slightly, holding the stick in front of your body with one hand. Use the other hand to catch or knock the puck away. Watch the puck at all times.
   — Place the stick squarely in front of the puck to stop it. Use your feet, legs, stick, and even your chest to stop the puck.
   — Clear the puck by hitting or kicking it to the side.

2. *Goalie Practice:* One player in each group is the Goalie and stands between the cone markers. The other players, take one shot at a time to shoot the puck along the floor, between cones, having the Goalie stop it.
   — Practice right and left forehand and backhand shots. Try Wrist Shots and Slap Shots. Pick the open spaces to shoot at, not the Goalie. Keep your stick blade lower than hip level!
   — After ten shots, change goalies. Continue until all players have been in goal.

GS–134 FACING OFF

FOCUS: Technique; reaction

EQUIPMENT: One floor hockey stick per player; one plastic puck per group

ORGANIZATION:

- Form groups of three players and have each player get a stick. Give each group one puck. Explain that the Face-off is used to start a game or to restart it after a goal has been scored or a rule has been broken.

DESCRIPTION OF ACTIVITY:

1. *Technique:* Two players, stand facing opposite sides about a stick length apart. Place your stick blades on the floor so that they are almost touching. Slide the lower hand down the stick shaft for more powerful control of the stick. Third player, drop the puck between the two players. Each player, immediately try to gain control of the puck. After four puck drops, change roles until everyone has had a turn dropping the puck.

   — Have the third player place the puck on the floor between the two players before the face-off and then simply say "Go!"

2. *The Face-Off Game:* (Divide the class into two even teams, and have each team facing the other, about 10 meters [90 feet] apart. Have players space themselves an arm's length apart. Have players number off consecutively from opposite ends. Teacher, hold the puck at the face-off circle.) When I call out a number, the two players with that number, come to the circle for a face-off. The winner of the face-off, either dribble or pass the puck back to your line to win a point for your team. Team Leaders, keep score.

3. *Sideline Goalies:* Play as for Face-Off Game, but whoever gains control of the puck at the face-off tries to shoot it past the opposition's sideline players, who act as goalies.

VARIATIONS:

a. *The Face-Off Game:* For a large class, have more than one game going on at the same time. Instead of dropping the puck, place them on the floor between the players and blow a whistle to start.

b. *Hickey-Hockey:* Place the puck on the floor. When the number is called, each player hits the floor on his or her side of the puck, then the opponent's stick. Do this three times, calling "hickey-hockey one!" the first time; "hickey-hockey two!" the second time and "hickey-hockey three!" the third time the stick hits the floor. On the third hit, each player tries to get control of the puck.

c. Call two numbers at a time and add the rule that at least one pass must be made between the two players before attempting to score.

1.

1 ②' 3 4 5 6 7 8 9 10 11 12

12 11 10 9 8 7 6 5 4 3 ②' 1
2.

1 2 3 4 ⑤' 6 7 8 9 10 11 12

"5!"

12 11 10 9 8 7 6 ⑤' 4 3 2 1
3.

"HICKEY - HOCKEY 1!"

GS-135 DEFENSING—OFFENSING

FOCUS: Dodging; checking techniques

EQUIPMENT: One hockey stick per player; one plastic puck per player; cone markers

ORGANIZATION:

- Dodging is the skill of keeping control of the puck and evading a checker. Checking or tackling is the skill of taking the puck away from an opponent. Have players get a stick and a puck and find a free space.

DESCRIPTION OF ACTIVITY:

1. **Dodging Technique:** On the signal "Go!" dribble the puck to the right; to the left; forward and backward. On the signal "Dodge," dodge around an imaginary checker. Try to choose the right moment to execute your dodge to beat an opponent; then push the puck to one side of the checker and move around to the other side of the opponent to regain control of the puck.
2. **Checking Techniques:** Find a partner; then one partner carry the puck toward the stationary partner, who will try to take it away from you. Try to dodge and "fake out" your partner. If the tackle is successful, change places.
   — **Poke or Jab Check:** Hold the stick with one hand and poke or thrust it forward to knock the puck away from the opponent's stick.
   — **Sweep Check:** Move your stick in a sweeping motion to check the puck away and secure control of it.
   — Practice these techniques with a partner.
3. **Keep-Away with Tackling:** (Mark out small play areas with cone markers.) Play two-on-two in a confined area. You may lightly check each other, but the stick blade must not come above the waist. No body contact is allowed. Use split vision to keep your eyes on the puck and opponent.
4. **Hockey Pirates:** Refer to GS-130 for a description of the game.

GS-136 ZONE HOCKEY

FOCUS: Lead-up game; positional play

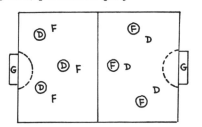

EQUIPMENT: One floor hockey stick per player; one plastic puck per game; cone markers and two hockey nets; two sets of colored pinnies per game

ORGANIZATION:

- Zone Hockey develops positional play and space awareness. It can be played in smaller areas allowing for several games to be set up at the same time. Mark out the play area with cone markers and erect the nets. Divide the class into teams of six to eight players. Have players collect a floor hockey stick and a team pinnie and position themselves on the play area as shown, as either Forwards, Defense, or Goalie. After five minutes of play, have players change positions and then continue the game.

DESCRIPTION OF ACTIVITY:

1. Start the game with a face-off at center between two opposing Forwards. Forwards and Defense, you must play in your own zone. *For example*: The Forwards of team "A" play in the same half of the play area as the Defense and Goalie of the opposition team.
2. Players, you may not cross the center line to play in the other zone but can pass the puck back and forth over the center line. Look for the open player.

GS–137 SIDELINE HOCKEY

FOCUS: Lead-up game; team positional play

EQUIPMENT: One floor hockey stick per player; one plastic puck per game; two large folding mats per game; two sets of colored pinnies per game

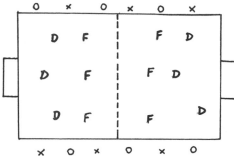

ORGANIZATION:

- Place a tumbling mat behind each endline of a large rectangular area, about 32 meters × 20 meters (100 feet × 60 feet). Divide the class into teams of six to nine players. Have players collect a floor hockey stick and a team pinnie and position themselves on the play area as shown: have one half of the team on the court, as either Forwards or Defense (there are no Goalies); have the other half space themselves along the sidelines as shown. Players change positions after every three minutes of play.

DESCRIPTION OF ACTIVITY:

1. Each team, try to score a goal by shooting the puck to hit the opposition's mat. Court players, you may pass to your sideline players at any time.
2. Start the game with a face-off at center between two opposing Forwards. After each goal, restart the game with a face-off.
3. Sideline players, help your team by keeping the puck in the playing court and passing to your own players. You may not pass to another sideline player.
4. A puck that goes out-of-bounds over the endline and that does not hit the mat is put back into play by the defending team.

GS–138 MAD BALL HOCKEY

FOCUS: Lead-up game; team play

EQUIPMENT: One floor hockey stick per player; two to four plastic pucks (or tennis balls); four hockey nets (or eight cone markers); two sets of pinnies; one whistle

ORGANIZATION:

- Position hockey nets in the middle of both ends and at each side of the play area. Divide the class into two equal teams and distribute one set of pinnies to each team. Assign each team one end net and one side net to defend. At the start of the game use two pucks; then as skill improves, add another and then another until four pucks are in use. Position each puck in the middle of the play area. Two goalies for each team stand in front of the nets. All other players scatter.

DESCRIPTION OF ACTIVITY:

1. To begin the game, four players, two from each team, stand on either side of the pucks ready to face off. When the whistle blows, try to gain control of the puck and pass it to your teammates to try and score in either of the opposition's goals.
2. Goalies, keep track of how many goals the other team has scored. After five minutes of play, the team with the fewer goals scored against it wins. Play a new five-minute game with new goalies.
3. Look for players who are "open." Clear to open spaces to receive a pass. Keep your stick below the waist at all times and the puck traveling low along the ground.

GS–139 FLOOR HOCKEY, THE GAME

FOCUS: Regulation game; rules

EQUIPMENT: One floor hockey stick per player; one plastic puck per game; two sets of colored pinnies per game; marking cones (if outside); two goalie nets

ORGANIZATION:

- If the game is played in a large gym, use the basketball court boundary lines and center circle as the playing court. In a small gym, the ball is alive off the walls. If outside, mark off a large rectangular court with marking cones. Position the two Goalie's nets and mark out the Goalie's crease (a restraining area around the goal, for the goalie's protection). No player or equipment may enter this area. Mark off the four "X's" on both sides of the goals, for face-offs.

DESCRIPTION OF ACTIVITY:

1. A team consists of one Goalie, two Defensive players, and three Forwards. No more than six players per team may be on the floor at any time.
2. A Face-off at center between the two Center Forwards is used to start the game and to restart the game after a goal has been scored.
3. Play two eight-minute halves, with a two-minute halftime to change ends.
4. Goalie, you may stop shots with hands, feet, or stick and must release it to either corner within three seconds. You may not throw or shoot the puck toward the opposition's goal.
5. Defensive players, you cannot go forward of the center line. The Center Forward, you may go back and forward over the center line, but the other two Forwards, you must stay in your opponent's half of the court.
6. Raising the puck higher than knee level results in a penalty shot on goal. A penalty shot may be shot from anywhere outside the Goalie's crease; the puck is dead after the shot. Play continues with a center face-off.
7. If the puck gets trapped against the wall or other equipment, a face-off takes place at the nearest "X."
8. The following fouls result in the puck being given to the opposition at the place where the foul occurred:
   — touching the puck with the hands
   — swinging the stick above waist height
   — the Goalie playing the puck forward
   — a player other than the Goalie in the Goalie's crease
   — the Guards or Forwards moving across the center line
   — stepping on, holding, or lying on the puck

   The defending team must retreat five meters (5 yards) when the puck is put into play after a foul.
9. Players committing the following personal fouls are given a two-minute penalty for the first offense and expelled from the game for the second:
   — tripping with the stick or foot
   — pushing or body checking
   — hacking or striking another player with the stick
   — bad language

VARIATIONS:

a. All defensive and offensive players may move anywhere on either side of the center line.
b. Play Mini-Hockey Games in smaller court areas of three-on-three; four-on-four; five-on-five.

GS—140 FOUR STATIONS HOCKEY

FOCUS: Stick handling; accuracy shooting; passing; goaltending

EQUIPMENT: Four hockey nets;
seven deckrings;
six plastic bleach bottles;
eight bladeless hockey sticks;
six hockey sticks;
three folding mats;
three hockey pucks or balls;
floor tape or cone markers;
one whistle

ORGANIZATION:

• Partition the play area into four equal smaller areas and set up the suggested stations in each area. (If available, use benches turned over on their sides to mark off the four areas.) Then divide the class into four equal groups and assign each group to a station. Rotate groups every five to seven minutes on the whistle signal. Demonstrate the skill involved at each station. Emphasize safety at all times. At the finish, have each group put away the equipment.

DESCRIPTION OF ACTIVITY:

1. *Area 1, Ringette Hockey:* Play three-on-three or four-on-four hockey using a deckring, bladeless hockey sticks, and a net at opposite ends for each team.

2. *Area 2, Hockey Shoot:* (Position two nets in one quarter of the play area so that they are well spaced apart. Mark a shooting line 5 meters [15 feet] away from one net, and another shooting line 6 meters [20 feet] away from the other net.) Take turns trying to score a goal, using the Wrist Shot.

3. *Area 3, Deckring Shot:* (Set up two identical stations with three plastic bottles in a triangle formation about one giant step from a wall. Use floor tape or cones to mark off the shooting line four giant steps away.) Take turns using the bladeless stick to send the deckring toward the bottles. How many bottles can you knock over in three tries?

4. *Area 4, Goalie Challenge:* (Position three folding mats, standing upright so they won't fall over, as goalie nets. Ensure that they are well spaced apart.) Each player, in turn, take five shots on goal to try and score. Goalie, how many saves can you make? Take turns goaltending and shooting.

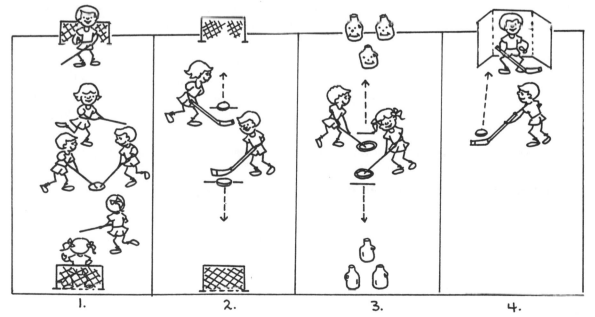

1.   2.   3.   4.

FOCUS: Hand–eye coordination; footwork; dexterity; visual tracking

EQUIPMENT: One 15-centimeter (6-inch) utility ball per player; one wall target per pair; floor tape

ORGANIZATION:

• Players explore striking the ball with an open hand. Have each player get a ball and stand facing a wall, about 3 meters (10 feet) away.

DESCRIPTION OF ACTIVITY:

1. Let the ball bounce once; then hit it against the wall. Hit the ball high against the wall; medium height; low. Catch the ball in two hands each time. Change hands and repeat. Can you hit the ball to the wall, let it bounce once off the wall, then hit it back to the wall? How many times can you do this without missing?

2. Try to hit the ball with your right hand, then with your left, then the right, etc. Can you keep this going without stopping? Start close to the wall; then move farther away from the wall. Always be in control!

3. *Handball Target:* (Tape targets on the wall so that two can share a target.) Try to hit the target with your right hand five times; then left hand five times. Bounce the ball first; then strike it.

4. *Two Square:* (Use floor tape or paint to mark out as many 1-meter by 2-meter [4-foot by 8-foot] courts and a center line as needed. Have players pair off. Each pair gets a ball; players then stand facing each other in one side of the two-square court.) One partner, start the game by bounce serving the ball: Drop the ball and hit it on the first bounce with your open hand into the other player's square. Continue hitting back and forth until one player misses. Play to five points. Then challenge another player.

   — *Rules:* On the line is in; ball must clear the center line and bounce in the other player's side; either hand or both hands may be used; ball must be hit after the first bounce.

   — Remember to be in Ready Position and keep your head up. Try to use either hand to hit the ball. Referee yourselves and keep your own score. Play fairly.

5. *Four Square:* (Use masking tape to mark out as many 2.5-meter [8-foot] square courts as you have groups of four players. Divide the court into four smaller squares and name each square A, B, C, and D. Form groups of four players; then have each player stand in the ready position in one of the squares of the court.)

   — Player in Square A, bounce serve the ball with one or two open hands to a player in any of the other three squares. Whoever receives the ball, allow it to bounce; then hit it with one or two open hands to a player in any other square. You may go out of your square to hit the ball. The game continues with players hitting the ball, after one bounce, from square to square until one player fails to return the ball or a point is scored.

   — The receiver scores a point whenever the previous player's ball hits a line or goes out-of-bounds; the previous player strikes the ball down.

   — The ball must be arched; the previous player hits the ball with a fist.

   — The server scores a point whenever the receiver misses the ball or the receiver holds the ball.

   — The game is restarted after a point is scored by a bounce serve from the player in Square B, then Square C, Square D, and then by Square A again. The first player to earn five points wins the game.

GS-142 USING A PADDLE OR RACQUET

FOCUS: Handshake grip; ready position; striking

EQUIPMENT: One paddle per player; one tennis ball, paddle ball or whiffle ball per group

ORGANIZATION:

• Have each player get a paddle. Review and demonstrate the Ready Position and the Handshake Grip; then allow players to practice the grip while slide-stepping in the Ready Position.

DESCRIPTION OF ACTIVITY:

1. *Handshake Grip:*
   — Hold the paddle out from your body, waist high, so that the head is vertical to the ground and the handle is pointing to your bellybutton.
   — Grip the paddle handle as if you were shaking hands with it; thumb and forefinger form a V-shape along the top of the handle and point to the edge of the paddle head. Spread your fingers so that they are comfortable.
   — Hold the throat of the paddle with the other hand.

2. *Ready Position:* Plant your feet shoulder-width apart, bend the knees, keep your head up and weight evenly distributed on both feet. Hold your paddle in your dominant hand using the Handshake Grip, and place your other hand on the throat of the paddle.

3. *Pivoting Technique:* Stand in the Ready Position. Without moving your left foot, step forward with your right foot; then step backward; to one side; to the other side, and return to the Ready Position. Repeat with the right foot as the pivot foot.

4. *Facings:* Hold your paddle in the Handshake Grip in the ready position at all times as you slide-step around the play area. When I call the name of an object, such as the door, chalkboard, bench, that wall, stop quickly in the ready position and pivot to face the object. Do not cross your feet as you slide-step.

5. *Paddle and Ball Tasks:*
   — Dribble the ball to the floor. Start low to the floor; then gradually dribble higher and higher. Keep the ball under control at all times.
   — Place the ball on your paddle. Try to bounce the ball about 30 centimeters (12 inches) in the air each time.
   — Alternately bounce the ball against the floor and then off your paddle into the air. How long can you alternate bounces without stopping?
   — Now walk around the play area while: bouncing the ball on the floor with your paddle; bouncing the ball off your paddle into the air; alternately bouncing the ball on the floor and into the air.

6. *Circle Bat:* (Form circles of six to eight players. Each group gets a whiffle ball, or tennis ball, and all players stand in the Ready Position, holding the paddle in the Handshake Grip.) Bounce the ball once; then bat it to any player across the circle. Players, allow the ball to bounce once before you hit it back across the circle.
   — Challenge other groups to be the first to hit the ball thirty times.

FOCUS: Forehand and Backhand stroke technique; footwork; partner work

EQUIPMENT: One paddle per player; one whiffle ball, racquetball, or tennis ball per player; several benches

ORGANIZATION:

• Revise and demonstrate the Forehand and Backhand strokes. Constantly remind players to use the Handshake Grip. Review the grip with players who use the "frying pan" grip (holding the handle with the paddle horizontal to the ground.) Emphasize that players are to return to the Ready Position after making each stroke and to watch the ball. To start, have players pair off, each collect a paddle and a ball to share, and then find a free space. Have players pantomime the stroking action first.

DESCRIPTION OF ACTIVITY:

1. *Forehand Stroke:* Hold the paddle in the Handshake Grip with a firm wrist. Turn the shoulder of the nonhitting arm toward your partner. Place the foot opposite your hitting hand in front, and the other foot behind. Now, holding the paddle vertically, pull it back and then swing it forward toward the imaginary ball, and follow through.

2. *Backhand Stroke:* Hold the paddle in the Handshake Grip; then slide your hand around the handle so that your first knuckle is on top of the leading edge of your racquet. Turn the shoulder of your hitting arm toward your partner. Step forward on the foot that is on the same side as your hitting arm and, holding your paddle vertically, swing it forward waist high; then follow through toward your target.

3. *Footwork:* Stand in Ready Position facing me. Pivoting on your right foot, step your left foot across in front of your right so that your left shoulder is at right angles to the target; then perform a forehand stroke. Step back to Ready Position. Repeat several times.

   — Now, pivoting on your left foot, step your right foot in front so that the back of your right shoulder faces the target. Do a backhand stroke. Repeat.

   — Now perform the appropriate footwork and stroke as I call out "Forehand!" or "Backhand!"

4. *Partner Practice:* One partner, get a ball and stand opposite your partner about 5 meters (15 feet) apart. Toss the ball so that it bounces in front of your partner's dominant side. Your partner, from Ready Position, pivots and makes a Forehand stroke to hit the ball back to you. Repeat five times, catching the ball each time.

   — Toss the ball to your partner's other side so that your partner can make a backhand stroke on that side. Repeat five times.

   — Change roles after the ten hits.

5. *Wall Stroking:* Stand facing a wall, about 3 to 4 meters (9 to 12 feet) away. Drop the ball and hit it against the wall using forehand strokes. Try to send the ball above a 1-meter (3-foot) line on the wall. Catch the ball each time; then repeat.

   — Instead of catching the ball each time, allow it to bounce once off the floor; then hit it back to the wall. Can you do this continuously?

   — Repeat using Backhand strokes.

6. *Rebound Ball:* With a partner, take turns hitting the ball against the wall using both Forehand and Backhand strokes. Hit the ball softly at first to establish control and for an easier return by your partner.

VARIATIONS:

Have players hit the ball across a bench while practicing the strokes.

FOCUS: Bounce and Drop serve techniques; partner work

EQUIPMENT: One paddle per player; one whiffle ball, paddle ball, or tennis ball per pair; one bench per pair; wall or floor tape

ORGANIZATION:

• Tape a line on the wall 60 centimeters (2 feet) above the floor. Have players find a partner, get a paddle each and a ball to share, and then stand side by side in the Ready Position, facing a wall. Explain the term *serve*.

DESCRIPTION OF ACTIVITY:

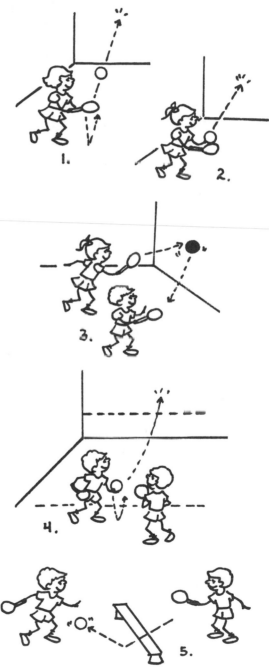

1. *Bounce Serve:* Step forward with the foot opposite your serving hand. Hold the ball in your other hand. Drop the ball and allow the ball to bounce once; then swing your paddle forward to strike the ball against the wall using the Forehand Stroke. Take turns with your partner. Repeat using the Backhand Stroke.

2. *Drop Serve:* Hold the ball at chest level in your other hand. Drop the ball in front of your body: As it drops and before it hits the floor, use a Forehand Stroke to strike the ball with the paddle. Take turns hitting the ball. Repeat Drop Serves using the Backhand Stroke.

3. *Serving Practice:*
   — Serve ten Bounce serves to the wall. Then serve ten Drop serves.
   — With a partner, take turns using the Bounce Serve to serve the ball to the wall. One partner serves the ball; the other catches it and serves again.
   — Repeat using the Drop Serve.
   — Stand facing your partner across a bench. Drop-Serve and Bounce-Serve the ball, allowing it to bounce once before you catch it and serve it back to your partner.

4. *Wall Ball:* With your partner, stand facing the taped line on the wall. One player, serve the ball to the wall above the line. Partner, you may play the ball off the wall, or after the first bounce. A point is scored each time your partner fails to return the ball. If you win a point, you get to serve next. The ball must hit the wall above the taped line.

5. *Bench Ball:* Stand facing your partner across a line. One partner Drop-Serve the ball; the other partner, allow it to bounce once before you catch it; then serve it back to your partner. Repeat, using the Bounce Serve.
   — Play a game to five points. Use the Bounce Serve to start and keep serving as long as you win the point. Use forehand or backhand strokes to hit the ball back to your opponent.

FOCUS: Lead-up games; cooperation

EQUIPMENT: One paddle per player;
one whiffle or tennis ball per pair;
floor tape;
two balance benches per game;
one coin

ORGANIZATION:

- Tape lines on the walls about 1 meter (3 feet) above the floor; then tape other lines on the floor in front of the wall lines and about 3 meters (10 feet) from the wall. Form groups of three players. Each player gets a paddle; then give each group a ball and have them go to a wall line.

DESCRIPTION OF ACTIVITY:

1. *Group Wall Ball:* Stand in file formation behind the floor line and face the wall line. First player, bounce the ball and serve it to the wall above the line; then quickly step aside so that the second player can hit the ball after it bounces once. Third player do the same, and continue. Join the end of the file after you play your shot. Count the number of times your team hits the wall above the line in one minute.

2. *Zigzag Game:*
   — *Practice:* Each team of three find another team of three to play with. Collect two benches and place them end to end; then line up on either side of the benches as in the diagram. Hit the ball over the bench to the next player so that the ball moves along in a zigzag pattern from player to player and back again. Allow the ball to bounce once before striking.

   — *Game:* Challenge other groups. Move back two steps to increase the distance. Make as many hits in a row as you can. Count aloud the number of hits made. When you miss, start counting again from zero.

3. *Floor Ping-Pong:* (Play Floor Ping-Pong according to the basic rules of ping-pong. Tape as many 3-meter × 1.5-meter [10-foot × 5-foot] courts as you will need for pairs; then have players find a partner and get a ball to share. Toss a coin to determine who will serve first.)

   — Begin the game with a bounce serve from your right-hand court. Hit the ball with the paddle over the center line (the net) and into your opponent's right-hand court. Your opponent may then return the ball so that it lands anywhere in your court. Continue to play according to the basic rules of ping-pong.

   — Each player serves for five points at a time, then serve changes to the other player.

   — The ball must arch before landing; it cannot be struck downward. Lose a point if the ball hits a line or goes out-of-bounds or a player fails to return a ball.

   — Play to eleven, fifteen, or twenty-one points.

VARIATIONS:

a. Play with ping-pong paddles and a ping-pong ball.

b. Play doubles. Players alternately hit the ball.

c. Arrange a tournament.

FOCUS: Basic badminton strokes

EQUIPMENT: One badminton racquet per player;
one badminton bird per player;
four cone markers per group;
floor or wall tape;
wall targets

ORGANIZATION:

- Review the Ready Position and Handshake Grip. Explain and demonstrate the forehand and backhand strokes with a badminton racquet and bird. Introduce the Overhead Clear, and allow ample time for players to practice these skills. Tape 1-meter (3-foot) square targets to the wall, 1 meter (3 feet) from the floor. Have each player get a badminton racquet and a badminton bird.

DESCRIPTION OF ACTIVITY:

1. **Drop Serve:** Find a place along the wall and stand facing it. Gently hold the feathers of the badminton bird between your fingers and hold it out in front of you. Check that you have the racquet in the Handshake Grip. Drop the bird and hit it toward the wall, using the Drop Serve.

   — Hit the bird low; a medium shot; then a high shot.

   — Take ten shots using the forehand stroke.

   — Try ten shots using the backhand stroke. Remember to watch the bird!

2. **Target Practice:** Stand 3 meters (10 feet) from a wall target and hold the bird by its feathers. Drop the bird and try to hit the target with the bird.

   — Try five Forehand Strokes, then five Backhand Strokes. How many times can you hit the target?

3. **Bird in the Air:** Hit the bird into the air, alternating with your forehand and backhand on opposite sides of your racquet. How many times can you hit the bird in a row? Can you keep the bird in the air while walking around the play area?

   Continue to hit the bird while changing position from standing to kneeling, to sitting, to kneeling, and standing again.

4. **Keep It Up:** (Form circles of three or four players.) Hit the bird to each other and try to keep it up as long as possible. Call "Mine!" when you intend to hit the bird.

   — Count the number of hits your group makes; then try to beat your score.

   — Challenge other groups to beat your best score.

5. **Keep-It-Up Relay:** (Form teams of three or four players. Have each team stand in files at one end of the play area, in front of a row of four cones.) Take turns weaving in and out of the cones while hitting the bird in the air. If the bird drops, pick it up and continue. Return to your group and flip the bird to the next player. Continue until all players have had two turns.

6. **Overhead Lob or Clear:** Stand with your nonracquet shoulder facing the target and nonracquet foot forward. Draw the racquet back with your elbow fully bent; then throw the racquet directly overhead as your elbow straightens. As the racquet approaches the bird, straighten the arm and snap the wrist forward. Hit the bird directly over the racquet shoulder, with the racquet face angled slightly upward to force the bird high and keep into the other court.

   — Find a partner and together practice the overhead lob.

GS–147 PADDLE TENNIS

FOCUS: Lead-up game; court awareness; forehand-backhand strokes

EQUIPMENT: One paddle per player; one tennis ball or whiffle ball per two players; badminton court and net

ORGANIZATION:

• Paddle Tennis is played on a badminton court with the net lowered to 92 centimeters (3 feet) and may be played as singles or doubles. A whiffle ball or tennis ball is ideal for this game. Emphasize that players check the Handshake Grip and come back to the Ready Position after all shots. Encourage players to use Forehand, Backhand, and Lob strokes.

DESCRIPTION OF ACTIVITY:

1. *Singles:*
   — Server, stand behind the baseline on the right-hand side of the court and bounce-serve the ball across the net into the receiver's right back court.
   — Receiver, you must let the ball bounce once before hitting it back over the net. From then on, it may be played by either player, on the "fly" or after a bounce. On the line is in.
   — *Scoring:* Server, keep serving until you commit a fault or fail to return a ball. Play to eleven, fifteen, or twenty-one points.
2. *Doubles:*
   — When you loose the serve, it goes to a member of the other pair. Take turns.
   — Use the long and wide badminton court for doubles.

GS–148 GOODMINTON

FOCUS: Lead-up game; badminton strokes; team work

EQUIPMENT: One badminton racquet per player; one badminton bird per game; volleyball court, poles, and net

ORGANIZATION:

• Goodminton is best played on a volleyball court with the 2.5-meter (8-foot) net lowered if necessary. Form two teams of six players: play three players up front and three in the back court as in volleyball.

DESCRIPTION OF ACTIVITY:

1. *Service:* Play begins each time with a serve by the player in the back right court position. The serve must not touch the net.
   — Server, keep serving as long as you are winning points. When you lose the serve, the other team gets to serve.
   — Before a new serve, the players on the serving team only, rotate one position in a CW direction.
2. *Faults:* If the serving team commits any of the following, it loses the serve; this is called "side out." If the receiving team commits any of the following, the serving team earns one point:
   — touching the net with racquet or body
   — reaching over the net with any part of the racquet or body
   — touching the floor on the opponent's side of the net
   — catching or holding the bird
   — a team hitting the bird more than three times in a row
   — any player hitting the bird twice in a row
   — illegally serving

3. Play to nine, eleven, or fifteen points. A two-point lead is needed to win.

GS-149 TENNIS BALLS AND TENNIS CANS PLAY

FOCUS: Visual tracking; hand–eye coordination; manual dexterity

EQUIPMENT: One tennis ball per player; one tennis can per player

ORGANIZATION:

• To further develop visual tracking and refine hand–eye coordination, children are challenged to tossing a tennis ball upward and catching the ball in the can by themselves, then with a partner. Emphasize keeping eyes on the ball until it is in the tennis can and "giving" with the ball as it lands in the can. Have each player collect a tennis ball and can; then find a free space. Check for good spacing.

DESCRIPTION OF ACTIVITY:

1. Toss your tennis ball upward with one hand, let it bounce once; then catch it in the can held by your other hand. Try this trick several times. Switch hands and repeat the task.

   — Can you catch the ball in the can without letting it bounce off the floor? Try several times; then switch hands and repeat.

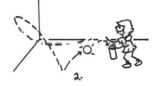

2. Go to a wall. Toss your tennis ball up onto the wall. Let it bounce once off the floor; then try to catch it in the can. Practice five times. Switch hands and try again.

3. Who can toss the ball up, spin around once, then catch it in the tennis can on the first bounce? Do this trick again, but turn in the opposite direction. Switch hands and try again.

4. Let me see you toss the ball up, kneel down, and catch the ball in the tennis can on the first bounce. Do this trick again, but this time sit down. Switch hands and repeat the trick.

5. Hold the tennis can upside down and rest the tennis ball on the bottom of the can. Show me how you can balance the ball in this way while walking; jogging; galloping; skipping; side-stepping.

   — Now try to send the ball upward, quickly flip the can over in your hand, and catch the ball in the can on the first bounce. Can you catch the ball in the can before it bounces?

6. Who can toss the tennis ball under one leg and catch it in the can? Can you toss the ball from behind your back and catch it in the can?

7. Find a partner. Can you underhand-toss a tennis ball to each other and catch it in your tennis cans on the first bounce? on no bounces?

8. Invent a trick of your own. Invent a partner trick.

GS–150 CONTROL DRIBBLING

FOCUS: Footwork; dribbling technique

EQUIPMENT: One soccer ball per player; several cone markers

ORGANIZATION:

• Dribbling is a series of short kicks or taps along the ground, usually alternating the feet to contact the ball. This allows the dribbler to maintain possession of the ball. Scatter several cone markers throughout the play area; then have players get a ball and stand 3 meters (10 feet) from a wall.

DESCRIPTION OF ACTIVITY:

1. *Dribbling Technique:* Use the inside of the foot, not the toe, and keep the ball close in order to maintain better control. Short kicks or taps should be used so that you can "feel" the ball at all times without actually looking at it. Try not to break your running stride, and move in a straight line.

2. *Practice:* Dribble the ball around the play area without touching a cone, another ball, or another player as follows:
   — Use only the inside of either foot.
   — Use only the outside of either foot.
   — Use the inside and outside of either foot.
   — On signal "Change!" exchange your soccer ball with another player and continue.

3. *Shuttle Dribble Relay:* (Form teams of five or six players and have them stand in shuttle formation, one half facing the other about 15 meters [50 feet] away, standing in file formation.) First player, dribble the ball to the opposite file, pass the ball to the next player, and go to the end of the file. How many crossings can your team make in two minutes?

4. *Shadow Dribble:* Find a partner and stand alongside each other with your ball at your feet, in an open space. On the signal "Go!" one player dribble the ball around the play area changing directions, speed, and body movements, while your partner tries to mimic your every action. On the signal "Change!" switch roles.

5. *Square Dribble:* (For each group of four players, mark out a square, with sides about seven or eight steps, and place a cone on each corner. Assign each team to a square and have the four players form a file behind one of the cones.) On the signal "Go!" first player in the file, dribble your ball around the square, circling around each cone as you go. When you reach the first cone, the second player may go; then the third player, and then the fourth. On the signal "Change!" (after three circuits), reverse direction and continue.

6. *Follow-Your-Pass:* (Form groups of six to eight players and have them stand in a circle facing inward. Have each group get a ball.) Using the inside of the foot, pass the ball across the circle to an opposite player; then follow your pass and take the position of that player, who will have vacated that spot by the time you get there. Call out the name of the player to whom you are passing. *Remember the rule*: Kick first, then follow your pass.
   — *Challenge:* Which group can complete thirty passes first?

GS-151 TRAPPING THE BALL

FOCUS: Stopping the ball technique; ball control

EQUIPMENT: One soccer ball per player

ORGANIZATION:

- Have the players find a partner. Present the following techniques and have players practice them in their pairs.

DESCRIPTION OF ACTIVITY:

1. **Sole of Foot:** Keep your heel close to the ground and raise your toe. Crouch slightly with body relaxed. Trap and then quickly prepare to pass.

2. **Inside of Foot:** Lean slightly toward the oncoming ball. Bend your knee to form a wedge with the ground and draw your foot back as it contacts the ball.

3. **Outside of Foot:** This trap is more difficult to master. Lean toward the oncoming ball and contact the ball with the outside of the foot. Place the other foot away from the ball to allow kicking foot a free swing at the ball.

4. **Trap with Shins:** Use this trap when you have plenty of time. Face the oncoming ball; bend both knees toward the ground, forming a wedge between your shins and the ground.

5. **Inside of Leg:** Use this trap to control a low bouncing ball or low pass. Keep the trapping foot close to the ground; then turn toward the oncoming ball, crouch slightly with a bent knee, and wedge the ball between your lower leg and the ground.

6. **Chest:** Use this trap to control a high pass. Arch your back to contact the ball. Let your body sink down and backward so that the ball will drop slowly to the ground. Girls, you may cross your arms for protection, but your arms cannot be used to play the ball.

7. **Stomach:** At contact, lean forward and draw in your abdominal muscles to cause the ball to drop forward.

8. **Top of Foot:** Use this trap to control a dropping ball. Raise your foot and stop the ball in the wedge made by your instep. At contact, draw your foot downward.

9. **Trapping Practice:** Toss the ball up at eye level. Allow it to bounce; then, raising your arms sideways for balance, try to trap the ball using the top of one foot; the top of the other foot; the sole of one foot; the sole of the other foot; repeat each trap ten times.

   — Stand about 3 meters (10 feet) from the wall. Toss the ball to a point about 1 meter (3 feet) up the wall and trap the rebound after the first bounce using the inside of your leg; your shins; your chest; your stomach. Repeat each trap ten times.

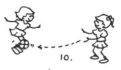

10. Find a partner and stand about 5 meters (16 feet) from each other. Take turns throwing the ball to your partner's chest, stomach, and thighs. Trap the ball and control it using the chest and stomach traps, the inside of leg trap, and the trap with the shins; then kick it back to your partner. After five throws, change roles.

GS–152 BASIC SOCCER KICKS

FOCUS: Kicking techniques; footwork; passing; trapping   **EQUIPMENT:** One soccer ball per player

ORGANIZATION:

• The Instep Kick is the most powerful kick in soccer and, along with the Toe Kick, is used for distance kicking. The Inside-of-the-Foot Kick is generally used for passing but may also be used to score goals. Demonstrate these kicking techniques; then allow players to practice in pairs.

DESCRIPTION OF ACTIVITY:

1. ***Inside-of-the-Foot Kick:*** Place your nonkicking foot beside the ball; then draw your kicking foot back, turning the toe outward. The inside of your foot is now at right angles to the ball's line of flight and the sole is parallel to the ground. Contact the ball with the inside of your foot and follow through in the direction of the kick, straightening the knee.

2. ***Practice:*** Find a partner and stand 5 meters (15 feet) apart. Kick the ball back and forth to each other, using the inside-of-the-foot kick. Receiving partner, trap the ball with the inside-of-the-foot trap. Can you kick-pass the ball so that your partner does not have to move? Remember to trap the ball before you kick it. Now try to kick the ball with the inside of the other foot and trap the ball with the inside of this foot. Who can kick the ball with one foot and trap with the other?

   — Moving in general space, kick-pass the ball to each other. Remember to get the ball under control before you pass the ball back.

3. ***Center-Kick Game:*** Form groups of three players and collect two soccer balls. First and second players, each with a ball, stand facing about 10 meters (30 feet) apart; the third player, stand in the middle. First player, kick to the middle player, who will trap the ball and return it to you; then second player, kick to the middle player. Change places every ten kicks that the center player is able to return. Try to use either foot to kick the ball. Use the sole-of-the-foot trap.

4. ***Instep Kick:*** Approach the ball from an angle, two or three steps behind the ball. Place your nonkicking foot beside the ball about 15 centimeters (6 inches) away from it. Swing your kicking foot from the hip, back and then forward. Point the toe down and heel up, keeping your ankle rigid. Contact the ball with the lower part of the shoelaces underneath the ball, snapping the lower leg forward at the knee. Follow through in the direction of the kick and straighten the knee. Hold your arms out to the side for balance.

   — Show me how you can kick the ball with the toes of your foot. This is called the Toe Kick.

   — Face a wall about 6 meters (20 feet) away. Practice the Instep Kick by kicking the ball to the wall and trapping the rebound. Practice Toe Kicks as well. After every ten kicks, move another giant step away from the wall until you are ten meters (30 feet) or ten giant steps from the wall.

   — Face a partner about 10 meters (30 feet) away. Practice these kicks using your best foot, then your other. Can you kick the ball directly to your partner? Use different traps to bring the ball under control.

GS–153 TARGET KICKING CHALLENGES

FOCUS: Accuracy kicking; trapping; cooperation   **EQUIPMENT:** One soccer-type ball per pair;
two cones per pair;
one hoop per group;
one wall target per pair

ORGANIZATION:

- Have players pair off. Each pair collects a ball and two cones and then finds a free space. Check for good spacing.

DESCRIPTION OF ACTIVITY:

1. ***Goal Kicking:*** Place the cones one giant step apart on the floor; then pace three giant steps away from the cones.

   — Try to kick the ball between the two cones to your partner.

   — Explore using the different kicks you have learned.

   — Explore placing the cones closer together, or stepping farther away from them.

2. ***Hoop Kick:*** (Form groups of three. Players in each group collect one ball and a hoop, then find a free space. Check for good spacing.) Player A, stand in the middle holding the hoop vertically on the floor and out to one side. Player B, try to toe-kick the ball through the hoop. Player C, trap the ball; then take a turn at toe-kicking the ball through the hoop. Start close enough so that your kicks go through the hoop. Gradually move further away. Change the hoop holder after every five kicks. Continue until everyone has had a turn at holding the hoop. Repeat using Instep Kicks and the Inside-of-the-Foot Kicks. Kick with either foot.

3. ***Kicking a Moving Ball:*** (Mark off several 1-meter [3-foot] square targets on the walls, 30 centimeters [1 foot] above the ground; also mark off a line 4 meters [12 feet] from the target. Have players find a partner, get a ball each, and stand about 6 meters [20 feet] from the wall targets.) In turn, dribble your ball to the line; then kick it at the target using the instep kick. Watch the ball as your foot contacts it; then field the ball and take nine more kicks. Repeat ten Instep Kicks with the other foot; then repeat using Inside-of-the-Foot Kicks.

4. ***Passing Shuttle:*** (Form teams of six players. Divide each team in half and have each half stand facing the other 10 meters [30 feet] apart. Set up two cones, 2 meters [6 feet] apart and between the two groups.) The first player, dribble the ball forward; then kick it between the cones to the second player and run to the end of the opposite file. Second player, repeat the pattern, and so on.

   — Which team can be the first to complete thirty kick-passes through the cones?

5. ***Performance Checking:*** Have one partner make ten Inside-of-the-Foot Kicks at a low wall target or hockey net, while the other partner keeps track of the number of kicks that hit the target. Teacher records the scores; then the partners switch roles. Repeat for the Toe Kick and Instep Kick.

FOCUS: Dribbling; kicking accuracy

EQUIPMENT: One or more partially deflated soccer balls per game; one soccer ball per player; one wall target per pair; six to eight bowling pins per game; nine long ropes and garbage cans (boxes)

ORGANIZATION:

• These games further reinforce dribbling and kicking skills.

DESCRIPTION OF ACTIVITY:

1. *Circle Soccer:* (Divide the class into teams of eight to ten players. Have the two teams form a large circle, with each team facing the other across the circle. Players should be about arm's length apart. One team is given the partially deflated ball.) On signal "Go!" kick the ball, trying to send it past the opposing players below the waist. Score one point each time the ball is kicked through the opponent's side of the circle. Play to five points; then challenge another team.

2. *Soccer Dodgeball:* (Form teams of about five players. One team move to the middle of the circle. The other teams, form a circle around them.) Circle players, try to kick the ball to hit the inside players below the knees. Inside players, you may not touch the ball with your hands, except to protect your faces. Teams, take turns in the middle for two minutes each, and count one point each time an inside player is hit. No one is eliminated. The team scoring the most points wins. Remember, keep your kicks low to the ground! Also, remember to trap the ball first, then kick it!

3. *Bowling Pin Soccer:* (Form teams of five players and have the teams stand side by side facing each other on opposite lines, about 10 meters [30 feet] apart. Place a row of pins across the middle of the play area between the teams and give each team three soccer balls.) Players, kick the balls from behind your line and try to knock down as many bowling pins as you can. Trap the ball before kicking and keep your kicks low. You may pass to a teammate who is in a better position for a kick at the pins. The team knocking down the most pins wins. Reset the pins and start again.

4. *Cone Marker Golf:* (Create a golf course with five, seven or nine holes by placing cone markers around a large area. Design the course so players must kick around obstacles [buildings, trees, fences, posts, etc.]. Create tee-off circles with long ropes near each cone; then number the cones and issue each player a score card. Form groups of two or three players and assign each group a starting tee.) Tee-off with a punt kick from inside the rope circle. Kick the ball to hit each cone (or roll into a box or garbage can) in order around the course and keep your score. Any kick can be used, and each kick or "golf shot" is counted. Tally your score at completion of course. Lowest score wins!

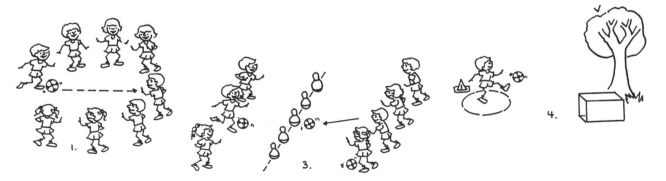

FOCUS: Technique and practice

EQUIPMENT: One soccer ball per group; whistle

ORGANIZATION:

- Tackling is a legal move to take the ball away from an opponent. Explain the technique of tackling, have players practice the skill, and then play End Ball in an area 10 × 20 meters (30 × 60 feet). To begin, have players pair up, each pair with a soccer ball to share, and find a free space.

DESCRIPTION OF ACTIVITY:

1. **Technique of Tackling:** The tackle may only be made from the front or from the sides, with the feet or the shoulders. Using the hands or tackling from behind is illegal. Face your opponent and watch your opponent's feet. Keep your weight evenly balanced on both feet with the knees bent, so that you may move quickly in any direction. Make your tackle when your opponent is off balance or about to kick or pass. Once you have gained possession of the ball, pass to a teammate.

2. **Practice:** Stand facing each other about 5 meters (15 feet) apart. One partner with the soccer ball, dribble toward your other partner, who tries to tackle the ball and gain possession. Take turns dribbling and tackling.

3. **Soccer Pirates:** (Choose one third of the class to be "Pirates" without a ball; the other two thirds scatter, each player with a ball.) On signal "Pirates are coming!" each Pirate try to steal a ball without touching another player. The player whose ball is stolen becomes the new Pirate. Who can last the game without becoming a Pirate?

4. **End Ball:** (Divide into teams of four players: two on offense and two on defense.) Offensive team, bring the ball from one endline to the other, dribbling and passing to each other. Defensive team, try to tackle a player with the ball or intercept. Score one point each time the ball is dribbled (not kicked) over the endline. If the ball goes out-of-bounds, the offensive team gets possession of the ball at that spot. Change the offense and defense after three attempts to score a point.

— Play three-on-three.

FOCUS: Goalkeeping techniques; kicking accuracy; partner and group work

EQUIPMENT: One soccer ball per pair; two cone markers per pair

ORGANIZATION:

- Explain and demonstrate the following techniques; then have the players practice the skills. To soften the kick for the goalkeeper, use sponge soccer balls or partially deflated soccer balls.

DESCRIPTION OF ACTIVITY:

1. *Technique:*

    — *Stance:* Stand with feet shoulder-width apart and lean forward slightly with your weight on the balls of your feet. Raise your hands in front of your body at chest level, ready to stop the oncoming ball. Keep yourself between the goal and the ball. Watch the play and move out from the goal to stop the ball.

    — *Stopping a Ground Ball:* Turn sideways and kneel on the knee closer to the ball, positioning yourself directly in front of the ball. "Give" with the hands as the ball contacts your hands.

    — *Stopping a Ball at Chest Height:* Move quickly into the path of the ball with outstretched hands. As contact is made, pull the ball toward your chest. Smother the ball with your chest and shoulders to secure the ball.

2. *Diving After a Ball:* If the ball is low, land so that your body is between the ball and the goal. With outstretched hands, pull the ball quickly into the body, bringing the knees up and the head down to protect the ball. If the ball is high and wide, try to tap or punch the ball out, around, or over the goal. Hit with the palms (best) or with the closed fist.

3. *Dribbling to Put the Ball Back into Play:* Dribble the ball with two hands; then either throw the ball into play, or punt. Learn to dribble without looking at the ball.

4. *Throwing the Ball into Play:* The Throw-in is more accurate than the kick. Use either the "Baseball Throw" or the "Sling Throw" with the throwing arm fully extended and the ball cradled between the arm and the wrist. Throw to a nearby teammate.

5. *Punting the Ball:* Guide the ball downward with both hands toward the kicking foot. Swing the kicking leg through. Contact the ball with the kicking foot on the instep (shoelaces), in an upward motion. Follow through with the kicking foot pointing toward the target. Finish by rising up on the toes of the nonkicking foot.

6. *Thrower and Goalie:* (Form pairs. Have each pair collect a ball and two cones and set up the cones 2 meters [6 feet] apart, as a goal; then set up a throwing line about 5 meters [15 feet] in front of the goal. If indoors, set up the goal against a wall. In each pair, one player is the Goalie, the other the Thrower.) Thrower, throw the ball to the Goalie to stop: Throw the ball low (a ground ball); waist or chest high; high; wide. Goalie, adopt the Goalie Stance, field the ball; then dribble and instep kick the ball back; or throw the ball into play, or punt the ball back to your partner.

7. *Two-on-Two Soccer:* Form groups of four; each pair in the group, set up your own goal, 15 meters (16 yards) away from the other pair's goal. On each team, one partner is the Goalie; the other is a Forward. Change roles often. Play to five points; then challenge another pair.

8. *Three-on-Two:* (Form groups of five players: three players on offense and two on defense. Set up two cones as a goal and mark out a goal area.) Offensive players pass and dribble the ball to get a good shot on goal. No player is allowed in the goal area. Take turns at being on offense, and change positions often.

GS–157 GOAL-KICKING GAMES

FOCUS: Passing; dribbling; goalkeeping; goal kicking

EQUIPMENT: One soccer ball per three players; two cone markers per three players; two sets of pinnies

ORGANIZATION:

- Teach the Give and Go play first; then play the game Three-on-Three. Form groups of three players and have them set up goals with their two cone markers. No. 1 player is the Goalie; No. 2 stands about 6 meters (20 feet) from the goal. Player No. 3 stands with the ball about 10 meters (30 feet) from the goal.

DESCRIPTION OF ACTIVITY:

1. *Give and Go:* Player No. 3, pass the ball to No. 2 and run toward the goal. No. 2, trap the ball with the foot and pass it back to No. 3, who receives it in front of the goal. No. 3, take a shot on goal. All change places after five kicks.

2. *Three-on-Three:* (Form teams of six to nine players. Have each team put on pinnies and line up on opposite sidelines of the play area.) The first three players from each team, come to the middle for a face-off (the ball is dropped between two players). From then on, try to score by kicking the ball through the opponent's line of players.

   — Sideline players, use goalkeeper techniques to stop the ball. The six middle players, trap, pass, and dribble to score.

   — After a point has been scored, or after 1½ minutes, middle players return to the sidelines and the next three players take over in the middle. Continue until all players have played.

   — Sideline players trap the ball and kick it back to a teammate.

GS 158 THE THROW-IN

FOCUS: Technique; practice; partner work

EQUIPMENT: One soccer ball per pair

ORGANIZATION:

- The Throw-in is taken when the ball goes out-of-bounds. An opponent of the player who last touched the ball takes the Throw-in from outside the sideline. Explain and demonstrate the Throw-in technique; then have players choose a partner, get a ball, and stand about 5 meters (15 feet) apart.

DESCRIPTION OF ACTIVITY:

1. *Technique of the Throw-In:* Place both hands behind the ball and throw the ball from behind your head. A part of both feet must also be in contact with the ground until the ball is released. Keep both feet parallel, or place one foot slightly ahead of the other, behind the sideline. Bend your body well back at the waist to add power. Rock your weight from your heels, to the balls of your feet, to your toes as the throw is made.

2. *Running Throw-In:* (Used to add power to the throw and to save time.) Take several running steps before releasing the ball. Make sure that both feet are in contact with the ground as the ball is released.

3. *Throw-In to a Partner:* Stand facing your partner. Using the Throw-in technique, throw the ball to each other. Thrower, throw the ball to land below the receiver's knees. Receiver, trap the ball using one of the traps learned; then kick-pass the ball back to the thrower. After ten Throws-ins, change positions.

FOCUS: Technique; practice; partner and group work

EQUIPMENT: One volleyball or other light ball per player

ORGANIZATION:

- Heading a ball is hitting the ball with the front or side of the forehead. Heading is used to pass to a teammate, pass over an opponent's head, to prevent a goal, to shoot for goal, as a trap, or to change the direction of the ball. Use volleyballs, light sponge balls, or slightly deflated soccer balls in the early stages of teaching heading.

DESCRIPTION OF ACTIVITY:

1. *Heading Technique:*

   — *Preparation:* Lean back, bend the trunk, and extend the head forward toward the ball and keep the eyes open.

   — *Contact:* As the head and trunk come forward and the neck muscles are tensed, swing both arms back for balance, and take the ball on the forehead at the hairline. To change the direction of the ball, hit it on the side of your forehead and twist your head in the direction you want the ball to go.

   — *Jump Heading:* Jump to make contact with the ball at the top of the jump.

   — *Downward Head:* At the moment of contact with the ball, snap your head forward and downward to put your chin on your chest.

   — *Safety:* Keep your eyes open at all times and line the ball up with your forehead; not the top of your head (this usually results in a headache). Remember that <u>you</u> hit the ball. Don't let the ball hit you. To lessen the impact, snap the head out toward the ball.

2. *Practice:*

   — Hold the ball in two hands. Watch the ball continuously as you touch your forehead at the hairline with the ball.

   — Toss the ball up slightly above your head, and tap the ball up and out with your forehead.

3. *Wall Drill:* Stand about two steps away from a wall. Throw the ball high on the wall; then head the ball back to the wall. Repeat ten times.

   — Turn sideways and try to head the ball back to the wall using the side of your head. Turn to use the other side of the head. Watch the ball at all times.

4. *Triangle Drill:* (Form groups of three players. Have each group get a ball and stand in a triangle about 2 meters [6 feet] apart.) Player No. 1, toss the ball to No. 2, who heads it to No. 3. Player No. 3, catch the ball and toss it to No. 1, who heads the ball to No. 2. Player No. 2, catch the ball and toss it to No. 3 to head to No. 1. Continue the pattern: tossing, heading and catching. Reverse the direction. Remember to move so that your body is facing the oncoming ball when heading.

GS-160 PUNT KICKING

FOCUS: Technique; distance kicking; partner and group work; related game

EQUIPMENT: One soccer ball per player; several colored beanbags; one coin; six cone markers

ORGANIZATION:

- Conduct this lesson outdoors, if possible. The punt kick, used by the goalie, can be made from the stationary position or on the run. Explain and demonstrate the punt kick; then have players practice. Have them find a partner and stand 10 meters (30 feet) apart.

DESCRIPTION OF ACTIVITY:

1. **Punt Kick Technique:**
   — Hold the ball with both hands at waist level in front of your body and directly over your kicking leg.
   — Take three steps forward, starting with your nonkicking foot.
   — Look at the ball. Lean over it as you guide it down over your kicking foot.
   — Swing your kicking foot forward and contact the middle of the ball with your instep (shoelaces).
   — It should feel as though you are kicking "through the ball," with your foot pointing toward the target. Finish by rising on the toes of your nonkicking foot.

2. **Free Practice:** Punt the ball back and forth to your partner. Observe each other's technique and coach each other.
3. **Group Kicks:** (Form groups of four to six players. Have the first group, the Kickers, line up behind the end line of the field; all others scatter over the field to act as retrievers.) The Kickers, take five kicks each and try to kick the ball as far as possible. The Retrievers, mark the farthest spot where the ball lands, using the beanbags; then roll the balls back to the Kickers. Take turns at being the kicking group.
   — Try the punt with a walking then a running approach.

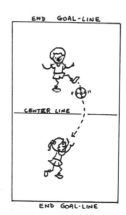

4. **Forcing Back:** (Divide the class into two equal teams and have each team scatter on opposite sides of the soccer field, marked out with cones. Toss a coin to see which team will be the first to punt the ball.)
   — Try to punt the ball across the other team's goal line to score a point. The first team to get three points wins the game.
   — To start, the team with the ball may choose any player to punt the ball. The first kick is taken at a point 18 meters (20 yards) back from the middle line.
   — Players on the other team, kick the ball back from the spot where the ball was first touched. If the ball is caught, the receiving team, you may advance five paces to take a kick.
   — If the ball is caught by a player in the end zone, no point is awarded and the game continues.
   — The player who fields the ball should take the kick or give a player who hasn't kicked the ball yet a turn.

VARIATIONS:

a. To increase participation, use more than one soccer ball.
b. Substitute a football for the soccer ball.

GS–161 VOLLEY KICKING

FOCUS: Technique; practice; partner work; related games

EQUIPMENT: One soccer ball per pair; three softball bases per game; one home plate; four bases per game; one volleyball court, net, poles; one large light ball (beachball)

ORGANIZATION:

• The Volley Kick is performed while the ball is in the air. Explain and/or demonstrate the technique; then have the players practice before playing the related game. To begin, have players pair off and each pair get a ball, then scatter in a free space.

DESCRIPTION OF ACTIVITY:

1. *Technique:*
   — Kicker, run forward to meet the oncoming ball. Keep your eyes on the ball as you plant your nonkicking foot; then swing the kicking foot forward to meet the ball in the air.
   — Kick the ball on the instep (shoelaces). As you lean forward at the waist, follow through with the kicking foot in the direction of the target.
2. *Practice:* Find a partner and stand 5 meters (15 feet) apart, facing each other. First player, throw the ball to your partner for him or her to Volley Kick back to you. Try the Volley Kick five times with each foot; then change. Strive for control. Change roles and repeat.
3. *Kickball Soccer:* (Form teams of about nine or ten players. The fielding team takes the regular softball positions on the field, with the Pitcher holding the ball. The kicking team lines up behind home plate.)
   — First player on the kicking team, stand just in front of home plate, ready to Volley Kick the ball thrown by the pitcher. As soon as the ball is kicked, Kicker, run around as many bases as you can. You get one point for first base; two points for second base; . . . six points for six bases.
   — Player fielding the ball, stand still and hold the ball until all the fielders line up behind you. As soon as they are lined up, dribble the ball around them back to the head of the line; then call "Stop!"
   — Runner, on "Stop!" stop where you are and count the number of bases passed and return to the kicking team.
   — After everyone has had a turn on the kicking team, teams change roles.
4. *Beachball Soccer:* (Play this game on a 8 × 16 meter [25 × 50 foot] area or on a volleyball court, using a large, light ball [beachball]. The object of the game is for each team to send the ball back and forth over the net so that it touches the ground on the opponent's side. Adjust the height of the net according to the players' ability.)
   — Server, start the game by lightly punting the ball over the net. From then on, the ball may be volley kicked or headed as many times as necessary by one team to get it over the net. The ball must not be touched by arms or hands while in play.
   — A point is scored when the opposition fail to return the ball over the net properly. Only the serving team can score.
   — *Variation:* Allow the ball to bounce once before being kicked or headed.

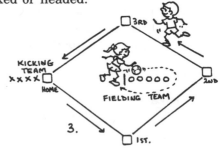

GS–162 SOCCER STATION WORK

FOCUS: Dribbling; kicking; passing; trapping; heading

EQUIPMENT: Four soccer balls; one garbage can; one bleach bottle or cone; four cone markers; one chair

ORGANIZATION:

- Divide the class into four teams of four to six players. Set up the four stations as outlined. Explain the activities at each station. Allow about four minutes at each station; then have teams rotate CCW to the next station.

DESCRIPTION OF ACTIVITY:

Station 1. Dribble and Shoot: From behind the line, dribble in and out of the cones to move close to the chair. Shoot the ball through the legs of the chair, retrieve the ball on the other side, dribble around the last cone and then back to the line to pass to the next player. Continue.

Station 2. Head the Ball: Form two files of two or three players in shuttle formation 3 meters (9 feet) apart. No. 1 head the ball to No. 2, who heads the ball into the garbage pail. No. 1 and No. 2, change sides and the game continues. Other players, help by retrieving loose balls.

Station 3. Hit and Run: Four players, form a semicircle. No. 1 with the ball, start in the center behind the bleach bottle. No. 1, kick to No. 2, who kicks back trying to hit the bottle. No. 1, then kick to No. 3, who kicks to hit the bottle. When four and five have had a turn, No. 5, take one's place in the center. Continue. Center player, reset the bottle if knocked down.

Station 4. Shot on Goal: Form two files of two or three players facing each other on opposite sides of the goal (2 cones about 1 meter [3 feet] apart). No. 1, kick the ball through the goal to be fielded by No. 2. Then No. 2, trap the ball and shoot at goal for No. 3 to trap and kick. After your turn, go to the end of the opposite file. Continue.

GS–163 SOCCER OBSTACLE COURSE

FOCUS: Dribbling; ball control

EQUIPMENT: One soccer ball per player; four cone markers; one hoop; one bench; one chair; one set high jump stands and bar; floor tape

ORGANIZATION:

- Form groups of four to six players and have each group set up an obstacle course as shown.

DESCRIPTION OF ACTIVITY:

1. *Obstacle Course:* When the first player gets to the bench, allow the next player to go. Suggestions:
   - dribble around the cones 3 meters (9 feet) apart
   - dribble through the chair
   - pass the ball to the bench and receive the rebound
   - dribble around the cone
   - dribble under the bar, jump over the bar, and retrieve the ball
   - dribble to circle the cone
   - take a shot on goal (hoop taped to the wall)
   - retrieve the rebound and dribble back to the start
2. Each team design your own soccer obstacle course.

GS–164 MANY-GOAL SOCCER

FOCUS: Lead-up games; soccer skills; positional play; offense and defense

EQUIPMENT: Four portable goals (or cone markers); two or more partially inflated soccer balls (utility balls or sponge balls); one set of pinnies per team

ORGANIZATION:

- Form two equal teams and have one team wear the pinnies. Play on a soccer field if outdoors, and on a basketball court if indoors. Assign an adjacent end goal and a side goal to each team to attack. The teams will defend their goals. Have teams choose a goalie to stand at each goal. Change goalies frequently.

DESCRIPTION OF ACTIVITY:

1. To start, each team get a ball and place it at the center. On the signal "Go!" kick the balls into play, trying to score a goal at either of the opposition's goals.

2. You may touch the ball with any part of your body except your arm from shoulders to fingertips. Only the goalies can handle the ball. If a player touches the ball with hands or arms, the other team gets a free kick.

3. Indoors, the ball may be played off the walls. Each team keeps its own score.

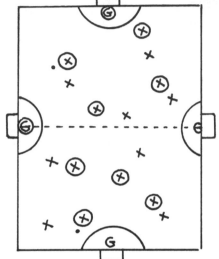

GS–165 ZONE SOCCER

ORGANIZATION:

EQUIPMENT: See GS-164.

- Mark out the field and place cones to mark the three center lines as shown. Form two teams of eight to twelve players per team. Each team divides into Forwards and Backs and takes up the field positions in the diagram. Have the two Centers toss a coin to see which team kicks off.

DESCRIPTION OF ACTIVITY:

1. The Center who won the toss, kick off from the center of the field. Then the offensive Forwards, try to kick the ball across the opponent's goal line. The defensive Backs, try to prevent the offensive Forwards from scoring by tackling or interception; then gain possession of the ball to score across their goal line.

2. Only the Forwards can score; you may go anywhere but must not cross back over your own center zone line. Backs, you may not cross over your own center zone line. Forwards and Backs, change positions every five minutes.

3. If the ball goes out of bounds, it is thrown in by an opponent at the spot where it crossed the line.

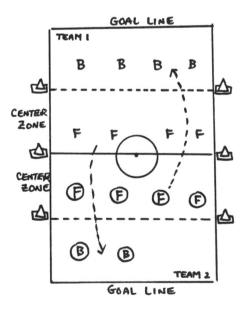

GS–166 FOUR-A-SIDE SOCCER

FOCUS: Lead-up game; offense and defense; the throw-in

EQUIPMENT: One soccer ball per game; four cone markers; one coin; one set of pinnies per game

ORGANIZATION:

- Use a 12 meter × 20 meter (13 yard × 22 yard) play area and place two cones 3 meters (10 feet) apart in the middle of each endline as goals. Form two teams of four players and have each team occupy half of the play area. Toss a coin to see who kicks off first.

DESCRIPTION OF ACTIVITY:

1. Start the game with a kick-off at center; then try to score a goal by kicking the ball between the opposition's cones. The other team, try to intercept the ball and score.

2. After a goal, the opposite team kicks off from the center. The kick-off must be kicked to a teammate first; from then on, the ball may be kicked by any player.

3. The other team is awarded a free kick after rough play or when an opposition player touches the ball with the hands.

4. The opposition team throws the ball back into the play area if it goes out over the sidelines or endlines. To throw the ball in, a player must hold the ball overhead in both hands and have both feet in contact with the ground throughout the throw.

GS–167 SIX-A-SIDE SOCCER

EQUIPMENT: See GS-166.

ORGANIZATION:

- Mark out the field to the following dimensions: Field—60 meters × 40 meters (190 feet × 120 feet); Goals—4.5 meters (15 feet); Center Circle—5 meters (15 feet) diameter; Goal Circle—15 meters (45 feet) radius. Form two teams of six to eight players per team (six players on the field and one or two substitutes). Each team divides into three Forwards (near the center line), two Halfbacks (halfway between the center line and the goal line, and one Goalie (in front of the goal). Have the two Center Forwards toss a coin to see which team kicks off. Forwards, Backs, and Goalie, change positions every five minutes.

DESCRIPTION OF ACTIVITY:

1. The Center who won the toss, kick off from the center of the field. From then on, players may move in any part of the field and any player may score. Pass the ball to your teammates to score a goal. The ball must not be played with the hands, except by the Goalie.

2. If the ball goes out of bounds, the throw-in is taken by an opponent at the spot where it crossed the line.

3. If the attacking team causes the ball to go out over the endline, a defensive player kicks it back into play from the endline. If the ball was last touched by a defender and goes over the endline, an attacker kicks it back from a corner.

4. For excessively rough play, a penalty kick is awarded at that spot.

GS–168 SOCCER RULES

FOCUS: Knowledge of the game

ORGANIZATION:

- Teach the following information in the classroom. A knowledge of the rules of the game will allow players to understand the need for proper skill development and the necessity of avoiding bad habits. Teachers should modify these rules to suit their own conditions. Reducing the size of the play area, playing with a smaller or lighter ball, increasing the number of players on teams are but a few ways of modifying the rules to meet the needs of the players. Emphasize the importance of maintaining positions and not blindly following the ball. Point out that short accurate kicks between players are better than long upfield kicks.

DESCRIPTION OF ACTIVITY:

1. *The Field:* For elementary schools, modify the size of the playing area to 75 meters × 55 meters (80 yards × 60 yards). Place the center spot 9 meters (10 yards) out; the goal area 4.5 meters (5 yards) out; and the penalty area 14 meters (15 yards) out from the goal line.
2. *Team Positions:* A team consists of eleven players. The Goalkeeper prevents the ball from going in goal; the two Fullbacks are defensive players; the five Forwards advance the ball and try to score goals; the three Halfbacks advance and retreat with the play.
3. *The Game:* The team winning the toss gets the choice of kicking off or which end to defend. Play eight-minute quarters with two-minute breaks and a five-minute break at halftime. Change ends at the half. Allow unlimited substitutions for elementary soccer.
4. *For Girls:* Play all the rules, but when blocking a ball, girls are permitted to fold arms across the chest to meet the ball or play it with the shoulder.
   — Kicks: On all the following kicks, the opposing players must be 6.5 meters (8 yards) away.
5. *The Kick-Off:* Taken at center field at the start of each period of play, or after a goal has been scored. Each player must stay in his or her own half of the field until the ball has been kicked. The ball must be kicked toward the opponent's goal line.
6. *Goal Kick:* If an offensive player causes the ball to go behind the defending team's goal line but not into the goal, the defending team is awarded a goal kick, which is taken from within the goal area, usually by the Goalie or Fullback.
7. *Corner Kick:* If a defensive player causes the ball to go behind his or her own goal line, the offensive team is awarded a corner kick, to be taken inside 1 meter (1 yard) of the nearest corner of the field.
8. *Direct Free Kick:* A Free Kick from which a goal may be scored is awarded after an intentional Penal offense has occurred, such as:
   — charging an opponent dangerously
   — charging from behind
   — jumping at an opponent
   — kicking or tripping an opponent
   — holding, striking, or pushing an opponent
   — handling the ball with arm or hand (except the goalkeeper)
9. *Throw-In:* If a player causes the ball to go over one of the sidelines, the other team is awarded a Throw-in at that point on the sideline where the ball crossed. Throw-in rules include:
   — the thrower must be outside the playing field
   — both feet must be in contact with the ground
   — the ball must be thrown from over the head with both hands
10. *Offside:* If in the opponent's half, an attacking player must have at least two opponents (including the goalie) in front of him or her at the time the ball was passed ahead. Penalty: an indirect free kick, from which a goal may not be scored directly.

GS-169 THROWING AND CATCHING SKILLS

FOCUS: Throwing and catching; gripping the ball

EQUIPMENT: One softball per player; one softball glove per player

ORGANIZATION:

• Review and demonstrate the techniques for gripping the ball and using a glove to catch a ball. Review the overhand throwing technique. Allow players to practice at a wall. Have each player get a ball and stand about 4 meters (12 feet) from a wall. Check for good spacing.

DESCRIPTION OF ACTIVITY:

1. ***Full-Hand Grip:*** If you have smaller hands, use this grip. Space your thumb and fingers evenly around the ball and hold it with your finger pads, not in the palm of your hand. You should be able to see "daylight" between the ball along the side.

2. ***Two-Finger Grip:*** Place your thumb on the underside of the ball and your index and middle fingers on top. Your third and fourth fingers support the ball along the side.

3. ***Using a Glove:*** Put the glove onto your nonthrowing hand. Put your fingers into the four glove fingers. Check that your fingers are not too deep in the glove: The back strap should come across your knuckles. The glove will protect your hand and increase the catching area.

4. ***Practice Tasks:***
   — "Snap" the ball into the pocket of your glove with short hard throws. Repeat several times.
   — Toss the ball into the air and catch it in your glove. Repeat. How high can you toss the ball and still catch it?
   — Underhand throw the ball at a wall and catch the rebound with your glove.

5. ***Overhand Throwing:***
   — ***Stance:*** Stand with your nonthrowing shoulder to the wall and your feet comfortably apart. Hold the ball in the Full-Hand or Two-Finger Grip.
   — ***Throwing Action:*** Shift your weight to the rear foot. At the same time, swing your throwing hand up behind your shoulder so that the ball is just above your ear. As you step forward with your front foot, bring your throwing arm forward with your elbow leading. Snap your wrist forward and down as you release the ball and follow through in the direction of the wall. Keep your eyes on an imaginary target throughout the throw.

6. ***Catching the Ball:*** Stand with your feet comfortably apart and your knees slightly bent. Move in front of the oncoming ball, watch it, and catch with both hands. If the ball is low, catch with your fingers pointing down. If the ball is high, catch with your fingers up. Watch the ball enter your glove and trap it with your free hand, bending your elbows to soften the ball's impact.

7. ***Practice Tasks:***
   — Mime the throwing and catching actions several times; then overhand throw the ball at a wall at an imaginary target. Can you catch the ball before it hits the ground?
   — How quickly can you make the catch, then throw the ball back to the wall? Try low throws; higher throws.
   — Turn your back to the wall. Show me how quickly you can pivot to face the wall and still throw a ball at your target.

GS—170 OVERHAND THROWING TASKS

FOCUS: Throwing and catching on the move; for distance; partner work

EQUIPMENT: One softball per pair; one softball glove per player; one softball base per pair

ORGANIZATION:

• Explain the technique of softball throwing and catching described below. To allow players to practice, have them find a partner and stand 6 meters (20 feet) apart.

DESCRIPTION OF ACTIVITY:

1. *Throwing Practice:* Stand facing your partner; throw and catch the ball. Aim at your partner's chest and watch the ball at all times. After each five successful throws and catches, move back a step each, and repeat.

   — Throw the ball high to make your partner move under the ball.

2. *Throwing on the Move:* (Find an open space.) Move around in your space, throwing the ball back and forth to your partner. Change direction often. Throw the ball wide, so your partner will have to reach to catch the ball.

3. *Throwing for Distance:* Find your throwing range. Move away from each other, throwing and catching until you can no longer successfully throw or catch the ball.

GS—171 SIDEARM THROW

FOCUS: Sidearm throwing technique; partner work

EQUIPMENT: See GS-170.

ORGANIZATION:

• The Sidearm Throw is used for shorter and quicker throws than the Overhand Throw and is the most effective throw for infielders (for example, from shortstop to second baseman; from pitcher to first baseman). Explain the technique; then allow players to practice. Have them find a partner and stand about 5 meters (16 feet) apart.

DESCRIPTION OF ACTIVITY:

1. *Throwing Action:* Extend your upper throwing arm out diagonally and down from your shoulder and your forearm straight up from your elbow. Swing your arm forward with the forearm parallel to the ground. Release the ball and follow through with your arm across your body.

2. *Practice:* Stand facing your partner; throw sidearm to your partner aiming at your partner's chest. When catching, watch the ball all the way into your glove. After five successful throws and catches, move back a step each, and repeat.

3. *Throw to First:* (Have partners collect one base and one ball and find an open space.)

   — Partner A, stand on the base with one foot contacting the base; then throw ground balls to partner B.

   — Partner B, field the balls thrown by A; then throw sidearm back to A.

   — Partner A, watch the path of the incoming ball; step toward it with one foot and stretch forward to make the catch while keeping the other foot in contact with the base. Change roles after ten throws.

GS–172 THROWING AND CATCHING GAMES

FOCUS: Overhand and sidearm throwing; catching

EQUIPMENT: One softball per pair; one softball glove per player; four bases

ORGANIZATION:

• Form teams of six to eight players; then have each team form a circle about 6 meters (20 feet) diameter, with players well spaced. Have players get a glove each and one ball per team.

DESCRIPTION OF ACTIVITY:

1. **25-Up:** Players, try to complete twenty-five consecutive overhand throws and catches by passing to a teammate across the circle. You may not throw to a player alongside you. Count your score out loud. Can you make twenty-five throws before the other teams do? If the ball is dropped or misthrown, start counting again from zero. Try to establish a pattern to your throwing by throwing to the same player each time if possible; for example: No. 1 throws to No. 4; No. 4 throws to No. 7; No. 7 throws to No. 2; No. 2 throws to No. 5; No. 5 throws to No. 8; No. 8 throws to No. 3; No. 3 throws to No. 6; No. 6 throws to No. 1.

— Repeat using the Sidearm Throw.

2. **Around the World:** (Form groups of five players: One Batter, One Catcher, and Three Base players.) Batter, stand with one foot on the home plate. On the signal "Go!" from the Catcher, try to run to touch a foot to all the bases and home plate again before the base players can throw the ball to first, second, third base, and then back to home plate. Take turns at being the Batter. Rotate positions after each turn.

FOCUS: Ready position; visual tracking; fielding technique; throwing

EQUIPMENT: One softball per player; one softball glove per player

ORGANIZATION:

- Review and demonstrate the fielding techniques; then allow players to practice. For correct fielding technique, players should turn to face the ball and move into the path of the ball; watch the ball constantly until it falls into the glove; use both hands to trap the ball; and "give" with the hands to cushion the ball's impact. Have players find a partner and collect a glove each and a ball to share.

DESCRIPTION OF ACTIVITY:

1. **Catching a Low Ball:** Position yourself so that you are directly in front of the oncoming ball and kneel on one knee. Form a basket with your hand and glove, your little fingers touching and pointing down. Keep your eyes on the ball until you feel it in your glove; then "give" with your hands to cushion the ball's impact. If the ball rolling toward you is a grounder, turn your side to it, place your front knee on the ground, and field the ball in front of that knee.

2. **Catching a High Ball:** To catch a fly ball, put your thumbs together and raise them to your chin. Follow the path of the ball until it hits your glove; then "give" with your hands. Bend your knees slightly as you catch.

3. **Partner Tasks:**

   — Stand about 6 meters (20 feet) apart and throw sidearm grounders to each other.

   — Throw the ball to each other, making it bounce once before it reaches your partner.

   — Collect another ball so that you have one each. Throw grounders to each other at the same time.

   — At a wall, one partner overhand throw the ball to the wall for the other partner to catch; then reverse roles.

   — Using two softballs at the same time, throw a high (fly ball) to your partner, who must move under it to make the catch. Repeat ten times.

4. **Pick-Off:** Put one ball away, One player, throw fly balls to your partner. Partner, after you catch the fly ball, quickly throw the ball back to your partner, using the Overhand Throw. Repeat ten times. Repeat again using the Sidearm Throw.

5. **Fielding Triangle:** Form groups of three and stand in a triangle formation. First player, throw the ball along the ground toward the second player, who quickly fields the ball and throws a grounder to the third player. Repeat with high throws. Remember to watch the ball constantly until it falls into your glove, trap with both hands, and give with your hands and arms to cushion the ball's force.

6. **Grounders Relay:** (Divide the class into teams of six players; then have each team stand in shuttle formation about 5 meters [15 feet] apart. Give each of the six players a number; then explain the relay procedure. One file of players throws grounders while the other fields the ball and throws overhand to the first players. Have one team demonstrate the action.)

   — Player 1, throw a grounder to Player 2 on the opposite side and cut to the right to run and follow your throw; then stand at the end of the opposite field.

   — Player 2, field the ball; then throw it overhand to Player 3. Run, cutting to the right to follow your throw, and stand at the end of the opposite file.

   — Player 3, field the ball; then throw a grounder to Player 4.

   — The relay continues until each player has thrown and caught a grounder twice.

   — Count the number of times your team exchanges the ball within two minutes. Can you beat that number as I time you again?

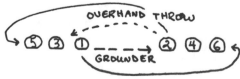

GS-174 BASE RUNNING_____

FOCUS: Base running and tagging technique; agility; team work

EQUIPMENT: Four bases per group or four cone markers

ORGANIZATION:

• Review the Infield Base Positions and softball terms *diamond, Infield,* and *Outfield*. Demonstrate tagging technique and have players practice base tagging through team activities.

• Divide the class into two groups. Have each group get four bases and place them in the form of a softball diamond. Have each group practice running around the bases and tagging with one foot.

DESCRIPTION OF ACTIVITY:

1. ***Base-Running Warm-Up Circuit:*** Starting with one foot on home base, first runner, sprint to first base, then jog to second base, sprint to third, and jog home, touching the inside of each base with your foot as you go. Swing out slightly as you run and avoid turning at right angles. As soon as the previous runner reaches second base, the next runner may go. Repeat the circuit four times.

2. ***Base-Tagging:*** (To practice, have players form groups of four, get two bases per group, and place them 15 meters [45 feet] apart.) First player, begin with your foot on the base. Sprint to the next base to "tag" it by stepping on it on the right side (to avoid colliding with the baseman). Tag the base with either foot, but do not break stride. As soon as the first player has reached first base, the second runner, you may go, and so on until all runners have run five times.

3. ***Round-the-Bases Relay:*** (Place one base in each corner of a 15-meter [50-foot] square; then place a cone in front of each base. Form four equal teams and have each team stand in file formation behind a cone inside the square.) On signal "Go!" each player, in turn, run CCW to touch all four bases with one foot; then return to your team to tag the next runner. The first team to complete the relay and sit cross-legged wins. As you run, swing out slightly from the base path. When approaching each base, lean into your turn, to tag the inside edge of the base.

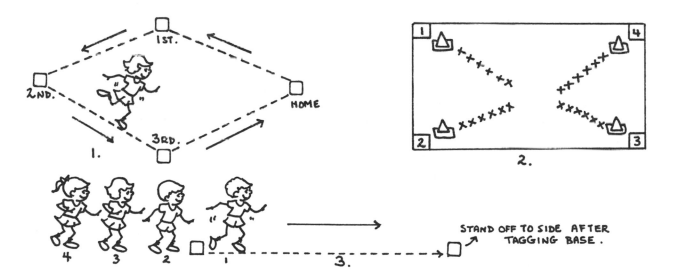

FOCUS: Technique; accuracy; partner work

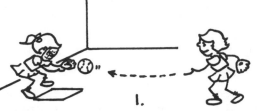

EQUIPMENT: One softball per pair;
one base per pair;
one softball glove per player;
catcher's mask, body protector;
one wall target per pair;
one hoop per pair;
wall or floor tape

ORGANIZATION:

- Demonstrate how to wear a catcher's mask and body protector; then have players find a partner and, together, get a softball and base to share. Pairs place the base near a wall and one player, the Catcher, crouch behind the base; the other player, the Pitcher, stands 8 meters (24 feet) away. Have players increase the distance apart as skill improves.

DESCRIPTION OF ACTIVITY:

1. **Positions:**
   - **Catcher:** You should be just beyond the range of the swinging bat. Squat with feet shoulder-width apart and one foot ahead of the other. Watch the ball and hold your glove up as the target for the pitcher.
   - **Pitcher:** Aim the ball at the Catcher's glove. Try to pitch the ball over the plate and between the top of the batter's knees and armpits.

2. **Pitching Practice:**
   - **Underhand Pitching Action:** Begin with your feet together; hold the ball in both hands, facing the batter. Bend forward slightly at the waist. Now separate your hands, hold the ball between your fingers and your thumb, and swing your pitching arm back keeping your arm close to your body; then swing the ball arm forward and, at the same time, step forward on the foot opposite your throwing arm. Watch your target as you deliver the ball.
   - **Windmill Pitching Action:** As you step forward with the opposite foot to the pitching arm, swing your pitching arm up and over your head, behind your back; then forward to follow through with your arm toward the batter.
   - Practice underhand pitching: pitch the ball to the catcher ten times; then change roles and repeat. Practice the windmill pitching action the same way.

3. **Back-Catching Practice:** (Form groups of three players: a Back Catcher, a Pitcher, and a player at first base.) Pitcher, pitch the ball to the Catcher; Catcher, then throw to first base; First Base, throw back to the Pitcher. Repeat ten times; then change roles and repeat.
   - How fast can you move the ball around the three positions?

4. **Target Pitching:** (Tape several wall targets to the wall about 60 centimeters [2 feet] from the floor—enough targets for every two players.)
   - Get a ball, stand 3 meters (10 feet) from the wall target, and pitch it at the target. How many times can you hit the target in ten tries using the Underhand Pitch?
   - How many times can you hit the target in ten tries using the Windmill Pitch?
   - Find a partner and get a hoop. One partner, stand at the wall and hold the hoop to one side at waist level. Your partner pitches the ball through the hoop. Change roles after five throws. Keep changing until you have pitched a total of twenty pitches each. Count your score out of twenty pitches and report your score to me to record.
   - Gradually step farther away from your target and repeat the above target pitches.

FOCUS: Stance; grip; swing technique; bunt technique; group work

EQUIPMENT: One softball per group; one home plate per group; one softball glove per player; one bat per player; one base per group of four

ORGANIZATION:

• Review and demonstrate batting technique and then allow players to practice the stance, grip, and swing. Introduce the Bunt, which is a gently hit ball directed into the infield but away from infield players. It is used to make a base hit; to advance a base runner (called a sacrifice bunt); or during a critical time in the game. Demonstrate bunting technique and then allow players to practice.

DESCRIPTION OF ACTIVITY:

1. *Grip:* Hold the bat firmly, with your hands together near the "butt" of the bat, with your dominant hand on top of the other. Move your hands up the bat, called "choking up" on the bat, if more comfortable. Hold the bat off your shoulder with the trademark facing up.

2. *Stance:* Stand with your feet shoulder-width apart and your knees slightly bent. Turn your nondominant side toward the pitcher so that you face home plate. Point the bat over your rear shoulder, bend your elbows, and hold your hands out from your body. Practice a swing to see that the end of the bat reaches just past the far side of home plate. Step back if it reaches too far over the plate.

3. *Swing:* Focus your eyes on the ball. As the ball leaves the pitcher's hand, shift your weight to your back foot. Begin your swing by rolling your hips forward and stepping into the ball. Swing your bat parallel to the ground and step forward onto your front foot as you contact the ball. Continue to swing the bat in a wide arc around your front shoulder. Batter, do not cross your hands as you grip the bat; swing with a smooth, continuous motion. Remember, do not throw your bat after hitting the ball!

4. *Strike Zone:* (Form groups of four to five players: Batter, Catcher, Pitcher, and two Fielders. Number players consecutively to establish the order of rotation and have them take up positions.) With batter standing at base, pitcher, make five pitches into the strike zone (over the plate and between armpits and knees). The first two pitches are practice pitches, which the batter will not try to hit; the next three pitches, the batter will try to hit. Rotate positions every five pitches.

5. *Bunting Technique:* Start in the batting stance. As soon as the ball is pitched, bring your rear foot forward and square your body to the Pitcher. At the same time, slide your upper hand about halfway up the bat, with your fingers holding the bat parallel to the ground, just behind the hitting surface. As the ball contacts the bat, "give" with the bat to soften the hit. Try to angle the bat to direct the ball inside either foul line and within fair territory.

6. *Practice Tasks:* Find a partner and collect a bat and ball.
   — Without the ball, practice bunting. Check each other's technique.
   — Find a partner. One partner pitch, the other bunt. Change roles after five bunts.

7. *Bunt and Run:* (Form groups of four players: a Batter, a Pitcher, a Catcher and a First Baseman.) Bunt and run to first base. Rotate positions after every five bunts.

FOCUS: Reinforce basic softball skills; station work

EQUIPMENT: Softballs;
softball gloves;
softball bats;
bases;
stopwatches;
tires, rope, targets

ORGANIZATION:

• Set up six softball stations as illustrated; then form groups of three to four players. Assign each group to a station. Rotate groups to the next station after three or four minutes. Throughout the activity, observe players closely and correct technique where necessary.

DESCRIPTION OF ACTIVITY:

1. **Station 1, Base Running:** Each player in turn, run the bases in order while another player times you. Try to beat your time on the next run.

   — Two runners go at the same time. Start at opposite corners of the diamond, and time each.

2. **Station 2, Fielding Fly Balls:** One player, throw fly balls to the other players, who call for the ball and try to catch it in the glove. Change throwers every five throws. Count the number of fly balls caught.

3. **Station 3, Pitching:** (Tape 42-inch × 19-inch targets to a wall, about 50 centimeters [20 inches] above the ground. This is the strike zone. Mark off a pitching line, 11 meters [35 feet] from the target.) Take turns to pitch ten underhand pitches to the target. Score one point for every hit on the target.

4. **Station 4, Batting:** Work in pairs. One partner pitch; the other bat. Each batter, make five hits into fair territory. Count the number of good pitches it takes to make five hits.

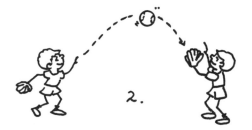

5. **Station 5, Fielding Grounders:** With a partner and one ball, stand facing each other about 8 meters (25 feet) apart. Throw ten grounders to each other. Count the number of successful catches out of ten.

6. **Station 6, Accuracy Throwing:** (Use a tire or hoop suspended from a basketball backboard frame [or tree] as the target. The tire should be about 50 centimeters [20 inches] above the ground.) Take ten overhand throws at the tire. Score two points for throwing through the tire; one point for hitting the tire.

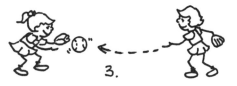

GS-178 SEMICIRCLE SOFTBALL

FOCUS: Lead-up game; batting; fielding; pitching; catching

EQUIPMENT: One bat per game; one softball per game; six cone markers

ORGANIZATION:

- Form two teams of six to eight players for each game. One team bats, while the other fields. Place a semicircle of cones about 15 meters (45 feet) from home plate. Have the batting team line up behind the home plate. The fielding team comprises a pitcher, a catcher, and the remainder, who form a semicircle in the outfield behind the cones.

DESCRIPTION OF ACTIVITY:

1. Batters, try to score a point by batting the ball past or over the semicircle of cones.
2. If the ball is caught or stopped at the cones by the fielders, then no point is scored.
3. Change pitcher and catcher often so that all may get a turn. Change sides after each player on the batting team has batted.
4. Play to three, five, or seven innings.

GS-179 FREEZE THE RUNNER

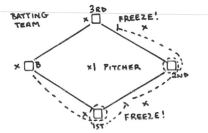

EQUIPMENT: One softball; one bat; one softball glove per fielder; full set of softball bases

ORGANIZATION:

- Set up the bases as for softball. Divide the class into two equal teams: the batting team and the fielding team. Have the fielders position themselves around the bases and in the field area. The pitcher is a member of the batter's team.

DESCRIPTION OF ACTIVITY:

1. Pitcher, pitch to your batter. Batter, hit the ball into the field; then run to first base, circling around it completely without touching it, and continue to the next base, and so on.
2. Fielder, field the ball; then throw it so that every fielder catches the ball. The fielder who is last to catch the ball shouts "Freeze!" This is the signal for the base runner to stop immediately. If caught between bases, the base runner must go back to the last base touched.
3. After the next batter hits the ball, the frozen base runner (or runners) continues to circle around each base until reaching home plate and scores one run but must stop again on the signal "Freeze!"
4. There are no outs. Everyone wins! After everyone on the batting team has had a turn at bat, the fielding team will bat.
5. Change the pitcher for every new batter so that everyone gets to bat and pitch.

GS-180 KNOCK-PIN SOFTBALL

FOCUS: Lead-up game; fielding; base running; batting

EQUIPMENT: Four bowling pins (or bleach bottles); three bases; one pitcher's plate; one bat and ball; gloves

ORGANIZATION:

• Set up four bowling pins or bleach bottles: one on the outside corner of first, second, third bases, and home plate, each 11 meters (35 feet) apart; then place the pitcher's plate 9 meters (28 feet) from home plate. Form two equal teams: batters and fielders. Number the players consecutively to establish batting order and fielding positions. Batters stand to one side, boy–girl in file formation. Fielders stand in regular softball positions and the pitcher gets a ball and stands at the pitcher's plate.

DESCRIPTION OF ACTIVITY:

1. The pitcher, pitch the ball to the first batter. Batter, after your hit, run around all the bases in order, to touch home plate, before the fielders can retrieve the ball and pass it to players at first base, second base, third base, and then to home plate.
2. Base players, knock down the bowling pin at your base before throwing the ball to the next base. Score one run for each player who makes it home before all the pins are knocked down.
3. Batter, you are out when a fielder catches a fly ball; all pins are knocked over before you reach home plate; or you knock over any of the pins.
4. The fielding team goes to bat after every player on the batting team has a turn. Rotate fielding positions after each inning.

GS-181 WHACK-O

FOCUS: Lead-up game; all softball skills

EQUIPMENT: One bat; one Nerf™ ball; one home plate; several gloves

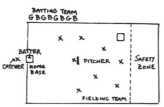

ORGANIZATION:

• The playing area has a Home Base and bases about 15 meters (45 feet) apart. Set up home plate and another base 15 meters (45 feet) apart; then form two equal teams, batters and fielders. The fielding team consists of a pitcher, a catcher, and the rest, fielders.

DESCRIPTION OF ACTIVITY:

1. The pitcher pitches underhand to the batter. Batter, try to hit the ball and run to the Safety Zone and, if possible, return home again before a fielder retrieves the ball and tags you.
2. Batter, if you are tagged, you are out, but if you reach home without being tagged or hit, your team scores one run. If it is not safe to return home, you may stay in the Safety Zone.
3. Batter, you may hit the ball in any direction and must run as soon as you hit the ball. If you miss the ball twice or hit a fly ball that is caught, you are out. You are out if you throw the bat.
4. Runners, you may not steal home; however, as soon as there are three in the Safety Area, the first runner must run Home to score a run for his or her team. The other runners may try to run Home as well or stay. Runners may run only after the ball has been hit by the batter but may not run when a fly ball is caught.
5. Change roles after all batters have had a turn to bat. After three innings, the team that scores the most runs wins the game.

GS—182 DOUBLE SCRUB

FOCUS: Lead-up game; all softball skills

EQUIPMENT: Two bats; one softball; one home plate and three bases; several gloves

ORGANIZATION:

• For this game, the ideal is nine to eleven players. Each position is numbered as shown in the illustration. Have each player draw a number from one to eleven to determine the starting positions. Regular softball positions are used.

DESCRIPTION OF ACTIVITY:

Scrub is played using regular softball rules except for the following modifications:

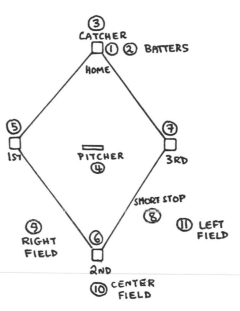

1. There are two Batters to start the game. Batters try to work together as a pair. Batters, after you hit the ball, you have two choices: Run to first base (if you get to first base safely, you may then walk directly to third base) or run for a Home Run all the way around the bases.

2. Second Batter, try to get on base yourself and try to get the first Batter home. Fielders, if you catch a fly ball, you exchange places with the Batter.

3. When a Batter is out, all players rotate one position: from Batter to Right Field, to Center Field, to Left Field, to Third Base, to Short Stop, to Second Base, to First Base, to Pitcher, to Catcher, to Batter.

4. Play until all players have played all positions.

GS—183 SLO-PITCH

EQUIPMENT: See GS-182.

ORGANIZATION:

• Each game consists of two teams of ten players: a batting team and a fielding team. The fielding team has a Catcher, Pitcher, First Base, Second Base, Third Base, and a Shortstop, and any number of Outfielders. The extra player is the "Rover," who plays in the outfield usually to field line drives.

DESCRIPTION OF ACTIVITY:

Slo-Pitch is played using regular softball rules except for the following modifications:

1. Pitcher, you must pitch a slow underhand toss with at least, but not more than, a 3-meter (10-foot) arch from the ground. Any other pitch is called a strike. If the pitch lands in the strike box, it is counted as a strike.

2. Base Runners, you may not lead-off (leave the base before the ball is pitched). If you do, you are automatically out. Once the ball has been hit, you may run.

3. Batter, you must take a full swing at the ball. If you are hit by a pitched ball, it is called a "ball." You are out if you try to bunt. You are also out if you hit a foul ball on your third strike.

4. An inning is finished after three batters are out, or once through the batting order, whichever comes first.

GS—184 CRICKET SOFTBALL

FOCUS: Lead-up game; all softball skills

ORGANIZATION:

- This game is best played outside. Form two teams of six to eight players: a batting team and a fielding team. The fielding team has two Pitchers, who stand in the middle of the two bases, which are about 16 meters (50 feet) apart: Each Pitcher faces a Batter at a base. Behind each base, place a bowling pin. All other Fielders, scatter around the field.

EQUIPMENT: Two bats; two bases; two bowling pins; one softball per game

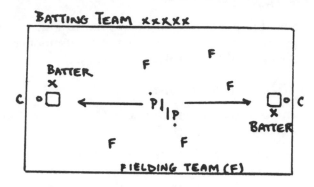

DESCRIPTION OF ACTIVITY:

1. Pitchers, take turns pitching to a Batter to try and knock over the pin at that end.
2. Batter, try to score a run by hitting the ball, then running, carrying your bat to touch the opposite base with your bat, before the fielding team can knock down a club at either end.
3. When one batter hits the ball, both have to run to exchange bases before a pin is knocked down. You may run as many times as you can before a club is knocked down. Each time you successfully change places, you score a run.
4. Batter, if after you hit the ball and run to the other base the pin is knocked down before you get there, you are out.
5. After a pin has been knocked down, that Batter is replaced by a new Batter. The new Batter must face the next pitch.
6. After a fly ball is caught, the Batter is automatically out.

GS—185 DECOVE ROUNDERS

EQUIPMENT: See GS-184.

ORGANIZATION:

- Decove Rounders is named after its originator, Jim Decove. Form two equal teams of six to eight players. Number the players consecutively to establish batting and fielding positions. Set up the bases as for softball and have the batting team stand off to one side. During the game, rotate the fielding positions after each hit.

DESCRIPTION OF ACTIVITY:

1. Each team stays at bat until the number of runs it has scored equals the number of players on the team.
2. Fielders, in order for your team to get to bat, you must help the batters score the correct number of runs. Your job is not to tag batters out but to keep them on base.
3. The pitcher tosses the ball to the first batter on the other team. If the batter misses three pitches in a row, he or she goes to the end of the line to await the next turn.
4. If the batter hits the ball, he or she may run to the bases, according to the kind of hit: A grounder means a run to first base; an infield fly means a run to second base; and an outfield fly means a run to third base. Base runners advance toward home plate according to what the next batter hits.
5. The fielding team must stop a grounder or catch a fly ball before the batter is allowed to stay on the base.
6. The inning continues until the batting team scores points equal to the number of players on the team.

GS-186 SOFTBALL RULES AND REGULATIONS

FOCUS: Knowledge of the game; field positions

ORGANIZATION:

• Explain the following rules and regulations to the players, starting with the field positions.

DESCRIPTION OF ACTIVITY:

1. *Playing Field and Positions:* The official softball diamond has 20-meter (60-foot) baselines and a 15-meter (46-foot) pitching distance. For elementary and junior high grades, the diamond may be adjusted down to 15-meter (45-foot) baselines and a pitching distance of 11 meters (35 feet).

2. *Teams:* Teams consist of nine players; a Catcher; a Pitcher; First, Second and Third Basemen; a Shortstop; and a Right, Center, and Left Fielder.

3. *Batting Order:* Players may bat in any order. For convenience, have players bat according to their field positions. Once a batting order has been established, it may not be changed, even if players change field positions.

4. *Pitching Rules:* The Pitcher must face the batter and stand with both feet on the pitching rubber. The ball must be held in front with both hands. The Pitcher is allowed only one step forward and must deliver the ball while making the step.

   — The ball must be thrown underhand. The Pitcher is not allowed to fake or make any motion toward the Batter without delivering the ball.

   — The Pitcher is not allowed to pitch the ball until the Batter is ready.

   — *A Strike:* A "strike" is a pitch, thrown over the plate, between the knees and shoulder of the batter.

   — *A Ball:* A "ball" is a pitch that does not go through the strike zone.

5. *Batting:* The Batter may swing at a pitched ball or let it go by. If the Batter misses a pitched ball, it is a "strike." A ball hit into foul territory is called a strike unless the Batter already has two strikes.

6. *A Fair Ball:* A fair ball is a batted ball that settles in fair territory between the foul lines (that is, between home plate and first base and between home plate and third base).

   — A ball that rolls over a base or through the field into fair territory is also a fair ball.

   — Fly balls that drop into fair territory beyond the infield are fair balls.

7. *A Foul Ball:* A foul ball is a batted ball that lands outside the foul lines between home and first and between home and third, or a fly ball that lands in foul territory beyond first or third base.

8. *A Fly Ball:* Any fly ball is a high batted ball that can be caught either in foul territory or fair territory for an out. A fly ball cannot touch the ground.

9. *Base Running:* The Runner is not allowed to "lead off" (that is, the Runner must stay on the base until the ball leaves the Pitcher's hand); otherwise, he or she is out. The Batter may advance to first base if he or she:

   — hits a fair ball and gets on the base before the ball does;

   — is "walked," (that is, receives four called balls);

   — is hit by a pitched ball;

   — is interfered with by the Catcher when batting.

(continued)

— The Base Runner may advance after a fly ball is caught. He or she may advance one base on the first overthrow at first or third base. On an overthrow at second, with the ball rolling into center field, the Runner may advance two bases.

— The Runner may try to steal a base as soon as the ball leaves the Pitcher's hand. The Runner must advance to the next base when forced to do so by another Base Runner.

— A Runner may advance to the next base on a fair hit that is not caught on the fly.

— A Base Runner may return to his or her base without being put out after a foul ball has not been caught.

— A Runner may overrun first base without being penalized. However, on all other bases, that Runner must maintain contact with the base or be tagged out.

10. *Outs:* A Batter is out if he or she:

— has three strikes;

— is tagged out at first;

— hits a fair or foul fly ball that is caught;

— hits a third strike and the Catcher catches the ball;

— bunts a foul ball on the third strike;

— throws the bat more than 3 meters (10 feet);

— steps on home plate when batting;

— interferes with the Catcher, who is trying to catch a fly ball or put out a Runner coming home;

— fouls a ball to the Catcher that rises above the Catcher's head and is caught.

11. *A Base Runner Is Out if he or she:*

— leaves the base before the ball leaves the Pitcher's hand;

— leaves the base before a fly ball is caught and the Fielder tags him or her, or that base, before the Runner returns;

— is forced to run to the next base, but the Fielder with the ball touches that base first;

— is tagged when off base;

— is hit by a batted ball when off base;

— passes another Runner;

— deliberately interferes with a field player;

— fails to touch a base and the Fielder touches him or her before he or she can return;

— touches a base that is occupied by another Base Runner.

12. *Scoring:* The game lasts for five or seven innings. An inning is completed when both teams have had a turn at bat. One run is scored each time a Base Runner runs a complete circuit of the bases (first, second, third, home) in that order.

— If the third out is a forced out, no run is scored, even if the Runner touches home plate before the "out" occurred.

GS–187 SPRINTING

FOCUS: Running technique

EQUIPMENT: Track, open area, or gymnasium

ORGANIZATION:

- Review and demonstrate good running technique. Emphasize that runners concentrate on good running form rather than speed, that they run on the balls of the feet with the body leaning forward, head up and still, and drive with the arms. Have players run side by side in groups of four or five. As soon as one group reaches the halfway point of the play area, the next group may start.

DESCRIPTION OF ACTIVITY:

1. **Sewing Machine:** Run lightly on the spot, on the balls of your feet. Start slowly, gradually increasing speed and using the correct running technique; then gradually decrease your speed. Repeat several times.
2. **High Knee Lift:** Start by running on the spot, lifting your knees high with each step. Hold your hands out in front at waist level and try to hit the palms with your knees on each step. Move forward, stepping on the balls of your feet and lifting with knees. Keep your head up and look straight ahead.
3. **Sprint Technique:** Run in an upright position, looking directly ahead of the finish line. Bend your elbows at right angles and brush your hips with your hands as you drive them forward. Place the thumb of each hand on your forefinger and relax your hands. Use a high lift of the thighs and pump your arms while running. Run with a forward lean on the balls of your feet using a stamping motion.
4. **Practice:** (Form groups of four or five runners. Have runners run side by side down the track, in "waves," using the correct sprinting technique.) As soon as one wave reaches the halfway point of the 100-meter track, the next wave may start.

GS–188 STRIDING

FOCUS: Striding technique; acceleration

EQUIPMENT: Track, open area, or gymnasium; several cone markers

ORGANIZATION:

- Review and demonstrate the Striding technique; then have players practice. Have players stand side by side along a starting line in groups of four or five, on a 100-meter track or in a gym. As soon as one group reaches the halfway point, the next group may start.

DESCRIPTION OF ACTIVITY:

1. **Striding Technique:** From a standing start, slowly run forward with an exaggerated stride and arm action. Kick your feet out in front as you run, reach forward with your foot, and snap your foot down on the track. Gradually increase the pace to the halfway mark; then gradually slow down until you reach the finish. Stride back to the starting line and repeat.
2. **Jogging and Striding:** Start with an easy jog; then stride. Alternate jogging and striding to the finish line; then stride back to the starting line at a strong pace, pumping your arms and increasing your pace to full speed at the starting line. Repeat.

FOCUS: Standing and sprint start techniques

EQUIPMENT: Track, open area, or gymnasium; two hoops per group; one beanbag per group

ORGANIZATION:

- Form groups of three or four runners and have groups line up behind the starting line.

DESCRIPTION OF ACTIVITY:

1. **Standing Start Technique:** Place the toe of the leading foot just behind the starting line. Place the other foot a comfortable distance behind. Lean forward; then push off quickly with the back foot. Take small quick steps as you continue to lean forward. Keep the weight on the balls of the feet and the toes. Throw the leading arm (same side as the leading leg) vigorously forward on your first step. Continue to pump with the arms, and keep low. Run for a short distance; then jog back to the start.
   — Experiment to see which foot you would rather have in front.

2. **Quick Off the Mark:** Take a Standing Start position. On signal "Go!" explode into your run and sprint to the 30-meter mark. Pretend to run through a tape at top speed, with your head up and your knees high. Jog back to the starting line. Repeat.

3. **Beanbag Race:** (Each group collects two hoops and a beanbag and stands about 18 meters [60 feet] apart.) Stand in Standing Start position, in file formation behind the first hoop with the beanbag inside the hoop. On signal "Go!" first runner, pick up the beanbag, sprint to the second hoop, place the beanbag in the hoop, sprint back to tag the second runner, and join the end of the line. Second runner, sprint to the second hoop, pick up the beanbag, and return it to the first hoop. Continue until all players have had two turns.

4. **The Crouch Start:**
   — **Position:** Place the toe of your front foot about 20 centimeters to 30 centimeters (5 to 12 inches) behind the starting line and the knee of the rear foot beside the front foot.
   — **"On Your Mark!":** Place the thumb and forefinger of each hand behind and parallel to the starting line, shoulder-width apart. Your remaining fingers form a high arch so that your shoulders are as high as possible. Straighten your arms and fix eyes on a spot 1 meter (3 feet) ahead.
   — **"Get Set!":** On the word "Set!" take and hold a deep breath. Raise your hips so that they are slightly higher than your shoulders. Shift your weight forward onto your hands and extend your rear leg. Your front knee should form a right angle. Continue to look at a spot 1 meter (3 feet) ahead.
   — **"Go!":** On "Go!" push off with your back leg. Quickly swing your leading leg through and take a short stamping step as you lean forward. At the same time, vigorously throw your leading arm (same side as your leading leg) forward. Rise gradually as you pump your arms and run forward taking quick steps.
   — Don't try to beat the gun. Think about the action of running.
   — Strive to get all the body parts working together smoothly.
   — Repeat No. 2 and 3 activities using the Sprint Start.

GS-190 THE SPRINT ACCELERATION AND FINISH

FOCUS: Finish technique; acceleration; practice

EQUIPMENT: Track or open area; finish-line tape (wool yarn); starting blocks (optional)

ORGANIZATION:

- Review the Crouch Start; then have runners practice, in pairs, accelerating from the start and finishing technique.

DESCRIPTION OF ACTIVITY:

1. **Individual Starting Practice:** Find a spot on the track and practice the crouch start on your own. Say to yourself "On your mark!" "Get set!" "Go!" Run about 20 meters (60 feet) three or four times.

2. **Acceleration:** Now in waves of four runners, run on the spot, slowly at first; then gradually increase speed as you run down the track, lifting your knees high and keeping upright. Get to top speed at about the 30-meter (100-foot) mark (cone marker); then gradually slow down. Jog together back to the starting line. Repeat. Remember the following sprinting tips:

   — Keep your head still; do not bob or weave. Focus on a point ahead as you run.

   — Think about pumping with the arms and driving upward with the knees.

   — Cup your hands naturally and do not clench your fists.

   — Run fast and relaxed; do not strain.

3. **Finish Technique:** Hold your normal sprinting action until you are well past the finish line. Run "through" the finish line as if you had another 20 meters (60 feet) to run; then gradually slow down. Do not lunge at the tape.

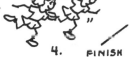

4. **Sprint Challenge:** (Set up a finish-line tape 30 meters [100 feet] from the starting line.) Find a partner and stand side by side. When it is your turn, listen for the signals "On your mark!" "Get set!" "Go!" Race your partner to the finish line; then jog back to the start down the sidelines. Change partners and repeat.

5. **Overtaking:** Stand with your partner behind the starting line. Commence running around the track. One runner, run about 5 meters behind your partner; speed up to sprint past your partner to run 5 meters ahead; then your partner sprints past you. Continue around the track. When about 30 meters from the tape, the rear runner, shout "Go!"; then both sprint for the finish line, to cross with proper technique.

6. **Face Down Sprints:** Lie alongside your partner, face down on the track, with your hands and head behind the line. On the signal "Go!" spring to your feet and run 50 meters through the finish line. Repeat several times.

   — Repeat, lying on your backs with head touching starting line.

GS–191 WIND SPRINTS

FOCUS: Sprinting; jogging, endurance

EQUIPMENT: Six cone markers;
finish-line tape (or wool yarn)

ORGANIZATION:

• This activity is a good way to build cardiorespiratory endurance. Review the Sprint Start and Finish techniques and sprinting form; then have runners find a partner and line up in pairs behind the starting line. Runners run together, alternating sprinting and jogging down the track. Place cone markers about 50 meters (150 feet) apart and have each runner in turn hold the finish line for the next pair.

DESCRIPTION OF ACTIVITY:

1. When your pair is called to the starting line, get into the Sprint Start position. On the signals "On your mark!" "Get set!" "Go!" sprint at top speed to the first marker; then gradually slow to a jogging pace until you reach the second marker. Accelerate to top speed again. When you reach the third marker, slow to a jog for another 50 meters. Finally, sprint at top speed to run through the finish line.
2. Runners, remember to run on the balls of your feet and lift your knees high when sprinting. Pump vigorously with your arms to gain maximum speed quickly.

GS–192 SHUTTLE RELAYS

FOCUS: Standing or crouch starts; sprinting; baton changing

EQUIPMENT: One baton per team; one or two stopwatches

ORGANIZATION:

• Add these activities to your track program to increase participation. Review the Standing Start and the Crouch Start; then explain and demonstrate the shuttle method of exchanging batons. Form teams of four to six runners and have one player on each team get a baton. Allow players to practice with their team.

DESCRIPTION OF ACTIVITY:

1. *Baton-Changing Shuttle Relay, Standing Start:* Half of each team stand in a file facing the other half behind a line about 50 meters (150 feet) away. First runner, hold the bottom of the baton in your right hand. On the signal "Go!" run to the other file, and pass the baton to the receiver's right hand with a downward motion. Receiver, stand behind the line with your right palm open and facing upward. Watch the baton as it approaches. If the baton is dropped, quickly pick it up and continue. As the exchange is made, you will pass each other right shoulder to right shoulder.
   — Which team can finish first after every runner has had two turns?
2. *Crouch Start Relay:* Repeat the Shuttle Relay using the Crouch Start, but without the baton. When it is your turn to run, go down on the mark, get set, and go when the incoming runner touches you on the right shoulder. The first team back in original positions after two turns wins.
3. *Twenty Crossings:* Repeat the Shuttle Relays until the teams complete twenty laps. Waiting teammates, count the number of crossings run.

GS-193 RELAY RACING

FOCUS: Baton exchanging; exchange lane

EQUIPMENT: One baton per team;
one beanbag per team

ORGANIZATION:

• Explain and demonstrate the Left-to-Right baton changing technique; then form teams of four runners; number the runners 1, 2, 3, and 4, and have them stand one behind the other about 16 meters (50 feet) apart. The first runner on each team gets a baton. At first, have runners practice with their team at a slow pace to learn the baton exchange technique.

DESCRIPTION OF ACTIVITY:

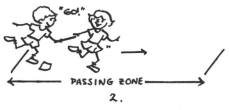

1. *Left-to-Right Baton Exchange Technique:*

— First runner, hold the bottom of the baton in your left hand, run, and pass it into the right hand of the runner ahead with an upward motion.

— Continue to the other three runners, passing with the left hand and receiving in the right.

— Receiver, while facing the front, reach back with the fingers and thumb of the right hand facing down, and start to run when the incoming runner is about 4 meters (13 feet) away. Shift the baton to your left hand as you run. Repeat.

— Exchange the baton while both runners are near top speed with both arms fully extended.

2. *Checkmarking:* Take a beanbag and place it on the ground ahead in the passing zone (see diagram). Incoming runner, when you reach the checkmark, call "Go!" for the receiver to start running.

GS-194 CONTINUOUS RELAY

FOCUS: Racing; passing the baton; team effort

EQUIPMENT: Circular track with four lanes;
One baton per team of four runners

ORGANIZATION:

• Divide the class into six even groups and distribute the groups evenly around the oval track at stations A, B, C, D, E, and F. Number the runners in each group; 1, 2, 3, and 4. All the ones are a team; all the twos are a team, and so on. Have the four runners at station A get a baton each.

DESCRIPTION OF ACTIVITY:

Continuous Relay:

— Runners 1, 2, 3, and 4 at station A, go down into the Sprint Start position on your marks behind the starting line. On the signal "Get Set!" "Go!" sprint to station B, and exchange the baton with your next runner.

— Runners at station B, pass to the runners at station C, and so on around the track.

— When you have exchanged the baton, stay at that station and line up in your same lane. When the baton comes around again, carry it to the next station and so on until every runner is back in his or her original position.

— Remember, runners, to shift the baton from the right hand to the left while on the run. Receiver, hold your hand steady and do not look around.

FOCUS: Interval training technique; aerobic endurance

EQUIPMENT: Track or open space; one stopwatch per pair

ORGANIZATION:

• Explain and demonstrate the difference between sprinting, middle distance, and distance running. All races from 800 meters to 1,500 meters (approximately one mile) are considered middle distance. Distance running is any distance over the mile. Middle distance running develops muscular endurance, cardiorespiratory endurance, and leg strength. Find a partner and get a watch.

DESCRIPTION OF ACTIVITY:

1. *Technique:* Run with the body more erect. Strike the ground with the heel first; then rock onto the toes for the push off. The arm action is relaxed and rhythmical and not as vigorous as in sprinting. Breathe naturally.

2. *Interval Training:*

— *Week 1.* In pairs, run for 100 meters (110 yards); walk for 100 meters; run for 100 meters; walk for 100 meters, and so on. Repeat.

— *Week 2.* Repeat, running for 200 meters and walking for 100 meters.

— *Week 3.* Repeat, running for 300 meters and walking for 100 meters.

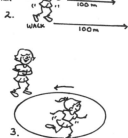

3. *Progressive Training over 1,600 Meters:* Time your partner as he or she runs around the track for one lap, 400 meters (440 yards). Change roles and repeat. Time your partner over two laps. Change roles and repeat. Then time your partner over one lap. Change roles and repeat. When finished, you will have run 1,600 meters. Add your lap times to get your training time.

4. *Five-Minute Run:* Run over a selected course for five minutes. Speed is not important; keep a steady pace. Slow down if you have to, but try to keep moving.

5. *Scottish Mile:* (Form groups of ten to twenty runners and have groups line up in file formation around the circular track or gym.) On the signal "Go!" start running around the track. As you run, last runner, sprint on the inside of the group to the front of the file to take the lead. As soon as you take the lead, the next runner at the end of the file sprint to take the lead, and so on until each runner has been the leader.

— Run at a slow jog.

— Run at half pace. Sprint to get to the front of the file to take the lead.

GS-196 LONG JUMPING

FOCUS: Approach; takeoff; flight; landing

EQUIPMENT: Several long jump pits with take-off boards; several measuring tapes; one rake; two beanbags per jumper; one long rope per pit

ORGANIZATION:

• Have jumpers gather around the long jump pit. Explain and demonstrate technique: the approach, take-off, flight, and landing. Explain the procedure for establishing checkmarks: in order to establish consistency in hitting the take-off board correctly. Emphasize that jumpers need gain as much speed and height as they can: "Speed + Height = Distance." Have them form groups of four to six jumpers. In each group, jumpers pair up and get two beanbags each, then gather around the pit. Set up other track and field practice stations to avoid line-ups and to increase participation. Have each group in turn come to the long jump pit. Other groups practice previously taught skills. Rotate stations every five minutes.

DESCRIPTION OF ACTIVITY:

1. *Technique:*
   — *Approach:* Start from the same spot each time with both feet together. Increase your speed to reach the take-off board at top speed.
   — *Take-off:* Hit the board with the same take-off foot each time. Spring off that foot, rolling from your heel, to the ball of your foot, to your toe. Prepare for the take-off by "gathering" with your arms (throwing them upward vigorously with a circular motion). At the same time, bring your rear leg up and forward, and look up.
   — *Flight:* Try to gain as much height as you can. "Hang" in mid-air.
   — *Landing:* Reach forward with your legs, arms, and trunk, and as your heels hit the sand, quickly fling both arms back to force your whole body forward.
2. *Take-Off-Foot Practice:* Stand with your feet together on the approach track. Break into a slow run; then hit the take-off board with your left foot and land on both feet. Repeat, jumping from the right foot. Which foot would you rather jump from? Use it as your take-off foot each time.
3. *Establishing Checkmarks:* Set your beanbag marker at the edge of the track, about 30 meters to 37 meters (100 to 120 feet) from the take-off board. Start with both feet together opposite the checkmark. Take a step forward with your take-off foot; then run down the approach and "through" the board (make no effort to jump). At the halfway point, 15 meters to 19 meters (50 to 60 feet), have your partner check the spot where your take-off foot lands. Repeat several times to establish this checkmark.
   — Run through again, hitting the halfway checkmark, and then have your partner check to see if you are hitting the take-off board correctly. Repeat many times, trying to hit the checkmark and the board consistently. Any part of the foot protruding over the front edge of the board is a foul, and the jump will not be measured; otherwise, measure from the front edge of board to nearest point of touch in the sandpit.
   — Use the measuring tape to measure your halfway checkmark and your starting mark. Record these measurements and measure them off whenever you long jump.
4. *Flight:* Run toward the pit; then as you take off, try to gain as much height as possible as you leave the board. Jump from the same take-off foot each time. Use your arms to increase the height as you jump.
5. *Height and Distance:* Sprint down the track toward the pit. Try for height and distance. Try to jump over a rope held lightly across the pit. Can you jump over it if we raise it higher? Take turns holding the rope.

Game Skills / **321**

FOCUS: Basic pattern of steps; technique   **EQUIPMENT:** Open area or gym

ORGANIZATION:

• The Triple Jump, also called the Hop, Step, and Jump, is related to the Long Jump and is divided into five basic steps: Run-in; take-off; hop; step; and jump. Explain and demonstrate these steps; then have the jumpers practice. Emphasize that jumpers use their arms for balance. Remind them not to get too much height in the first Hop, and to try for height on the Step and Jump.

DESCRIPTION OF ACTIVITY:

Technique:

1. *The Run-In:* This is similar to the Long Jump. Get enough speed to ensure a good take-off.

2. *The Take-Off:* Hit the board with a heel-toe action, "gathering" with the arms as in the Long Jump.

3. *The Hop:* The Hop should not be too high, as height tends to undo the forward momentum needed for the Step and Jump to follow. Hold your head erect and land on the same foot used for the take-off. Land on the ball of the foot and toe, rock back to the heel, roll forward, and lift, in preparation for the Step. Try to keep your momentum moving forward.

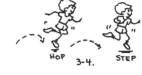

4. *The Step:* Swing the free knee forward and upward vigorously to start the Step. Keep this knee high to maintain balance. Land on that foot on the ball of the foot and the heel; then roll forward with the knee bent in preparation for the final Jump.

5. *The Jump:* The Jump is similar to the Long Jump. Get as much height as possible and land on both feet.

6. *Hopping Practice:* Stand in a free space and practice hopping from your left foot and landing on your left. Practice hopping from your right foot and landing on your right. Which one is more natural?

— Take a short run followed by a hop, landing on the same foot.

— Form lines of five to six jumpers. In your lines, hop across the play area, taking long hops on the same foot. Hop back on the other foot.

7. *Stepping Practice:* Start on your take-off foot; then take long exaggerated steps, one after the other, lifting with the arms on each step.

8. *Jumping:* Stand on your non-take-off foot. Use your arms to get as much height and distance as possible as you jump onto both feet.

— Form lines and continue to jump across the play area. Return the same way.

9. *Hop, Step, and Jump:* From a standing start, hop, step, and jump across the play area. Do not try for distance, but try to feel the rhythm of the Triple Jump.

GS–198 TRIPLE JUMP, MORE PRACTICE

FOCUS: Step-sequence technique; leg strength

EQUIPMENT: Open area, gym, or triple jump pit; three hoops per six jumpers; three mats per six jumpers; three cone markers per group of six jumpers

ORGANIZATION:

• Review the basic Triple Jump steps; then have the jumpers practice them as a sequence. Have jumpers scatter over the play area.

DESCRIPTION OF ACTIVITY:

1. Stand in a free space and practice the pattern of the Hop, Step, and Jump. Now practice the Hop, Step, and Jump from a short run-in.

2. *Triple Jump in Hoops:* (Form files of five or six jumpers behind a starting line, and arrange three hoops in front of each file as in the diagram.)

   — *Follow the Leader:* Hop from the line into the first hoop, step into the second hoop, and jump into the third. Move the hoops farther apart and repeat.

3. *Triple Jump Between Mats:* (Arrange three small mats in a line in front of each group, with spaces in between; see diagram.)

   — With a running start, hop, step, and jump into the spaces between the mats. Return to the start and repeat.

4. *Reach the Markers:* (Place cones on the floor or ground, in front of a line [or take-off board] at the following distances apart: 1.6 meters–2.4 meters–2.4 meters (5 feet–8 feet–8 feet.)

   — Run in, take off from behind the line (or take-off board) to hop, step, and jump at each of the cones. Try to get a bounce-bounce-bounce, smooth and relaxed action.

   — Cones may also be set at the following distances to suit the jumpers.

   1.8–2.7–2.7 meters (6–9–9 feet)

   2.1–3.0–3.0 meters (7–10–10 feet)

   2.8–3.7–3.7 meters (9–12–12 feet)

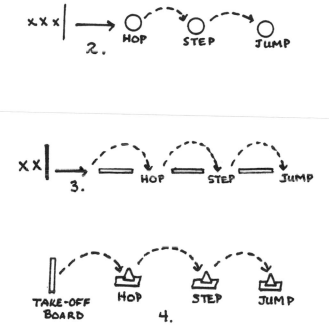

GS–199 HURDLES

FOCUS: Hurdling technique

EQUIPMENT: Low hurdles or improvised hurdles

ORGANIZATION:

- Hurdles may be improvised by placing a wand or broom handle on two wooden blocks, two cardboard boxes, or two cones. Training should start at a height of about 60 centimeters (25 inches); then gradually increase the height. There should be six hurdles, spaced over 55 meters (60 yards) as shown. Form groups of three or four hurdlers. Have them get a hurdle to share and find a free space.

DESCRIPTION OF ACTIVITY:

1. ***Technique of Hurdling:*** Look up the track, not at the hurdle. Sprint to the hurdle. Take off about 1 meter to 1.5 meters (3 to 5 feet) in front of the hurdle. Lean forward and straighten your lead leg, turning your toes up as it goes over, and at the same time stretch forward with your opposite hand.

   — Raise the trailing leg over the hurdle. Bend it at right angles at the knee. Turn the toes up and out. Once over the hurdle, snap your leading foot down quickly, and at the same time throw your leading arm around and back. Try to "step over" the hurdle, not "jump" it.

2. ***Establishing the Lead Leg:*** Stand 10 meters (11 yards) away from the hurdle; then run over the hurdle, placing your left leg in front. Run over the hurdle again with your right leg leading. Which leg is more comfortable as your lead leg? That leg is your leading leg from now on!

3. ***Hurdling Action, Free Space:*** Find a free space, stand on your take-off leg, and practice the hurdling action without a hurdle. The three movements are:

   — lift the lead knee up, extend the leg straight forward vigorously, and reach forward with the leading arm

   — lift the trail leg over, horizontal to the ground

   — snap the lead leg down quickly and throw the lead arm back

   Repeat this action over and over again.

4. ***Hurdling Action, Over One Hurdle:*** Face the hurdle; step over the hurdle using the correct style, always leading with the same leg and leaning forward at the waist. Move farther back and try the whole action at a faster pace.

5. ***Hurdling Action, Over a Series of Hurdles:*** Place two hurdles in a row. Sprint to the first hurdle; take three or five steps between and hurdle the second. Develop good technique before adding more hurdles. Continue to add more until you can hurdle the full set of six in good style.

   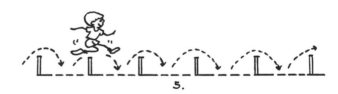

GS-200 SCISSORS-STYLE HIGH JUMPING

FOCUS: Scissors technique; leg strength

EQUIPMENT: Two or more sets of high jump standards; two or more plastic or metal training bars; foam landing pits

ORGANIZATION:

- Most high jump styles today require a foam landing pit; however, the Scissors Style can be taught using only a sandpit. Explain the Scissors technique and have players practice; then form groups of four or five players. Have them gather near a high jump pit.

DESCRIPTION OF ACTIVITY:

1. *Scissors Technique:* Approach the bar at about a thirty-degree angle. If you take off with your left foot, approach the bar from the right. Move to the opposite side for a right-foot take-off. Choose whichever side you prefer. Take five to ten springing steps as you approach. Take off at about arm's length from the bar. Kick high the leg nearer the bar and swing your arms up as if you are about to sit on the bar. Lift your rear leg over the bar in a scissors movement. Straighten your legs as you go over the bar to complete the scissors action. Land on your leading foot; followed by your take-off leg.
   — Jumpers, jump over the middle of the bar!
2. *Practice:* Stand three to five steps away from the bar on the side you prefer. With the bar set at waist level, run and jump using the Scissors Style. If you knock the bar, replace it, and continue. As you improve, raise the bar.
3. *Scissors Relay:* (At least two jumping pits are required. Each group stands in file formation at a pit.) On signal "Go!" first player in line, run in and jump the bar using Scissors Style, run back to the line, touch next player, and go to end of line. Continue until all jumpers have had five turns. Replace the bar if you knock it down and continue. The first team to finish wins.

GS-201 STRADDLE-STYLE HIGH JUMPING

FOCUS: Straddling technique; leg strength

EQUIPMENT: See GS-200.

ORGANIZATION:

- The straddle style is also called the "Belly Roll." When a foam landing pit is available, the Straddle and the Flop styles are preferred high-jumping methods. Explain the four stages of the Straddle-style; then, to allow for maximum participation, have at the most only five or six jumpers at each set of standards during practice. Rotate groups to other events while waiting.

DESCRIPTION OF ACTIVITY:

1. *Approach:* Run toward the bar from the left side at about a 30- to 45-degree angle. Take five to seven steps as you approach, running high on the balls of your feet until the next to last step. As this right foot rocks from heel to toe, lower yourself for the "gather" (circle the arms upward), plant your left foot (take-off foot), and bend at the knee. The last three steps are longer and quicker as you prepare to "gather."
   — Remember to jump over the middle of the bar. The "planted" foot is the jumping foot and the last foot to leave the ground.
2. *Take-Off:* Swing your right leg up and begin to turn your tummy toward the bar. Swing both arms up in front of the bar, leading with left arm.
   — *Clearance:* At the top of your jump, look down at the bar and roll over onto your tummy to "lie along the bar." Your right leg is the first to go over the bar. Lift your leg high and out of the way.
   — *Landing:* Land on your right leg or on your right side and back.
3. Practice the Straddle technique as for Scissors style.

GS–202 FLOP-STYLE HIGH JUMPING

FOCUS: Flop-style technique; back flexibility; leg strength

EQUIPMENT: Foam landing pits; four folding mats per station; high jump standards and crossbars

ORGANIZATION:

• Practice only on foam "pits," no smaller than 3 meters × 3 meters (9 feet × 9 feet) and not thinner than 30 centimeters (2 feet). Place the pit directly below the crossbar with the front edge in line with the jump standards. As an added safety measure, place folding mats around the sides and back of the foam pit. To avoid the foam pit from sliding, place a folding mat under it as well. Introduce jumpers to the feeling of arching backward when jumping by having them practice the Flop Style without high jump standards or bar. Jumpers take turns practicing the technique.

DESCRIPTION OF ACTIVITY:

1. *Standing Flop:* Stand at the edge of a foam landing pit with your back to the pit. Throw your arms up and back, spring off both legs, and throw yourself backward. Arch your back as you fall backward and land on your upper back. Roll off the pit and repeat, taking turns.

2. *Running Flop:* Stand facing the pit. Take only three to five steps as you run to the pit in a slightly curved path. Throw your arms up and back and spring off both feet to gain as much height as you can. Land on the pit on your upper back and shoulders, with both legs and feet dangling overhead. Roll off the pit and repeat.

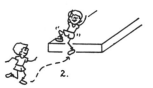

3. *Approach:* Place the bar at about waist level. Approach the bar from the same side as you would for the Scissors-Style high jump. If you are using a left-foot take-off, approach the bar from the right. For a right-foot take-off, approach from the left. Take three to five steps as you run to the bar at a 30- to 40-degree angle and with a slightly curved path so that you rotate naturally during your jump.

4. *Take-Off:* The take-off is similar to the basketball lay-up. Swing the inside knee up high as you swing your arms upward. Rotate your body so that your back is to the bar, arch your back as you rise over the bar, raise your hips, and flick your legs up and over the bar as you fall toward the landing pit.

5. *Landing:* Look toward the bar as you land on your upper back and shoulders. Roll backward off the landing pit.

6. *Practice:* Stand facing a low bar at a distance of 1 meter (3 feet). Take one step, plant your foot, and rotate to clear the bar. Land on your upper back, flipping your feet out of the way to prevent knocking the bar. After several successful tries, raise the bar another 2 or 3 centimeters (1 inch).

7. *Run-in Approach Practice:* Try the flop after a three- to five-step running approach to the bar. Raise the bar again after several successful jumps.

— Gradually lengthen the run-in to seven to nine steps and have jumpers approach in a full semicircle.

— Remember to swing your arms vigorously upward to help lift the body. Flop over the middle of the bar.

GS-203 SHOT PUTTING

FOCUS: Shot putting technique; shot put circle

EQUIPMENT: Shot put circles;
one 4-foot light rope;
two 6-inch nails;
6-pound shots

ORGANIZATION:

- ***Construction of a Shot Put Circle:*** Tie the end of a light rope around a 6-inch nail. At a distance of 105 centimeters (3 feet, 6 inches) from the first nail, tie a second 6-inch nail. Drive one nail into the ground and describe a circle with the other. Place a board against the leading edge of the circle. Explain and demonstrate the putting technique using a right-handed demonstrator. (All directions are to be reversed for left-handed putters.) Have the putters gather around the back end of the shot put circle and practice, one at a time.

DESCRIPTION OF ACTIVITY:

1. ***Gripping the Shot:***
   - Hold the shot at the base of the fingers, not in the palm of the hand.
   - Place the fingers directly behind the shot. Flex the wrist backward and hold the elbow out at a 45-degree angle.
   - Hold the nonthrowing arm upward and outward in a natural position for balance.
   - Cradle the shot into the side of the neck, with the palm of the hand pointing forward.

2. ***Shot Putting Technique:***
   - Stand near the rear of the circle. Take all your weight on the right leg and raise the left leg so that the left toe merely touches the ground. Nestle the shot against the side of your neck and raise the left arm out to maintain balance.
   - Lower your whole body over the right leg. At the same time, bend at the knee and raise the left leg forward to balance completely on the right leg.
   - In one movement, push forward vigorously with the right leg, shifting the left leg through the air at the same time, to take a hop onto the right foot to the middle of the circle. Keep low as you hop. This is called the "Glide."
   - Drive upward with the right leg; then rotate your trunk to land on your left foot as you push hard with your right (shot) arm upward and forward. Push the shot off the fingers with a high elbow action.
   - Continue the left rotation. As soon as the shot has left your hand, switch the position of your feet to bring your right foot close to the front of the circle.

3. ***Standing Put:*** The Glide (the hop across the circle) is omitted from the Standing Put. Check to see that you have the correct grip on the shot. From a standing position in the middle of the circle, push the shot along its proper line of flight (about forty degrees to the ground). Move your arm in a straight line. Rotate your trunk, hold your elbow high, extend your arm, and flick your fingers to release the shot.

4. ***Practice the Glide:*** Drive with the right leg to land on the right leg. Keep the nonputting arm up and out. Do not deliver the shot, but practice the Glide Hop.

5. ***Glide and Put:*** Practice the Glide across the circle and the putting action without the shot.

6. ***Practice the Glide and the Put:*** Using the 6-pound shot, practice the Glide and the Put. Concentrate on good form. Measure your puts from the edge of the circle to the closest mark made by the shot. Repeat, trying to beat your previous performance.

GS–204 TRACK AND FIELD STATIONS

FOCUS: Organization; maximum participation; station work

EQUIPMENT: See suggested stations.

ORGANIZATION:

• Divide the class into groups of five or six children and choose a leader for each group. Have the same number of events as groups. Select a variety of running, throwing, and jumping events. Set up the chosen events and arrange the equipment; as children will be dispersed, safety will be of paramount importance. Explain and/or demonstrate what is required at each station. Explain the rotation pattern at the conclusion of each station practice. Prior to commencing practice, have the class warm up properly, using exercises from Section 2, "Fitness Activities." During practice, circulate to each event, to coach and encourage; or stay at one station and concentrate on coaching that event. Position yourself so that you can observe all stations at the same time.

DESCRIPTION OF ACTIVITY:

Select the desired number of Stations from the following:

Station 1. Sprints: 60 meters, 100 meters, 200 meters

Station 2. Running Long Jump

Station 3. Circular Relay: 4 × 50 meters

Station 4. Shot Put: Use a 6-pound shot

Station 5. Triple Jump

Station 6. Middle Distance Run: 400 meters

Station 7. High Jump: Scissors, Straddle, or Flop

Station 8. Hurdles

GS–205 TRACK AND FIELD SPORTS TABLOID

FOCUS: Organization; track and field skills; team work

EQUIPMENT: Six long ropes; high jump equipment; stopwatch; one whistle; hurdle equipment; four beanbags and deckrings; box; cone markers; medicine ball; chalkboard and chalk

ORGANIZATION:

• Refer to SG-46 in Section 6 for organization of a Tabloid Sports Program. The objective is for each team to score as many points as possible at each station, within a given time limit (for example, three minutes). Divide the class into teams of five or six children and choose a leader for each team. From previously taught activities, select a variety of novel running, throwing, and jumping events, such as Three-Legged Races, Sack Races, or the more formal events as follows. Set up the chosen events and arrange the equipment. Explain the scoring system and the length of time at each station. Explain the rotation pattern at the conclusion of each station. Start and stop the activity with the whistle. Prior to commencing the Tabloid, have the team leaders warm up their teams. Position yourself so that you can observe all stations at the same time. A sample tabloid follows.

(continued)

DESCRIPTION OF ACTIVITY:

Station 1, Sprint: From behind the line, sprint around the cone marker (50 meters away) and back to tag the next runner. Score one point for each round trip.

Station 2, Middle Distance Run: (300 meters to 400 meters) (Have a helper time the runners.) All runners, start at the same time, behind the line. Timer, call out the times at five-second intervals as the runners cross the finish line. Score points based on finish time.

Station 3, Running Long Jump: (Place three ropes across the pit) Score one point for jumping beyond the first rope; two points for jumping beyond the second; and three points for the third.

Station 4, Triple Jump: (Organize as for Running Long Jump.)

Station 5, High Jump: (Use three pits if available and set the bars at three different heights.) Choose the height you wish to jump, then jump, one at a time. Score one point for the lowest height jumped; two points for the middle height; three points for the highest. Take as many turns as you can in the time limit. Add the scores.

Station 6, Hurdles: (Place three hurdles in a row 15 meters apart, in front of line.) Take turns going over the three hurdles. When finished, tag the next hurdler and continue. Score one point for every hurdle jumped. If a hurdle is knocked over, count one point, but the hurdle must be reset before continuing.

Station 7, Beanbag Race: (Place a cardboard box behind a starting line and four deckrings 5 meters [15 feet] apart, in a row, in front of the box. Inside each deckring, place a beanbag.) Each runner, in turn, run to get a beanbag, grab it, and run back to place it in box. Continue until all four beanbags are in the box. The next runner, place beanbags back in deckrings, one at a time. Continue in this way. Score one point for each trip.

Station 8, Medicine Ball Throw: (From a starting line space three cones in a row, about 8 meters [25 feet] apart.) First player, throw the medicine ball from the starting line as far as you can. Second player, retrieve the ball and throw from where it landed (not rolled). Then the third player throw, and so on. Score one point each time the ball lands past a cone marker. When the ball lands beyond the last cone, throw back toward the starting line.

Special Games

Special Games activities develop leadership, cooperation, self-esteem, creativity, and a sense of fair play. The emphasis throughout these activities is on fun and team work, not winning or losing.

The fifty-four Special Games in Section 6 are organized into Relays, Low-Organized Games, and Tabloid Sports.

(*continued*)

SG-1 EQUIPMENT SHUTTLES

FOCUS: Equipment manipulation

EQUIPMENT: One basketball per team;
one soccer ball per team;
one jump rope per team;
one hoop per team;
one hockey stick and puck per team;
one medicine ball per team;
four cone markers

ORGANIZATION:

• Form teams of four to six players. To arrange teams in shuttle formation, have half the players stand facing the other half across a distance of about 10 meters (30 feet). Mark a starting line for each half of the team with cone markers and give a basketball to the leader of each team.

DESCRIPTION OF ACTIVITY:

Ball Shuttle:

1. On signal "Go!" leader, run and dribble the basketball toward the other half of your team. Hand the ball to the first player there and go to the end of the file. Remember to stay behind your starting line until you receive the ball.

2. The player with the ball, dribble it back to the other half of the team, hand it to the first player, and join the end of the file.

3. Continue the relay in this way until everyone has had a turn and all players are in their starting positions, sitting cross-legged. The team to finish the task the quickest is the winner.

VARIATIONS:

a. **Soccer Shuttle:** Have each player dribble a soccer ball across to the first player in the opposite file; then join the end of that file.

b. **Skipping Shuttle:** Each player jumps rope across to the first player in the opposite file.

c. **Hockey Shuttle:** Each player stickhandles a puck across to the first player in the opposite file.

d. **Medicine Ball Shuttle:** Each player carries a medicine ball across to the first player in the opposite file.

e. **Obstacle Shuttle:** Set up cone markers, chairs, or pins between the two shuttle files and have each player zigzag through the objects using the equipment to the opposite file.

V(a)   V(b)

V(c)   V(d)

V(e)

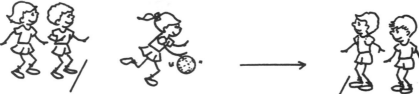

BALL SHUTTLE

FOCUS: Coordination; cooperation

EQUIPMENT: Two cone markers per team; one short rope per pair

ORGANIZATION:

- Use cones to mark a starting line and a turning post 10 meters (30 feet) apart; then form teams of six to nine players. Players should get into groups of three with teammates of equal size. The threesome stand side by side, in file formation behind the starting line. Ensure that the turning post is located a minimum of 1.7 meters (8 feet) from any wall or obstruction. Establish traffic patterns: Have the runners go around the turning post from the right (CCW) and return across the line on the right side as well, facing the file of team members. Adjust the hopping distance to the ability level of the class.

DESCRIPTION OF ACTIVITY:

1. Each threesome, holding each other around the waist, raise your right legs and hop together toward the cone marker, around it, and back to your team. Remember to keep your inside legs lifted from the floor while hopping.

2. The second threesome, repeat this action as soon as the first group is across the starting line. Continue in this way until everyone has had a turn at each position (middle player, right-hand player, left-hand player).

3. The first team to finish with all its players in cross-leg sit position in file formation wins the relay.

VARIATIONS:

a. ***Three-Legged Race:*** Have players pair off with someone of equal size. Partners stand side by side, holding onto each other's waists, with adjacent ankles tied comfortably together with a 1-meter (3-foot) length jute rope. Allow pairs to practice moving as a single unit, keeping the same rhythm.

b. ***Five-Legged Relay:*** Form teams of six or nine players per team. Have players in each team get into groups of three with teammates of equal size. The threesome stand side by side, in file formation at the starting line, facing a turning line 10 meters (30 feet) away. Outside players join outside hands under one leg of the middle player and gently lift it off the floor, and hold inside hands around the middle player's waist. Middle player balances and supports self by placing arms around the outside players' shoulders. If there is an unequal number of players in the teams, have the extra player join a threesome to form a foursome, or join in yourself to make another group of three.

Repeat relay three times until everyone has had a turn at each position.

SG–3 SPOKE RELAY

FOCUS: Cooperation; agility

EQUIPMENT: Lively music;
tape or record player

ORGANIZATION:

• Form teams of six to eight players. Each team forms a circle and players get into back-lying position with their heads toward the middle of the circle and their legs spread apart. Have players join hands to form the hub of the wheel; their bodies are the spokes. Players on each team then number off.

DESCRIPTION OF ACTIVITY:

1. On signal "Go!" first player, stand up and run CCW over the other players' legs until you reach your spot. Lie down there. As soon as you are lying down again, the second player will quickly stand up and repeat your action.
2. Continue in this way until each teammate has repeated the Spoke Relay twice. The first team to hook-sit in a circle, facing outward, with legs outstretched, wins the game.

VARIATION:

Have each team form a circle and sit with legs outstretched, their backs to the middle, with hands behind and feet together. Players' backs form the hub of the wheel; their legs are the spokes.

SG–4 CHARIOT RELAY

EQUIPMENT: Two cone markers per team

ORGANIZATION:

• Use cones to mark a starting line and turning post, 10 meters (30 feet) apart; then form teams of six to nine players. Each team forms several chariots of three players: two players form the chariot by standing side by side and joining inside hands; the third player is the driver and stands behind them, holding the players' outside hands. Each team should have at least two chariots. Remind chariots of the traffic pattern: Go around the marker from the right side (CCW) and return to cross the finish line on the right side.

DESCRIPTION OF ACTIVITY:

1. On signal "Go!" first chariot, run forward, around the marker, and back across the starting line. The second chariot may then go. Remember to keep your hand-hold throughout the relay.
2. Continue the race until each chariot has made three round trips and each player of the group of three has been a driver.
3. The first team to finish wins.

VARIATION:

Zigzag Chariot Relay: Set up a zigzag course of cone markers or chairs so the chariots must maneuver in and out.

FOCUS: Agility; strength; coordination

EQUIPMENT: Eight cone markers;
one basketball per team;
one hoop per team;
one jump rope per team;
one bench per team

ORGANIZATION:

• Form teams of four or five players and have each team stand in file formation behind a starting line. Mark four lines in front of and parallel to the starting line, all spaced 3 meters (10 feet) apart. Ensure that teams are well spaced to avoid collisions. Place the slower, less skilled players in the middle of the team. If an unequal number occurs in the teams, have a player go twice.

DESCRIPTION OF ACTIVITY:

1. On signal "Go!" each player, in turn, run forward and perform a different stunt at each of the four lines; then return to your team and tag the next runner. Continue until all players have performed the stunts. The first team to complete the relay and sit cross-legged in file formation at the starting line is the winner.

2. Suggestions for stunts:
    — Do twelve Cross-Over Straddle Jumps at the first line.
    — Do eight Knee Push-Ups at the second line.
    — Do eight Curl-Ups at the third line.
    — Do eight Burpees at the fourth line.

    — Jump and do two heel clicks at the first line.
    — Lie down and jump up four times at the second line.
    — Hold a "Stork Stand" balance for eight counts (count in time with the music's beat) at the third line.
    — Do a Log Roll across the fourth line, three roll-overs in one direction, then three roll-overs back.

VARIATIONS:

a. **Equipment Stunt Relay:** For each team, place a jump rope on the first line; a hoop with a basketball inside on the second line; and a bench on the third line. Each player, in turn, runs to the first line and jumps the rope thirty times; dribbles the basketball twice around the hoop in each direction at the second line; vault-jumps over the bench five times at the third line; performs two forward rolls on a mat at the fourth line.

b. Each team makes up a four-stunt relay that everyone performs. Teams take turns to present their stunt relay on succesive days.

SG–6 SIAMESE TWINS

FOCUS: Cooperation; coordination

EQUIPMENT: One stick per team; four cone markers per team

ORGANIZATION:

- Form teams of six to eight players per team. Have players in each team pair off and stand in file formation behind a line, facing a row of cone markers that are spaced 2 meters (6 feet) from each other. The first pair of each team straddles the stick, back to back, holding it with both hands in front. The front partner faces the cone markers, while the rear partner faces his or her team. Ideally, the sticks should be 5 centimeters (2 inches) doweling, cut into 1.2 meters (4 feet) lengths.

DESCRIPTION OF ACTIVITY:

1. Each pair, in turn, zigzag in and out of the cone markers, around the end cone marker, and zigzag back to your team across the starting line, to give the stick to the next pair in line.
2. Continue in this way until each pair has gone twice. On your second turn, front and rear partners change positions on the stick.

3. The first team to complete the relay and stand in starting position wins.

SG–7 WHEELBARROW RELAY

FOCUS: Partner work; arm-shoulder and leg strength

EQUIPMENT: Four cone markers

ORGANIZATION:

- Arrange teams of six or eight players in file formation behind a starting line and facing a turning line, about 5 meters (15 feet) away. Have players in each team pair off with someone who is of equal size. Have two players demonstrate the "wheelbarrow" position: One partner gets into the all-fours position; the other partner stands directly behind the kneeling partner. The standing partner then positions himself or herself between the partner's legs and grasps the partner's legs, holding them just above the knees, close to his or her hips. Adjust the "walking" distance to the ability level of the class.

DESCRIPTION OF ACTIVITY:

1. On the signal "Go!" the first pair "wheelbarrow" their way to the turning line. Once across the line, exchange roles and return to the file.
2. The next pair be ready to go as soon as the first pair crosses the starting line.

3. Continue in this way until everyone has had a turn. The first team to complete the relay and cross-leg sit in pairs is the winner.

VARIATION:

Scooter-Push Relay: One partner lies on his or her front on a scooter, gripping the sides of the scooter, while the other partner holds the lying partner's legs just above the knees and gently pushes him or her to a turning line. Here the two exchange roles and return to the starting line.

SG-8 AROUND-THE-WORLD RELAYS

FOCUS: Speed running; fair play

ORGANIZATION:

- Form teams of five or six players. Have teams make one big circle, with each team being one quarter of the circle and all circle players facing outward, spaced arm's length apart. Each team numbers off its members: 1, 2, 3, . . . , 5 or 6.

DESCRIPTION OF ACTIVITY:

1. On the signal "Go!" the first players, run CCW around the outside of the circle to your starting position and tag the second players, who repeat the circle run. Continue until everyone in your team has had a turn.
2. The first team to complete the activity and sit cross-legged in their quarter of the circle is the winner.

VARIATIONS:

a. Have players run CW around the circle.
b. Repeat relay using manipulative equipment such as deckrings, beachballs, or playground balls, which must be handed off from one player to the next.
c. *Circle Bounce Relay:* Have players, in turn, bounce a large playground ball around the circle.
d. For a smaller class, form a large circle with one team occupying each half of the circle. Number each team off and perform the relay as above.

SG-9 TUNNEL RELAY

EQUIPMENT: One medicine ball per team;
one cone marker per team

ORGANIZATION:

- Form teams of six players and have each team stand in file formation behind a starting line. The leader of each team holds a medicine ball.

DESCRIPTION OF ACTIVITY:

1. On the signal "Go!" leader, run with the medicine ball around the cone marker, join the front of your file, turn your back to the team, and roll the medicine ball backward through the open legs of your teammates to the end player. You can assist the ball as it rolls through your legs.
2. End player, pick up the medicine ball; run around the cone marker and back to your team. Join the front of your team and roll the medicine ball through.
3. Continue until the leader, as last player, runs a second time and returns to the front of the team. The first team cross-leg sitting behind the leader is the winner.

VARIATION:

Use a basketball and have players, in turn, dribble around the cone markers.

SG-10 RUN, ROLL, AND SET RELAY

FOCUS: Running; tumbling

EQUIPMENT: One folding mat per team;
one beanbag per team;
four cone markers

ORGANIZATION:

• Form teams of four or five players and arrange each team in file formation behind a starting line and facing a mat, located lengthwise, 6 meters (20 feet) away. Place a beanbag just in front of each mat nearest the team.

DESCRIPTION OF ACTIVITY:

1. On signal "Go!" the first player, run toward the mat, pick up the beanbag, and hold onto it while you do a forward roll along the mat; then set the beanbag near the far edge of the mat. Quickly run back to your team to tag the next player and join the end of your file.

2. The second player, run to the beanbag first, pick it up, and, holding onto it, do a forward roll on the way back, set the beanbag in its original spot, and then return to tag the third player in your team.

3. Continue in this way until everyone has had a turn. The first team to finish in file formation, cross-leg sitting, wins.

SG-11 BOX BALL RELAY

FOCUS: Cooperation; passing and receiving

EQUIPMENT: One ball per team;
one large box or container

ORGANIZATION:

• Divide the class into teams of four or five players and have players in each team number off 1, 2, 3, 4. Place a large box in the center of the play area and put the balls inside of it. Position the teams on each of the four sides of the play area, equal distance from the box, as shown. If there is an unequal number of players in the team, have a player go twice.

DESCRIPTION OF ACTIVITY:

1. On the signal "Go!" each player, in turn, race to get a ball from the box, stand facing your team, and pass it to each team player, who receives it and quickly passes it back to you. Then quickly return the ball to the box and "give five" to the next player on your team, who repeats the activity.

2. The first team to complete the task and cross-leg sit wins.

VARIATIONS:

a. Vary the type of pass used: Chest Pass; Bounce Pass; Push Pass.

b. *Box Ball Score:* Call out a number. The players with that number race to get a ball out of the box, pass it to each team player in turn, and return it to the box. The first player to return to his or her team in his or her original position scores a point for the team.

SG–12 SNOWSHOE RACE

FOCUS: Agility; coordination; fair play

EQUIPMENT: Twelve beanbags per team; four benches

ORGANIZATION:

- Place benches parallel to each other and about 3 meters (10 feet) apart; then form three equal teams of six to eight players. Have each player get two beanbags and hold one beanbag in each hand. The beanbags are the player's snowshoes. Ensure that players are well spaced to avoid collisions. Emphasize that players play fairly, keeping those beanbags under their feet while snowshoeing. Each team then stands in file formation behind a line that is 3 meters (10 feet) from the first bench.

DESCRIPTION OF ACTIVITY:

1. On signal "Go!" the first player, put a beanbag under each foot and snowshoe toward the first bench. When you reach it, pick up your beanbags, jump over the bench, and put your snowshoes under your feet again.
2. Continue to the next bench and repeat the action. As soon as you reach the second bench, the next player in your team may go.
3. When you reach the last bench, run around the outside of the benches and back to your team. Jog in place until it is your turn again.
4. When all players on your team have completed the course twice, jump up together and yell "Shazaam!" Who will be the first team to finish?

SG–13 GRECIAN FLURRY RELAY

FOCUS: Cooperation; running

EQUIPMENT: One parachute per team

ORGANIZATION:

- Form teams of sixteen players per team. Arrange each team in shuttle formation, with two groups of four comprising each half of the shuttle and facing the other half, 20 meters (60 feet) away. Give the starting group of four a parachute, which players grip with right hands on the front arc of the parachute and hold overhead with the rest of the chute trailing behind.

DESCRIPTION OF ACTIVITY:

1. On signal "Fly!" the starting group, run, holding the parachute high in the air, toward the opposite half of the shuttle. Hold the chute as high as possible so that the trailing end does not drag along the ground.
2. Second group, as the parachute comes toward you, grasp the rear trailing arc of the parachute with your right hands and run toward the third group. First group, let go of the parachute as soon as the second group has it in control; then join the end of this file.
3. Continue in this way, passing the parachute from one group to another. Which team can make the most number of crossings in three minutes?

VARIATION:

Have each group of four in a team, in turn, run around a turning point and back to the team to give the parachute to the next group.

FOCUS: Agility; leg strength; team work

EQUIPMENT: One bench per team;
one beanbag or deckring per team;
four cone markers

ORGANIZATION:

* Form teams of four or five players and have each team stand in file formation at a starting line. Place a bench opposite each team about 10 meters (30 feet) away.

DESCRIPTION OF ACTIVITY:

1. The first player on each team, get a beanbag, run to the bench, pass the beanbag under it, jump over the bench, and pick up the beanbag; then jump over the bench again and run back to hand the beanbag to the next player. Continue until everyone has had a turn.

2. (Place a beanbag 1 meter [3 feet] from each bench.) The first player, run to pick up the beanbag, jump over the bench, drop the beanbag on the other side of the bench, jump back over the bench, and return to tag the next teammate. Continue the relay in this way until everyone has had a turn.

3. The first player, place both hands on the bench, pick up the beanbag with your feet, swing the beanbag to the other side of the bench, and then run back to tag the next player, who repeats the same action. Continue until everyone has had a turn.

VARIATIONS:

a. When playing Bench Relays inside, have players run to touch an endline after jumping over the bench and before continuing with the other actions.

b. Each team creates its own Bench Relay. Have teams, in turn, demonstrate the activity involved; then everyone does the relay.

SG-15 OBSTACLE RELAY

FOCUS: Cooperation; general coordination

EQUIPMENT: Two chairs, one bench, and one table or box horse per team; hurdles or high jump standards; poles; three hoops per team; two cone markers

ORGANIZATION:

- Arrange each team of four or five players in file formation behind a starting line. Each team collects several obstacles (two chairs, one bench, one table or box horse, three hoops, and two hurdles) and arranges them in a row in front of their file, spacing them about 3 meters (10 feet) apart. Emphasize that players move through the obstacle course safely.

DESCRIPTION OF ACTIVITY:

1. Each player, in turn, go through the obstacle course and back around your team to your starting position. Return to tag the next player in line.

2. The first team to complete the course and cross-leg sit in their file is the winner.

3. *Suggestions for the obstacle course:* Go over one chair; under the second chair; hop along the bench from one end to the other; over the first hurdle; under the second hurdle; climb up and over the table or box horse; and in and out of three hoops.

VARIATIONS:

a. *Doubles Obstacle Course:* Have players pair off in their teams and go through the obstacle course twice, holding hands with their partner.

b. Have class design their own obstacle course using the equipment above.

SG-16 EVERYONE FOR YOURSELF

FOCUS: Throwing; running and dodging

EQUIPMENT: Two or three Nerf™ balls; several cone markers; three to four benches

ORGANIZATION:

• Use cones to mark off a large rectangular play area. Players scatter throughout this area. To begin the game, toss two balls into the play area.

DESCRIPTION OF ACTIVITY:

1. Any player may try to grab a tossed ball. The player with the ball has three seconds and may take three steps in any direction before throwing the ball at another player. The ball must hit below the waist.

2. If you are hit, you must sit on a bench until the player who hit you is also hit; then you may rejoin the game. Remember who hit you so that you can get back into the game. A loose ball may be picked up by any player.

VARIATIONS:

a. After six players are sitting on the benches, allow them all to return to the game.

b. Toss three Nerf™ balls into the play area and watch the activity level increase!

c. Establish the rule that a player with the ball may take only one "pivot step" in any direction.

SG-17 GHOST ZAPPERS

FOCUS: Throwing accuracy; running and dodging

EQUIPMENT: Set of banners; three utility balls (or sponge balls)

ORGANIZATION:

• Choose three players to be the Ghost Zappers; each wears a banner, holds a ball, and stands in the middle of the play area. The remaining players get into groups of three to four players, standing in a file and holding onto the waist of the player in front of them. Each group is a Ghost Train and the players are the Ghosts.

DESCRIPTION OF ACTIVITY:

1. The object of the game is for the Ghost Zappers to zap as many of the end Ghosts in the Ghost Trains as they can, in three minutes.

2. On the signal "Zap!" Ghost Zappers, throw your ball, trying to hit the end Ghost below the waist. The Ghost Train can protect the end Ghost by swinging away from the ball. The front Ghost, use your hands as well to block a thrown ball. Remember, Ghost Trains, to watch where you are going to avoid any collisions.

3. Any Ghost who lets go of the Train or who is hit below the waist with the ball becomes that Ghost Zapper's helper and wears a banner. The helper's job is to retrieve the ball after each throw and pass it back to the Ghost Zapper.

4. After three minutes, new Ghost Zappers are chosen, new Ghost Trains are formed, and the game is played again.

FOCUS: Alertness; fair play; throwing accuracy; catching

EQUIPMENT: One Nerf™ ball

ORGANIZATION:

- Have players stand in a circle formation, spaced arm's length apart and facing inward; then number off around the circle. Select one player to get a ball and stand in the center of the circle.

DESCRIPTION OF ACTIVITY:

1. Circle players, start jogging CCW around the circle. Center player, toss the ball overhead and call a number. Circle players, quickly move as far away from the center player as possible.

2. The player whose number is called, catch the ball on one or no bounces, and yell "Iceberg!" All players must then stop immediately and hold their positions.

3. Now player with the ball, throw it so that the ball hits a motionless player below the waist. If you miss, you get one spud and must toss the ball overhead again, calling a new number. If you hit a player, that player gets one spud and becomes the new center player.

4. When you have collected three spuds, you must come to me to perform a task (push-ups, jumping jacks, or sit-ups, etc.) before you can rejoin the game.

VARIATIONS:

a. If playing the game in a gym, have players stay on or inside the basketball boundary lines.

b. *Team Spud:* Divide the class into two teams and number off everyone from 1, 2, 3, etc. Play the game as above, keeping track of the number of spuds each team accumulates. Which team will collect the least number of spuds to win the game?

SG-19 DUEL BALL

FOCUS: Throwing accuracy; dodging

EQUIPMENT: Two sponge balls

ORGANIZATION:

- Form two teams of ten to fifteen players and have the players in each team number off. The two teams form a large circle, each team making up half the circle. Players space themselves evenly around their half of the circle. Place two sponge balls about 2 meters (6 feet) apart in the middle of the circle, on either side of a center line.

DESCRIPTION OF ACTIVITY:

1. Listen for your number. When you hear it, run to the center of the circle, pick up a ball, and try to hit the other player below the waist. You must stay in your half of the circle.
2. Circle players, retrieve the balls and throw them back to your teammate in the center.
3. If you hit the other player before he or she hits you, your team is awarded one point. Return to your place in the circle, and wait for another number to be called.
4. The game continues in this way until all players have had a turn. The team with the best score wins.

VARIATIONS:

a. Divide the class into smaller teams and have two games going at the same time.
b. Call out two numbers at a time. Partners must join inside hands and throw with outside hands, trying to hit the opposing pair.

SG-20 JUMP THE SHOT

FOCUS: Agility; alertness; leg strength

EQUIPMENT: One long rope per team;
one slightly deflated tether ball
or deckring per team

ORGANIZATION:

- To make a Jump-the-Shot rope, attach a tether ball to a rope that is about 5 meters (15 feet) long. If you do not have an old tether ball, any soft object such as a deckring or beanbag will do. Form equal teams of six to eight players. Each team stands in a circle, with players spaced at arm's length. One player on each team gets a Jump-the-Shot rope and stands in the center of the circle.

DESCRIPTION OF ACTIVITY:

1. Middle player, swing the rope slowly at first, CW so that your circle players know how far away from it they should stand to be able to jump over it. The rope should just pass under their legs. As you swing the rope, keep it low to the ground so that it is easy to jump.
2. Circle players, jump the rope each time it swings past you. If the rope hits your leg or you miss a jump, leave the circle and jog once around the play area; then rejoin the game.
3. Change rope turners every five turns.

VARIATIONS:

a. Have rope turners swing the rope CCW.
b. Vary the speed of the rope according to the ability level of the jumpers.
c. Have circle players join hands with a partner.
d. Have circle players bounce a ball as the rope is turned.

FOCUS: Throwing; catching; dodging

EQUIPMENT: One sponge ball;
set of banners

ORGANIZATION:

• Select one player to be IT, who wears a banner, holds a ball, and stands in the middle of the play area. All other players scatter around the play area. Remind players to watch where they are going to avoid collisions with other players. Encourage the IT team to pass to all its members, not to just those who can throw the ball the best.

DESCRIPTION OF ACTIVITY:

1. On the signal "Go!" IT, to start the game into action, move around the play area trying to hit a player below the waist. When you do so, that player must wear a banner and join the IT team.

2. Now IT players, you may throw the ball at a player within three seconds or pass the ball to each other to get into good position to hit a free player, but you can only take one pivot step from the place where you got the ball.

3. Free players, if you are hit, you must put on a banner and join the IT team. If you are hit while ducking, you must also join the IT team.

4. The ball cannot hit the floor or rebound off a wall and then hit a player. A player catching a thrown ball may throw it as far away as possible; however, if the ball is dropped, the player is considered to be hit.

5. The game continues until only one free player remains. This player becomes the new IT for the next game.

VARIATION:

Establish the rule that a player catching a thrown ball may "free" a player on the IT team.

SG-22 CHINESE WALL

FOCUS: Running and dodging; alertness

EQUIPMENT: Eight cone markers; several large folding mats

ORGANIZATION:

- Using the cones, mark out two parallel endlines that are 20 meters (60 feet) apart. Then mark out two parallel lines, 3 meters (10 feet) apart, across the center of the play area to represent the wall. Select three players to stand on the wall to defend it, and have the remaining players start on either endline.

DESCRIPTION OF ACTIVITY:

1. On the signal from the wall defenders, "Scale the wall!" players run and try to cross the wall to the opposite endline without being tagged with a one-hand touch by the defenders.
2. Defenders, you may not leave the wall, but may travel anywhere along it.
3. Players, if you are tagged by a defender, you must remain on the wall and help to defend it on the next crossing. Remember, do not attempt to cross the wall to the other endline until defenders give the signal.

VARIATIONS:

a. Have players wear flags (tucked into the back of their waistbands), which the defenders try to pull out as players run across to the opposite endline.
b. Place large folding mats across the center area to act as the "wall." Ensure mats are hooked together on the velcro sides and any flaps are facing downward.
c. Allow players to cross the wall at their choosing, but they must touch the opposite endline before attempting another crossing.

SG-23 FORDING THE STREAM

FOCUS: Cooperation, ingenuity

EQUIPMENT: One table and chair; one mat and long rope; four beanbags; two deckrings; one scooter; two cone markers

ORGANIZATION:

- Use cones to mark out a starting line and a finish line, (the two "banks" of a stream), about 20 meters (60 feet) apart. Divide the class into teams of five to six players. Evenly space teams along the starting line. Each team receives a table, a chair, a mat, a long rope, four beanbags, two deckrings, one scooter, and two cone markers.

DESCRIPTION OF ACTIVITY:

1. On the signal "Ford the Stream!" each team, using all the above equipment, must maneuver the equipment and team members from one "bank" to the other, without getting wet. No contact can be made with the floor by any player throughout the challenge. Each team is allowed one minute to develop a "plan of action."
2. If a player gets wet (touches the floor), then that player's team receives a five-second "freezing" penalty and cannot move forward.
3. The first team to get all the equipment and players behind the finish line on the other bank wins.

VARIATION:

Vary the equipment used according to what is available to you.

FOCUS: Dodging; throwing and catching; fair play

EQUIPMENT: One Nerf™ ball per team; several cone markers

ORGANIZATION:

• Use the cones to mark out a large rectangular court, with a center line and about 1.7 meters (8 feet) "out" area behind each endline, as shown in diagram. Divide the class into two equal teams and have each team occupy one half of the play area. To start the game, toss a ball into each half of the court.

DESCRIPTION OF ACTIVITY:

1. The object of the game is to be the first team to hit all the opposition players. The ball must hit a player below the waist and must be thrown within five seconds; otherwise, it is awarded to the other team.

2. A "hit" player must go to the opposition's "out" area. Here a player can field any ball that comes into this area, but then must throw it back to a teammate in his or her half.

3. Court players are not allowed to step outside their court to retrieve a ball; "out" area players are not allowed to step inside the court.

4. If you catch a ball thrown by an opposition player in his or her court that is traveling through the air, you may bring one of your end area players back to your court. However, if you drop the air ball, you are considered hit.

5. A throw must be a direct hit; the ball cannot hit the floor or rebound off a wall and then hit a player. If you are hit while ducking, you must go to the opposition's "out" area.

VARIATION:

To increase the challenge, have players in the "out" area throw the ball with their nondominant hand or roll it at opposition players.

SG–25 FRENCH CRICKET

FOCUS: Batting; throwing accuracy; catching

EQUIPMENT: One cricket bat per group; one small utility ball per group

ORGANIZATION:

• Divide the class into groups of six to eight players. Each group forms a circle, with players evenly spaced around it. One player, the Batter, holds a bat and stands in the center about 4 meters (12 feet) away from the circle players. Give the ball to a circle player to start the game.

DESCRIPTION OF ACTIVITY:

1. Circle players, throw the ball and try to hit the Batter below his or her knees, or catch a fly ball hit by the batter. If you do so, you become the new Batter.
2. Batter, use your bat for defense. Keep the bat near the floor so you can react quickly to a ball coming toward your lower body. If the ball hits you below your knees, you must change positions with the thrower.
3. Circle players, you may pass the ball around the circle before throwing it, trying to catch the batter out of position.

VARIATIONS:

a. To ensure that everyone gets a turn in the center, change the Batter after every five throws by the circle players.
b. Make a Cricket Bat with one flat side.
c. Have the Batter protect a cone marker or a garbage can placed in the center of the circle.

SG–26 QUADRANT DODGEBALL

FOCUS: Throwing; catching; dodging

EQUIPMENT: Two sponge balls; several cone markers; one set of banners

ORGANIZATION:

• Mark out a large square, with 20-meter (60-foot) sides. Divide the square into four quadrants, as shown in the diagram. Divide the class into two equal teams and have one team wear the banners. Half of each team position themselves in diagonally opposite quadrants. Each team has a ball. Emphasize that players play fairly and remain loyal to their team.

DESCRIPTION OF ACTIVITY:

1. On the signal "Go!" each team, try to hit players of the opposition team below the waist. Score one point for every player your team hits.
2. Hit players, you must stand outside of your quadrant and may only field balls for your team.
3. A ball must hit you directly below the waist to count as a hit. If you catch a thrown ball without it touching a wall or floor, you may call one of your hit players back into your quadrants. Players, you can move freely from one of your quadrants into another.
4. The team who has the most hits after a certain time is the winner.

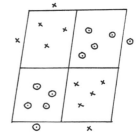

VARIATION:

Add another ball to the game.

FOCUS: Running and dodging; alertness

EQUIPMENT: One set of banners;
several cone markers;
any small object such as a marble,
piece of chalk, button, ping-pong ball

ORGANIZATION:

• Use cones to mark a play area with a center line that suits the players' level of running ability. Form two equal teams and have one team wear the banners. Each team stands side by side in its half at the center line, facing the other team. Flip a coin or choose a number to decide which team receives a small object, representing the "football," at the start of the game. Encourage teams to be "sneaky" when deciding how the football will be carried and who will carry it.

DESCRIPTION OF ACTIVITY:

1. The offensive team, with the "football," has ten seconds to meet in a huddle to decide on the team's game plan: Who will carry the object in his or her hands? How can you fake it to look like everyone in your team is carrying it?

2. On the signal "Go!" offensive team players, run toward the opposite end of the play area. Meanwhile, defensive team players, try to gag the opposition with a one-hand touch.

3. Offensive players, if you are tagged, open your hands and show what you are carrying. If your hands are empty, freeze on the spot. If you have the object, the teams change roles and the other team gets the "football."

4. Offensive player, if you are carrying the "football" and reach the end of the play area without being tagged, shout "Touchdown!" Your team then earns one point. The other team gets the "football" and the game continues.

SG-28 ROYAL COURT

FOCUS: Throwing and catching; dodging; fair play

EQUIPMENT: Two sponge balls; several cone markers

ORGANIZATION:

- Use cones to mark out a large rectangular play area and center line. Form two equal teams and have each team scatter in their own half of the play area. Each team selects a King or Queen, who stands behind the opposition's endline. Begin the game by rolling a ball into each team's court, then signaling "Go!"

DESCRIPTION OF ACTIVITY:

1. The object of the game is to be the first team to hit all the opposition players.
2. Players hit below the waist, go to the opposition's end to help your King or Queen by fielding the ball for him or her, or fielding a ball and throwing it back to your own court players.
3. Only the King or Queen is allowed to throw the ball at the opposing team.
4. Court players, you are not allowed to step outside your court to retrieve a ball; end area players, you are not allowed to step inside the court.
5. If you catch a ball while it is traveling through the air, you may bring one of your end players back to your court. However, if you drop an air ball, you are considered hit.

VARIATIONS:

a. For a faster game, allow any endline player to throw the ball at the opposition players.
b. Add another ball to the game.

SG-29 SPACESHIPS

FOCUS: Throwing accuracy; running and dodging; fair play

EQUIPMENT: Three hoops; three small utility balls

ORGANIZATION:

- Equally space three hoops lengthwise through the middle of the play area (galaxy). Choose three players to be the aliens. They each get a ball (meteorite) and stand with both feet inside the hoop (space station). The other players are the spaceships and stand in a line formation at one end of the play area.

DESCRIPTION OF ACTIVITY:

1. As Commander of the universe, I will call the spaceships to fly from one end of the galaxy to the other. Spaceships, as you travel through space, watch out for aliens, who will try to zap you with their meteorites. If a meteorite hits you below the waist, you are stranded in space and must sink to your knees.
2. Aliens, you must have both feet inside your space station when throwing a meteorite. Quickly retrieve a thrown meteorite and return to the space station before throwing it again.
3. Any spaceships who run out-of-bounds or fly outside the galaxy will become stranded there. Stranded spaceships, try to touch a flying spaceship to change roles with that player. Remember, you can only move your upper body; your lower body is frozen to the spot! Continue until all spaceships are stranded in space.

VARIATION:

Use different signals to call the spaceships across the galaxy: all girl spaceships; all boy spaceships; all spaceships wearing green; all spaceships wearing sweat pants or shorts.

FOCUS: Passing and receiving skills

EQUIPMENT: Four cone markers per game; one small utility ball per game; one set of banners per game

ORGANIZATION:

• Use cones to mark out a square play area that has a maximum of 10-meter (30-feet) sides. For each game, you will need two teams of six to eight players. One team wears the banners. To start the game, toss a ball up between two opposition players at center, who try to bat the ball to a team player. The remaining players scatter around the jumpers, 2 meters (6 feet) away. Emphasize that team players can use the corners of the play area to trap an opposing player. Caution players that no dribbling, no running with the ball, and no body contact are allowed. Have players find an opposition player to guard throughout the game (man-to-man defense).

DESCRIPTION OF ACTIVITY:

1. The object of the game is to pass the ball around from team player to team player, trying to "corner" opposition players, then tag them with the ball to score points. The first team to get to five points is the winner.

2. Opposition players, you may not intercept the ball but should try to avoid being tagged by the ball-handlers.

3. The ball changes possession when:

   — the ball is dropped

   — a player holds the ball longer than three seconds

   — a player takes more than one pivot step while carrying the ball or attempting to tag an opposition player

   — a player steps or throws the ball out-of-bounds. The opposing team is awarded the ball at the place where the infraction occurs.

VARIATIONS:

a. Vary the type of ball used: sponge ball, utility ball, volleyball, basketball, football, beanbag.

b. Vary the type of pass used: chest pass, bounce pass, push pass.

c. Set up a "Corner Ball Tournament" and have teams challenge each other.

d. Allow defensive players to intercept the ball.

SG-31 STEAL THE STICKS

FOCUS: Running and dodging

EQUIPMENT: Twelve batons; several cone markers; one set of banners; four hoops; two baskets or boxes

ORGANIZATION:

- Divide a large rectangular play area in half using cone markers, and mark a line across each end and at center. Evenly distribute six batons or sticks (33-centimeter or 12-inch doweling, 12-millimeter [1-inch] in thickness) behind each line. Place a hoop on two diagonal corners of the playing area, the Prisons, and a hoop in the middle of each half, the Safe Homes. Place a basket on the other two diagonal corners for the Stick Boxes. Form two equal teams and have one team wear banners. To start, the players on each team stand side by side in their half at center, facing the opponents.

DESCRIPTION OF ACTIVITY:

1. The object of the game is to "steal" all the opponent's sticks and store them in the Stick Box before the other team can do the same.
2. On the signal "Go!" both teams, attempt to run to the opposition's endline and grab a stick without being tagged. If you succeed, you may carry it over your head back to your half, without being tagged. Place the stick in the Stick Box; then make another attempt!
3. If you are in the Safe Home in the opposition's half, you cannot be tagged, but only one player at a time can be in the hoop.
4. If you are tagged in the opponent's half, you become a prisoner and must go to the opponent's Prison, remaining there until a teammate frees you. When freed, both you and the player who freed you with a hand touch may return safely to your half by walking on the outside of the playing area.
5. A player can only free one prisoner at a time, and only one stick at a time can be taken from the opposition's endline.
6. The game ends when one team has collected all of the opponent's sticks or a certain time has elapsed. The team with the most sticks wins.

VARIATIONS:

a. Increase the challenge by allowing no sticks to be taken until all prisoners are freed first.
b. A player with an opposition's stick must try to make it back to his or her own half without being tagged.
c. Instead of sticks, place a flag on a stick in the ground in the middle of each endline. The object of the game is to steal the opposition's flag and carry it into their own half before the other team can do the same.
d. Scatter obstacles throughout the play area so that players can dodge around, over, under, or through them.

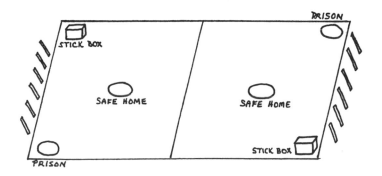

FOCUS: Throwing and catching; dodging

EQUIPMENT: Four sponge balls;
two to four banners;
six cone markers

ORGANIZATION:

• Use cones to mark off a large rectangular area and center line. Divide the class into two equal teams and have each team scatter in their own half of the play area. Each team must select two Doctors, who wear banners. To begin the game, roll a ball into each half of the play area.

DESCRIPTION OF ACTIVITY:

1. The object of the game is to hit both the opposition team's Doctors to win the game.

2. Opposing players, throw the ball at each other from your own half, trying to hit your opponents below the waist. A player hit above the waist or hit by a ball that bounces first, or who blocks a ball thrown toward the face, is not hit. You have five seconds to throw the ball.

3. A ball that hits a player while he or she ducks down is considered a hit. A player dropping a fly ball while attempting to catch it is also considered hit. If a player throws an air ball that is caught by an opposition player, then the thrower is considered hit and must drop to the floor at that spot. A player with the ball may use it to deflect another ball that is thrown at him or her.

4. Any hit player, immediately sit on the floor on that spot, as you are injured, until one of your team Doctors can pull you over the endline into the recovery zone. You may then rejoin the game. A Doctor may rescue only one player at a time.

5. The first Doctor to be hit becomes a regular player, and the game continues with only one Doctor.

VARIATIONS:

a. Choose your Doctors in secrecy so that the opposition must determine who the Doctors are.

b. Allow Doctors to throw the ball at the opposition as well.

SG—33 INVASION

FOCUS: Accuracy throwing; catching; dodging

EQUIPMENT: Several cone markers;
four sponge balls;
floor tape

ORGANIZATION:

• Use the cones to mark out a large rectangular area and center line. Use the floor tape to mark out an invasion line, lengthwise through the middle of the play area, as shown. Divide the class into two even teams. Have each team line up on their endline and quietly choose two Secret Agents per team. Evenly space four balls along the center line.

DESCRIPTION OF ACTIVITY:

1. On the signal "Go!" both teams rush toward the center line, quickly grab the balls, and try to hit the opposing players below the waist. Hit players, immediately drop to the floor in the back-lying position.

2. A Secret Agent player, rescue a dropped team player by grabbing him or her by the legs and dragging this player across your endline. Once behind this endline, the rescued player does five push-ups and then may rejoin the game.

3. Secret Agent, disguise yourself by acting like a regular player and throw the ball at the opposing team. However, if you are hit below the waist by an opposing player, you are no longer a Secret Agent but now a permanent regular player.

4. If a ball is caught by an opposing player, the thrower must drop into the back-lying position and wait to be rescued. If a player attempts to catch a ball but misses, or if a player ducks and is hit by a ball, then that player must drop and also wait to be rescued.

5. Once a team's Secret Agents are both hit, then the opposing team can "invade" into that team's half only along the invasion line and try to hit as many players as possible in one minute. Any player hit by an invader must cross-leg sit on the spot. Which team will invade first?

6. Remember, Invaders, you must stay on the invasion line, and you and your Secret Agents (in trying to rescue their own players in the opposition's court) risk getting hit by the opposing players.

VARIATION:

Add more "invasion" lines to increase the activity.

INVASION LINE

FOCUS: Throwing accuracy; catching; dodging

EQUIPMENT: Eight cone markers; eight whiffle balls; three sponge balls

ORGANIZATION:

• Evenly space four cone markers at each end of the play area. Place a whiffle ball on top of each cone marker and then place the sponge balls in the middle of the play area. Form two equal teams and have teams stand at opposite ends of the play area.

DESCRIPTION OF ACTIVITY:

1. The object of the game is to be the first team to knock down all the other team's balls.

2. On signal "Go!" players from each team, run to the middle of the play area and grab a sponge ball.

3. Without crossing the center line, throw the ball, trying to hit opposition players below the waist and knock down all the other team's whiffle balls.

4. Each team is allowed to have one player to guard each whiffle ball. Remove any cone and ball that are knocked down.

5. If you are hit, you must sit or stand at the side of the play area until the player who hit you is also hit or a teammate catches a fly ball. If you drop a ball, you are considered hit. If you duck, the ball may hit you anywhere; however, you may block a ball that is coming toward your face.

VARIATION:

Allow only one player to guard the four whiffle balls.

SG-35 BALLOON HANDBALL

FOCUS: Team work; hand–eye coordination

EQUIPMENT: Six cone markers; two inflated balloons of different colors; one set of banners

ORGANIZATION:

- Use cones to mark out a rectangular play area and a center line to create two halves. Form two equal teams and have one team wear the banners. Players on each team stand side by side in their half at center, facing the team on the opposite side. One player from each team then gets a balloon.

DESCRIPTION OF ACTIVITY:

1. On signal "BOP!" each team, try to bat the balloon over the opposition's goal line. At the same time, each team, try to stop the other team's balloon from reaching your goal line. Only an open hand may be used to bat the ball.
2. Score one point for each goal. The first team to get to five points wins.

VARIATIONS:

a. For a large class, use two balloons per team.
b. Play the game in pairs, who have inside hands joined and must bat with outside hands only.
c. Allow a player only two consecutive bats of the balloon before another player bats it.

SG-36 BLANKETBALL

FOCUS: Cooperation

EQUIPMENT: One sturdy blanket per team; several sponge balls

ORGANIZATION:

- Have players bring four old blankets, which should be about the same size and made of durable material. Form teams of six to eight players. Have each team evenly spread out around a blanket, with players firmly grasping the edges of the blanket. Place a sponge ball in the middle of the blanket. Ensure that teams are well spaced so that no interference occurs.

DESCRIPTION OF ACTIVITY:

1. Each team, working together, practice tossing the ball into the air and catching it on your blanket. How many tosses and catches can you make in this way?
2. Now pair up with another team, which positions itself about 4 meters (12 feet) from your team. Can you toss a ball back and forth from your blanket to the other team's blanket?
3. Now try this challenge: One team toss the ball high into the air, then quickly dash out of the way to let the other team dash under the falling ball and collect it in their blanket!

VARIATIONS:

a. Vary the type of ball used: small utility ball, volleyball, tennis ball.
b. Vary the type of "blanket" used: sturdy bedspread, large piece of light-weight canvas, small parachute, "fling-it" nets.
c. Have players pair up and use a towel to propel and catch a tennis ball together; then pass the ball to another pair.

SG—37 BUMP AND SCOOT BALL

FOCUS: Cooperation; volleyball skills

EQUIPMENT: Volleyball net or long rope and two posts per game; one beachball per game

ORGANIZATION:

- Divide the class into teams of six to eight players. For each game, have two teams position themselves on each side of a volleyball court. Give one team the beachball to start.

DESCRIPTION OF ACTIVITY:

1. The player with the ball, start the game by hitting the beachball over the net to the other team. Call "Mine!" if you intend to take the ball and play in your own space.

2. Whenever a player on one team hits the beachball over the net, he or she then scoots under the net to the other side.

3. The challenge is to make a complete change in teams with as few drops of the ball as possible.

SG—38 BASE-KET-BALL

FOCUS: Retrieving and passing; shooting; team work

EQUIPMENT: One basketball; chalkboard and chalk; several cone markers

ORGANIZATION:

- Form two equal teams of Batters and Fielders. One fielder, the Shooter, stands at the foul line of each basketball key. The other fielders, the Retrievers, scatter throughout the play area. One Batter gets a basketball and stands at home plate, which is in the middle of one side of the play area. The other batters stand in batting order just outside the sideline and wait their turn to bat. Mark a throwing line parallel to and 3 meters (10 feet) from the batter's sideline. Place cones at each corner of the play area. Allow each Shooter only one try to make a basket at a time. Adjust the shooting distance to the ability level of the class. After every four throws, change the Shooters so that everyone in the fielding team gets a chance at this position.

DESCRIPTION OF ACTIVITY:

1. Batter at home plate, throw the ball over the "throw line"; then run CCW around the cones. Try to reach home before a retriever can catch the ball and throw it to the nearest Shooter, who will try to make a basket.

2. If the Shooter shoots the ball into the basket before you reach home plate, you are out. If the Shooter misses, the ball is passed to another Shooter, who will try again. Fielders, continue retrieving and shooting the ball until the Batter reaches home.

3. You score one point for your team if you reach home plate before the other team can make a basket.

4. After all Batters have had a turn, change roles. The team with the best score wins.

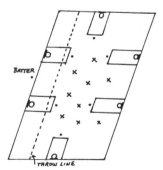

SG—39 HOOF BALL

FOCUS: Kicking skills; running and dodging

EQUIPMENT: Several cone markers; one sponge ball or slightly deflated soccer ball; chalkboard and chalk

ORGANIZATION:

- This is an indoor game that uses the walls of the play area. Use the cones to mark out a large rectangular play area, with a kicking line and endline about 1.7 meters (8 feet) from a front wall and an end wall. Divide the class into two even teams: the Kicking Team, who stands in file formation along one side wall, and the Fielding Team, who scatters throughout the play area. To start the game, one fielder holds the ball and stands about 4 meters (12 feet) away from the first Kicker, who stands in the middle of the kicking line. Have kickers alternate boy–girl in the kicking order. Change the ball roller every three rolls.

DESCRIPTION OF ACTIVITY:

1. Fielder, roll the ball toward the kicker. Kicker, kick the ball past the kicking line anywhere in the play area; then run quickly to the opposite endline without being hit with the ball. You have earned one point for your team. You may choose to stay behind the endline, or try to return to the kicking line to earn two runs for your team.

2. Fielding team, quickly retrieve the kicked ball and, without taking any steps, pass it to another teammate or throw it at the runner, trying to hit him or her below the waist to put the runner out. A fly ball caught by a fielder does not put the runner out.

3. Runners, you may stay behind the opposite endline as long as there are only two of you. Once a third runner approaches the endline, the first runner to get there must run back to the kicking line. You could all decide to run back to the kicking line if you dare!

4. After the Kicking team players have all had a turn, then the teams exchange roles. The team with the best score wins.

VARIATIONS:

a. Have Kicking and Fielding teams change positions every three outs.

b. Have batters strike a tossed ball with the heel of an open hand.

FIELDING TEAM

FOCUS: Team work; batting and fielding skills   **EQUIPMENT:** Four bases or cone markers;
one volleyball or sponge ball

ORGANIZATION:

- Set up the four bases to represent "home plate," first, second, and third bases in a softball diamond. Divide the class into two equal teams: the Batting Team and the Fielding Team. Have the Fielders scatter throughout the diamond and the Batters stand in file formation, well out of the way of the play, on a sideline. Emphasize that in this game there are no outs. Everyone wins! Remind runners to "freeze" as soon as they hear the "Iceberg" signal.

DESCRIPTION OF ACTIVITY:

1. One fielder, the Pitcher, toss the ball toward the Batter so that the ball bounces in front of home plate. Batter, strike at the ball with the heel of your open hand.

2. Batter, after hitting the ball, run around the bases in order, while the Fielding Team quickly retrieves the ball. After every fielder has touched the ball, the Pitcher yells "Iceberg!" This is the signal for the base runner to immediately stop, even if caught between two bases.

3. After the next batter hits the ball, the base runner continues his or her way around the bases, as does the batter, until they hear "Iceberg!"

4. The Batting Team, score one run each time a runner reaches home plate. After everyone on the Batting Team has had a turn at bat, then the Fielding Team will bat.

VARIATIONS:

a. Vary the distance between the bases according to the ability level of the class.

b. Vary the way the ball is propelled forward: Throw a football or Frisbee™; kick a soccer ball; hit a ball with a bat; shoot the ball with a hockey stick; bat the ball with a broomstick.

SG—41 COOPERATIVE ROUNDERS

FOCUS: Cooperation; batting and fielding skills   **EQUIPMENT:** Four bases;
one bat and softball;
one glove per fielder

ORGANIZATION:

• Set the bases around the softball diamond to represent home, first, second, and third. Divide the class into two teams: the Batting Team, who stands in file formation on the side of the field between third and home; and the Fielding Team, who takes up positions around the bases and in the field. Have Fielders rotate positions after every three batters.

DESCRIPTION OF ACTIVITY:

1. The object of this game is for the Fielding Team to help the Batting Team collect a required number of runs (that is, the number of runs must equal the number of batters).

2. Each Batter, in turn, attempt to hit the ball. If, after three pitches, you fail to hit the ball, just rotate back into order and you will have another turn.

3. Fielding Team, try to field the ball well, but do not try to put the Batter out. If a grounder is hit, the Batter advances one base; if an infield fly is caught, the Batter takes two bases; if an outfield fly is caught, the Batter gets three bases. When runners are on base, they just move to the next base as their teammates get hits.

4. The Fielding Team, you must stop the ball first; then the Batter may run to the bases.

5. A run is scored each time a runner reaches home base.

SG-42 BEACHBALL GOLF

FOCUS: Cooperation

EQUIPMENT: Twelve hoops;
one large beachball
(or balloon), per group of three

ORGANIZATION:

- Scatter the hoops around the play area; then have players form groups of three. Give each group a beachball.

DESCRIPTION OF ACTIVITY:

1. *Practice:* Bat the beachball back and forth to each other. Try to keep the ball in the air without letting it touch the floor.
2. *Game:* While continuing to bat the ball between you, one of the threesome must try to pick up a hoop, get the beachball to pass through it, put the hoop back on the floor, and continue on to another hoop. Count the number of hoops through which you batted the ball in three minutes. You may not run while holding the hoop or the beachball, and the ball cannot be hit twice in a row.

VARIATION:

Play the game in teams of two players.

SG-43 RICOCHET

FOCUS: Throwing accuracy; team work

EQUIPMENT: One 30-centimeter (12-inch) utility ball;
twenty 20-centimeter (8-inch) utility balls;
six cone markers

ORGANIZATION:

- Use cones to mark out a rectangular play area and a center line. Divide the class into two equal teams, who stand in a line formation on opposite endlines, facing each other. Give ten small utility balls to each team. Place the large utility ball in the center of the play area.

DESCRIPTION OF ACTIVITY:

1. On the signal "Ricochet, Away!" both teams, throw the balls at the large utility ball, trying to force it over the opposition's endline. You are not allowed to kick the ball. Make sure you share the small balls with other team members so that everyone participates!
2. Players, you may retrieve only those balls in your own half of the playing area. Before attempting to throw the retrieved ball at the big ball, you must touch your endline first.
3. The team that succeeds in sending the big ball over the opposition's endline wins.

VARIATIONS:

a. Place two large balls in the middle of the play area to increase the challenge level.
b. Use a beachball and beanbags.

SG—44 WHIP IT!

FOCUS: Throwing and catching; alertness

EQUIPMENT: Volleyball net (or long rope) and posts; four tennis balls; four tube socks

ORGANIZATION:

- Whip-It is a lead-up game to Volleyball. To play the game, you will need to make four Whip-Its by knotting a tennis ball in the toe of each tube sock. Demonstrate how to throw a Whip-It by circling it twice around in a CW direction; then tossing it up and outward with an underhand motion. Allow time for players to practice this throwing action. String a net or long rope between the two posts about 2 meters (6 feet) above the floor. Form two teams of six to eight players and give each team two Whip-Its. Players take up court positions of two lines of three or four players and rotate CW one position every minute. Remind players to stay in their own space and not try to hog the Whip-Its. Encourage players to take turns throwing the Whip-Its so that everyone gets involved in the game.

DESCRIPTION OF ACTIVITY:

1. The object of the game is to catch the Whip-Its before they hit the floor on your side of the net.

2. When I signal "Go!" toss your Whip-Its over the net, aiming for open spaces in the other team's court.

3. Call "Mine!" when you intend to catch the Whip-It. It must be then thrown from the spot where it was caught.

4. The other team scores a point whenever:

   — a Whip-It touches the floor of your court, the net, or the ceiling;
   — your team throws a Whip-It out-of-bounds; or
   — your Whip-It does not make it over the net.

VARIATION:

Whip-It Tourney: Have each team play all the others. The team with the best "defensive" score (that is, has the least number of points scored against them) is the winner.

FOCUS: Throwing and catching; team work

EQUIPMENT: One football; two basketball hoops; one set of banners; several cone markers

ORGANIZATION:

• Use cones to mark out a large rectangular playing area and a center line. Divide the class into teams of six to eight players. For each game, one team wears the banners. Start the game with a "jump-off" by two opposing players at center and the other team members in their own half. To avoid players cluttering around the football, teach the players to play "man-to-man" defense; that is, each player guards an opposition player. Adjust the size of the football to meet the ability level of the group. Girls will probably be more successful throwing a lighter, smaller ball. Encourage team players to pass to everyone in their team. Insist that at least one pass must be made to a girl.

DESCRIPTION OF ACTIVITY:

1. Team players, pass the ball to each other until you are in the opposition's court; then try to score points by throwing the football at the basketball hoop.

2. The "rule of threes" is in effect:

   — The ball must be passed, or a shot at a goal attempted, within three seconds.

   — A player is allowed to take a maximum of three steps in any direction.

   — A team must complete three consecutive passes before an attempt to score a goal can occur.

3. Opposing players try to intercept a pass and thereby gain possession of the football.

4. A player who throws the football through the basket or hoop earns two points for his or her team. One point is awarded if the football hits any part of the backboard, or the hoop rim, but doesn't go in.

SG-46 INTRODUCING TABLOID SPORTS

FOCUS: Teaching guidelines; class organization

EQUIPMENT: Station equipment; stopwatch and calculator; posterboard and marking pens; chalkboard and chalk; floor or masking tape; selection of lively music; tape or record player

ORGANIZATION:

• Tabloids are circuits of high-interest, low-skill, mass-participation activities that are challenging and fun! Choose eight activities from the following cards for each Tabloid and add ideas of your own. Set up equipment in stations around the play area, posting a sign at each station that can be easily read from a distance. Set up the scoreboard, mark starting lines with floor or masking tape, and select the music to be played. To begin, form as many teams of five to eight players as you have stations. Choose a leader for each team, and assign each team a number from one to eight. Explain the rules. Demonstrate the task to be performed at each station, or have each team demonstrate the task at its starting station. Allow each team to decide how it will organize itself at each station.

(continued)

VARIATIONS:

a. Choose sports or seasonal themes such as the Olympic Games, a Circus or Carnival, Christmas, Easter, or Halloween.

b. Practice game skills in tabloid format. Set up a Volleyball Tabloid; a Basketball Tabloid; a Soccer Tabloid; a Hockey Tabloid; a Track and Field Tabloid.

c. Adapt the tabloid activities so that they can be used outdoors as in a Winter Carnival or Beach Carnival Tabloid.

d. *Integration:* Combine several Grade 5 classes and run a Tabloid. As an Art project, have the children draw and paint pictures, depicting the theme of the tabloid and the station ideas.

SG—47 SETTING UP A TABLOID

EQUIPMENT: See SG—46.

ORGANIZATION:

• The objective is for each team to score as many points as possible within a time limit of two minutes or more at each station. When the music starts, players take turns at their activity. The leaders keep score for their team. When the music stops, everyone quickly sits cross-legged at their station in file formation, behind their leader and facing the scoreboard. The first team to do this earns three bonus points; the second team earns two points; and the third team earns one point. These points are added to the team score.

DESCRIPTION OF ACTIVITY:

1. Each team, in turn, call out your score when I call your team number. The team who yells the loudest and clearest score gets three bonus points!

2. After the scores are recorded on the scoreboard, rotate CW to the next station. Your team has twenty seconds to get organized before the music starts again.

3. When the music begins, try to score as many points as possible within the time limit at your new station. Be honest in keeping score!

4. After you have completed all eight activities, assemble near the scoreboard. Points will be tabulated and scores announced. Everyone, cheer for every team!

(The following activities give eight Station Ideas for a "general" Tabloid, followed by eight Station Ideas for Halloween and Olympic Tabloid themes.)

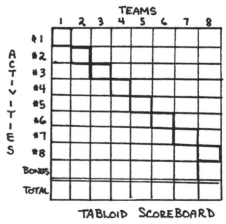

TABLOID SCOREBOARD

FOCUS: Volleying; agility; passing; rolling

EQUIPMENT: One beachball;
eight to ten hoops;
one medicine ball;
one cageball;
five cone markers;
masking or floor tape

DESCRIPTION OF ACTIVITY:

1. **Keep-It-Up:** (Have players form a circle. One player holds a beachball.) The object of this activity is to keep the beachball in the air. Don't let it touch the floor! You cannot hit the ball twice in a row. Score one point every time the ball is hit five times in a row.

2. **Stepping Stones:** (Place pairs of hoops in a row, with rows about 1.6 meters [5 feet] apart as shown. Tape each hoop to the floor. The team stands in file formation just behind a starting line.) The object of this activity is for each player to walk through the hoops on both hands and feet. Hands walk through the hoops on one side and feet walk through the hoops on the other side. When you reach the last hoop, stand up, run to your team to tag the next player, then go to the end of the file. Score one point for each player who finishes the task.

3. **Hot Potato:** (Mark a 3-meter (10-feet) circle with tape or ropes. Have players equally space themselves around the circle with the leader holding a medicine ball.) Pass the ball with control in a CW direction around the circle. Score one point each time the ball passes the leader.

4. **Cageball Weave:** (Place a line of five cones about 2 meters [6 feet] apart and in front of a starting line. Place the Cageball behind the starting line. The team is in pairs in file formation behind the line.) Each pair, in turn, roll the ball in and out of the cones, around the end cone, and back again the same way. Pass the ball to the next pair, who repeats the rolling pattern. Score one point for each round trip with the ball.

VARIATION:

Stepping Stones: Place twelve to sixteen hoops in a zigzag pattern on the floor so that they are touching, and secure to the floor with floor tape. Have players, in turn, step into the hoops as quickly as possible. When they reach the end, they must leap out of the last hoop to land on two feet, turn around, and step into the hoops again to tag the next player in the team. Score one point for each round trip.

FOCUS: Throwing accuracy; arm and leg strength

EQUIPMENT: One hoop or tire;
three sponge footballs or deckrings;
three junior basketballs or volleyballs;
basketball hoop and backboard;
two short ropes;
four large cone markers;
three plastic rings;
climbing frame, horizontal ladder;
several mats; landing pit;
floor or masking tape

DESCRIPTION OF ACTIVITY:

5. *Hoop-a-Basket:* (Tape a throwing line about 3 meters [10 feet] from a basketball hoop or use the foul line of the basketball key. Players stand in file formation behind the throwing line with the first three players holding the balls.) Each player, in turn, try to shoot the ball through the basketball hoop. Score one point for each basket.

6. *Flying Ace:* (Use a short rope to suspend a hoop from a basketball backboard and tie a second rope to the bottom of the hoop. Secure that rope to the floor with tape so that the hoop will not sway. Tape a throwing line 3 meters to 4 meters [10 feet to 12 feet] away from the hoop.) Each player, in turn, try to throw a football through the hoop. Score one point for each successful throw.

7. *Rickshaw Ride:* (Place a cone marker 10 meters [30 feet] away from a starting line. All players are just behind and facing the starting line. Three players stand side by side, and a fourth stands in front of the team.) Middle player, put your arms around the neck and shoulders of the other two players, who will join their outside hands beneath you. Fourth player, stand in front, lift the legs of the middle player, and hold the player's ankles at waist level. Move as a team in this way toward the cone marker, around it, and back to the starting line to score one point. Take turns in each of the four positions.

8. *Cross-the-River:* (Secure a ladder to the climbing frame in a horizontal position and at a height that is above the players' heads; then place mats directly below the ladder. Have each team stand in file formation beside the ladder.) Each teammate, in turn, swing from hand to hand beneath the ladder. If you must drop, continue crossing the ladder from that point. When you reach the end of the ladder, land softly on the mat, bending your knees; then the next player may go. Score one point for each crossing.

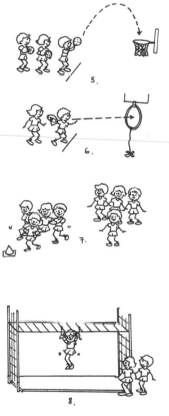

VARIATIONS:

a. *Flying Ace:* Have a player spin the hoop to increase the challenge level.

b. *Hoop-La:* Place three large cone markers in a triangle formation, equally spaced 1 meter (3 feet) from each other, and 3 meters (10 feet) from a throwing line. Each player, in turn, tosses three plastic rings toward the cone markers. Score one point for each ring that encircles a cone.

c. *Cat Walk:* Each player, in turn, climbs up the frame to the horizontal ladder, walks across it using his or her hands and feet to the other end of the frame, and jumps into the landing pit; then the next player goes. Score one point for each crossing.

FOCUS: Running; pulling; lifting; rope jumping

EQUIPMENT: One broomstick; five cone markers; four scooters; two short ropes; two folding mats; one long jump rope; one beachball (optional); one plastic spider (optional); floor or masking tape

DESCRIPTION OF ACTIVITY:

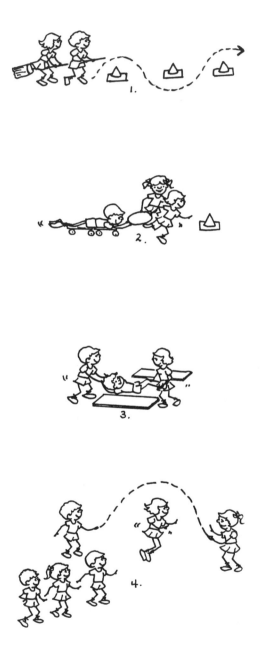

1. *Magic Broom Ride:* (Place four cones in a row, each 3 meters [10 feet] apart and 3 meters [10 feet] from a starting line. Have players in pairs, standing in file formation just behind the starting line. The first pair gets a broomstick.) Each pair, in turn, straddle the broomstick and ride it like a horse, weaving in and out of the cone markers, around the end cone, and directly back to the starting line. Score one point for each round trip.

2. *Ghost Riders:* (Have a rider lie on his or her front on two scooters [joined together by a rope] and hold onto a looped rope, which is pulled by one or two team players. Place a cone as a turning point about 10 meters [30 feet] in front of the starting line.) Pull each Ghost Rider around the end cone and directly back to the starting line so that the next one can go. If the cone marker is knocked over, it must be set upright before continuing. Take turns at being pulled and being the puller. Score one point for each Ghost Rider that completes the course.

3. *Coffin Carry:* (Place two folded mats about 4 meters [12 feet] apart. Tape a direction arrow between the mats.) One player, the "skeleton," lie down on your back on the first mat. Any number of players may hold onto the lying player's arms and ankles, safely carry that player to the other mat, and gently place the skeleton on the mat; then run back to the first mat to pick up the next skeleton. Everyone on your team should have a turn at being carried and being a carrier. Score one point for each skeleton carried from mat to mat.

4. *Spider Jump:* (Place a long rope on the floor. Two players stand at either end of the rope and start turning it. The other players stand in file formation nearby.) Each player, in turn, perform five jumps in the middle to score one point for your team. You may jump in "front door" or start in the middle. Everyone on your team should take turns at being the jumper and the rope turner.

VARIATION:

In *Spider Jump,* have the jumper hold a beachball or a toy spider while jumping. The jumper passes it to the next player after his or her fifth jump.

FOCUS: Agility; shooting accuracy; hanging; swinging; rolling

EQUIPMENT: One parachute; two benches; two box horses or tables; one landing pit or several mats; three deckrings; bleach bottles; one broom handle or bladeless hockey stick; eight beanbags and large piece of plywood; floor or masking tape; one or two climbing ropes; one nonskid mat and two large mats; two utility balls; one plastic laundry basket; one large cageball (2-meter or 6-foot diameter); several cone markers

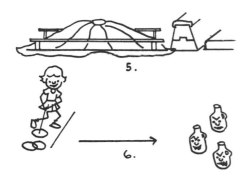

5.

6.

DESCRIPTION OF ACTIVITY:

5. *Haunted House:* (Spread the parachute flat along the floor and place upturned benches to hold down opposite sides of the parachute. Then place a box horse, followed by the landing pit, in line with the parachute. Have team line up in file formation in front of the parachute.) Each player, in turn, must try to get through the Haunted House as quickly as possible to score one point for your team by crawling under the parachute, climbing onto the box horse, and landing in the pit. As soon as the player ahead of you reaches the box horse, the next player may go.

6. *Jack-O'-Lantern Hockey:* (Place three bleach bottles, which represent the "jack-o'-lanterns," on crosses that you have taped in a triangular pattern about 4 meters [12 feet] from a shooting line. Place a broom handle and three deckrings near the shooting line.) Each player, in turn, take three tries to knock over the "jack-o'-lanterns" by shooting the deckrings with your broomstick at them. Other players, keep setting up the bottles when they are knocked over. Score one point for each bleach bottle knocked over.

7. *Witch's Fly:* (Place a box horse about 2 meters [6 feet] from the climbing rope; then position a crash pad on a nonskid mat under the rope. Check that the climbing rope is short enough to swing clear of the box horse. Place a laundry basket, with two utility balls in it, in the middle of the crash pad and under the rope. Lay a folded mat on either side of the crash pad. Players stand in file formation behind the box horse.) Each player, in turn, hold a utility ball between your ankles while standing on the box horse, then swing forward, dropping the ball into the laundry basket and landing safely on the crash pad. Score one point for each ball that lands in the basket.

8. *Giant Pumpkin Roll:* (Mark out a 5-meter [15-foot] diameter circle with the cones, spacing them about 2 meters [6 feet] apart, and place a large cageball outside of the circle. Have players stand outside a cone marker, evenly spaced around the circle and all facing the center.) Leader, quickly start the cageball rolling in a clockwise direction from player to player around the outside of the circle. Score one point each time the cageball passes the leader.

7.

8.

FOCUS: Strength; shooting accuracy

EQUIPMENT: One tug-o-war rope
(minimum 20 meters or 60 feet long);
several folding mats;
one scooter;
three deckrings;
three bleach bottles;
one bladeless hockey stick;
two crazy carpets and short rope;
several cone markers;
floor or masking tape

DESCRIPTION OF ACTIVITY:

1. *Luge Run:* (Use a long tug-o-war rope stretched out across the play area. Set a scooter on top of the rope at one end. Use folded mats as the "banks" of the course, as shown. Have the team in shuttle formation, at each end of the rope.) Each player, in turn, hook-sit on the scooter and hold on at the sides, while another teammate gently pushes you from behind along the tug-o-war rope to the other end. Here a new rider and pusher take over and repeat the activity. Everyone should have a turn at being a rider and a pusher. Score one point for each crossing.

2. *Deckring Shot:* (Set three bleach bottles on X's that you have taped in a triangular pattern, about 5 meters [15 feet] from a starting line. Place a bladeless hockey stick and three deckrings near the starting line.) Each player, in turn, take three tries to knock over the bottles by shooting the deckrings with your hockey stick at the targets. Other players, keep setting up the bottles when they are knocked over. Score one point for each bleach bottle you knock over.

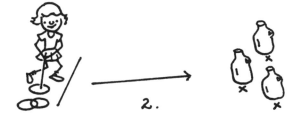

VARIATIONS:

Bobsled Ride: This activity is best done outside in snow conditions. Each player, in turn, sits or lies flat on a crazy carpet while two teammates pull the carpet by an attached rope in and out of cone markers, around the end cone, and directly back to the team. As soon as the first team crosses the starting line, the second team may go. Each player must take turns at being carried and being the carrier. Score one point for each round trip.

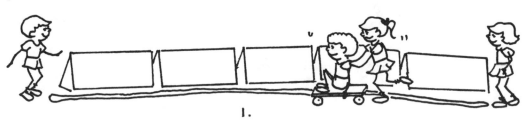

FOCUS: Springing; swinging; agility; sliding/rolling accuracy

EQUIPMENT: Springboard;
one boxhorse or table;
one crash pad;
three folding mats;
several cone markers;
one baton;
several benches;
one climbing rope;
six beanbags or deckrings;
floor or masking tape

3.

DESCRIPTION OF ACTIVITY:

3. ***Spring and Swing:*** (Set up a springboard just in front of a box horse, which is directly under a climbing rope. Place a crash pad with a nonskid mat under it, about 2 meters [6 feet] from the box horse. The safety mats are placed on both sides of the crash pad and between the box horse and crash pad. Mark a starting line about 5 meters [15 feet] from the springboard.) Each player, in turn, run toward the springboard, spring off it onto the box horse, grab the climbing rope, and swing out to safely land on the crash pad. Score one point for each landing.

4. ***Hurdle Relay:*** (Each half of the team stands in a file behind a line, facing the other half about 10 meters [30 feet] away. Evenly space five benches across the two shuttle files. The leader holds a baton in his or her right hand.) Each player, in turn, pass the baton to the front player in the opposite file by running to a bench and jumping over it, to cross to the opposite side. Score one point for each baton exchange.

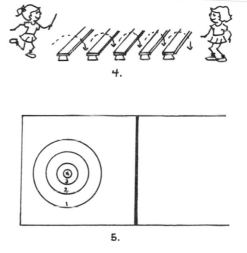

4.

5.

5. ***Curling:*** (Use floor tape to mark out four concentric circles, which represent the "House." Tape a "hog line," which is 5 meters [15 feet] from the Curling House. Team players stand in a file behind the hog line, with the leader holding three beanbags.) Each player, in turn, take three tries to slide your beanbags into the Curling House. Score points according to where your beanbags stop: The center circle, or "button" scores four points; the second circle, three points; the third circle, two points; and the largest circle, one point.

VARIATIONS:

a. ***Winter Olympics (Outdoors) Event—Schushlapping:*** A "Schushlap" is a 2.7-meter (8-foot), 2-inch by 4-inch stud, with six toe straps spaced evenly along the board. The strap can be short pieces of rope or leather, stapled at the sides so that one snowboot can slip into it. The team members slip one boot into a strap and use the other foot to push against the snow, as they "schushlap" their way from one cone marker to the other cone marker 10 meters (30 feet) away. The team, upon reaching the opposite cone marker, reverse feet and direction and return to the starting cone marker. Score one point for each crossing.

b. ***Curling (Outdoors):*** To set up the Curling event outside, have each player, in turn, roll a rubber utility ball over a smooth snow surface in an attempt to land the ball in the House, consisting of circles made with ropes. If using an ice surface, have players slide tin cans filled with water and frozen into a painted Curling House.

FOCUS: Jumping; speed running; accuracy throwing

EQUIPMENT: Floor or masking tape;
four high jump standards;
ten to twelve hoops;
seven small utility balls;
several short ropes;
several cone markers;
one volleyball;
several beanbags or deckrings;
one medium-sized box;
two laundry baskets;
one chair

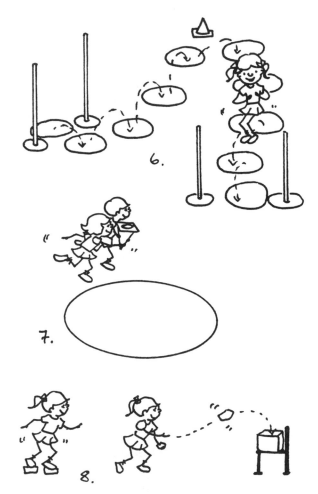

6. ***Super Slalom:*** (Space two high jump standards, 1.6 meters [5 feet] apart, at the start and finish of the course. These represent the "starting and finishing gates." Then tape ten hoops between the gates in a zigzag pattern on the floor, spacing them 1 meter [3 feet] apart. Set a cone marker near the halfway point.) Each player, in turn, jump with feet together and hands holding imaginary poles, from hoop to hoop. As soon as the player in front of you reaches the halfway point, the next player may go. Score one point for each player who completes the course.

7. ***Torch Run:*** (Use cones to mark out an oval track around the perimeter of the play area or tabloid stations. Have players in the team stand in pairs in file formation at the start/finish line, taped on the floor. Together, the first pair holds an upturned cone marker, which represents the "Olympic torch.") Each pair, in turn, hold the torch together and run as quickly as you can in a CW direction around the track, to hand the torch to the next pair. Score one point for each completed course.

8. ***Biathlon:*** (Have team stand in file formation behind a starting line, near a basket of beanbags and facing a throwing line, 6 meters [20 feet] away. Set a box on a chair, 3 meters [12 feet] beyond the throwing line.) Each player, in turn, place a beanbag under each foot and shuffle your way to the throwing line. Here toss the beanbags into the box. As soon as you reach the throwing line, the next player may go. Score one point for each beanbag that lands in the box.

VARIATIONS:

a. In ***Torch Run,*** place a volleyball on the torch and have players try to run the course without the ball dropping out.

b. In ***Biathlon,*** have players at the throwing line throw two balls at a wall target. Set a basket containing six utility balls near the throwing line.

Closing Activities

After a vigorous physical workout, the Closing Activity serves as a quiet, cool-down activity and leaves children ready to continue with classroom work. Section 7 presents forty-seven Closing Activities:

CA–1 SELF-ESTEEM BUILDERS

FOCUS: Self-esteem; class recognition

EQUIPMENT: Quiet background music; tape or record player

ORGANIZATION:

- These promoters of self-esteem show the children that you really do care for them as persons. Used often, they will help to promote a warm and friendly atmosphere in your lessons. Choose one or two of these Friendship Builders to use at the beginning, during, or at the end of the lesson. To teach, have children stand and face you.

DESCRIPTION OF ACTIVITY:

1. *Huddle Cheer:* Put your hands into the middle and give your team cheer.

2. *I Love You:* Say "I love you!" in sign language. With thumb and fingers extended, close your third and fourth fingers to your palm.

3. *I Really Love You:* Say "I really love you!" in sign language. With thumb and fingers extended, close your third finger to your palm and cross your first and second fingers.

4. *Respectful Greeting:* Stand tall facing the person or persons to be honored. On the signal "1, 2, 3!" form a fist, slap it into the palm of your other hand, and bow graciously from the waist. (Used to greet your class each morning and during the day.)

5. *High Fives:* Greet a partner by together jumping upward and slapping each other's hand. Now find another partner and give each other Low Fives. How would you give each other Medium Fives?

6. *Player of the Day:* (Use this self-esteem activity at the end of every physical education lesson.) Have players gather in a listening circle. Recognize a player in your class as the player of the day and have this player stand facing the class. Tell the class why you think this player of the day is so special: perhaps for cooperating with others, playing fairly, sharing equipment, being friendly, helping others, helping you, or trying hard to improve at a skill. When you have finished telling them, have the class give the player of the day a big "round of applause" by clapping their hands while moving them in a large circle. Ensure that each player in the class is given recognition at some time during the school year. You may wish to give a "Player of the Day" certificate to the boy or girl you have recognized.

VARIATIONS:

a. For homework, have the children teach the Friendship Builders to at least one other person.

b. Have players greet each other with High Tens; Low Tens; Medium Tens.

c. Have partners design a "friendship greeting" of their own and teach it to other partners.

CA–2 THE EYE RELAXER

FOCUS: Strengthening eye muscles; concentration

EQUIPMENT: Quiet background music; tape or record player

ORGANIZATION:

• Have players get a mat and cross-leg sit on the mat with trunk erect, looking straight ahead. Explain that all eye positions are to be held for five seconds. Count off the five-second intervals as they hold the positions. Explain that the eye is a very important muscle and that to exercise the eyes properly, children must take them through the full range of movement.

DESCRIPTION OF ACTIVITY:

1. Look as far to the right as possible without moving your head. Hold for five seconds.

2. Look across to the left side as far as you can for five seconds. Don't move your head.

3. Look up and hold for five seconds. Can you see your eyebrows?

4. Look down at something past your nose. Hold that position.

5. Without moving your head, trace a large circle with your eyes, in the same direction, three times. Now do the same thing, moving your eyes in the opposite direction.

6. Look at a spot far away in the distance and stare at it for five seconds. Can you zoom your gaze back now to stare at the tip of your nose? Hold for five seconds.

7. Imagine you are staring at a huge clock with all the numbers positioned around the rim of your eyes. When I call out a number, I want you to quickly shift your eyes to that position: 12 o'clock, 6, 10, 8, 3, 9, 1, 5, 7, 2, 11, 4, 12. . . .

8. Lie down on your back, relax with arms by your side, close your eyes, and look to the 6 o'clock position. Rest your eyes and listen to the music—no talking.

VARIATION:

While resting their eyes, explain the necessity of caring for their eyes, getting plenty of sleep and relaxation.

CA–3 "OLE MOTHER O'LEARY"

FOCUS: Cooperative singing

EQUIPMENT: None

ORGANIZATION:

• This action song is about how Mrs. O'Leary's cow kicked the lantern over in the barn and burned Chicago down in the 1800s and is sung to the tune "Hot Time in the Old Town Tonight." Have the children sit cross-legged inside a circle reasonably close to each other, facing you. Go over the song and the actions first; then have them join in and sing along with you.

DESCRIPTION OF ACTIVITY:

1. Follow me as I sing and do the actions of the song, "Ole Mother O'Leary":

   "Oh! Oh!, one fine night, when we were all in bed! (*lean head on hands and pretend to go to sleep*)
   Ole Mother O'Leary left the lantern in the shed! (*hang out a lantern*)
   The cow kicked it over and winked her eye and said! (*lean back, kick one leg, and wink*)
   There'll be a hot time in the Old Town Tonight! (*rub both hands together*)
   Fire! Fire! Fire!" (*stand quickly, raise one fist in the air as you yell "Fire!" "Fire!" "Fire!"; then quickly sit down*)

2. Repeat the song. Can you yell, "Fire! Fire! Fire!" much louder? I can hardly hear you!

VARIATION:

Divide into two groups. Have a contest to see who can yell "Fire! Fire! Fire!" louder and sit faster.

CA–4 MEMORY GAME

FOCUS: Memory and concentration

EQUIPMENT: Various objects such as balls, benches, hoops, ropes, beanbags, deckrings, and mats

ORGANIZATION:

• Have players find a spot alone and sit cross-legged. Scatter more objects than are needed around the play area.

DESCRIPTION OF ACTIVITY:

1. We are going to play a memory game in which you must remember every object that has been touched.
2. I will begin the game by touching an object, naming it, and then tagging a player. The tagged player must get up, touch and name the first object, and then touch and name a second object.
3. Before sitting down, the player then tags another player, who must touch and name the two previous objects, touch and name a third object, and then tag another player.
4. The game continues in this way until the last player touches and names every object that has been touched and named.
5. If you cannot name the objects touched, ask a player who has not had a turn to help you.

CA-5 LAUGHTER GAME

FOCUS: Leadership

EQUIPMENT: One nylon scarf or handkerchief

ORGANIZATION:

• Have the players sit cross-legged, close together in a circle; then choose a good-natured player to lead the game. That player gets a nylon scarf and stands in the middle of the circle.

DESCRIPTION OF ACTIVITY:

1. Leader, toss the scarf into the air and immediately break into a fit of laughter. Try to make everyone else laugh, too.
2. Continue laughing as long as the scarf floats in the air.
3. As soon as it touches the floor, everyone must immediately stop laughing and put on a sad face. Anyone who shows even the slightest hint of a smile after the scarf touches the floor is "out." Out players must lie down with chin on hands; they still may join in the laughter and may even try to make the sad players laugh.
4. I will be the laughter judge. Who will last the longest?

VARIATIONS:

a. Maintain the same leader throughout the game.
b. Use a balloon instead of a scarf.

CA-6 CHUCKLE BELLY

FOCUS: Cooperation

EQUIPMENT: None

ORGANIZATION:

• This activity gets the whole class "splitting their sides" with laughter. It is almost impossible for the class to go for thirty seconds without giggling. As soon as one starts, they all start. Arrange the players, one at a time, in the lying position, with each player's head resting on someone's belly.

DESCRIPTION OF ACTIVITY:

1. On the signal "Go," keep your eyes open and see if you can go thirty seconds without giggling, smiling, or laughing. Meanwhile, I am coming around to try and make you giggle by making faces, making weird sounds, telling funny jokes, and making funny actions.
2. Try the variations.

VARIATIONS:

a. *"Laugh and Pass It On":* While players are in the "Chuckle Belly" position, have everyone keep a serious face to start. Have the first player start laughing, then pass it on to the second, who passes it on to the third, and so on until all are roaring with laughter. Then have the first player quit and go to the exit, then the second, the third, and so on until they are all lined up.
b. *Fish Hook:* Form groups of four players. Lie in the "Chuckle Belly" position with your head on another player's belly to form a square. Tighten up all the muscles in your body and push back with your head. All players, now try to stand up, all at the same time and without turning. Count to ten and try again.

FOCUS: Balance; cooperation

EQUIPMENT: One beachball or large utility ball per pair

ORGANIZATION:

• Have players find partners who are approximately the same size. Have one of the partners collect a beachball and then find a free space.

DESCRIPTION OF ACTIVITY:

1. Place the ball between you and try these balances:

    — side to side

    — back to back

    — tummy to tummy

    — seat to seat

    — shoulder to shoulder

    — knee to knee

    — head to head

2. Can you do all those balances again as you move about the play area?

3. Show me how you and your partner can pick the ball up from the floor without the use of your hands, using your backs only; elbows only; tummies only; heads only.

4. *Beachball Circle:* Partners, form a circle; then try to pass the beachballs from partners to partners, around the circle, without using your hands.

5. *Beachball Train:* Two sets of partners, stand one behind the other with a beachball between each player. Move about like a train, with train noises. Can we link up all the trains to make one big train?

VARIATIONS:

a. With beachball balanced head to head, have the pairs touch: their toes; knees; the floor; turn around; kneel; etc.

b. Have pairs go through, over, on, or around obstacles, balancing the beachball between them. Use benches, standing hoops, cone markers, tables, and chairs as obstacles.

CA–8 MUSICAL MATS

FOCUS: Alertness

EQUIPMENT: One mat per player;
lively music;
tape or record player

ORGANIZATION:

• Have each player get a mat, scatter and stand on the mat.

DESCRIPTION OF ACTIVITY:

1. When the music starts, walk around the mats without touching them.

2. As soon as the music stops, quickly but carefully, jump onto a mat and remain there until you hear the music again.

3. Each time you walk around the mats, I will remove a mat or two or even three! Now you will have to share the space on the mat with others.

4. Let's continue the game in this way. How may mats do you think we will need in the end to hold the whole class?

VARIATIONS:

a. *Music Raft:* Each time a number is called, players get into groups of that number on a mat. If they can't get on a mat in the right group number, they do three jumping jacks. See how many players you can get onto a mat.

b. Use hoops or chairs and watch the fun! Discourage any foolery.

CA-9 TWEETIE

FOCUS: Alertness; listening skills

EQUIPMENT: Four cone markers

ORGANIZATION:

- Play in a rather small area. Secretly choose one player to be the "Tweetie." All other players scatter around the play area and stand with their eyes closed. If the game is slowing down, have Tweetie give a little chirp now and then.

DESCRIPTION OF ACTIVITY:

1. On the signal "Go," everyone walk slowly around the play area with your eyes closed.

2. Find someone's hand, shake it, and ask "Tweetie?" If you both ask "Tweetie," drop hands immediately and try to find someone else to ask "Tweetie," because the real Tweetie will remain silent throughout the game.

3. If you find a player who does not answer, you have found Tweetie; join hands and remain silent for the rest of the game.

4. Continue until everyone is holding hands with Tweetie.

VARIATION:

Reduce the size of the play area to speed up the action.

CA-10 THE IMPERSONATOR

FOCUS: Creativity; group work

EQUIPMENT: None

ORGANIZATION:

- Form groups of three to five players. Have each group find a free space and sit with players facing each other.

DESCRIPTION OF ACTIVITY:

1. Members, take turns to come out in front of your group and imitate a famous sporting, political, or entertainment personality.

2. When doing the impersonation, you are allowed thirty seconds only. You must not use your voice; only body movements and facial expressions.

3. The player who correctly guesses the answer becomes the next impersonator.

VARIATION:

Have each group take turns at doing an impersonation for the other groups to guess.

CA-11 LIMB ISOLATIONS _____

FOCUS: Body awareness; concentration

EQUIPMENT: One mat per player; quiet relaxing music; tape or record player

ORGANIZATION:

* Have players get a mat, find a spot alone on the floor, and lie down on their backs on the mat, with feet together and arms at their sides. Emphasize that players listen carefully to the directions and move arms and legs slowly and smoothly.

DESCRIPTION OF ACTIVITY:

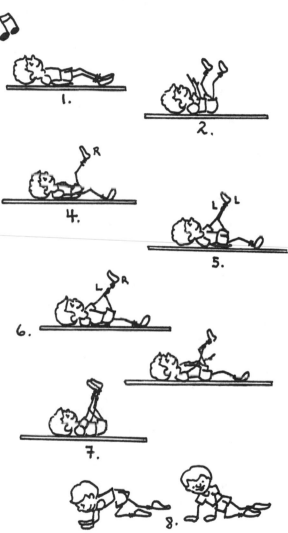

1. Relax . . . listen to the music . . . feel loose and lazy all over.

2. Raise both arms upward, keeping them straight. Now raise both legs upward, spread them apart, return arms to the sides, then bring your legs together and lower them to the floor.

3. Raise your right arm up, then your left arm; lower the right arm, now the left.

4. Raise your right leg into the air, then your left leg. Lower your right leg, now your left leg.

5. Raise your left arm and left leg at the same time; grasp the ankle with your left hand and hold for five seconds; then lower. Repeat stretch with your right leg and right hand.

6. Raise your right arm and left leg; grasp and hold for five seconds, then lower. Raise your left arm and right leg; grasp and hold for five seconds, then lower.

7. Raise both legs and arms upward; grasp ankles with hands and hold for five seconds, then lower.

8. Roll onto your tummy. Imagine that your head weighs 2,000 pounds (1000 kilograms). Slowly raise yourself to the standing position, with your head coming up last.

VARIATIONS:

a. Raise or lower the limbs to a count of four.

b. Have the players breathe in as they raise limbs; breathe out as they lower limbs.

CA–12 TALL TO SMALL

FOCUS: Cooperation; nonverbal communication   **EQUIPMENT:** None

ORGANIZATION:

- Form groups of six to eight players and have each group scatter in a restricted area and stand still. Make sure that the area is safe and there are no obstacles to trip over. Emphasize that there is to be no peeking!

DESCRIPTION OF ACTIVITY:

1. Close your eyes and keep them closed throughout the game. Now, while keeping your eyes closed and by feeling only, arrange yourselves in order of height from tallest to smallest in a straight line, without talking to each other.

2. When you have all found each other and linked elbows, open your eyes and see if you are lined up correctly. If you are, stay linked and walk to the exit door.

VARIATIONS:

a. Have the whole class arrange themselves from Tall to Small.

b. Boys form one group, the girls another.

c. Blindfolds may be used for each player.

CA–13 BIG FOOT

FOCUS: Cooperation   **EQUIPMENT:** Floor tape or two long ropes

ORGANIZATION:

- Form equal groups of six to eight players; then tape a starting line and a finish line 30 feet (10 centimeters) apart (or use long ropes to mark out the lines). Allow players to hold onto the player in front of them for balance. Emphasize that heels and toes must touch!

DESCRIPTION OF ACTIVITY:

1. On the signal "Go!" first player, stand with one heel on the starting line and place your other foot ahead of it so that you are standing heel to toe. The next player in your group, place one heel at the toes of your front foot and then stand heel to toe. Other players repeat until the whole group is standing heel to toe in a long line.

2. Which team can go the farthest? In other words, which team has the biggest feet?

VARIATION:

Big Foot Race: Have players stand in file formation as for Big Foot. On the signal "Go!" groups race to reach the finish line as follows: The player at the end of each group runs forward and stands heel to toe at the front of the file; the new last player repeats, and so on until the whole group reaches and crosses the finish line.

CA—14 SLOW-POKE

FOCUS: Body control

EQUIPMENT: Four cone markers;
slow music;
tape or record player

ORGANIZATION:

- This activity is a moving experience (barely). Form one long line of players along one side of the play area, facing the finishing line, about 3 meters (9 feet) away. Emphasize that players be good sports and accept the judge's decision as final.

DESCRIPTION OF ACTIVITY:

1. When the music starts, or on the signal "Go," everyone "race" to the other sideline as slowly as you possibly can, but you must be moving at all times. If you stop moving you are out of the race and can help point out anyone else who is moving.
2. The last one over the line wins.

VARIATIONS:

a. Use music to start and stop the race. If you run out of time, the player who is last when the music stops is declared the winner.
b. *Scooter-board Slow-Poke:* Play Slow-Poke on scooter boards.
c. *Bum-waddle Race:* Players line up in pairs and, holding inside hands, waddle to the finish line. Hands must not touch the floor. First over the line wins.

CA—15 POSTURE TAG

FOCUS: Running and dodging

EQUIPMENT: Two beanbags

ORGANIZATION:

- Choose one player to be the "Chaser," and another to be the "Runner." Both get a beanbag and place it on their heads. They stand tall with good posture: shoulders back, head up, and trunk lifted. Explain that if they maintain good posture, they will be able to keep the beanbag on their heads longer. All other players scatter, stand on the spot with good posture, prepared to run at any time. Remind stationary players that they must not interfere with the Chaser or the Runner.

DESCRIPTION OF ACTIVITY:

1. On the signal "Go," Chaser, try to tag the Runner. Runner, dash away, but try to keep the beanbag on your head. If the beanbag drops, replace it and continue.
2. Runner, to escape being tagged, you may place the beanbag on any player's head at any time. That player then becomes the new Runner and you take his or her place.
3. If the Chaser tags the Runner, we will choose a new Chaser.

VARIATION:

For a large class, have two sets of Runners and Chasers.

CA–16 OOH'S AND AAH'S

FOCUS: Concentration; cooperation; fair play   **EQUIPMENT:** None

ORGANIZATION:

- Form circles of eight to twelve players, all facing inward with hands joined. Choose a leader for each circle. Emphasize that players say their "Ooh's" and "Aah's" loudly and clearly, so everyone can hear, but squeeze hands gently.

DESCRIPTION OF ACTIVITY:

1. Leaders, begin the game by squeezing the hand of the player on your right, and say "Ooh!" That player then squeezes the hand of the player on his or her right, and so on around the circle.
2. Leaders, after the first signal is on its way, send a second signal by saying "Aah!" and squeezing the hand of the player on your left.
3. Both signals continue around the circle until they meet. That player is "zapped" and must run once around the circle before restarting the game.
4. Any player can reverse the direction when someone gives you an "Ooh" or an "Aah," by giving it back to them.
5. If both "Ooh" and "Aah" are traveling in the same direction, see if one can catch the other.

VARIATION:

Try "hip bumps" around the circle instead of a hand squeeze.

CA–17 CONCENTRATION

FOCUS: Alertness; listening; cooperation   **EQUIPMENT:** None

ORGANIZATION:

- Form groups of eight players and have them sit cross-legged in a circle. Have each group number off; the player with the number one is the Leader. Have players practice the "slap-slap," "clap-clap," "snap-snap" hand rhythm: Slap knees twice, clap hands twice, and then snap fingers twice. Continue to practice until players have got the slow, steady rhythm: "Slap-slap," "clap-clap," "snap-snap."

DESCRIPTION OF ACTIVITY:

1. Leaders of each group, start the rhythm: "slap-slap," "clap-clap," "snap-snap." The second time through, when you hear "snap-snap," call your own number and the number of another player in your group. For example: "slap-slap," "clap-clap," snap-"1," snap-"8."
2. The player whose number is called, wait until you hear the next "snap-snap," then call your number and the number of another player. You may even call the number of the player who just called yours.
3. Keep the rhythm going at a steady pace. If we get the rhythm going faster and faster, can you still do the hand actions and call the players' numbers? Let's give it a try!

VARIATION:

Concentration Challenge: Divide the class into two groups and have them challenge each other.

CA–18 FRAPPEZ

FOCUS: Cooperation; volleying skills

EQUIPMENT: One beachball or light plastic play ball per group

ORGANIZATION:

- Form groups of six to eight players per group. Have each group find a free space, form a circle, and space themselves arm's length apart. Check for good spacing of groups. Have one of the players get a beachball.

DESCRIPTION OF ACTIVITY:

1. When the music starts, the Leader, hit the ball into the air to any player, who in turn will hit it to another, and so on. The object of the game is to keep the ball in the air, by hitting with either hand, as long as possible.
2. No player is allowed to hit the ball twice in a row.
3. Count the number of consecutive hits in French: "une, deux, trois, quatre, cinq, six, sept, huit, neuf, dix!"
4. If the ball touches the floor, the count must begin all over again.
5. Which group will have the highest score by the time the music stops?

VARIATIONS:

a. Allow the ball to be hit with any body part.
b. Play the game in the kneeling position or sitting.
c. For advanced players, use a volleyball.

CA–19 ORBIT BALL

FOCUS: Cooperation; hand and foot striking

EQUIPMENT: An oversized beachball per group

ORGANIZATION:

- Form two groups of ten to twelve players and have groups form a double circle; one circle inside the other. Players in the outer circle stand with arms ready to tap the beachball. Players in the inner circle lie on their backs, heads pointing to the middle of the circle and legs raised overhead, ready to tap the beachball with their feet. Emphasize that players control the ball gently and that it should be tapped rather than kicked.

DESCRIPTION OF ACTIVITY:

1. Circle players, work together as you pass the beachball around the circle to put it into "orbit."
2. Try to keep the ball between the inside players, who tap it with their feet, and the outside players, who tap it back with their hands. Do not allow the ball to touch the ground. Call "Mine!" when you want to hit the ball.
3. Can you count the number of times the ball orbits the circle? Count out loud each time.
4. Inner and outer circles, change places. Can we beat our previous score?

VARIATION:

For a large class, set up two games.

CA-20 BLINDMAN'S BLUFF

FOCUS: Cooperation; trust

EQUIPMENT: One banner per player;
paper and pen;
one hat

ORGANIZATION:

- Have each player get a banner; then form groups of five or six players, who stand in a line. Write each number, one through six, on a small piece of paper, put in a hat, and have the members of each group select a number, which they must remember and not tell anyone else. Then have players blindfold each other with the banners; you may need to help blindfold the last few players.

DESCRIPTION OF ACTIVITY:

1. On signal "Go!" tell the other players in your group your number without talking! How will you do that? I'm sure you can find a way to communicate!

2. As soon as everyone knows the number of everyone in their group, change positions so that you are standing side by side in numerical order. Which group will be the quickest?

VARIATIONS:

a. Increase the size of the group to eight or ten players for additional challenge.

b. *Scrabble Challenge:* Have players in groups of seven stand side by side so that they correctly spell words such as "F-I-T-N-E-S-S" or "A-E-R-O-B-I-C."

c. *Alphabet Challenge:* Substitute the alphabet for numbers and give everyone a different letter. The whole class rearranges itself in alphabetical order while blindfolded.

CA–21 RATTLESNAKE

FOCUS: Alertness; listening; cooperation

EQUIPMENT: Two tin cans with pebbles per game; two blindfolds per game

ORGANIZATION:

- Form "snake-pits" (circles of ten to twelve players). Choose two of the players to go into the center, each holding a "rattler": a tin can containing several pebbles; one player is the "Rattlesnake"; the other is the "Victim." Both are blindfolded.

DESCRIPTION OF ACTIVITY:

1. On the signal "Go," to find out where the other is, each of the blindfolded players may shake the rattler at any time. When he or she does, the other must answer by rattling his or hers.

2. Rattlesnake, you are allowed to rattle only five times, but the Victim, you may rattle as often as you like.

3. Circle players, when the Rattlesnake or the Victim come near you, gently ease them back into the snake pit. Also help the Rattlesnake count the number of rattles.

4. If the Victim is not caught in five rattles, Rattlesnake and Victim, you both join the circle and a new Rattlesnake and Victim are chosen.

5. Circle players, you are allowed to shout advice and remarks to the Rattlesnake and the Victim, which will no doubt add to the confusion!

CA–22 TWO DEEP

FOCUS: Alertness; cooperation

EQUIPMENT: None

ORGANIZATION:

- Choose two players: one to be the "Walker"; the other to be the "Chaser." All other players, form a large circle, facing the center and standing about two arm lengths apart.

DESCRIPTION OF ACTIVITY:

1. On the signal "Go," the Chaser, try to tag the Walker, who can save himself or herself by stopping in front of any one of the circle players. This player immediately becomes a new Walker and can run wherever he or she wants to go to avoid being tagged.

2. The Chaser, if you tag the Walker, quickly change roles and continue the game.

3. The Walker and the Chaser, you may run in and out the circle players, but you must not touch them.

4. Circle players, you cannot interfere with the Walker or the Chaser.

CA–23 ROLLER DERBY

FOCUS: Cooperation

EQUIPMENT: One parachute per class;
one volleyball per class

ORGANIZATION:

- Have all players hold the parachute around the edge. Place a volleyball, or other light ball, on the chute.

DESCRIPTION OF ACTIVITY:

1. Raise the parachute with arms straight out in front of you. Now all working together, make the ball roll around the chute in a large circle. Control the ball by raising and lowering the chute. Don't let your hands touch the ball while it is on the chute.

2. Count the number of times the ball rolls around the chute before it rolls off. Let's try again. Can we beat our best score?

VARIATIONS:

a. *The Rocket:* Place the volleyball in the center of the limp chute; then all together quickly pull the chute toward you so that the ball shoots into the air like a rocket. Try to catch it again in the chute.

b. See Parachute Play in Section 5, for other cool-down games.

CA–24 SHU-SWAP

FOCUS: Social interaction; cooperation

EQUIPMENT: None

ORGANIZATION:

- "Shuswap" is the name of a lake in British Columbia, Canada. Have each player remove one shoe and place it in a pile.

DESCRIPTION OF ACTIVITY:

1. Everyone, pick up a shoe that isn't your own, hold the shoe somehow; then join hands and make one big circle.

2. Can you now find the owner of the shoe you are holding and return it, without breaking your hand hold? You may hold the shoe any way that you can, but do not put it in your mouth!

3. When all shoes have been returned, place the shoes in another pile and we'll start again.

4. After the last game, put your shoes back on and line up at the exit.

CA-25 SHARKS AND THE MINNOW

FOCUS: Passing and catching; cooperation

EQUIPMENT: Two large balls and one smaller ball

ORGANIZATION:

- Arrange the class in a circle. Explain that the small ball is the "Minnow" and the larger ones are the "Sharks."

DESCRIPTION OF THE ACTIVITY:

1. The circle players, pass the Shark balls (larger balls) around the circle to try and tag the player who is holding the Minnow ball (smaller ball). You may only pass the Shark balls from player to player around the circle, and they may be reversed at any time. However, the Minnow may be passed or thrown to any player in the circle.
2. Circle players, as you pass or throw the balls, call out "Shark" or "Minnow!"

VARIATIONS:

a. Play the game with two large circles.
b. Have each circle invent its own "Shark and Minnow" game!

CA-26 BLOW-BALL

FOCUS: Team work; arm and shoulder strength

EQUIPMENT: One ping-pong ball per group;
one mat per group;
four cone markers

ORGANIZATION:

- Form even teams of four to six players. Have the teams line up behind the starting line. In each team, have one player, the "Jockey," lie face downward on the mat while the other players in the team space themselves evenly around the mat and hold onto it.

DESCRIPTION OF ACTIVITY:

1. Teams, on the signal "Go," place the ping-pong ball on the floor in front of the Jockey, lift the mat (Jockey and all), and have the Jockey blow the ping-pong ball across the floor to race the other teams to the finish line, about 5 meters (15 feet) away.
2. Once the ball goes over the finish line, the Jockey becomes a Carrier, and another player lies on the mat. Continue until every player has had a turn.
3. Which team will be the first to finish?
4. Carriers, carry or drag the Jockey low to the floor. You must not touch or kick the ball.
5. Jockey, you are not allowed to touch the ball with your hands until over the line.

VARIATION:

Ruler Ball: Play as for Blow-Ball, but the Jockey bats the ping-pong ball across the line with a ruler.

CA–27 TARANTULA

FOCUS: Cooperation   **EQUIPMENT:** Four cone markers

ORGANIZATION:

- Mark out a starting and a finishing line. Form groups of three players and have them find their own space.

DESCRIPTION OF ACTIVITY:

1. Each group, tangle yourselves up by grasping hands under arms, over shoulders, or between the six legs. While in this position, half-squat down and spread your legs: You are now a "Tarantula." Move about the play area while maintaining your grip.

2. *Tarantula Race:* All Tarantulas, line up behind the starting line. On the signal "Go," see who can be first over the finish line without breaking up.

3. *Octopus Race:* Form groups of four players (eight legs) and repeat.

4. Let's try it with five players or even the whole class!

VARIATIONS:

a. *The Blob:* Have the entire class link arms and wind into a big spiral circle. Can you move like this, in step with each other, from one end of the play area to the other, without letting go?

b. *The Black Widow:* Have three players form each spider by standing back to back, squatting down, then moving together. Which spider group can move the quickest?

CA–28 CENTIPEDE

FOCUS: Cooperation   **EQUIPMENT:** Four cone markers

ORGANIZATION:

- Mark the start and finish lines with cone markers, 3 meters (10 feet) apart. Have players find a partner and assume the all-fours position, one behind the other.

DESCRIPTION OF ACTIVITY:

1. The front partner, support your feet on your partner's shoulders and take your weight on your hands. Back partner, take your weight on your feet and hands. Together move forward. Change places and repeat.

2. *Centipede Race:* All pairs, line up behind the starting line and centipede race to the finish line, about 3 meters (10 feet) away.

3. *Giant Centipede:* Four pairs, join together to make one Giant Centipede. Can your centipede stay together and not break up as you move around the play area?

4. *Monster Centipede:* The whole class, join together to make one huge Monster Centipede, where the "head" tries to catch and devour the "tail."

CA-29 BALANCE FEATHERS

FOCUS: Coordination and balance

EQUIPMENT: One balancing feather each; relaxing background music; tape or record player

ORGANIZATION:

• A "balance feather" is a peacock feather that can be purchased from Physical Education equipment suppliers. Have each player get a balance feather and take it to a free space. Emphasize the importance of handling the feathers with gentleness, as they are quite fragile. Ensure that players are well spaced to avoid any interference with other players. Emphasize that players need to concentrate on the feather, never letting their eyes leave it. Discourage any foolery!

DESCRIPTION OF ACTIVITY:

1. Balance your feather in the palm of your right hand; in the palm of your left hand. Now balance it on the back of each hand in turn.

2. Balance your feather on your index finger of your right hand; your left hand. Try balancing it on each of the other fingers.

3. Balance your feather on other body parts: elbow; shoulder; wrist; knee; forehead; nose; foot. On how many different body parts can you balance your feather?

4. Now try to transfer your feather from one body part to another without having the feather touch the floor. For example, can you transfer your feather from an elbow to the back of your hand?

5. Find a partner. Using one feather, try to transfer the feather from one partner to the other using different body parts.

6. Invent other balancing challenges. We will all try to perform your challenge.

VARIATIONS:

a. **Feather Challenge:** Set up a contest to see who can balance their feather the longest. Time the event, and provide opportunity for the record to be broken.

b. Wands (which are 1 meter [3 feet] in length and 6-millimeter [1/4-inch] doweling) can be substituted for balance feathers.

CA-30 SKIN THE SNAKE

FOCUS: Cooperation   **EQUIPMENT:** None

ORGANIZATION:

• Form teams of five to seven players. Have each team find a space and get into file formation behind a Leader. Make sure that there is enough room behind the teams for each player to lie down. Emphasize that players keep their legs in close while lying down. Remind players to keep the hand-hold at all times. Warn players to walk with legs wide apart to avoid treading on their teammates.

DESCRIPTION OF ACTIVITY:

1. Spread your legs apart; lean over, put your right hand forward to grasp the hand of the player in front of you; then put your left hand back between your legs, to grasp the extended hand of the player behind you. Hold the hands of both players throughout the game.

2. On the signal "Go," the last player, lie down as the rest of the team backs up over you, straddling you with legs apart. Then each player in turn, lie down for the team to shuffle backward over you until you are all lying down, still holding hands.

3. The last player (first to lie down), get to your feet; then straddle walk forward over the rest of the team, pulling each one in turn to the standing position until all are back in original positions.

VARIATIONS:

a. **Skin the Snake Challenge:** Which team can Skin the Snake the quickest and return to their original starting position without breaking the hand-hold?

b. **Class Skin the Snake:** Have the whole class form one long Skin the Snake line.

CA–31 THE HUMAN LOG ROLL

FOCUS: Cooperation

EQUIPMENT: Mats (optional)

ORGANIZATION:

- Form groups of six to eight players. Have the players in each group lie face down side by side, packed in tightly alongside each other, all facing the same direction, with arms extended out in front. They are the "human logs." Explain that the Log Roll works better if players stay very close together. Choose one Rider from each group and have the Rider lie down across the upper backs of the logs. Demonstrate the Human Log Roll; then allow groups to practice.

DESCRIPTION OF ACTIVITY:

1. On the signal "Go," logs, roll together in the same direction in order to give the rider a rather bumpy ride across your backs.

2. Rider, when you reach the end of the row of logs, lie face down beside the last player and join the logs. The log at the opposite end becomes the new rider, gently lies down on top of the logs, and begins to roll over their backs.

3. Continue in the same direction until your group has run out of space.

VARIATION:

On the signal "Reverse," reverse the direction in which the logs are rolling.

CA–32 SNAIL ROLL

FOCUS: Cooperation

EQUIPMENT: Mats (optional)

ORGANIZATION:

- Form groups of six to eight players. Have the players in each group lie face down and pack in tightly alongside each other, all facing the same direction, with arms extended out in front. Place a smaller player between two larger ones.

DESCRIPTION OF ACTIVITY:

1. Last player in the line, roll sideways onto your neighbor and keep rolling down all the bodies to the end. When you get to the end, join the line and lie on your front also. Then the next player at the other end can start rolling down the line.

2. Continue until your Snail runs out of space.

VARIATION:

Have a Snail race.

CA–33 TRUST FALLS

FOCUS: Cooperation; trust

EQUIPMENT: None

ORGANIZATION:

• The object of these activities is for all players to develop complete trust in each other.

DESCRIPTION OF ACTIVITY:

1. **Trust Fall:** (Form groups of three players. All players in each group stand facing the same direction, with one player about 18 inches [45 centimeters] in front of the other two. The two back players, the "Catchers," reach forward to almost touch the front player with their hands.) Front player, stiffen all the muscles in your body and slowly lean backward until you fall into the arms of the two back catchers. Try to keep your arms at your sides as you fall. Catchers, your hands should almost touch the falling player before he or she falls. Now catch the front player and push him or her gently to a standing position. Have the front player repeat the fall, but this time allow him or her to fall a little farther backward before you catch him or her. Let the player know that he or she can trust you. Change roles until all players in your group have experienced the Trust Fall.

2. **Circle of Friends:** (Form tight circles of six to eight players, standing shoulder to shoulder, with one player standing in the center.) The center player, stiffen your whole body, keeping arms rigid at the sides and feet still; then fall backward into the hands of the circle players. The circle players, gently push him or her in different directions across the circle. Players change positions and repeat.

CA–34 BUMPER-TO-BUMPER TUG

FOCUS: Cooperation

EQUIPMENT: None

ORGANIZATION:

• This is a nonrope version of tug-o-war that can be played by any number of players. Have players find a partner their own size and stand in a free space straddling a line.

DESCRIPTION OF ACTIVITY:

1. **Bumper-to-Bumper:** Stand back to back on either side of the line; reach forward between your legs to grab your partner's wrists. Try to pull each other over the line.

2. **Line Bumper-to-Bumper:** Class, divide into two groups, and stand back to back. One line, take a step to the right, while the other stands still, so that you are each covering a gap. Reach down between your legs, cross your arms, and hold the hand of the player behind you on the right and on the left. On the signal "Pull," try to pull the other line forward. You may not get very far, but it's fun trying.

CA–35 WALKING CHAIR

FOCUS: Cooperation; balance

EQUIPMENT: Wall

ORGANIZATION:

- Form groups of five to seven players and have each group stand close together in file formation near a wall. The last player in each file leans back against the wall. All players hold onto the waist of the player in front of them.

DESCRIPTION OF ACTIVITY:

1. **Wall Sit:** On the signal "1, 2, 3, Sit!" sit straight down to make a "lap" for the player in front of you, and sit in the lap of the player behind you so that everyone is comfortably seated. Hold for ten seconds; then stand. Try the Wall Sit again, but this time hold your hands above your head for ten seconds instead of around another player's waist.

2. **Walking Chair:** After the signal "1, 2, 3, Sit!" I will give the signal "1, 2, 3, Left, Right, Left, Right!" When your group hears this, slowly walk forward, beginning with the left foot, while still in the sitting position, chanting "Left, Right, Left, Right." Which group can walk the farthest without breaking up?

3. **The Unsupported Circle:** (Form a tight circle. Have the players stand very close together with their hands on the hips of the person in front of them, facing in a CW direction.) On the signal "Sit," everyone, sit down on the lap of the player behind you. Can you stay in this "unsupported circle" for ten seconds without collapsing? Remember to sit straight down and not to lean back as you sit. This will cause the circle to collapse. (You may need to shuffle the players toward the center to keep the circle tight.) On the signal "Hands up," everyone raise your hands in the air. Hold it for ten seconds.

4. **Walking Circle:** On the signal "Sit," sit down and hold onto the hips of the player in front of you. On the signal "1, 2, 3, Left, Right, Left, Right!" walk forward around the circle, beginning with your left foot, chanting "Left-Right, Left-Right!" Can you walk like this with your hands in the air?

VARIATIONS:

a. Try to pass a ball around the circle, first one direction, then the other.

b. Have the players walk around the circle in time as they sing a song.

FOCUS: Stretching and relaxation

EQUIPMENT: Relaxing music; tape or record player; mats (optional)

ORGANIZATION:

• Have all players lying down in the back-lying position.

DESCRIPTION OF ACTIVITY:

1. **Whole Body Stretch:** Extend your arms out in front and your legs behind. Make yourself as long as you can. Point your toes and extend your fingers. Hold for ten seconds and relax. Gently and smoothly roll over onto your front and repeat the stretch.

2. **Diagonal Stretch:** Still in the front-lying position, extend only your right arm and point only the toes of your left foot. Hold the stretch for ten seconds and relax. Stretch the left arm and the right leg in the same way. Hold for ten seconds and relax. Stretch both arms and legs again, and pull in your abdominal muscles. Hold for ten seconds and relax. Gently roll over onto your back and repeat the stretch sequence.

3. **Knee Hugs:** Pull your right leg toward your chest. Hold for twenty seconds. Repeat, pulling your left leg toward your chest. Be sure to keep your lower back flat and the back of your head on the mat, if possible. Don't strain. Now, pull your knee toward your opposite shoulder to stretch the hip area. Hold for twenty seconds and repeat on the other side. This time, pull both legs to your chest. Keep the back of your head on the floor; then raise your head up toward your knees. Hold for twenty seconds and repeat.

4. **Butterfly Stretch:** Relax with knees bent and out sideways, soles of your feet together. Hold this stretch for thirty seconds. Now, without forcing the stretch, gently "pulse" both your legs outward, back and forth about ten to twelve times, and no more than an inch (3 centimeters) in either direction. Repeat the stretch for another thirty seconds.

5. **Secretary Stretch:** Bring your knees together and rest your feet flat on the floor. Interlock your fingers behind your head, resting your arms on the floor. Now, lift your left leg over the right leg. Use your left leg to pull your right leg toward the floor until you feel a stretch along the side of your hip and lower back. Hold this stretch for thirty seconds; then relax. Keep your upper back, shoulders, back of head, and elbows flat on the floor. Repeat the stretch for the other side, crossing your right leg over your left and pulling down to the right.

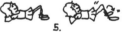

6. **How to Sit Up from the Lying Position:** From your back-lying position, bend both knees and roll over onto one side. While resting on your side, push with your hands to bring yourself into the sitting position. This method takes the strain off the lower back.

VARIATION:

Hanging Stretch: Use a bar that is above head height. Have players hang loosely on the bar using the over-hand grip for thirty-second intervals. Repeat three times.

CA–37 HUMAN KNOT

FOCUS: Cooperation **EQUIPMENT:** None

ORGANIZATION:

- If possible, arrange for an even number of players; the game works better this way. Form groups of ten to twelve players and have each group stand in a tight circle.

DESCRIPTION OF ACTIVITY:

1. Reach across the circle and join hands with any two players except those who are standing on either side of you.

2. Now, work together to untangle your hands so that everyone is standing around in a circle again holding hands. While you are untangling yourselves, remember not to let go of each other's hands.

VARIATION:

Choose one player to be the "Coach," who directs the undoing of the Knot.

CA–38 TUG-O-PEACE

FOCUS: Cooperation; arm and shoulder strength **EQUIPMENT:** None

ORGANIZATION:

- Form two equal teams of any number. Have the two teams face each other on opposite sides of a line so that each player is facing a gap. Using the wrist grip, players join right hands with an opposing player and left hands with another. End players will have one free hand.

DESCRIPTION OF ACTIVITY:

1. On the signal "Pull," both teams, try to pull the other team over the line.

2. There may not be a clear winner in this game, but it can be a lot of fun. If you want a winner, the winning team is best two out of three tries.

VARIATION:

Form teams of six to eight players. Have the teams challenge each other to a Tug-o-Peace.

CA-39 HOOK-ON TAG

FOCUS: Alertness; concentration   **EQUIPMENT:** None

ORGANIZATION:

• Choose two players: one to be the "Walker," the other to be the "Chaser". All other players find a partner, link elbows with the partner, and stand in a free space in the play area.

DESCRIPTION OF ACTIVITY:

1. On the signal "Go," the Chaser, try to tag the Walker. The only way you can move is by walking!

2. The Walker, you can save yourself at any time by hooking elbows with one of the standing players. The partner of the player you hook onto immediately becomes the new Walker and can quickly walk wherever he or she wants to go to avoid being tagged.

3. The Chaser, if you tag the Walker, quickly change roles and continue the game.

4. The Walker and the Chaser, you may walk in and out of the standing players, but you must not touch them.

5. Partners, you cannot interfere with the Walker or the Chaser. (Designate a new Chaser if the Walker is not tagged after a short time.)

CA-40 THE MAD ZAPPER

FOCUS: Alertness; fair play   **EQUIPMENT:** None

ORGANIZATION:

• Secretly choose one player to be the Mad Zapper, and explain to him or her how the game is played. All other players are the Detectives and scatter. Get players to "ham it up" as they slowly become paralyzed. Emphasize that zapped players must lie still and not speak for the rest of the game or reveal the Zapper's identity; quite a task for some players!

DESCRIPTION OF ACTIVITY:

1. All players, walk around the play area shaking hands with one another.

2. The Zapper, when you shake hands, press down firmly with your thumb on the wrist of that person. This is the signal that that player has been slowly "zapped" (paralyzed).

3. When zapped, stagger for a few steps, fall down, and lie perfectly still until the end of the game.

4. Detectives, if you get suspicious of who the Mad Zapper is, you can say "I know who the Zapper is!" If you can get another Detective to agree with you that that player is the Zapper, then you can both make the accusation. If you are correct, then the game is over. If it is not the Zapper, you are both zapped and fall to the floor.

5. Continue until someone identifies the Mad Zapper, or until only the Zapper and one other player are left.

CA–41 WING AND ROLL

FOCUS: Concentration; coordination

EQUIPMENT: Two balls of different colors per group

ORGANIZATION:

• Form teams of six to eight players. Have each team find a free space and sit in a circle facing the center and spaced an arm's length apart. Choose a Leader for each group to start the "ball rolling." Have the Leader hold the two different colored balls. The object is to establish a passing pattern among the players of the group.

DESCRIPTION OF ACTIVITY:

1. Leader, begin the passing pattern by "winging" (throwing) the white colored ball to any player who is not sitting alongside you. From then on, each player will do the same until each has received the ball and it has been returned to you.
2. Practice the pattern several times until you have learned it.
3. Leader, now add the second ball, the red one, to the pattern. Wing the white ball, and roll the red one. The same player should receive the white ball quickly followed by the red one.
4. Possible wing and roll pattern: Leader-Sean-Barbie-Susie-Andrea-Jon-Leader.

VARIATION:

Challenge: Which team can complete the most "Wing and Roll" patterns in two minutes?

CA–42 DOG AND A BONE

FOCUS: Alertness; friendly competition

EQUIPMENT: One towel per game

ORGANIZATION:

• Form equal teams of five or six players. Have the teams line up behind opposite endlines, about 10 meters (30 feet) apart, facing each other. Number the players in each line 1, 2, 3, 4, and so on, with the number ones at opposite ends. Place a "bone" (towel) midway between the two lines.

DESCRIPTION OF ACTIVITY:

1. When I call a number (for example, "3!") both number threes, leap forward and attempt to snatch the bone and return to your home line without being tagged by your opponent. If successful, you earn one point for your team. If your opponent tags you, the tagger's team gets the point.
2. Players, you may "feint" and jockey for position before making the snatch for the towel. Number one players, keep the score for your team.
3. Continue until each player's number has been called at least once.

VARIATIONS:

a. Have two games going on at the same time.
b. Use a beanbag or a runner instead of a towel.

CA–43 PROGRESSIVE RELAXATION

FOCUS: Total body relaxation

EQUIPMENT: One mat per player (optional); quiet relaxing music; tape or record player

ORGANIZATION:

• In this cool-down activity, players tense different muscle groups for ten seconds and then relax. Play relaxing music. Have each player get a mat and scatter around the play area. Players start by lying on their backs with legs slightly apart and arms at sides.

DESCRIPTION OF ACTIVITY:

1. Lie quietly on your mat and listen to the music. Try to relax every part of your body. Think of something pleasant.

2. Press your head against the mat; then relax.

3. Now, frown and move only your scalp upward. Yawn very slowly; then relax.

4. Squeeze your shoulder blades together; then relax.

5. Make fists with your hands and squeeze them tightly as you would a sponge; then relax.

6. Tighten your tummy muscles. Can you feel them tighten? Now relax.

7. Squeeze your buttocks together; then relax.

8. Press your legs to the floor; then relax.

9. Point your toes away from you; then relax. Pull your toes toward you. Now completely relax again.

10. Close your eyes. Breathe in deeply, then slowly breathe out, breathe in again, then let it out slowly with a long hissing sound—"Hisssssssssss!"

11. Without making a sound, open your eyes, stand up slowly, give a big "yawn," and stretch tall. Now move quietly to the exit door.

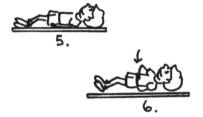
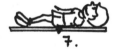

CA-44 TRUST WALK

FOCUS: Trust and cooperation

EQUIPMENT: One blindfold per player; benches; tables; chairs; gymnastic apparatus; high jump standards; and other obstacles

ORGANIZATION:

- This activity helps to build a trust relationship between players. Have players find a partner, collect a blindfold, and scatter. One player is blindfolded and the other stands behind and places hands on his or her shoulders.

DESCRIPTION OF ACTIVITY:

1. On the signal "Go," guide your blindfolded partner around the play area by applying pressure to the shoulders only, without talking. Try to avoid other players.

2. Guide your partner over, under, and around the various obstacles in the play area. Remember, guiding player, the safety of your partner is in your hands.

3. After two minutes, change roles with your partner.

VARIATIONS:

a. Have the guiding player talk to the blindfolded partner, but not touch.

b. Play the Trust Walk outdoors.

CA-45 SILENT BIRTHDAYS

FOCUS: Cooperation

EQUIPMENT: None

ORGANIZATION:

- Have the players form groups of six to eight players and scatter to their own space. Explain the activity; then allow the players time to discuss how they will communicate with each other.

DESCRIPTION OF ACTIVITY:

1. On the signal "Birthdays," close your eyes and line up in one line according to the month and day on which you were born, but there must be no talking.

2. When you are finished, open your eyes and check to see if you are in your correct order. As each group finishes, line up at the exit.

VARIATION:

Play Silent Birthdays in large groups of eight to twelve players.

FOCUS: Flexibility

EQUIPMENT: Relaxing background music; tape or record player

ORGANIZATION:

- Have participants stand in circles of ten to twelve players, facing inward and placing their hands on the shoulders of the person on either side of them. Choose a leader for each circle.

DESCRIPTION OF ACTIVITY:

1. *Circle Neck Stretch:* Slowly turn your head to the right and look over your right shoulder as far as you can. Hold for eight seconds. Repeat to the left side. Do this stretch sequence two more times.

2. *Circle Calf Stretch:* Bend your right leg forward and extend the other leg back. Gently press the heel of the back leg to the floor and hold stretch for twelve seconds. Reverse leg positions and repeat stretch. Do this stretch sequence two more times.

3. *Circle Lateral Leg Stretch:* Spread your legs wide apart so that each of your feet are touching a person's foot on either side of you. Now bend your right leg and lean to the right, keeping your left leg straight. Hold for twelve seconds; then repeat to the left. Repeat this stretch sequence two more times.

4. *Finger Walk Stretch:* Stand so that your feet are only 5 to 10 centimeters (2 to 4 inches) away from the person on either side of you. Walk your fingers down your right leg and try to touch the left foot (or lower leg) of the person on that side of you. Try to keep your legs straight. Return to starting position; then walk your fingers down your left leg and try to touch that person's right foot. If you cannot comfortably reach your foot, then bend your legs slightly. Repeat this sequence two more times.

5. *The Copy-Cat Stretch:* Stand, arm's length apart. Leader, go to the center and perform a slow stretching exercise, which everyone copies. When finished, call out the name of another player ("Copy-cat John!" or "Copy-cat Nicole!") who will come to the center to become the new Leader and perform another stretch, for everyone to copy. (Continue until everyone has had a turn in the center.)

VARIATION:

Have participants create a circle stretch and add it to the above routine.

CA-47 YOGA COOL-DOWN

FOCUS: Flexibility; relaxation; good posture

EQUIPMENT: One mat per player; quiet background music; tape or record player

ORGANIZATION:

• The following basic yoga routine includes a gentle warm-up, followed by relaxing stretches and breathing exercises. Have players get a mat and take it to a free space.

DESCRIPTION OF ACTIVITY:

1. *Sun Greeting:* Stand tall, with the palms of your hands gently pressed together at your chest. Now slowly breathe in as you raise your arms overhead; then slowly breathe out as you bring your arms sideways and down to your sides and bend slightly at the knees. Repeat three times.

2. *Pullover Stretch:* Stand with your feet shoulder-width apart, arms at your sides. Interlock your fingers behind your seat. Bend forward from the hips and raise your arms in back. Let your arms fall forward over your head as far as possible. Hold for ten seconds. Slowly return to starting position, keeping your hands clasped. Repeat three times.

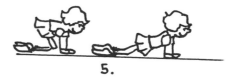

3. *Pelvic Tilt:* In hook-lying position on your mat, with feet hip-width apart and palms down, tighten your abdominal and buttock muscles. Now tilt your pelvis forward, letting your tailbone rise slightly from the floor. Hold for ten seconds. Return to starting position. Repeat three times.

4. *Arm Toner:* Begin in the all-fours position on your mat. Rotate your wrists outward and place your palms on the mat so the fingers point back to your legs. Keeping your palms in contact with the mat, lean your body weight back so that you feel a stretch along your forearms and wrists. Hold for ten seconds. Relax and repeat two more times.

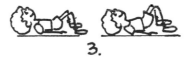

5. *Cobra:* Begin in front-lying position, with your palms on the floor at shoulder level. Supporting your weight on the palms, inhale and slowly raise your upper body, arching your back and tightening your buttocks. Look upward and hold for ten seconds; then exhale and slowly lower your body back to starting position. Repeat three times. (Watch that players do not raise their heads too far and thus hyperflex the back.)